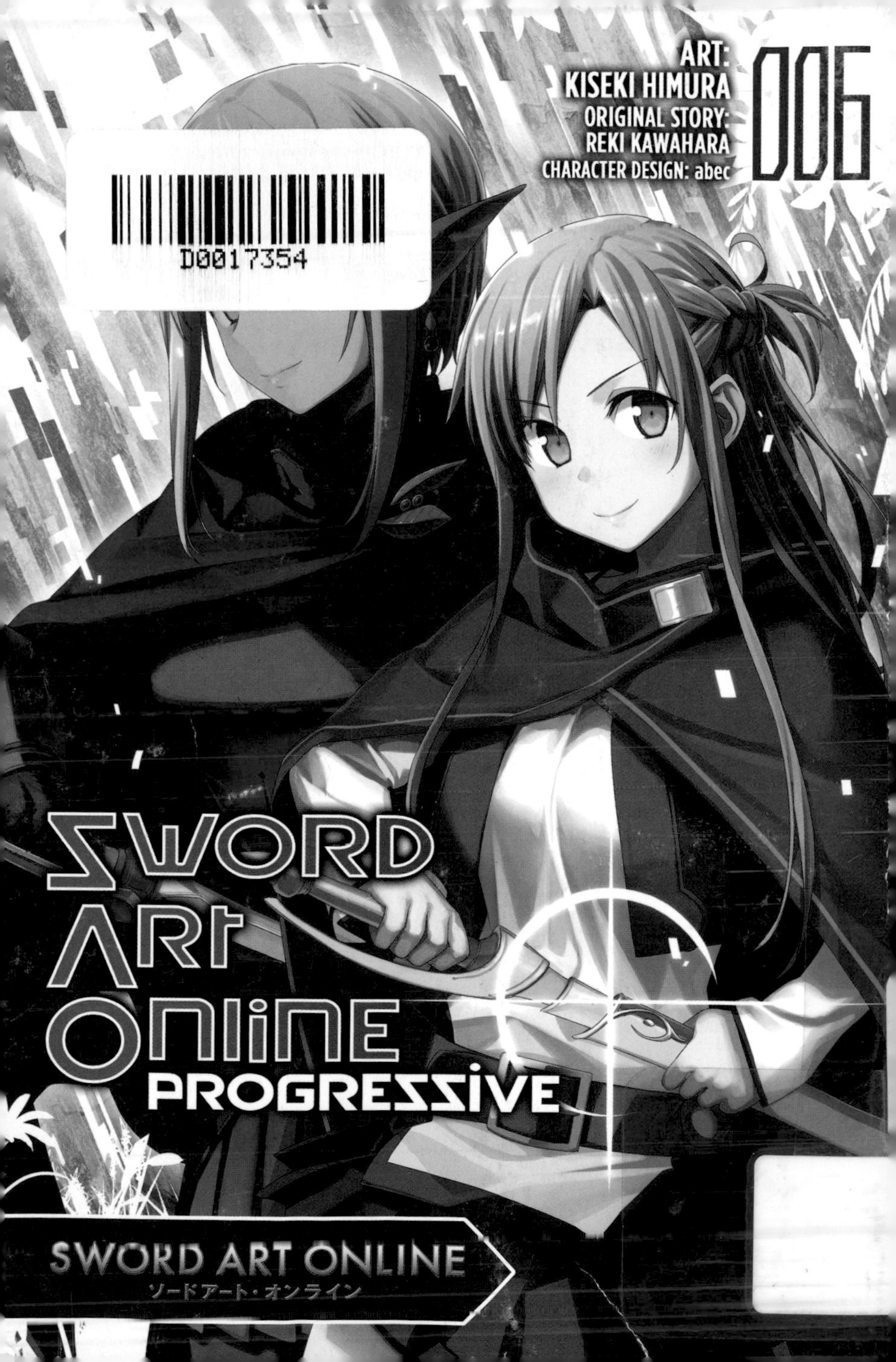
ART:
KISEKI HIMURA
ORIGINAL STORY:
REKI KAWAHARA
CHARACTER DESIGN: abec
006
SWORD ART ONLINE
PROGRESSIVE
SWORD ART ONLINE
ソードアート・オンライン

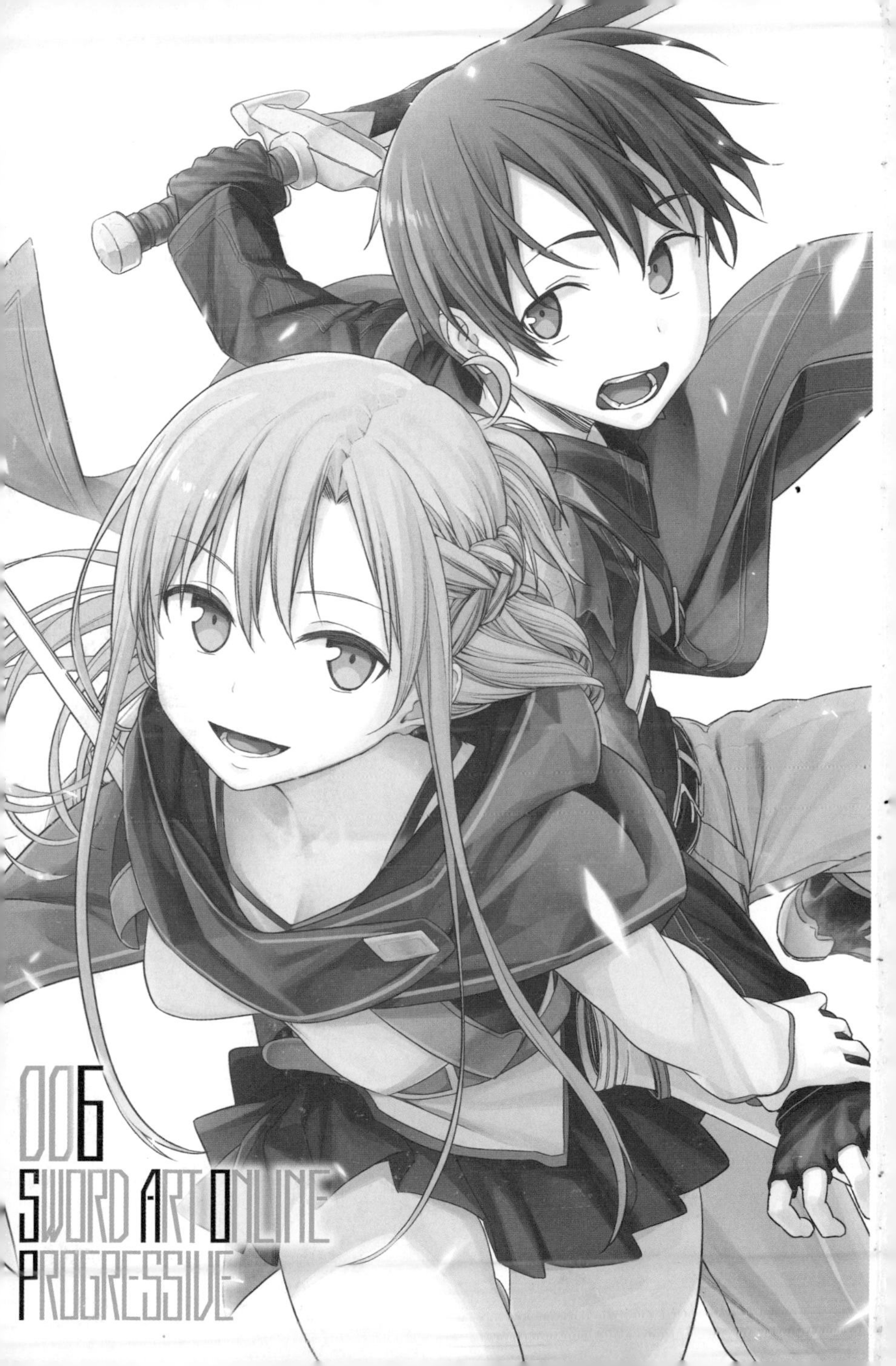
006
SWORD ART ONLINE
PROGRESSIVE

SWORD ART ONLINE PROGRESSIVE 006

CONTENTS

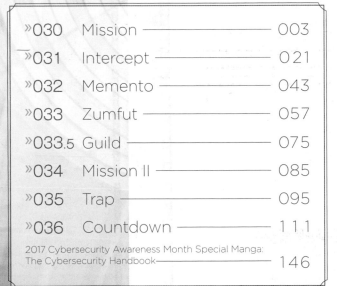

ART: KISEKI HIMURA
ORIGINAL STORY: REKI KAWAHARA
CHARACTER DESIGN: abec

#030: Mission

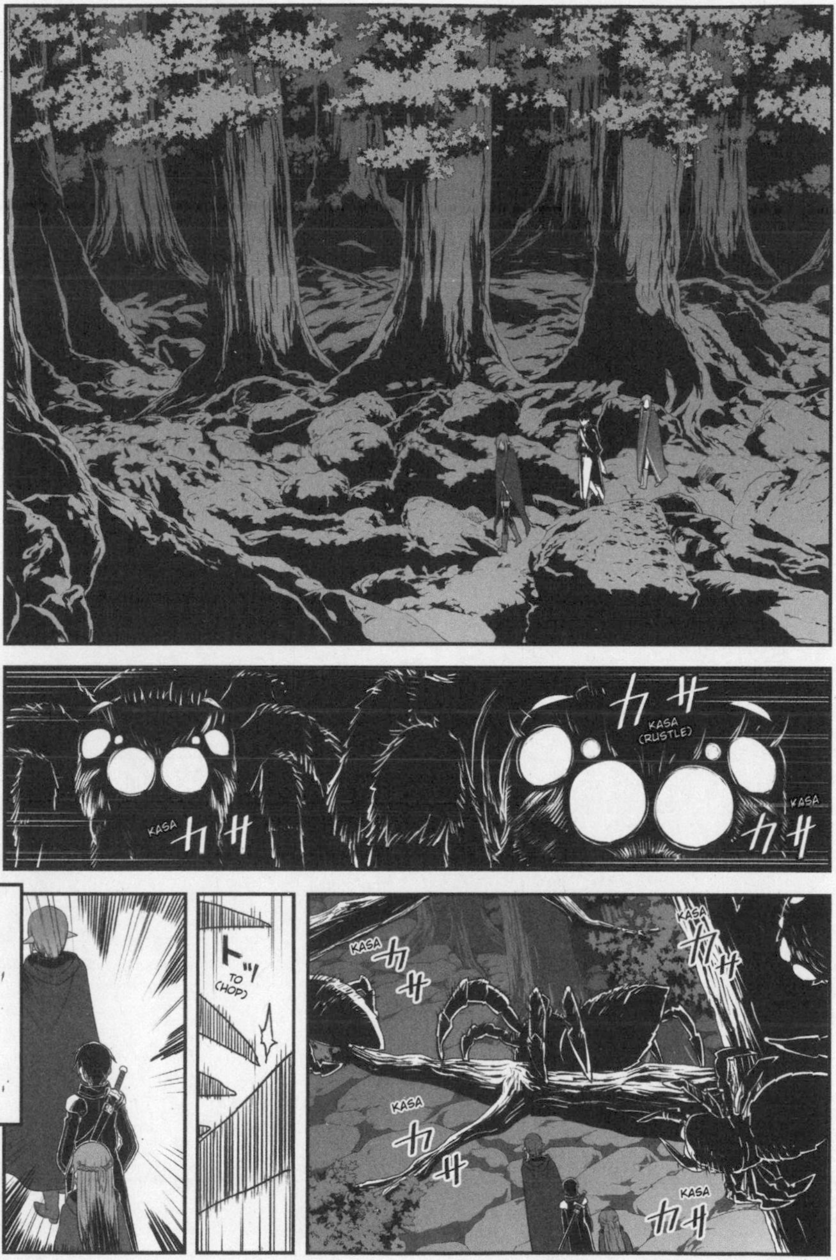
カサ
KASA (RUSTLE)
KASA
カサ
KASA
カサ
KASA
カサ
KASA
カサ
KASA
カサ
KASA
カサ
トッ
TO (HOP)

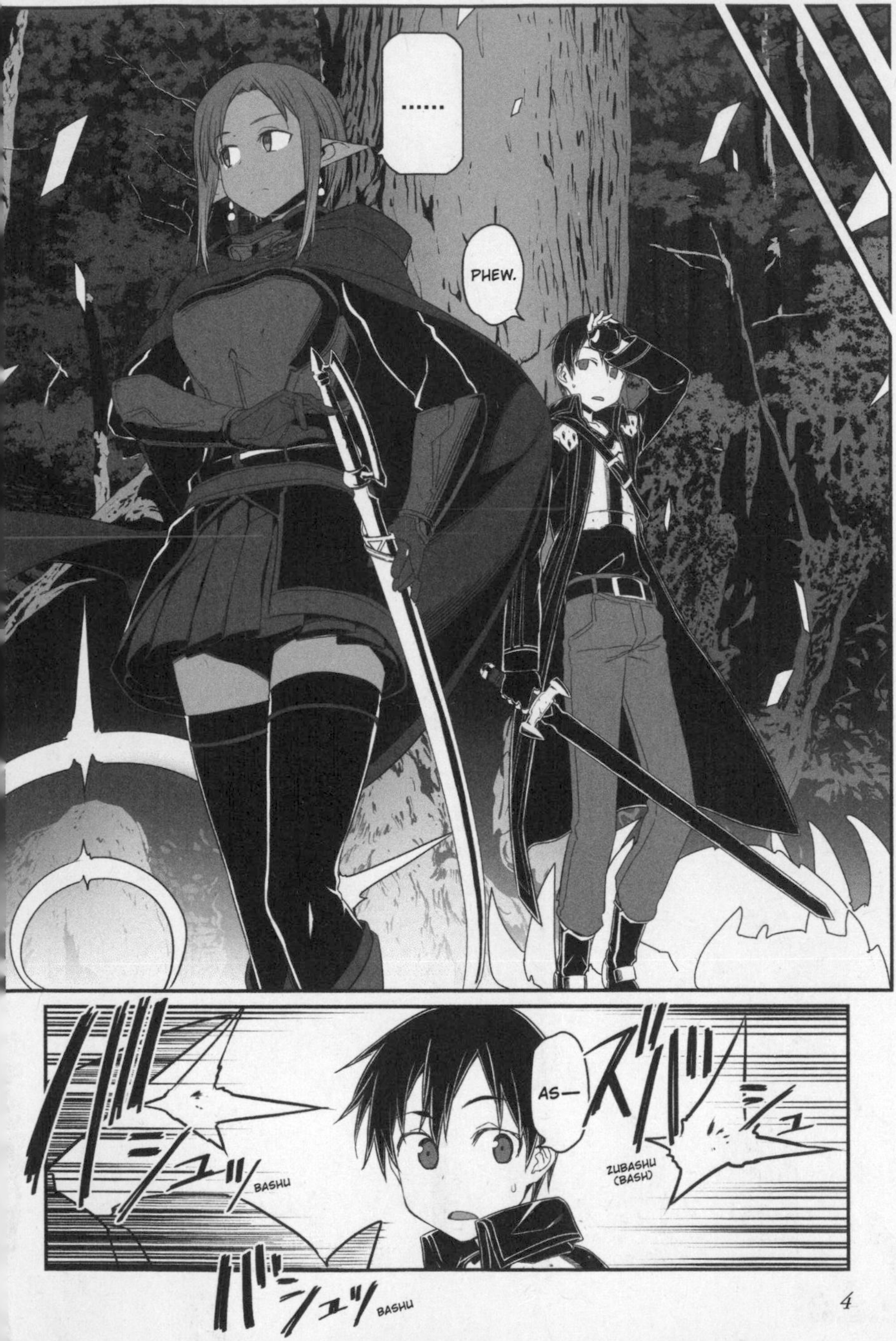

......
PHEW.
ズバシュ
ZUBASHU (BASH)
AS—
バシュッ
BASHU
バシュッ
BASHU

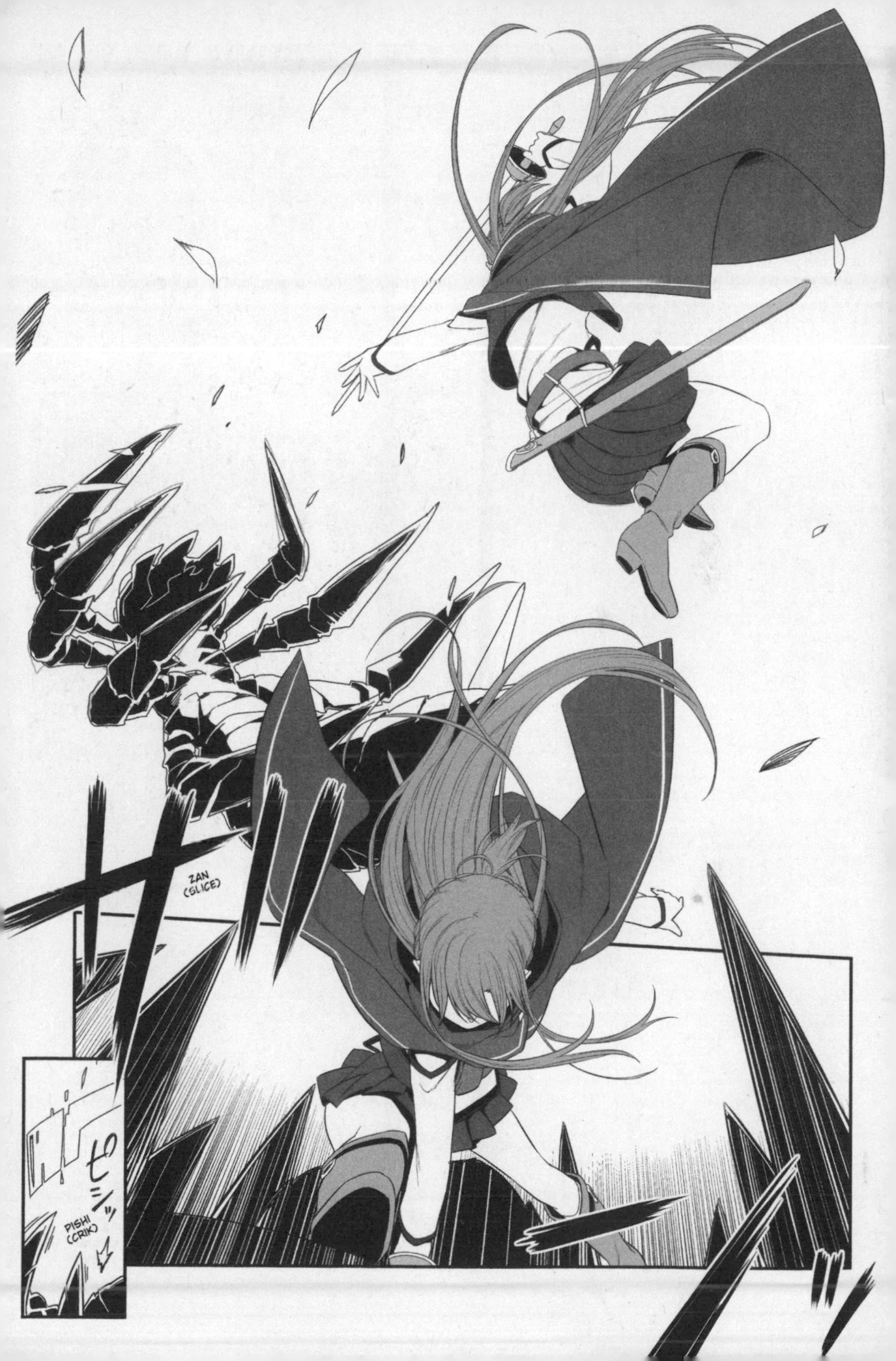
ZAN
(SLICE)
ピシッ
PISHI
(CRIK)

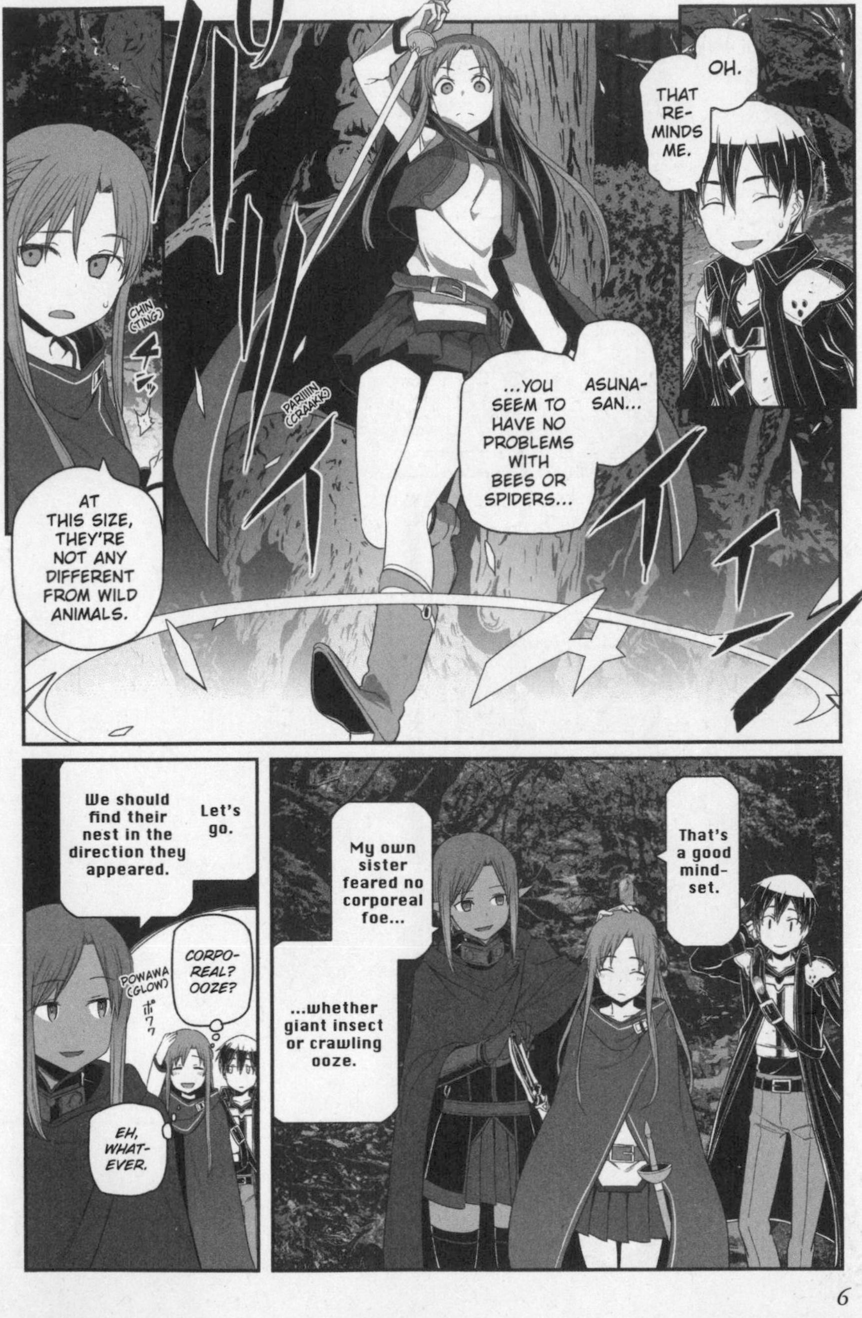
OH.
THAT RE-MINDS ME.
ASUNA-SAN...
...YOU SEEM TO HAVE NO PROBLEMS WITH BEES OR SPIDERS...
PARIIIIN (CRAAKK)
CHIN (TING)
AT THIS SIZE, THEY'RE NOT ANY DIFFERENT FROM WILD ANIMALS.
That's a good mind-set.
My own sister feared no corporeal foe...
...whether giant insect or crawling ooze.
Let's go.
We should find their nest in the direction they appeared.
CORPO-REAL? OOZE?
POWAWA (GLOW)
EH, WHAT-EVER.

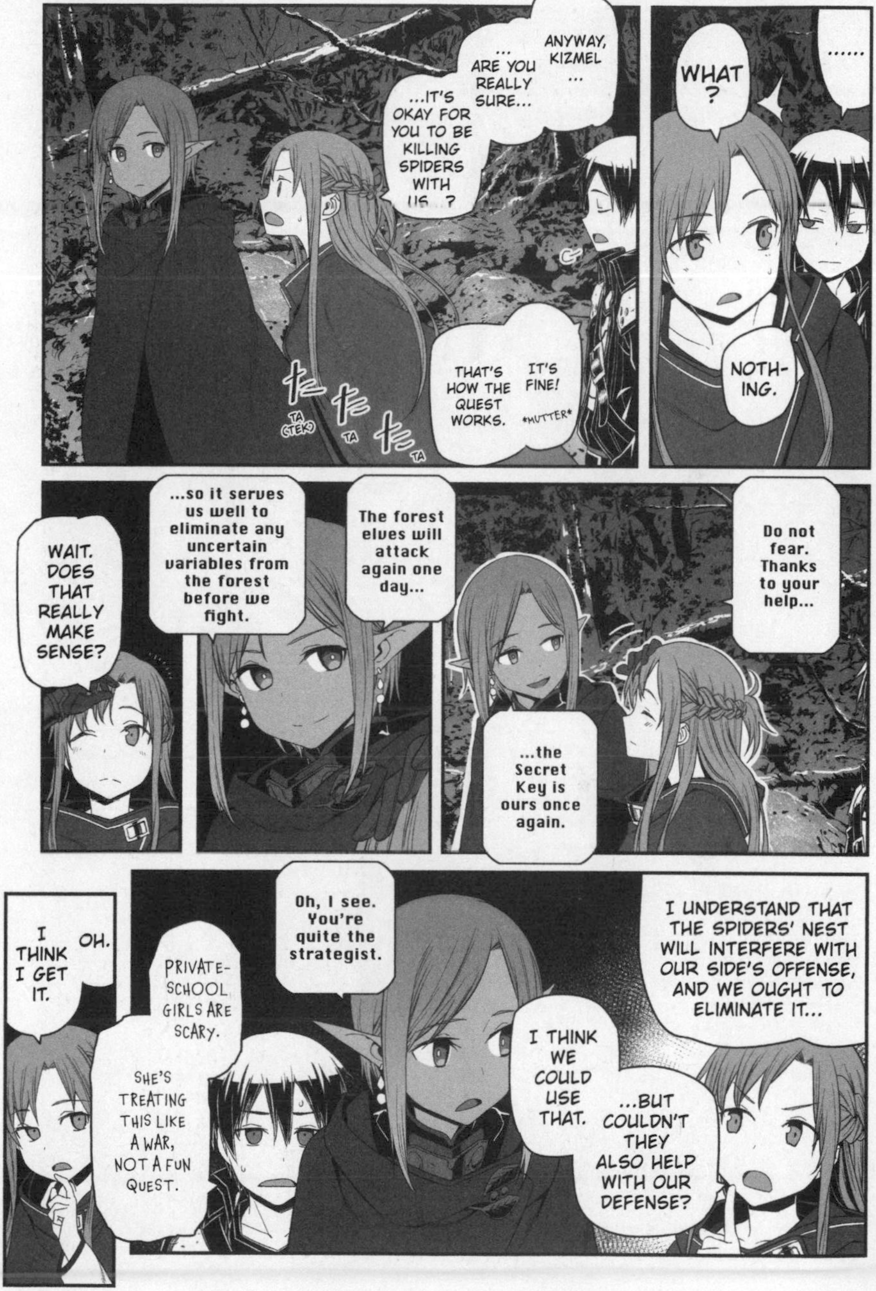
......
WHAT?
NOTHING.
ANYWAY, KIZMEL...
... ARE YOU REALLY SURE...
...IT'S OKAY FOR YOU TO BE KILLING SPIDERS WITH US...?
IT'S FINE!
THAT'S HOW THE QUEST WORKS.
MUTTER
TA (TEK)
TA
TA
Do not fear. Thanks to your help...
...the Secret Key is ours once again.
The forest elves will attack again one day...
...so it serves us well to eliminate any uncertain variables from the forest before we fight.
WAIT. DOES THAT REALLY MAKE SENSE?
I UNDERSTAND THAT THE SPIDERS' NEST WILL INTERFERE WITH OUR SIDE'S OFFENSE, AND WE OUGHT TO ELIMINATE IT...
...BUT COULDN'T THEY ALSO HELP WITH OUR DEFENSE?
I THINK WE COULD USE THAT.
Oh, I see. You're quite the strategist.
PRIVATE-SCHOOL GIRLS ARE SCARY.
SHE'S TREATING THIS LIKE A WAR, NOT A FUN QUEST.
OH.
I THINK I GET IT.

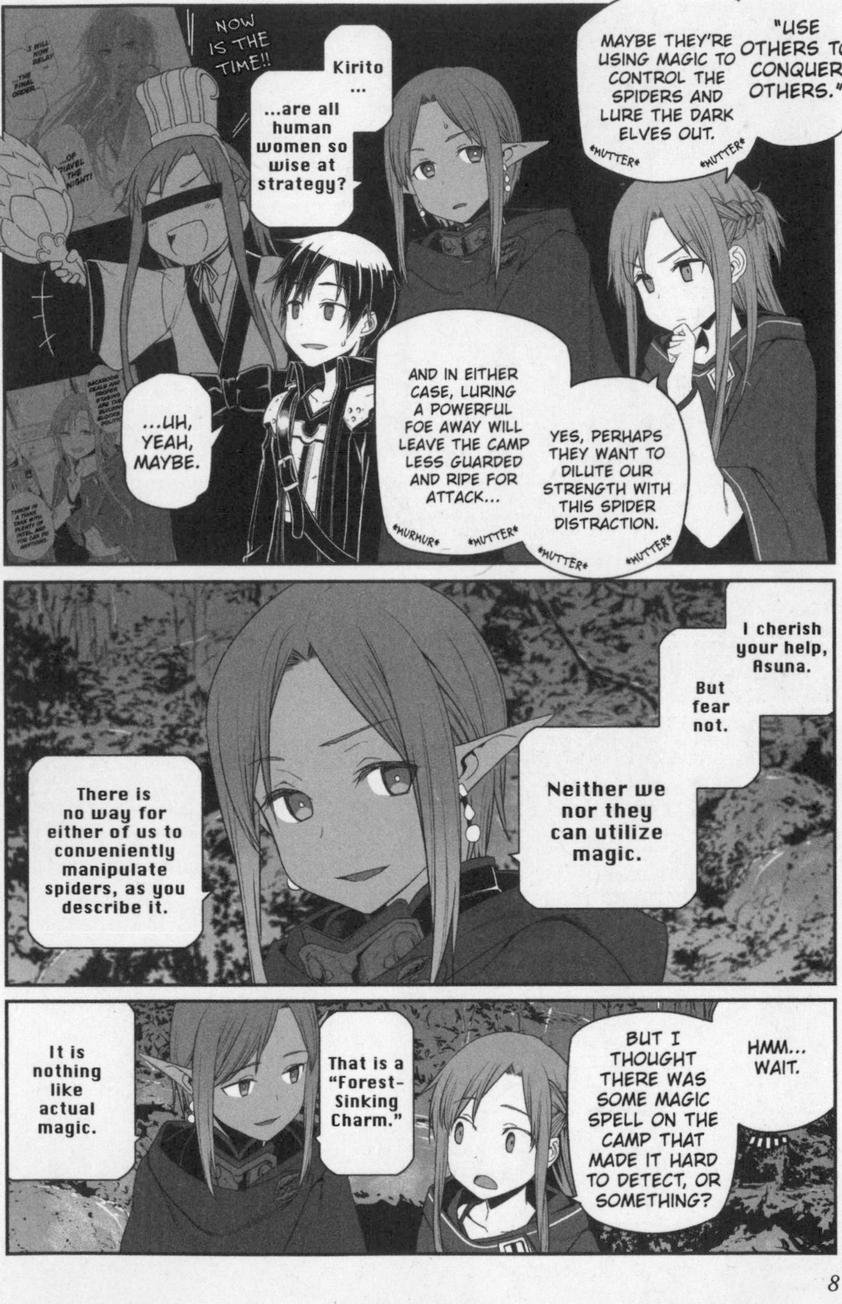
"USE OTHERS TO CONQUER OTHERS."
MAYBE THEY'RE USING MAGIC TO CONTROL THE SPIDERS AND LURE THE DARK ELVES OUT.
MUTTER
MUTTER
Kirito ...
...are all human women so wise at strategy?
NOW IS THE TIME!!
I WILL NOW RELAY ...
...THE FINAL ORDER...
YES, PERHAPS THEY WANT TO DILUTE OUR STRENGTH WITH THIS SPIDER DISTRACTION.
AND IN EITHER CASE, LURING A POWERFUL FOE AWAY WILL LEAVE THE CAMP LESS GUARDED AND RIPE FOR ATTACK...
MUTTER
MUTTER
MUTTER
MURMUR
...UH, YEAH, MAYBE.
THROW IN A THINK TANK WITH PLENTY OF INTEL, AND YOU CAN DO ANYTHING.
I cherish your help, Asuna.
But fear not.
Neither we nor they can utilize magic.
There is no way for either of us to conveniently manipulate spiders, as you describe it.
HMM... WAIT.
BUT I THOUGHT THERE WAS SOME MAGIC SPELL ON THE CAMP THAT MADE IT HARD TO DETECT, OR SOMETHING?
That is a "Forest-Sinking Charm."
It is nothing like actual magic.

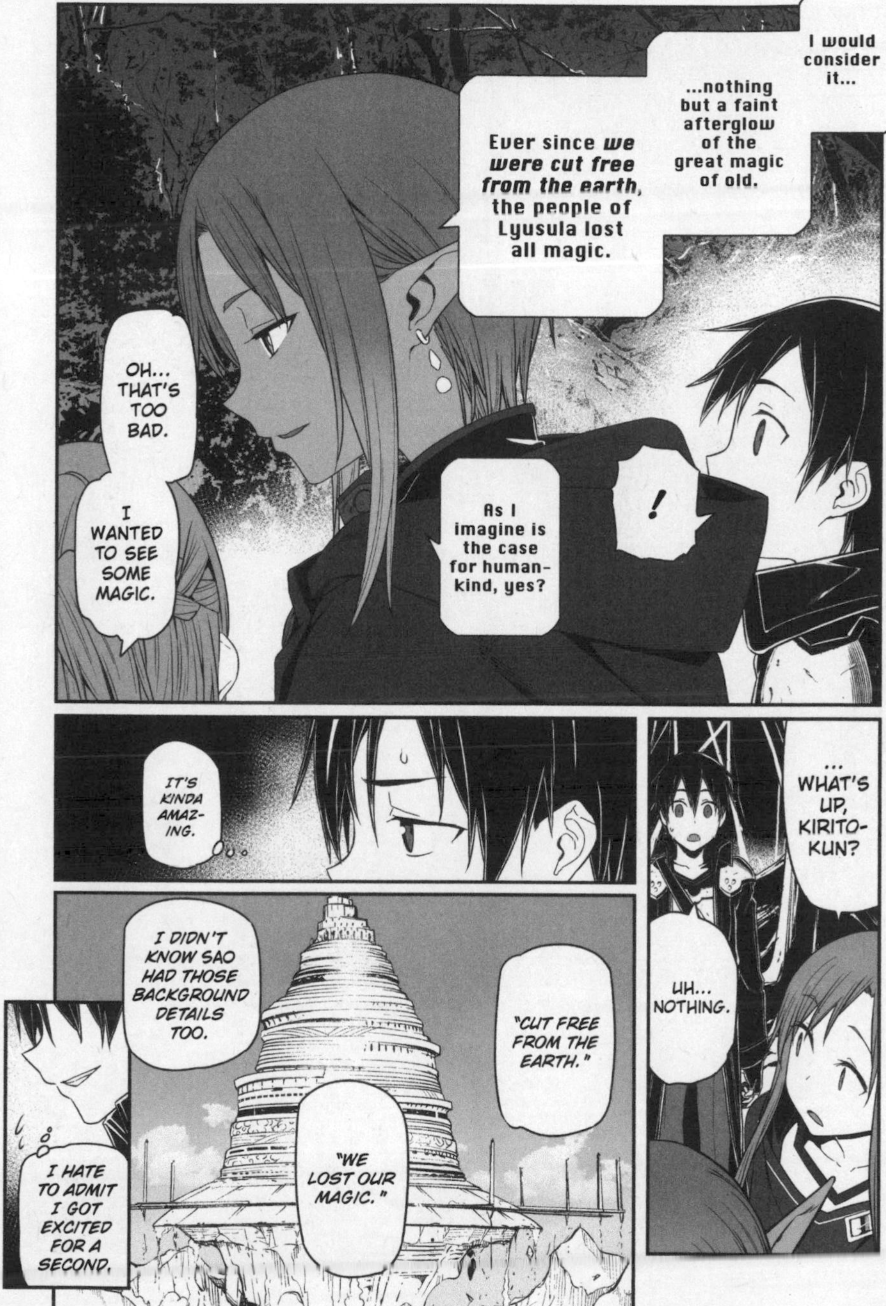
I would consider it...
...nothing but a faint afterglow of the great magic of old.
Ever since *we were cut free from the earth*, the people of Lyusula lost all magic.
!
As I imagine is the case for human-kind, yes?
OH... THAT'S TOO BAD.
I WANTED TO SEE SOME MAGIC.
... WHAT'S UP, KIRITO-KUN?
UH... NOTHING.
IT'S KINDA AMAZ-ING.
"CUT FREE FROM THE EARTH."
"WE LOST OUR MAGIC."
I DIDN'T KNOW SAO HAD THOSE BACKGROUND DETAILS TOO.
I HATE TO ADMIT I GOT EXCITED FOR A SECOND.

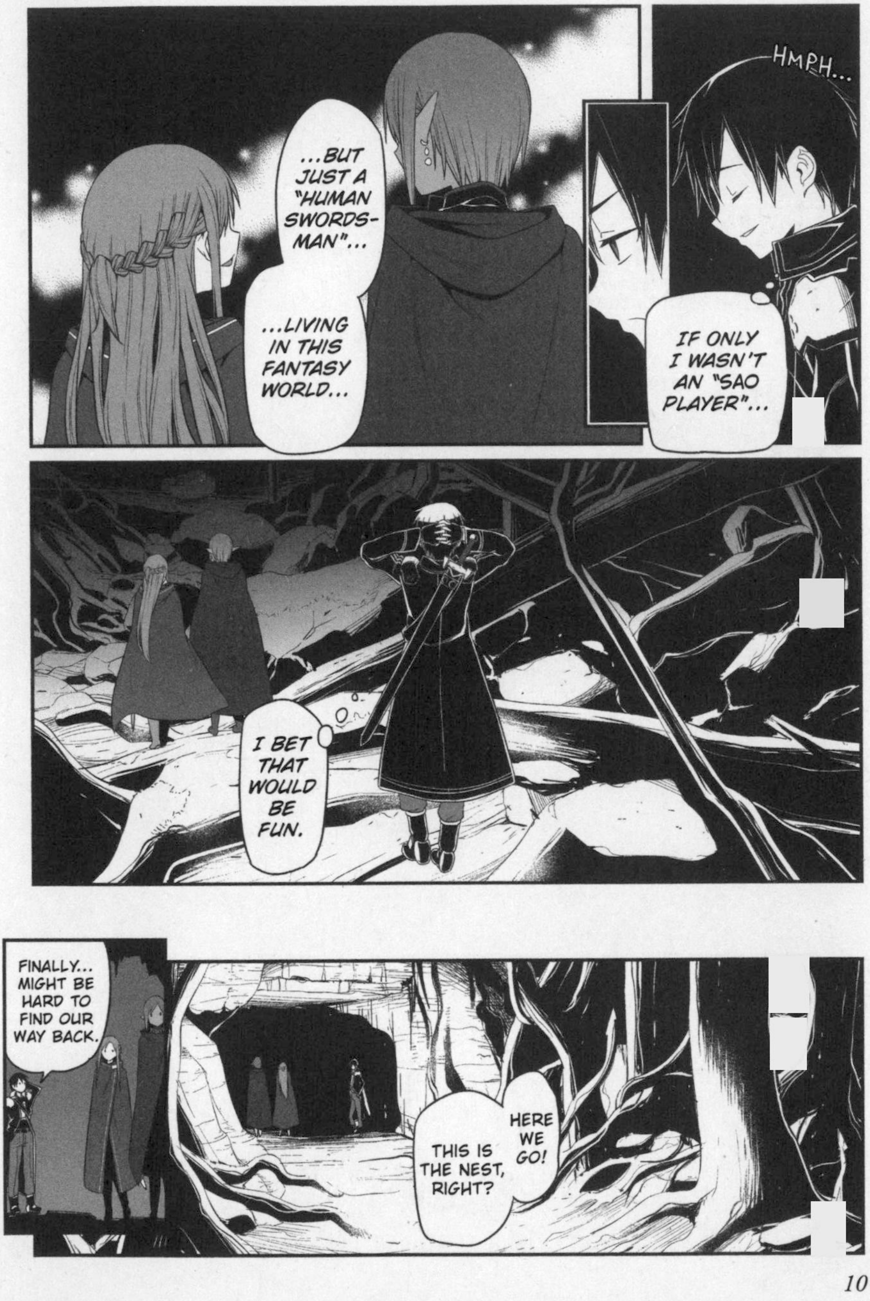
HMPH...
IF ONLY I WASN'T AN "SAO PLAYER"...
...BUT JUST A "HUMAN SWORDS-MAN"...
...LIVING IN THIS FANTASY WORLD...
I BET THAT WOULD BE FUN.
HERE WE GO!
THIS IS THE NEST, RIGHT?
FINALLY... MIGHT BE HARD TO FIND OUR WAY BACK.

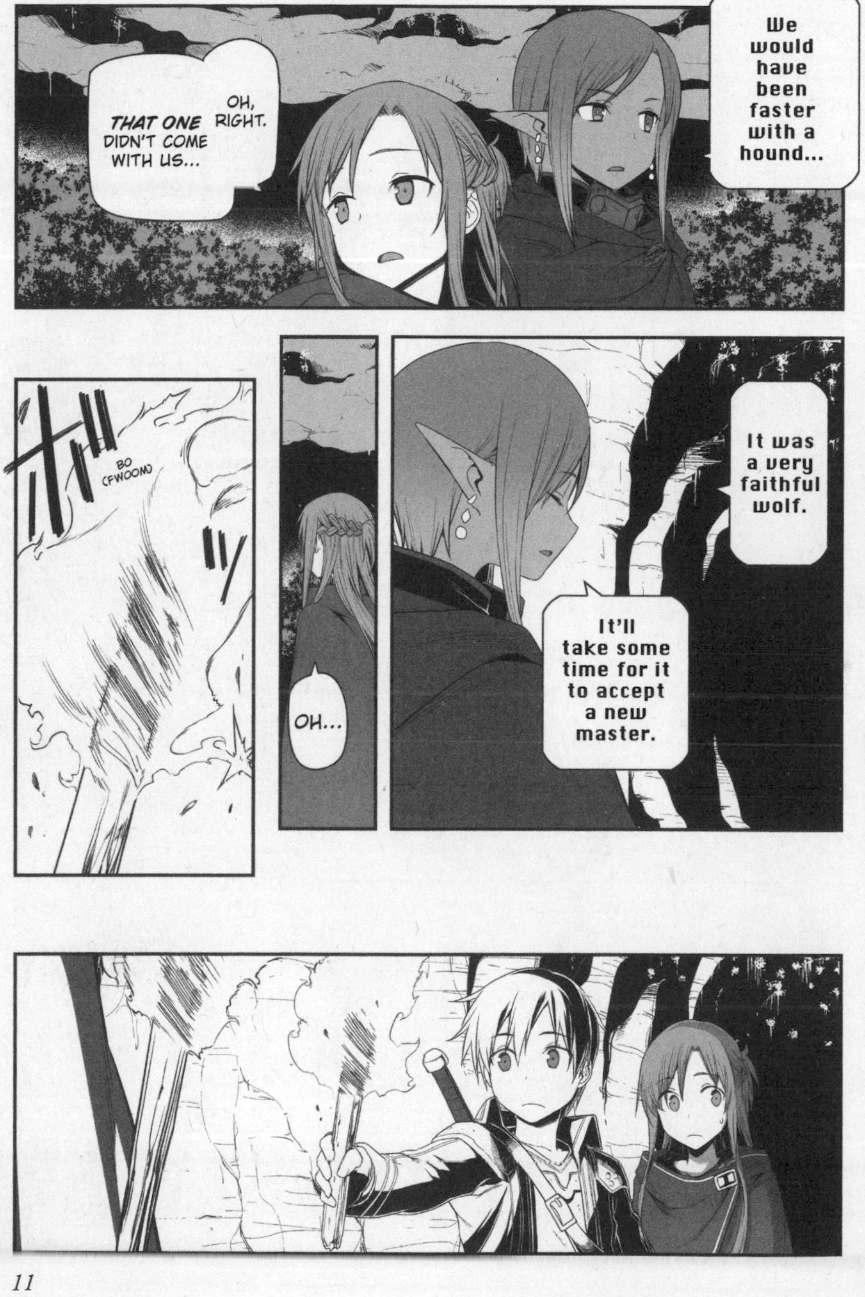
We would have been faster with a hound...
OH, RIGHT. *THAT ONE* DIDN'T COME WITH US...
It was a very faithful wolf.
It'll take some time for it to accept a new master.
OH...
BO (FWOOM)

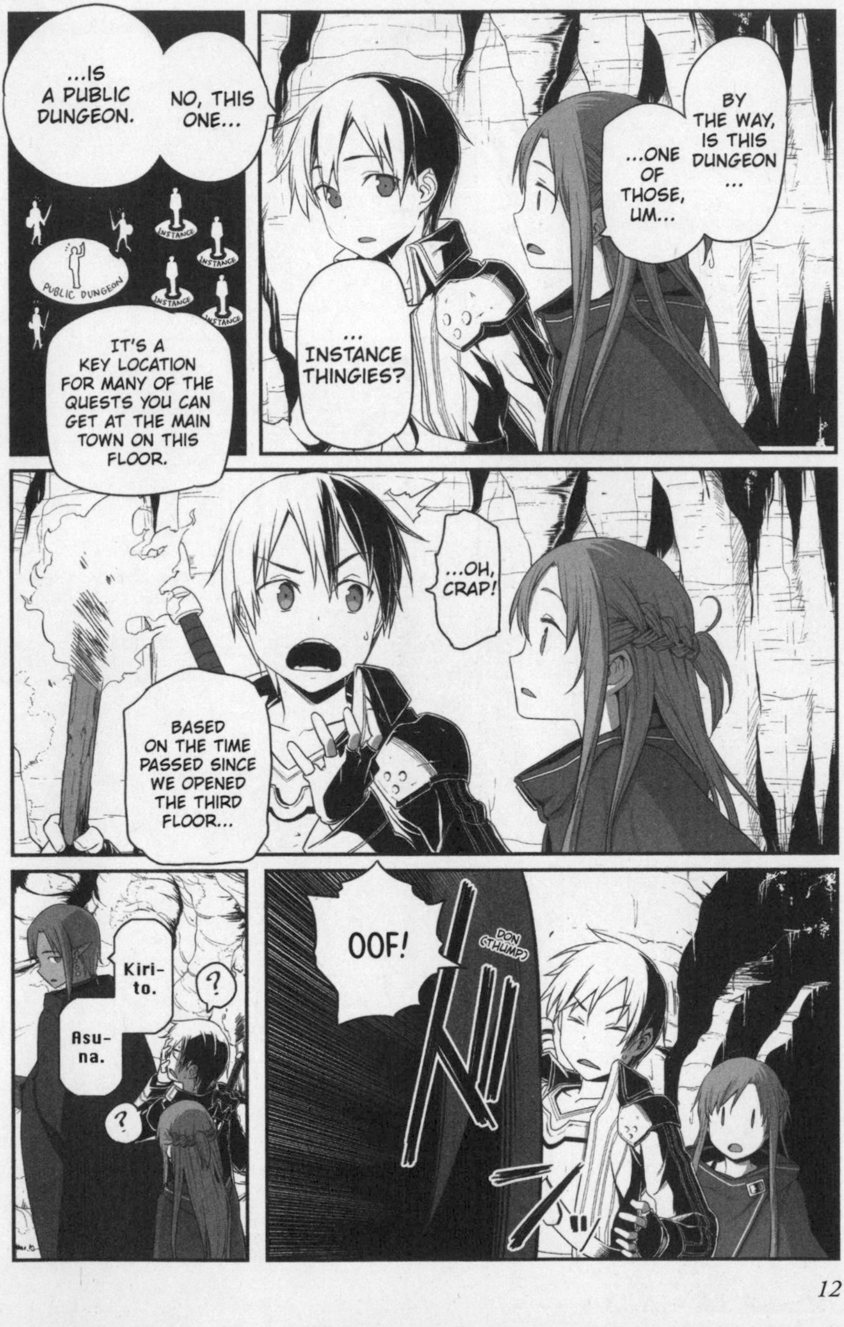
BY THE WAY, IS THIS DUNGEON...
...ONE OF THOSE, UM...
...INSTANCE THINGIES?
NO, THIS ONE...
...IS A PUBLIC DUNGEON.
INSTANCE
INSTANCE
INSTANCE
INSTANCE
PUBLIC DUNGEON
IT'S A KEY LOCATION FOR MANY OF THE QUESTS YOU CAN GET AT THE MAIN TOWN ON THIS FLOOR.
...OH, CRAP!
BASED ON THE TIME PASSED SINCE WE OPENED THE THIRD FLOOR...
OOF!
DON (THUMP)
Kiri-to.
?
Asu-na.
?

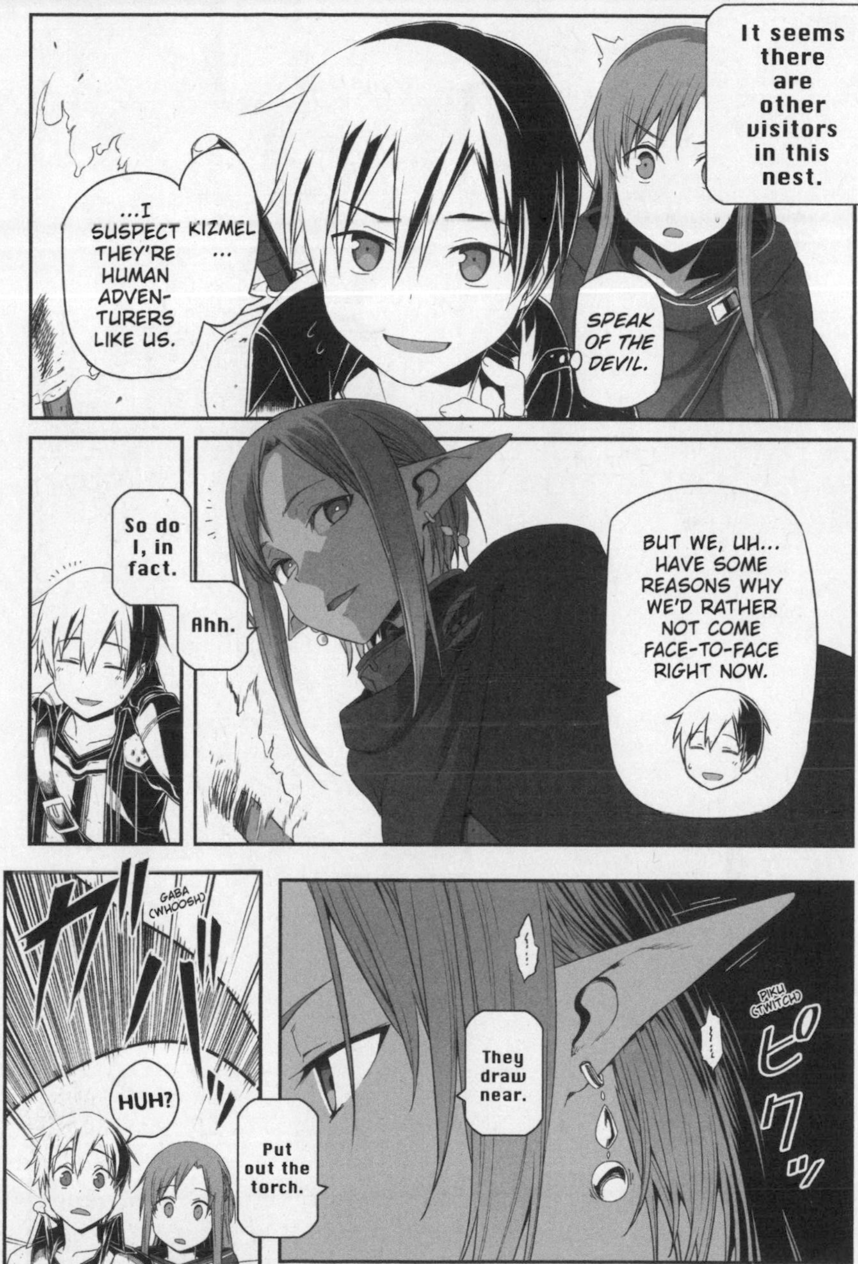
It seems there are other visitors in this nest.
SPEAK OF THE DEVIL.
KIZMEL...
...I SUSPECT THEY'RE HUMAN ADVENTURERS LIKE US.
BUT WE, UH... HAVE SOME REASONS WHY WE'D RATHER NOT COME FACE-TO-FACE RIGHT NOW.
So do I, in fact.
Ahh.
PIKU (TWITCH)
They draw near.
GABA (WHOOSH)
Put out the torch.
HUH?

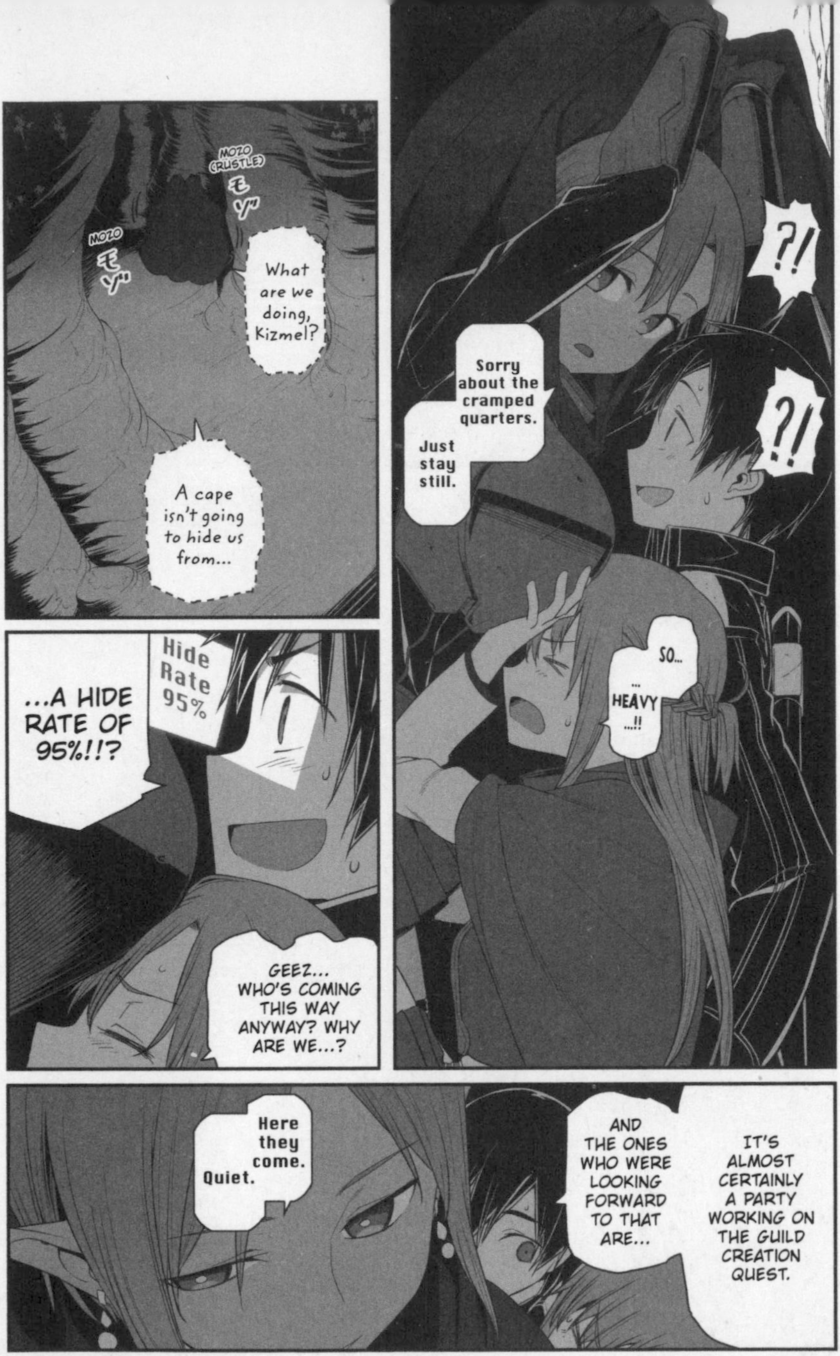
?!
?!
Sorry about the cramped quarters.
Just stay still.
SO... ... HEAVY ...!!
MOZO (RUSTLE) モゾ
MOZO モゾ
What are we doing, Kizmel?
A cape isn't going to hide us from...
Hide Rate 95%
...A HIDE RATE OF 95%!!?
GEEZ... WHO'S COMING THIS WAY ANYWAY? WHY ARE WE...?
IT'S ALMOST CERTAINLY A PARTY WORKING ON THE GUILD CREATION QUEST.
AND THE ONES WHO WERE LOOKING FORWARD TO THAT ARE...
Here they come. Quiet.

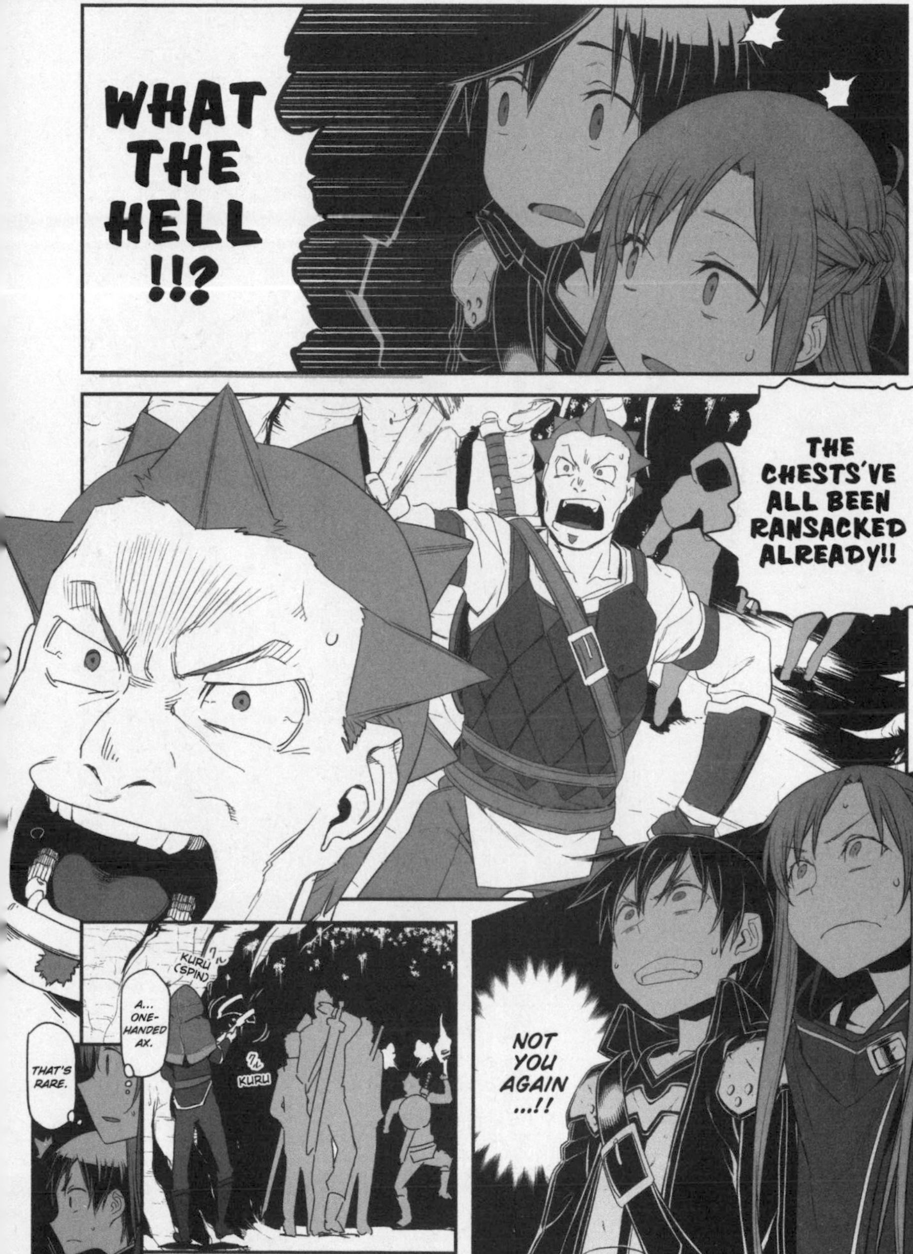
WHAT THE HELL !!?
THE CHESTS'VE ALL BEEN RANSACKED ALREADY!!
NOT YOU AGAIN ...!!
KURU (SPIN)
A... ONE-HANDED AX.
KURU
THAT'S RARE.

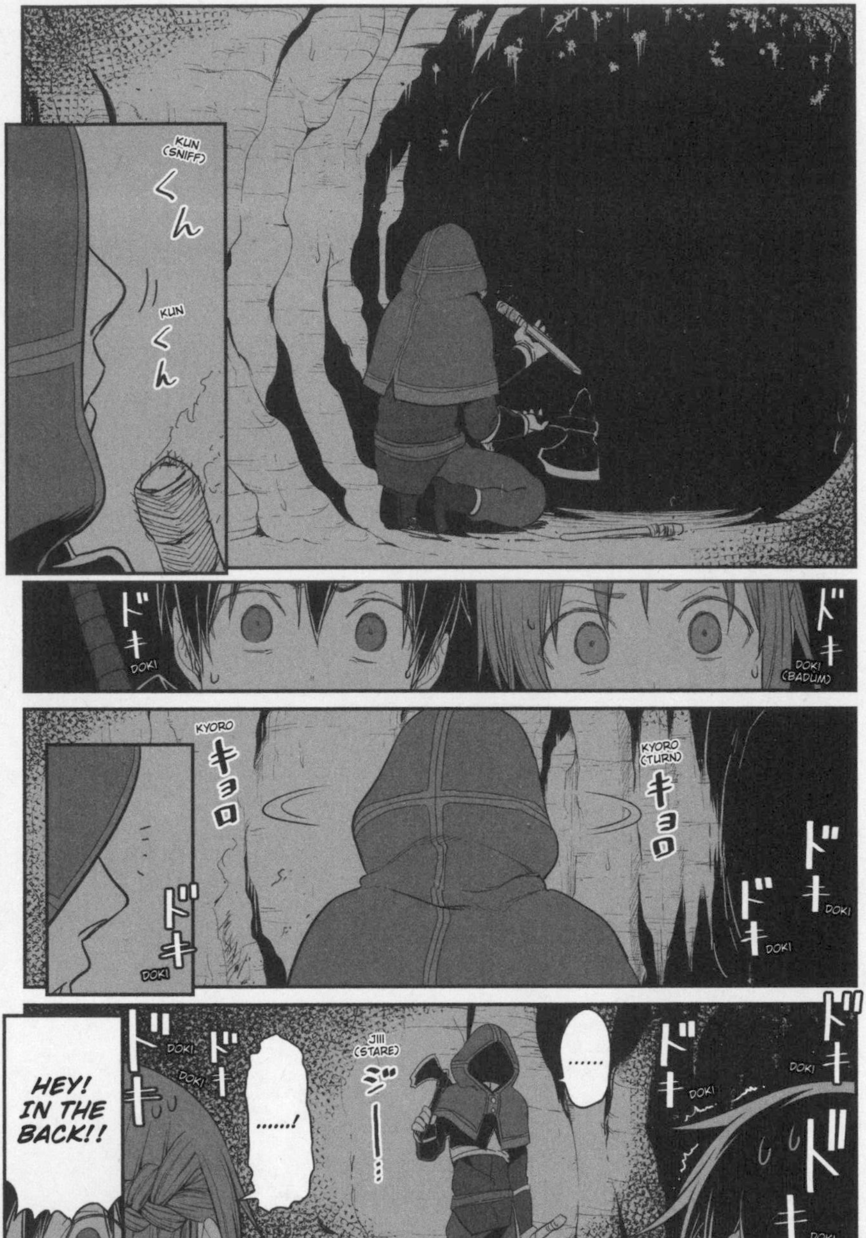
KUN (SNIFF)
くん
KUN
くん
ドキ
DOKI! (BADUM)
ドキ
DOKI
ドキ
DOKI
ドキ
DOKI
KYORO (TURN)
キョロ
KYORO
キョロ
ドキ
DOKI
ドキ
DOKI
ドキ
DOKI
ドキ
DOKI
......
JIII (STARE)
ジー...
......!
ドキ
DOKI
ドキ
DOKI
HEY! IN THE BACK!!

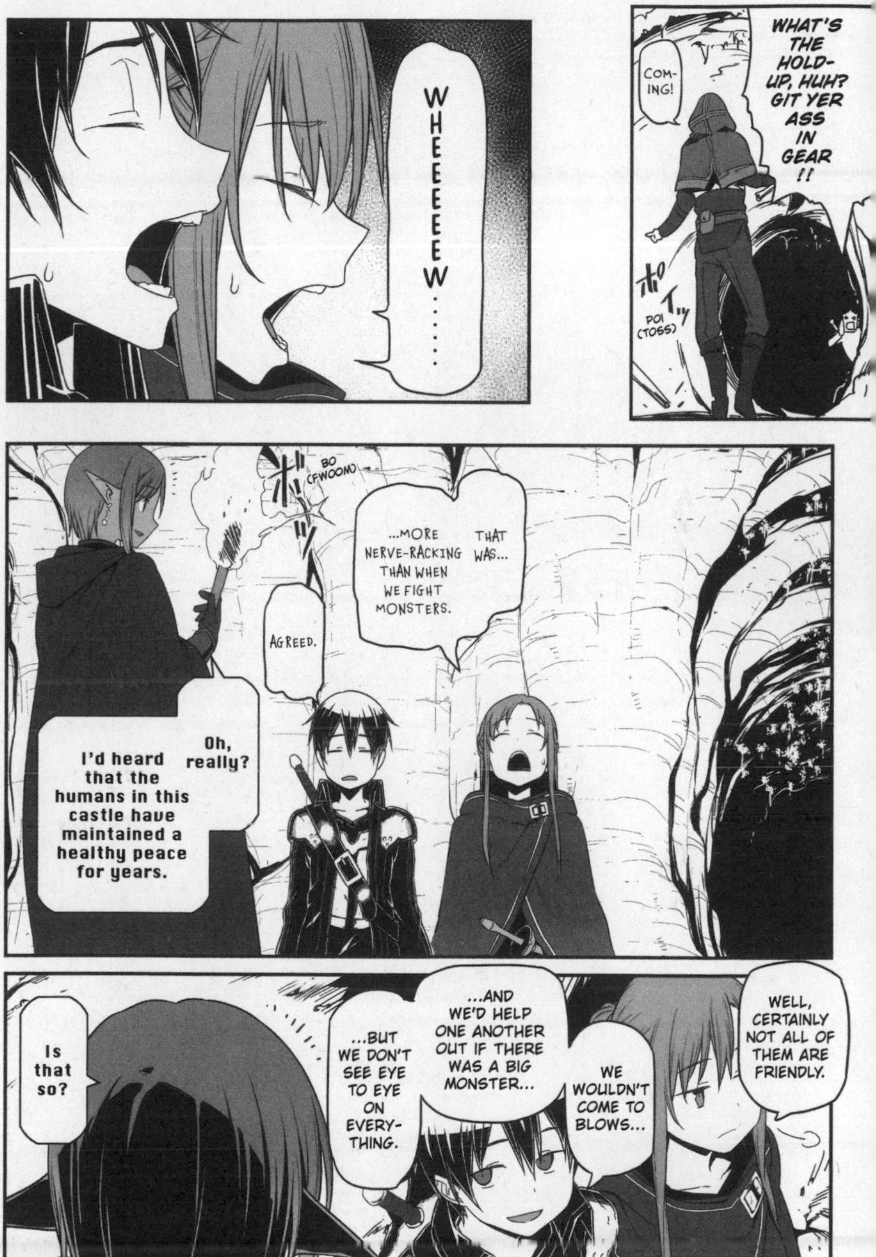
WHAT'S THE HOLD-UP, HUH? GIT YER ASS IN GEAR!!
COM-ING!
POI (TOSS)
WHEEEEEEW......
THAT WAS...
...MORE NERVE-RACKING THAN WHEN WE FIGHT MONSTERS.
BO (FWOOM)
AGREED.
Oh, really?
I'd heard that the humans in this castle have maintained a healthy peace for years.
WELL, CERTAINLY NOT ALL OF THEM ARE FRIENDLY.
WE WOULDN'T COME TO BLOWS...
...AND WE'D HELP ONE ANOTHER OUT IF THERE WAS A BIG MONSTER...
...BUT WE DON'T SEE EYE TO EYE ON EVERYTHING.
Is that so?

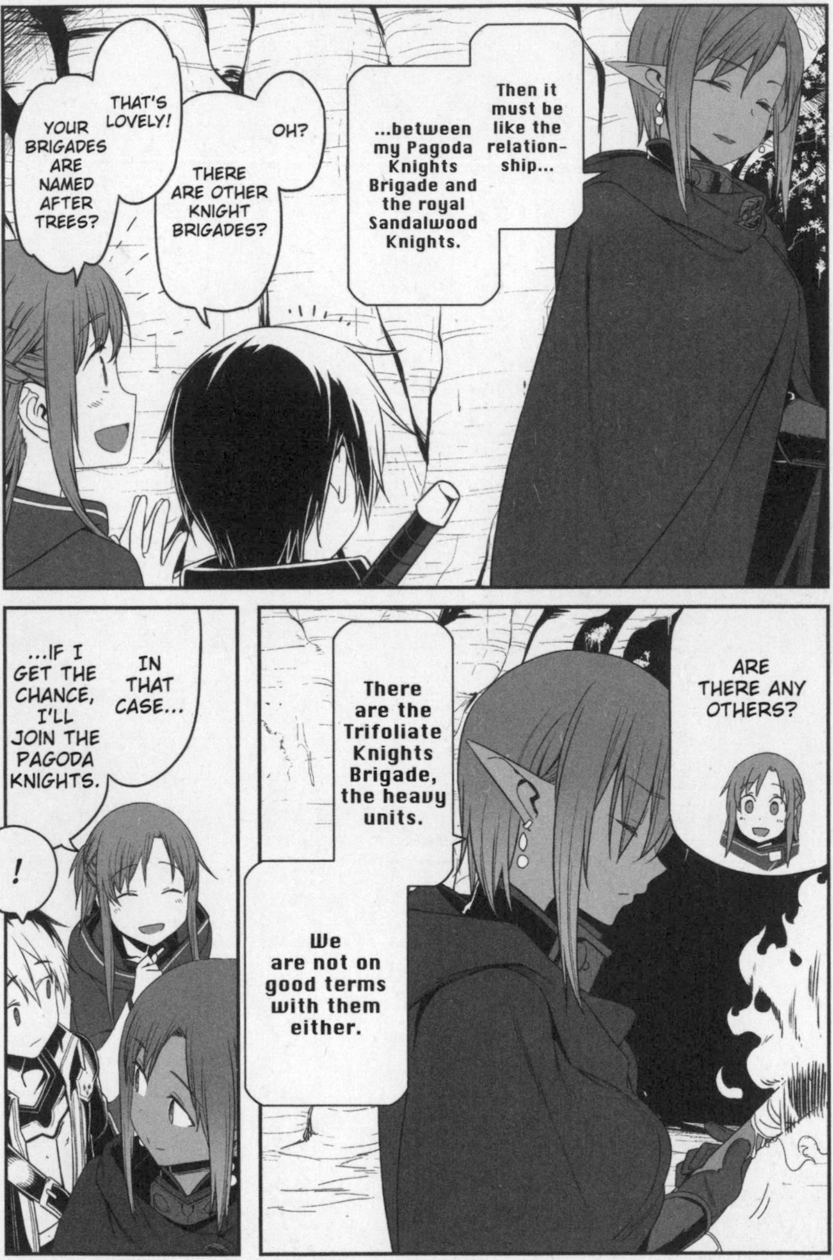
Then it must be like the relationship...
...between my Pagoda Knights Brigade and the royal Sandalwood Knights.
OH?
THERE ARE OTHER KNIGHT BRIGADES?
THAT'S LOVELY!
YOUR BRIGADES ARE NAMED AFTER TREES?
ARE THERE ANY OTHERS?
There are the Trifoliate Knights Brigade, the heavy units.
We are not on good terms with them either.
IN THAT CASE...
...IF I GET THE CHANCE, I'LL JOIN THE PAGODA KNIGHTS.
!

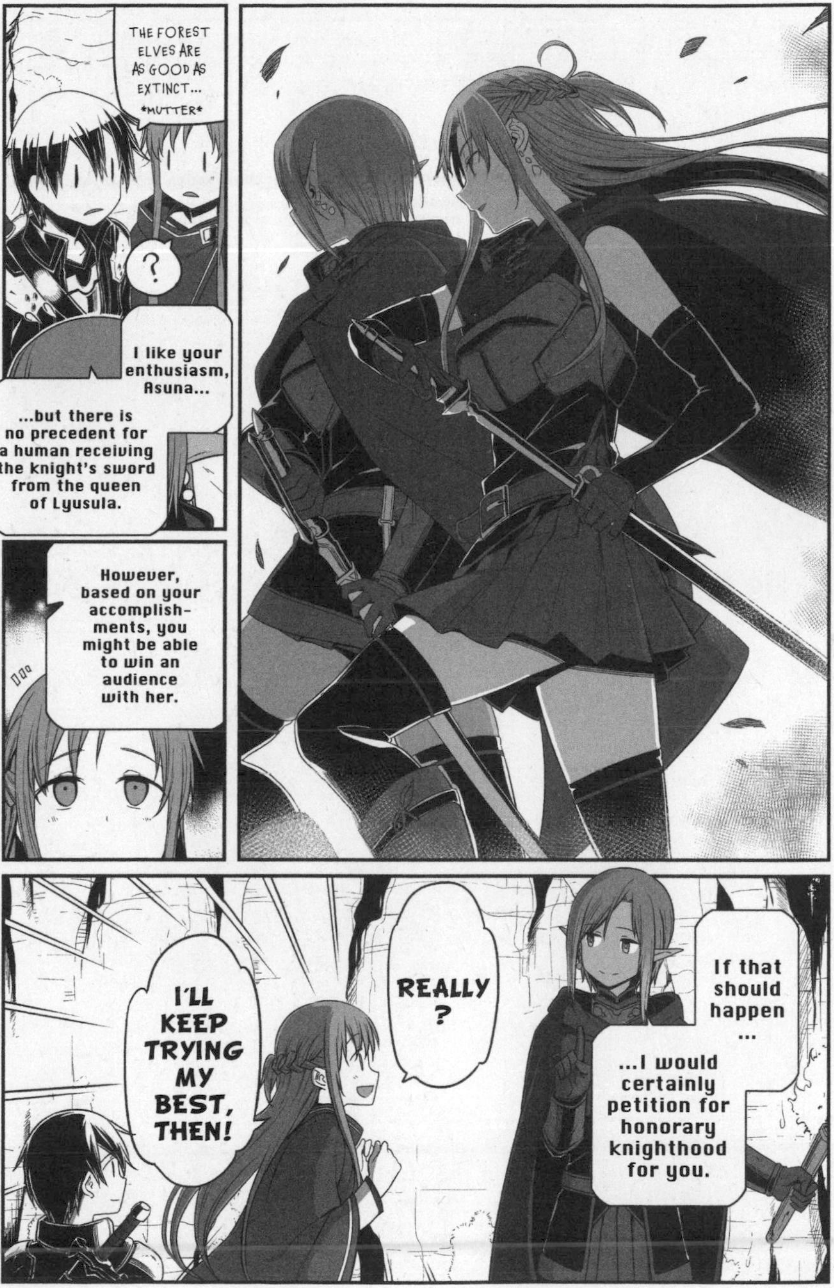
THE FOREST ELVES ARE AS GOOD AS EXTINCT...
MUTTER
?
I like your enthusiasm, Asuna...
...but there is no precedent for a human receiving the knight's sword from the queen of Lyusula.
However, based on your accomplish-ments, you might be able to win an audience with her.
If that should happen ...
...I would certainly petition for honorary knighthood for you.
REALLY?
I'LL KEEP TRYING MY BEST, THEN!

SWORD
ART
ONLINE
PROGRESSIVE

#031: Intercept

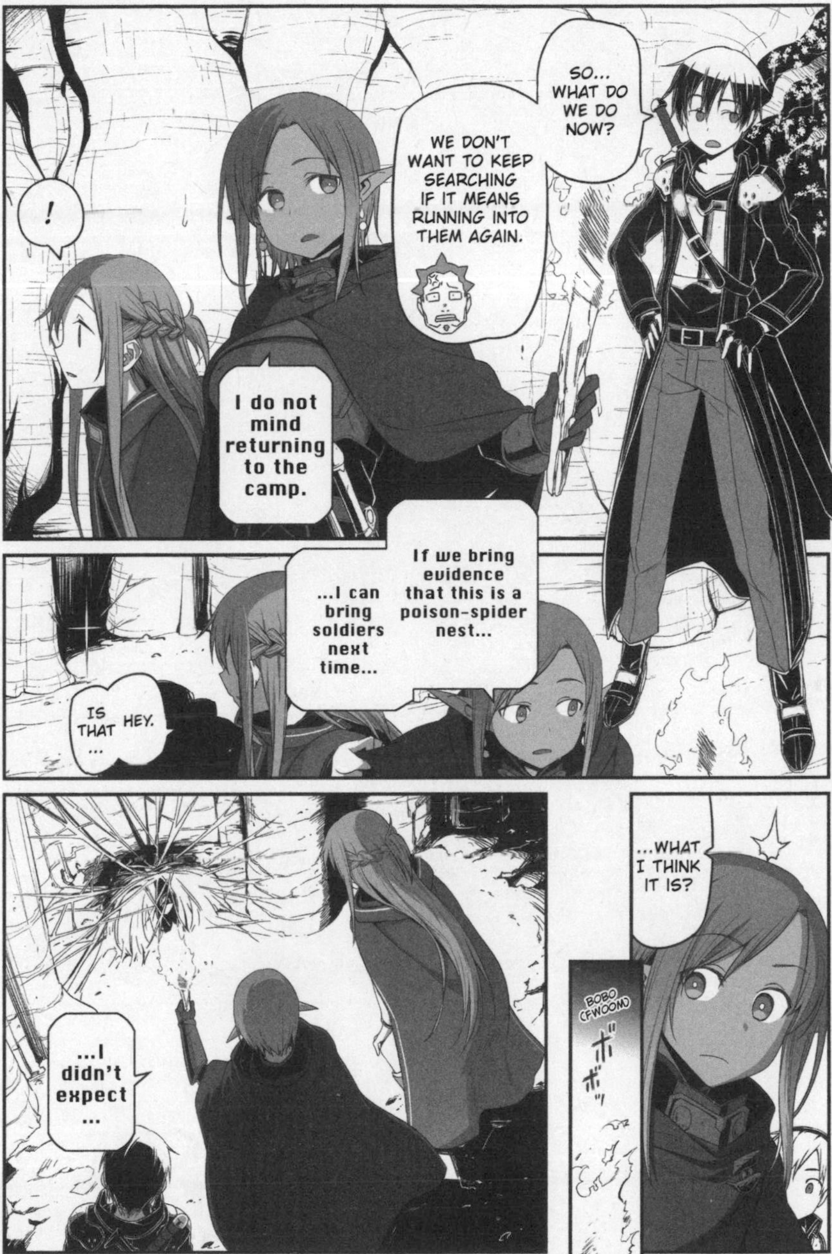
SO... WHAT DO WE DO NOW?
WE DON'T WANT TO KEEP SEARCHING IF IT MEANS RUNNING INTO THEM AGAIN.
I do not mind returning to the camp.
!
If we bring evidence that this is a poison-spider nest...
...I can bring soldiers next time...
HEY.
IS THAT ...
...WHAT I THINK IT IS?
BOBO (FWOOM)
ボボッ
...I didn't expect ...

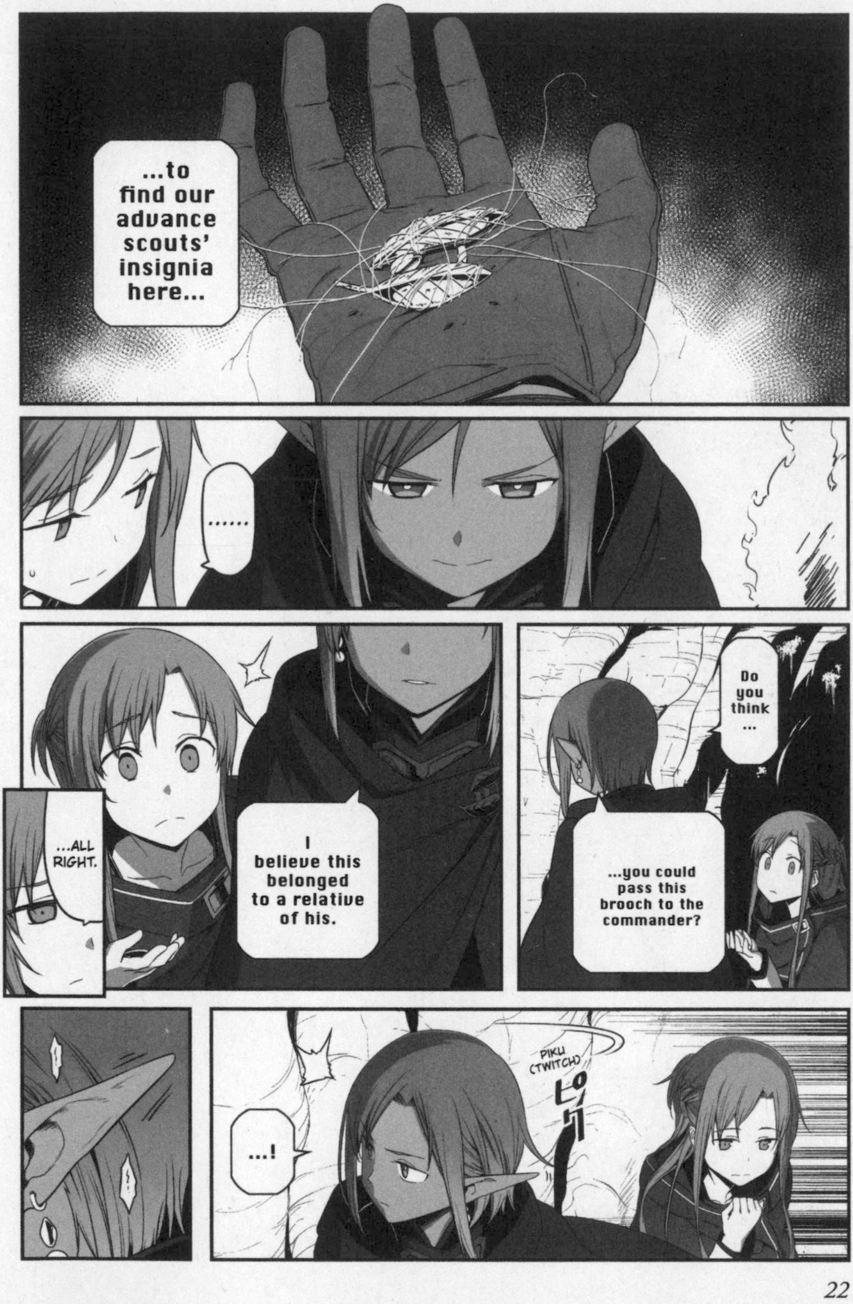
...to find our advance scouts' insignia here...
......
Do you think ...
...you could pass this brooch to the commander?
I believe this belonged to a relative of his.
...ALL RIGHT.
PIKU (TWITCH)
ピク
...!

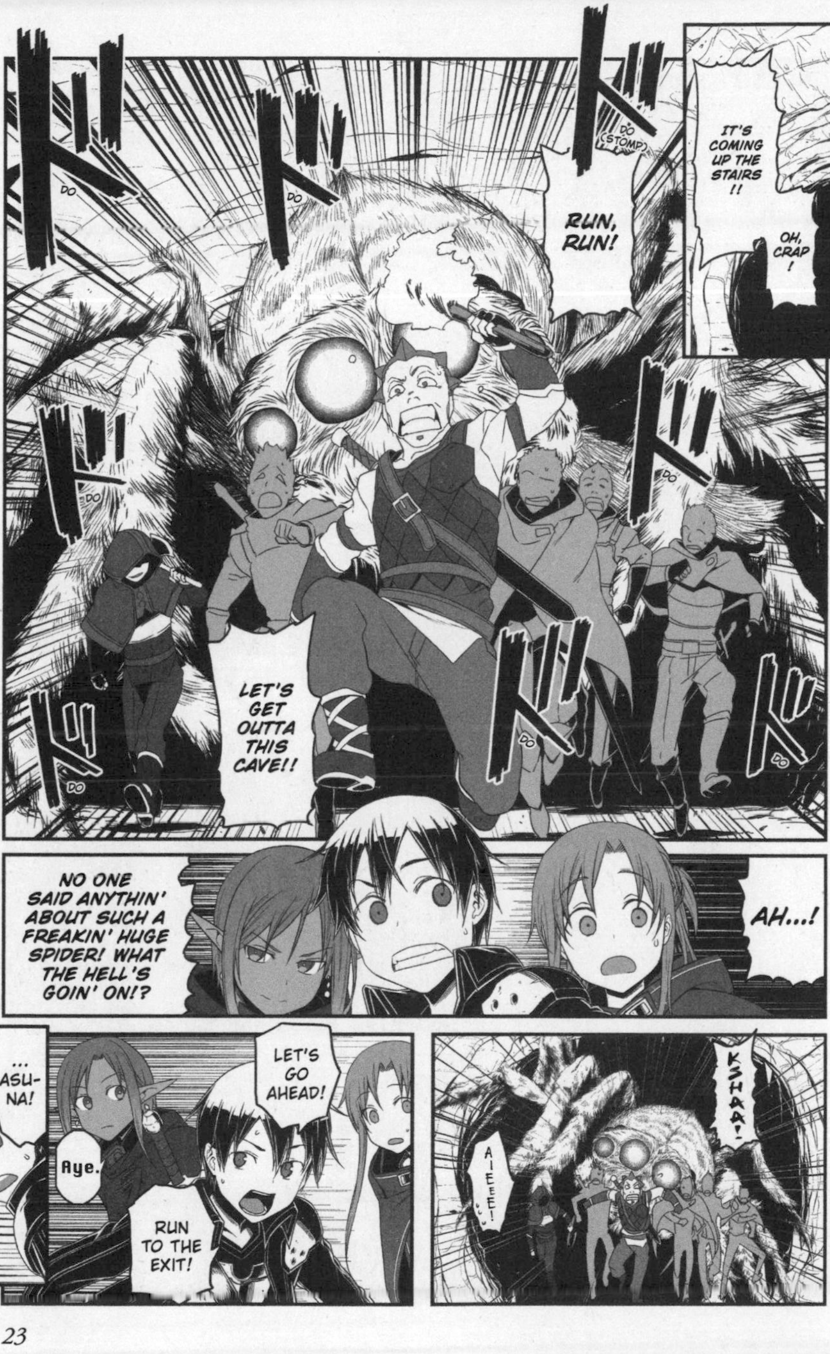
IT'S COMING UP THE STAIRS!!
OH, CRAP!
DO (STOMP)
RUN, RUN!
DO
DO
DO
DO
DO
DO
LET'S GET OUTTA THIS CAVE!!
DO
AH...!
NO ONE SAID ANYTHIN' ABOUT SUCH A FREAKIN' HUGE SPIDER! WHAT THE HELL'S GOIN' ON!?
KSHAA!
AIEEEE!
LET'S GO AHEAD!
... ASUNA!
Aye.
RUN TO THE EXIT!

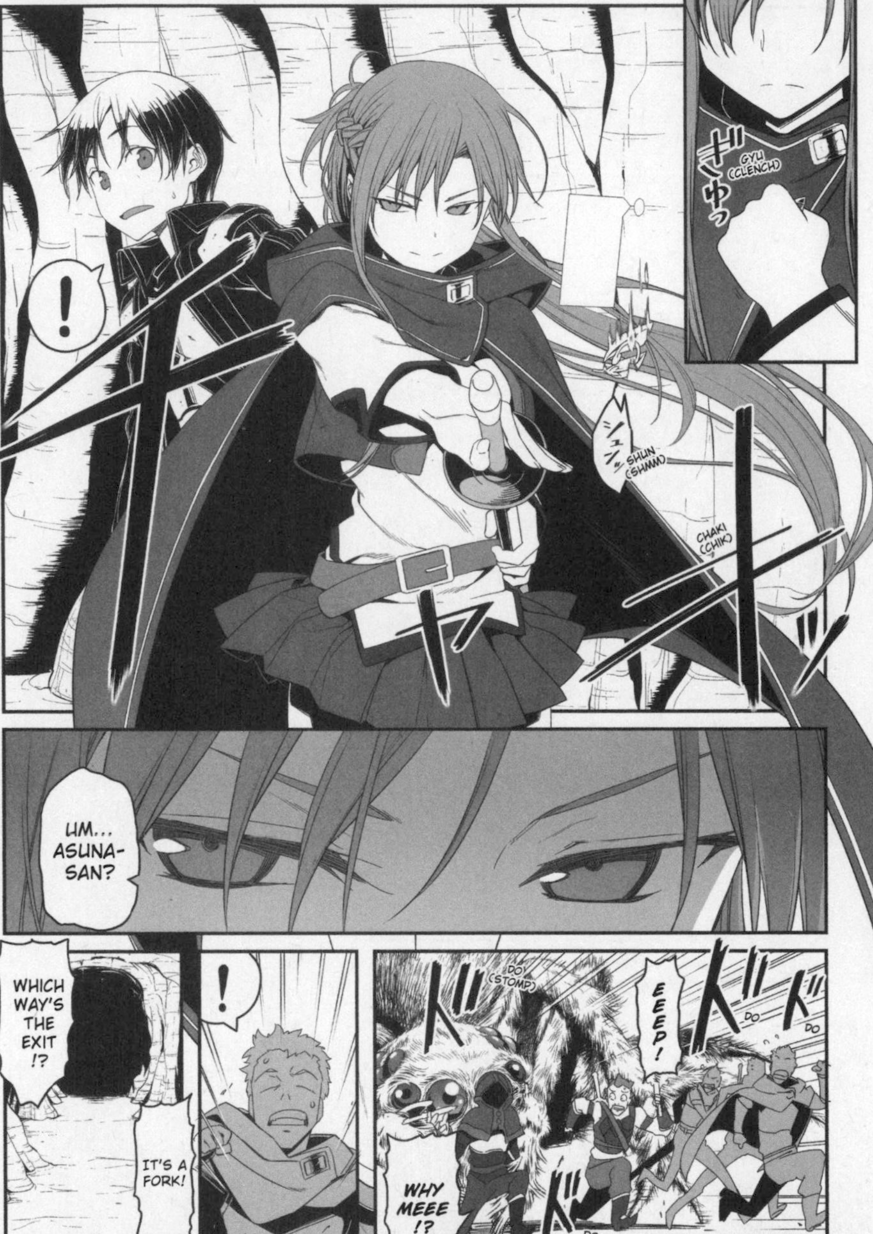
GYU (CLENCH)
SHUN (SHMM)
CHAKI (CHIK)
!
UM... ASUNA-SAN?
DOY (STOMP)
EEEP!
DO
DO
WHY MEEE!?
DO
!
WHICH WAY'S THE EXIT!?
IT'S A FORK!

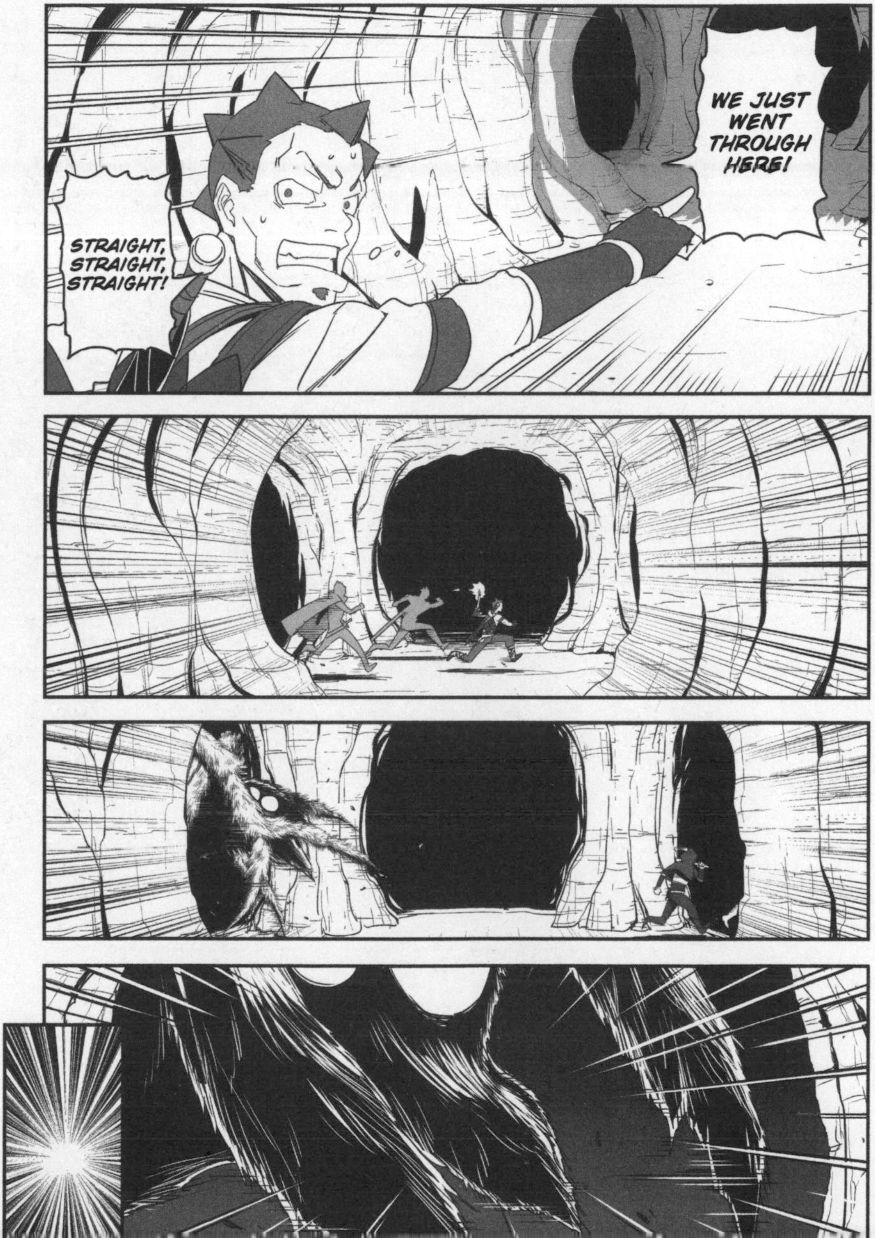
WE JUST WENT THROUGH HERE!
STRAIGHT, STRAIGHT, STRAIGHT!

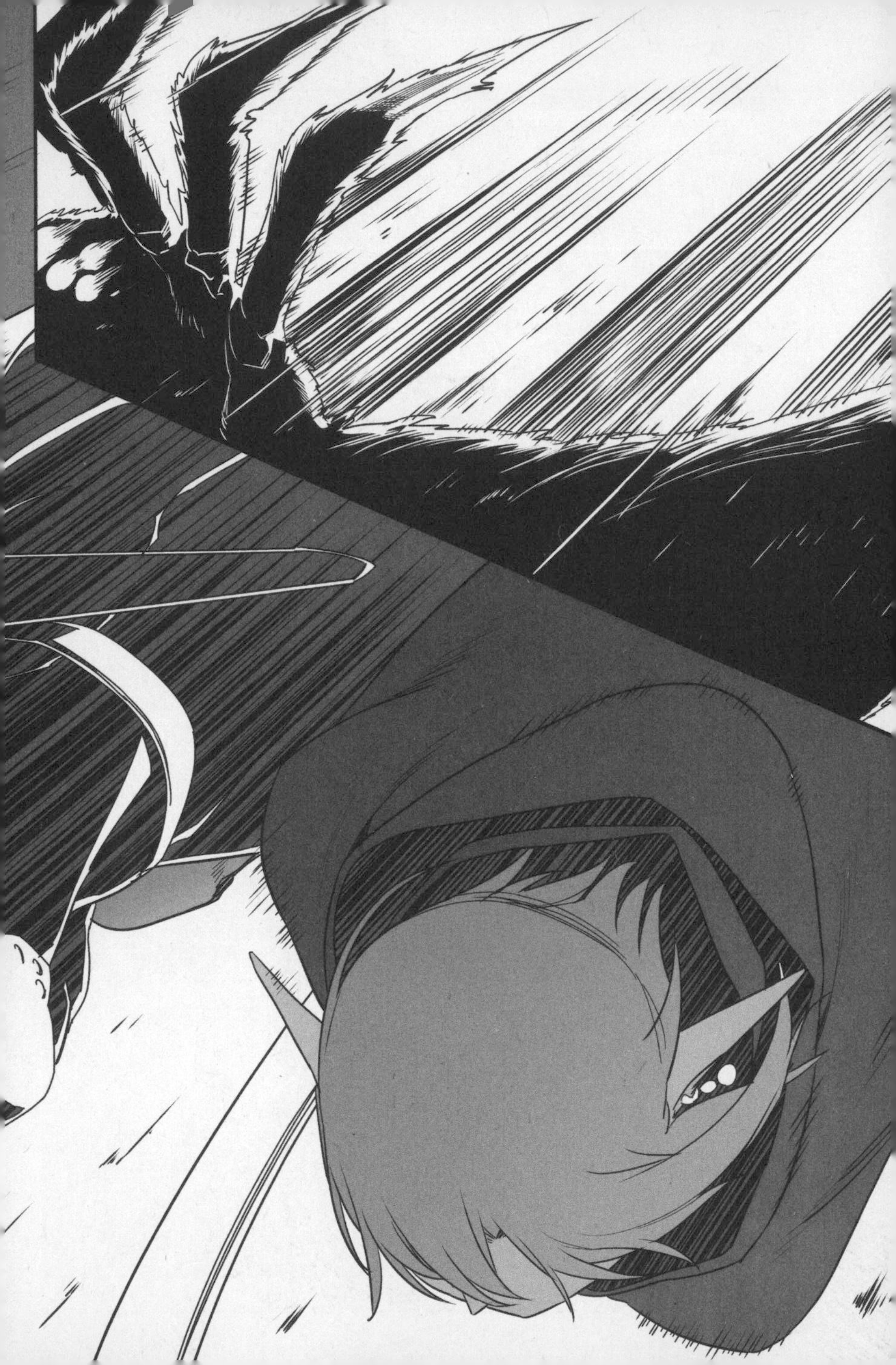

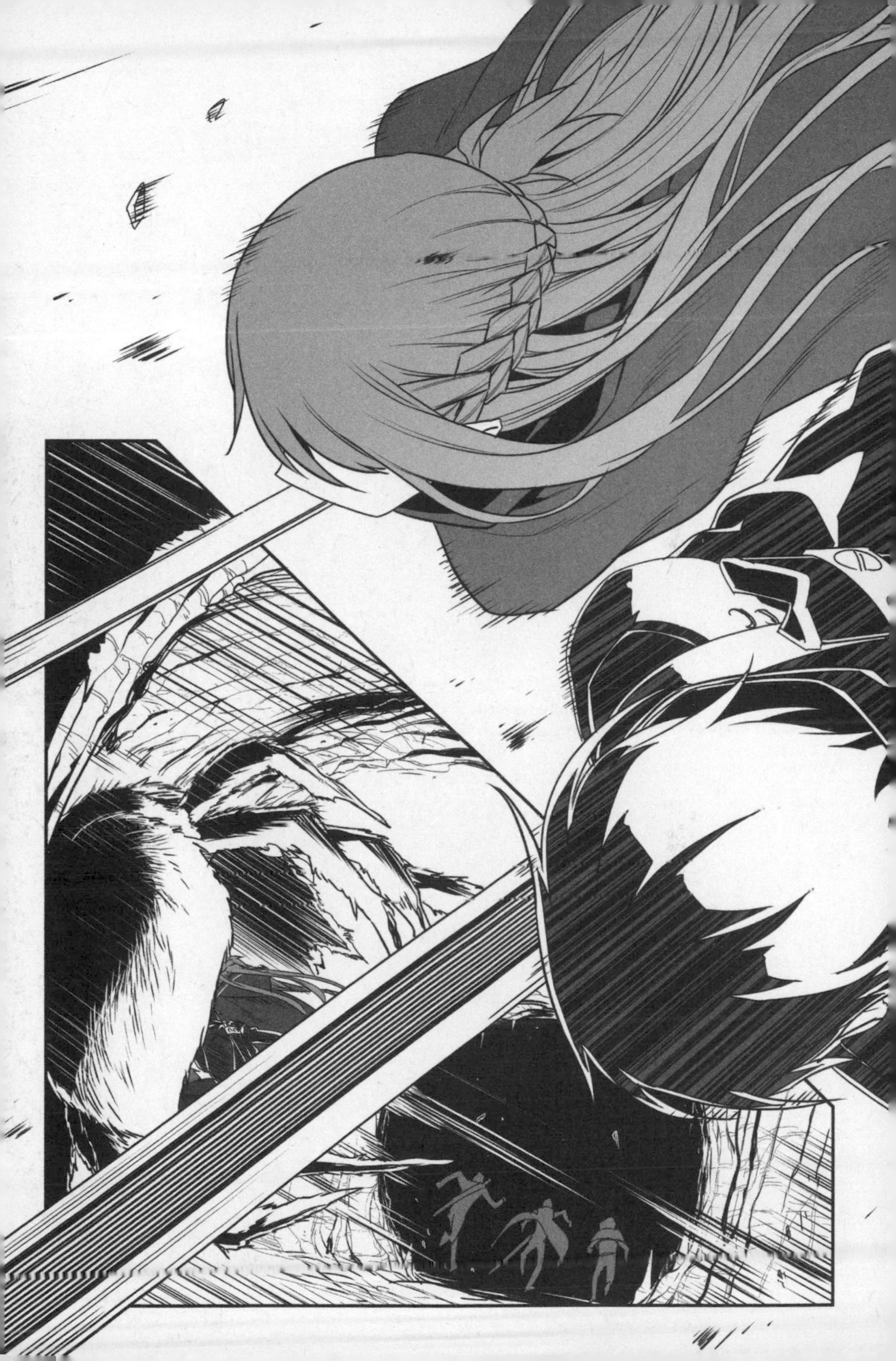

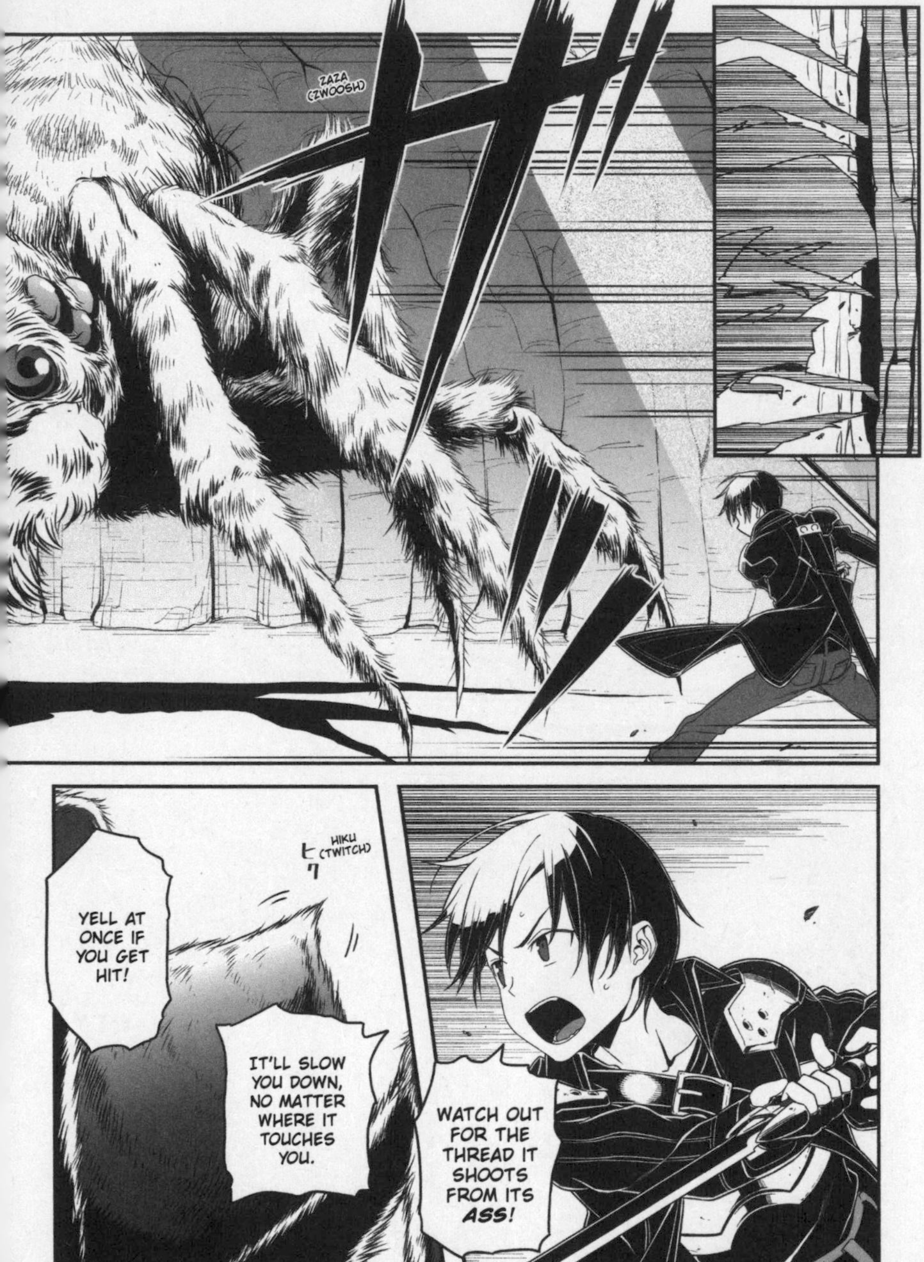
ZAZA (ZWOOSH)
WATCH OUT FOR THE THREAD IT SHOOTS FROM ITS ASS!
IT'LL SLOW YOU DOWN, NO MATTER WHERE IT TOUCHES YOU.
HIKU (TWITCH)
YELL AT ONCE IF YOU GET HIT!

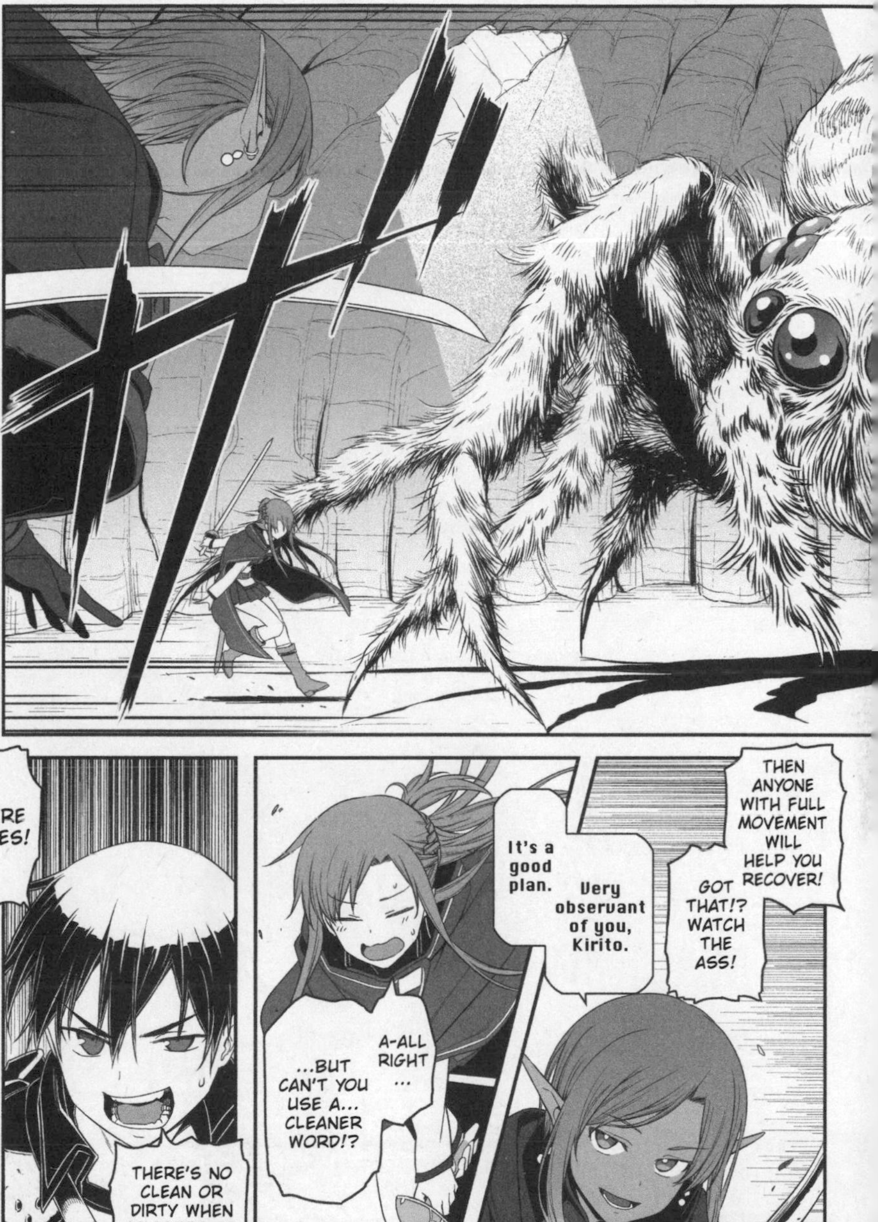
THEN ANYONE WITH FULL MOVEMENT WILL HELP YOU RECOVER!
GOT THAT!? WATCH THE ASS!
Very observant of you, Kirito. It's a good plan.
A-ALL RIGHT ...
...BUT CAN'T YOU USE A... CLEANER WORD!?
HERE GOES!
THERE'S NO CLEAN OR DIRTY WHEN IT COMES TO ASSES!

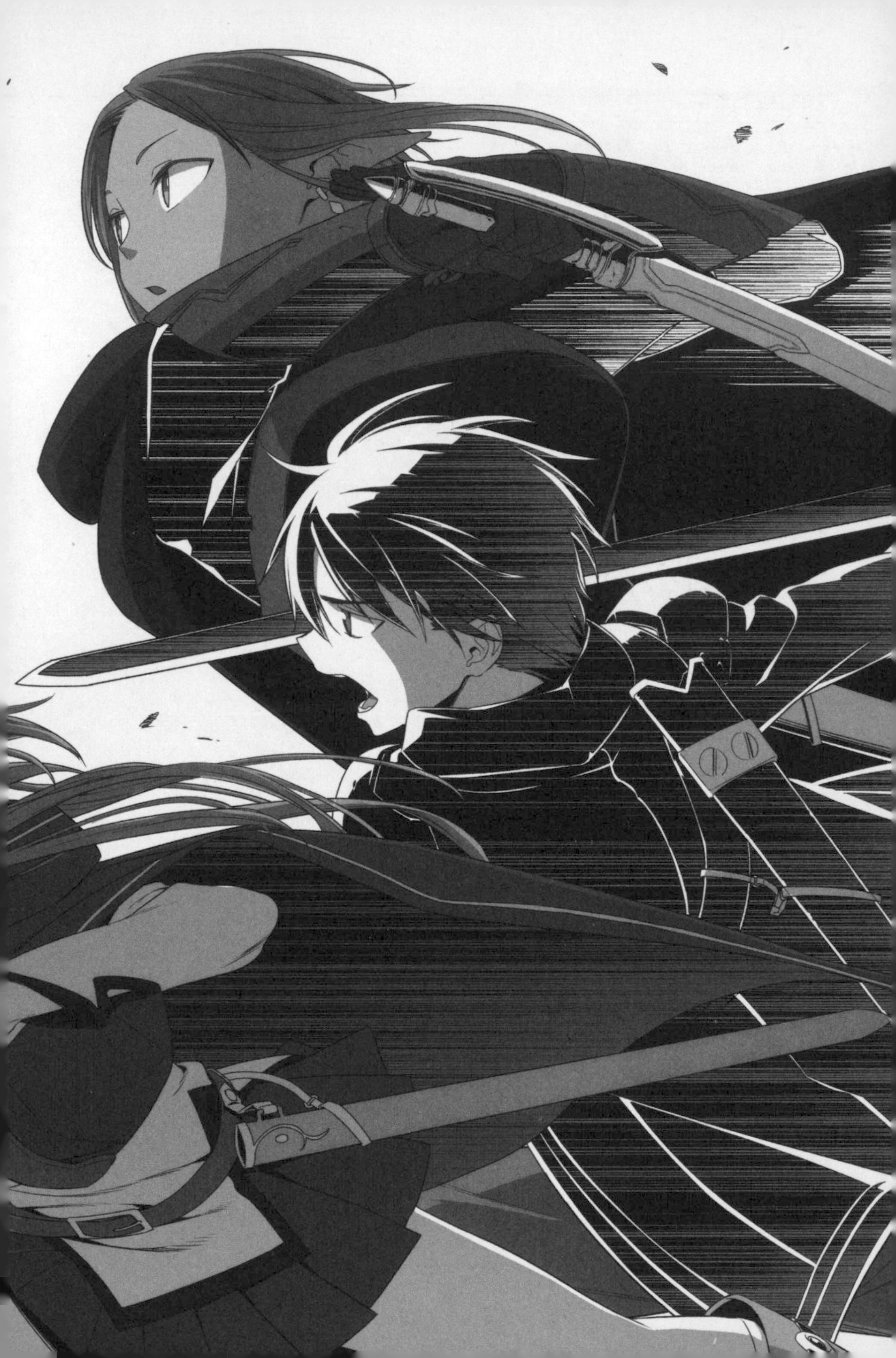

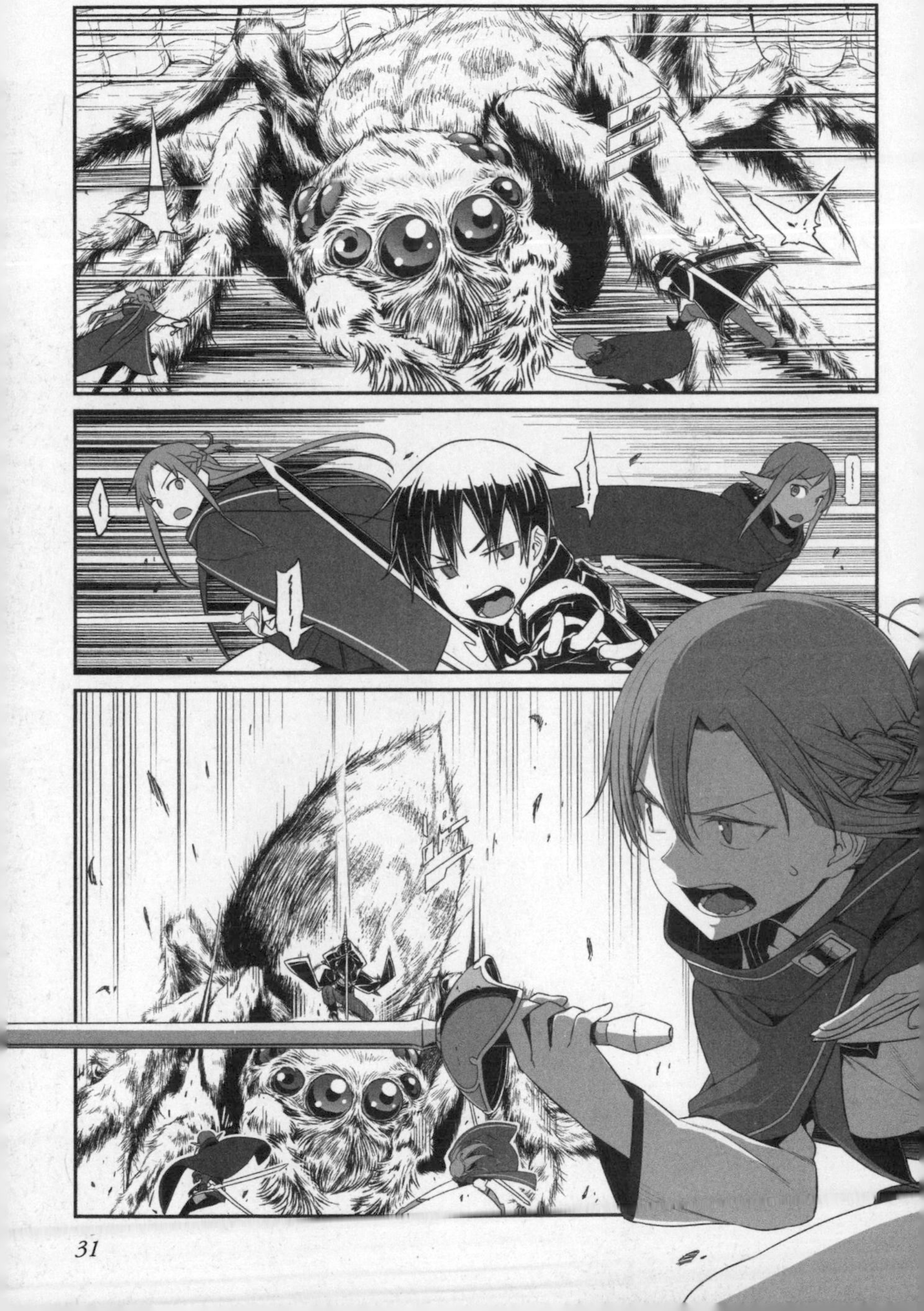

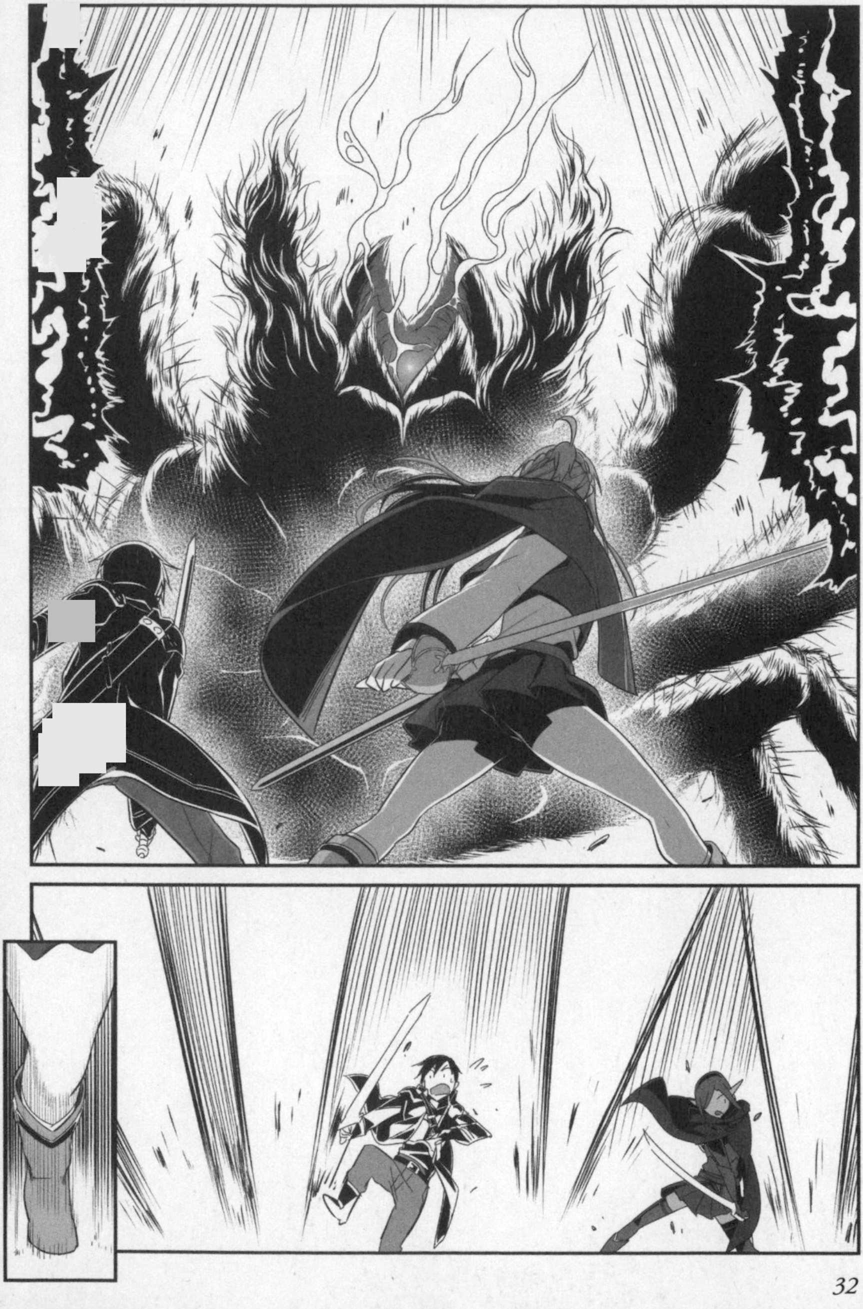

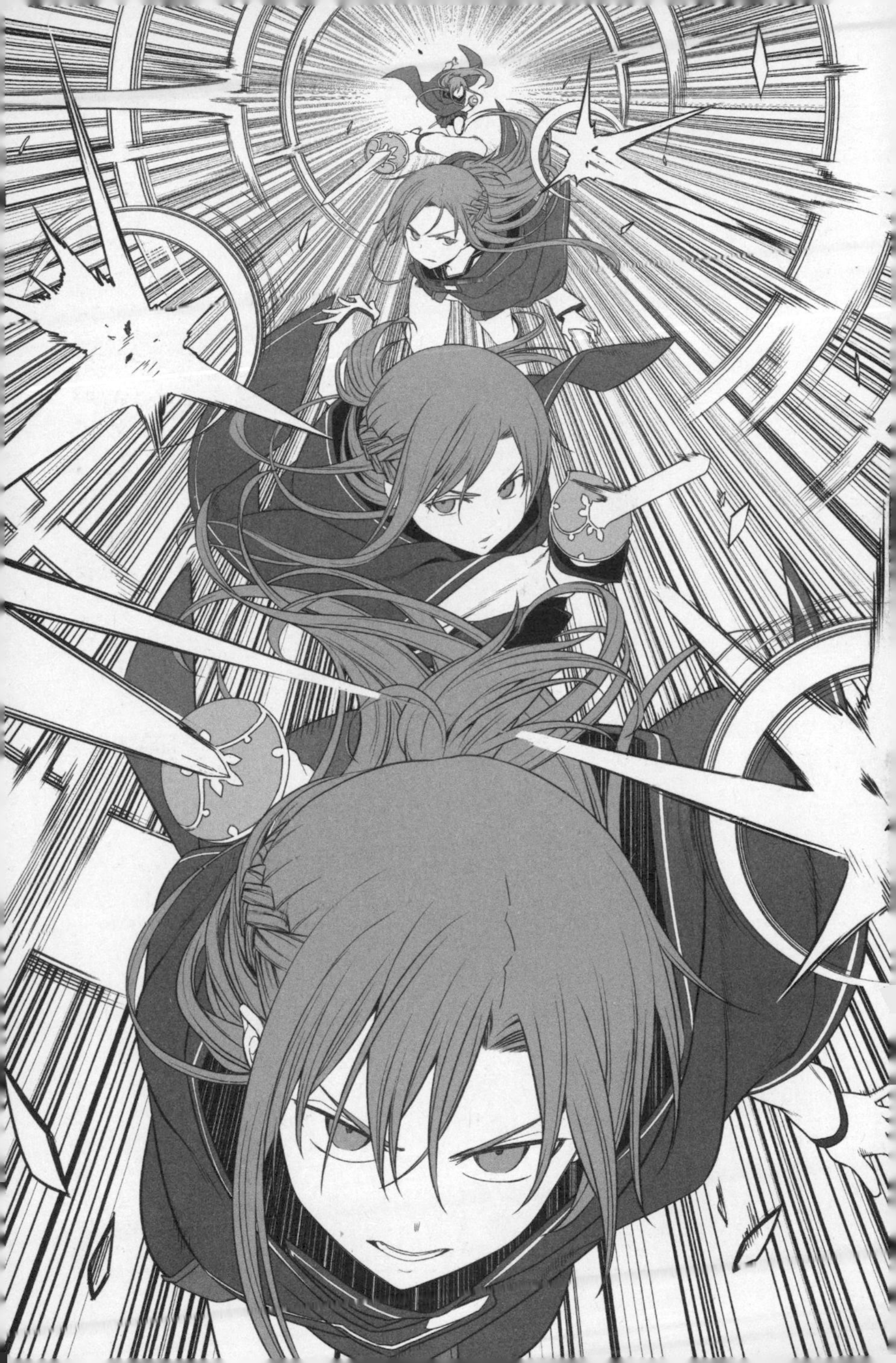

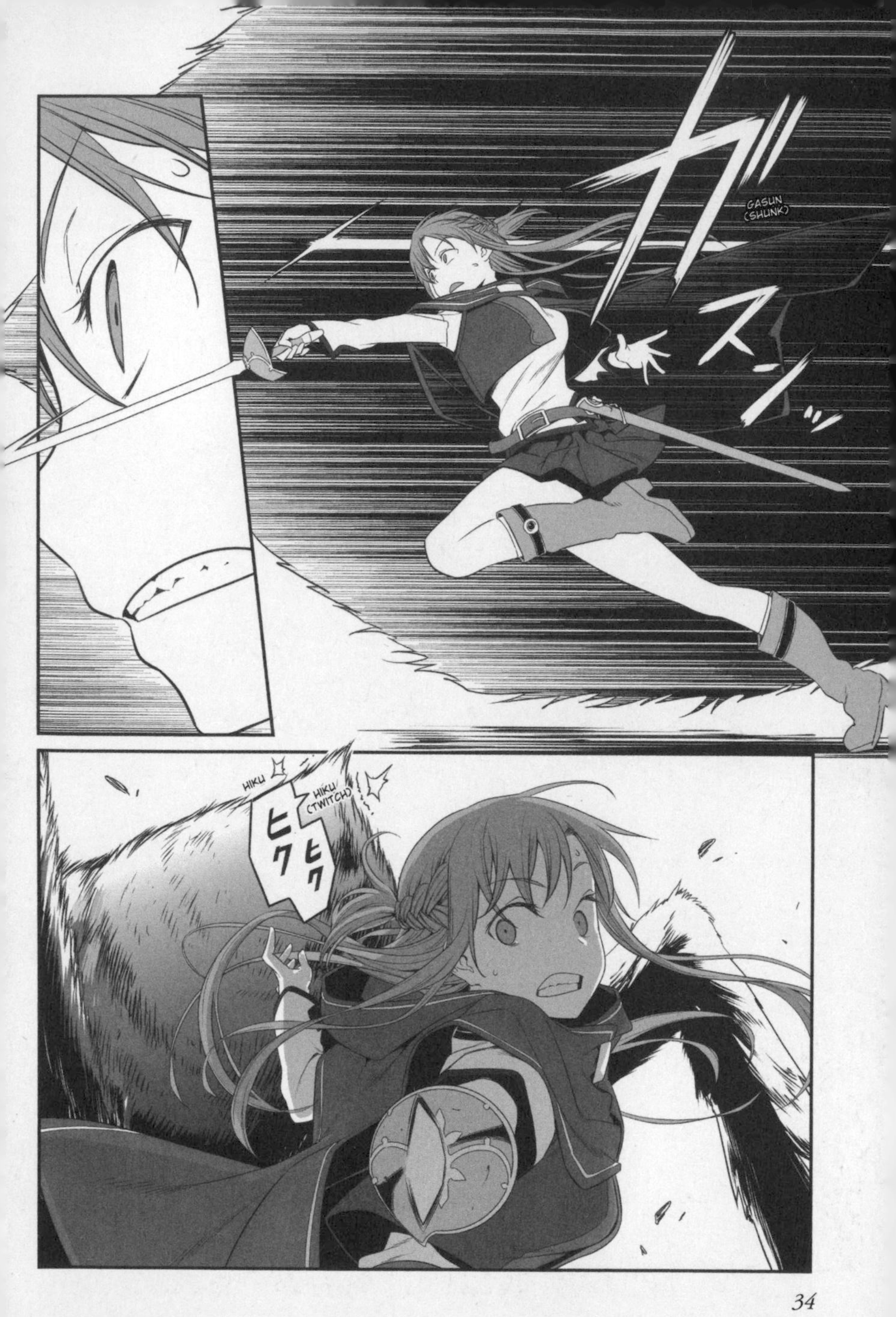
GASUN (SHUNK)
HIKU
HIKU (TWITCH)
ヒクヒク

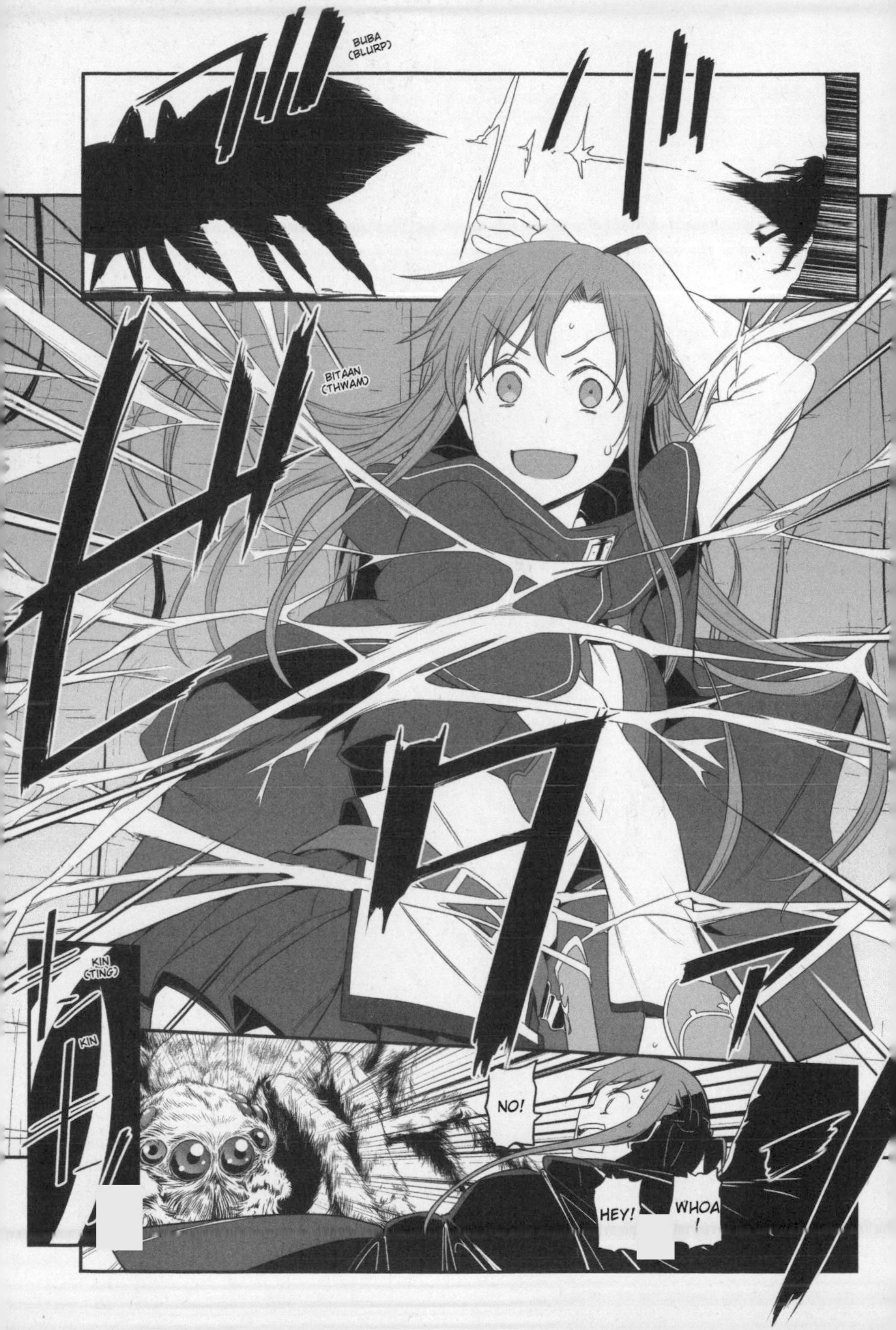
BUBA
(BLURP)
BITAAN
(THWAM)
NO!
WHOA!
HEY!
KIN
(TING)
KIN

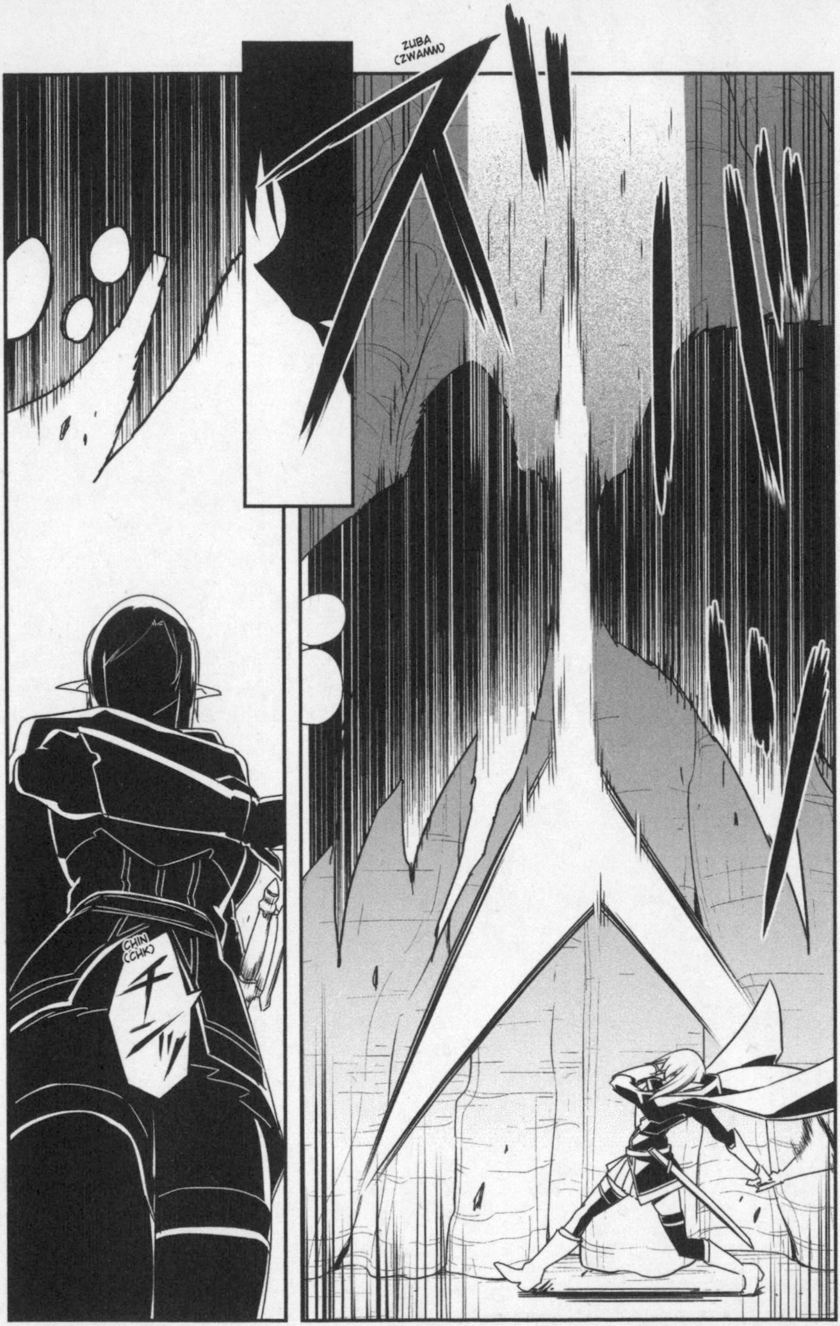
ZUBA
(ZWAMM)
CHIN
(CHK)

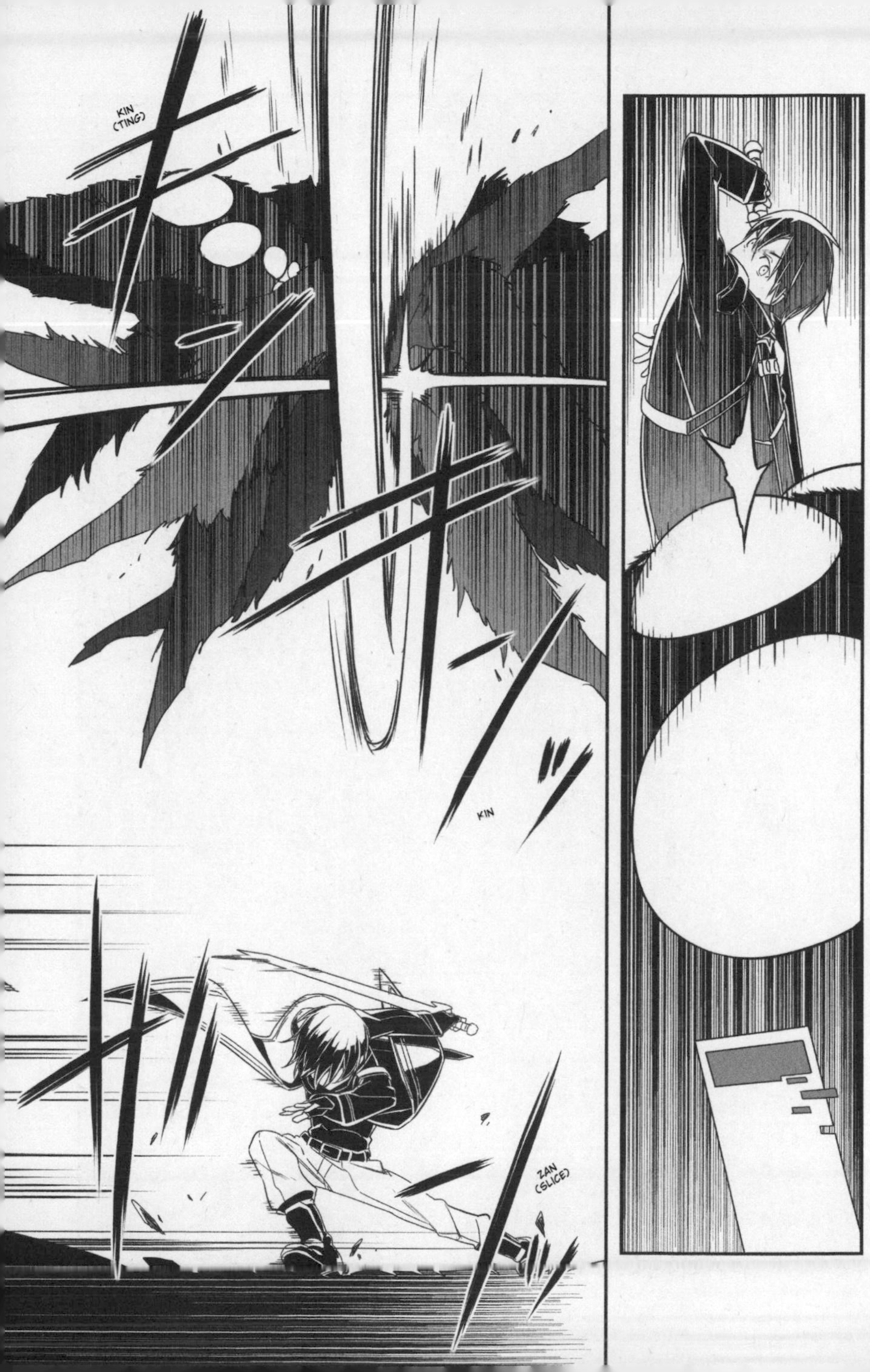
KIN
(TING)
KIN
ZAN
(SLICE)

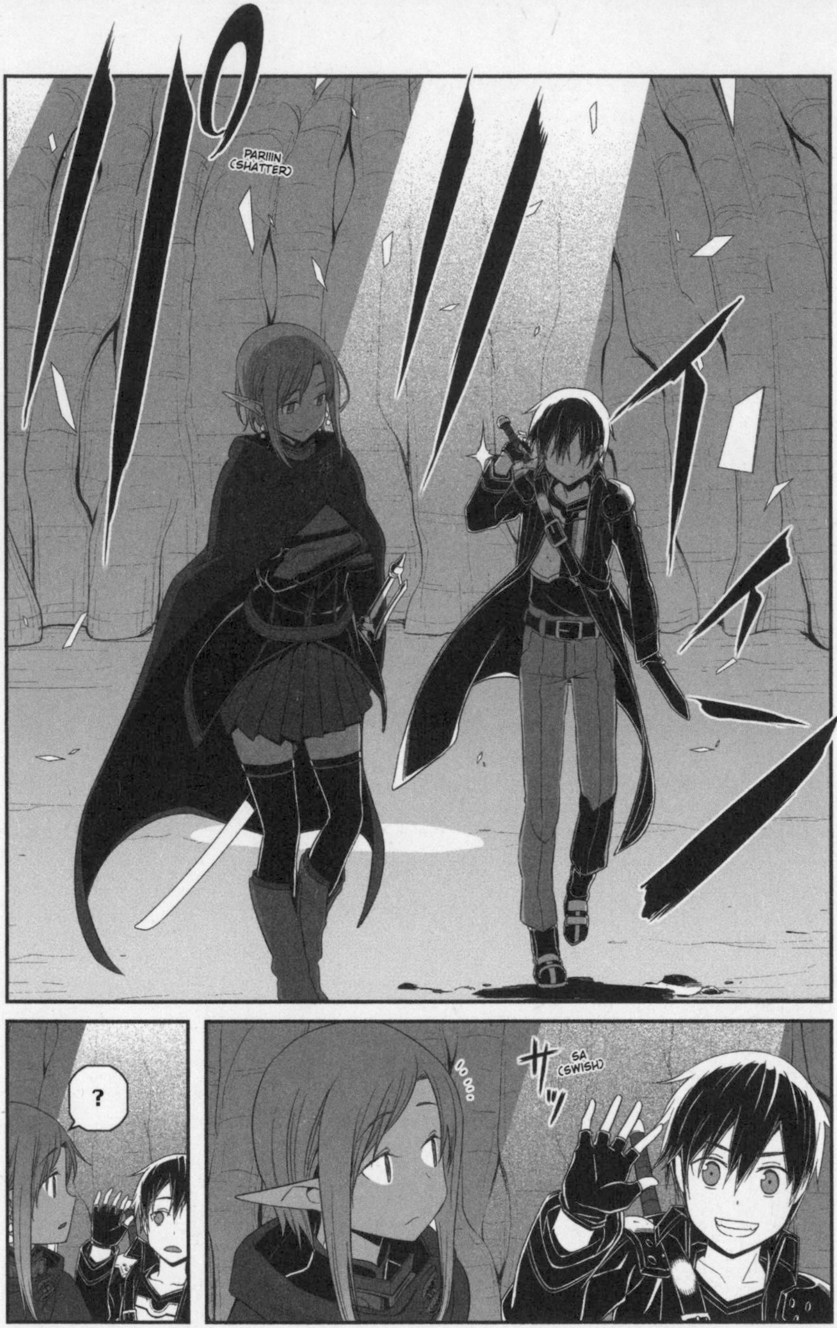
PARIIIN
(SHATTER)
SA
(SWISH)
?

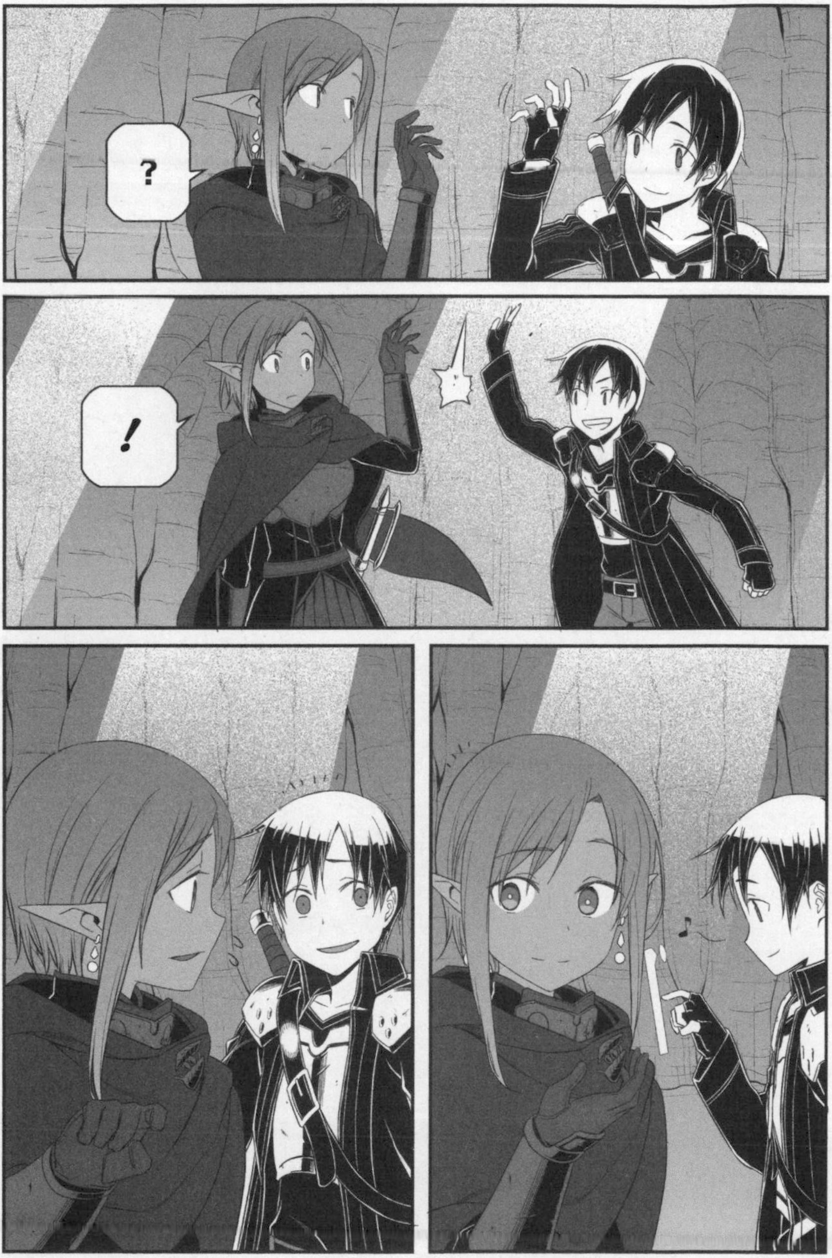
?
!

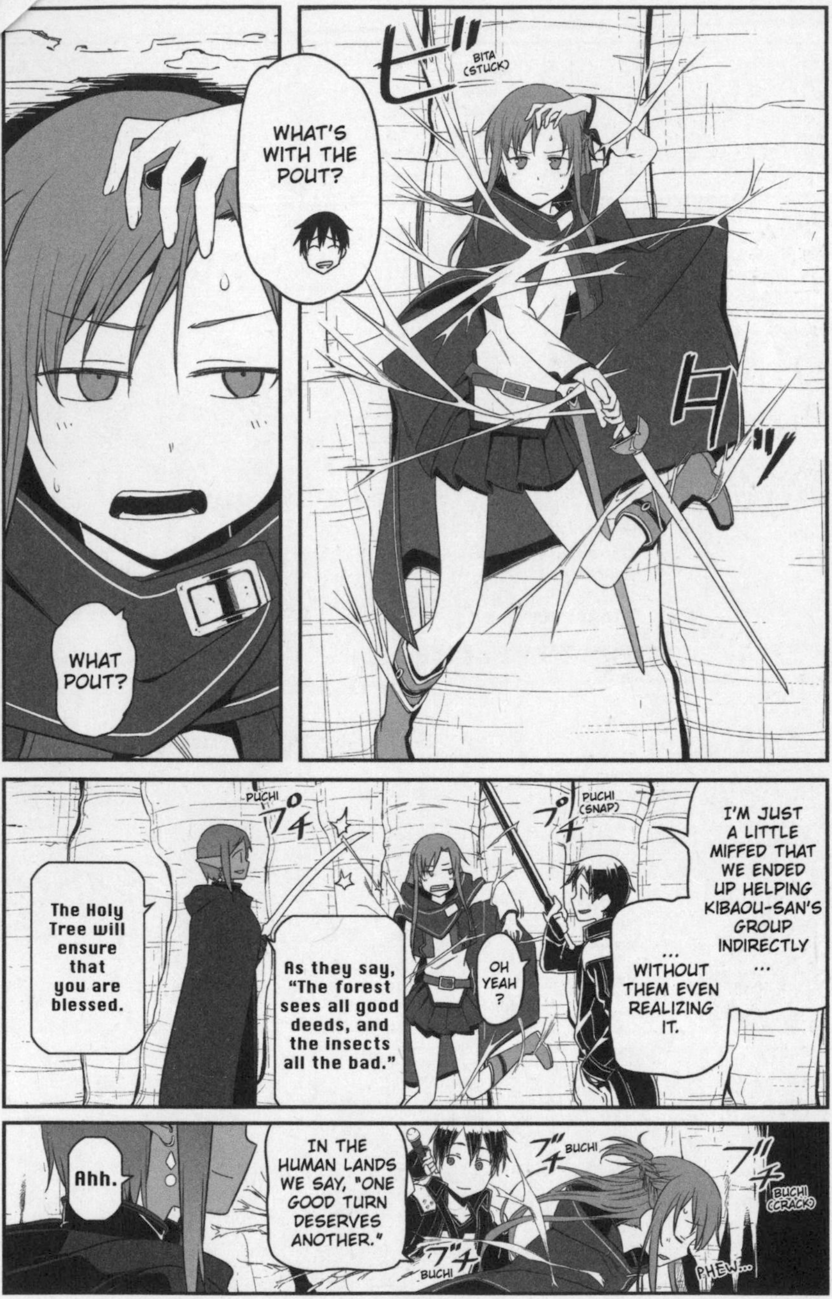
BITA (STUCK)
WHAT'S WITH THE POUT?
WHAT POUT?
I'M JUST A LITTLE MIFFED THAT WE ENDED UP HELPING KIBAOU-SAN'S GROUP INDIRECTLY ...
... WITHOUT THEM EVEN REALIZING IT.
PUCHI (SNAP)
OH YEAH?
PUCHI
As they say, "The forest sees all good deeds, and the insects all the bad."
The Holy Tree will ensure that you are blessed.
BUCHI (CRACK)
PHEW...
BUCHI
IN THE HUMAN LANDS WE SAY, "ONE GOOD TURN DESERVES ANOTHER."
BUCHI
Ahh.

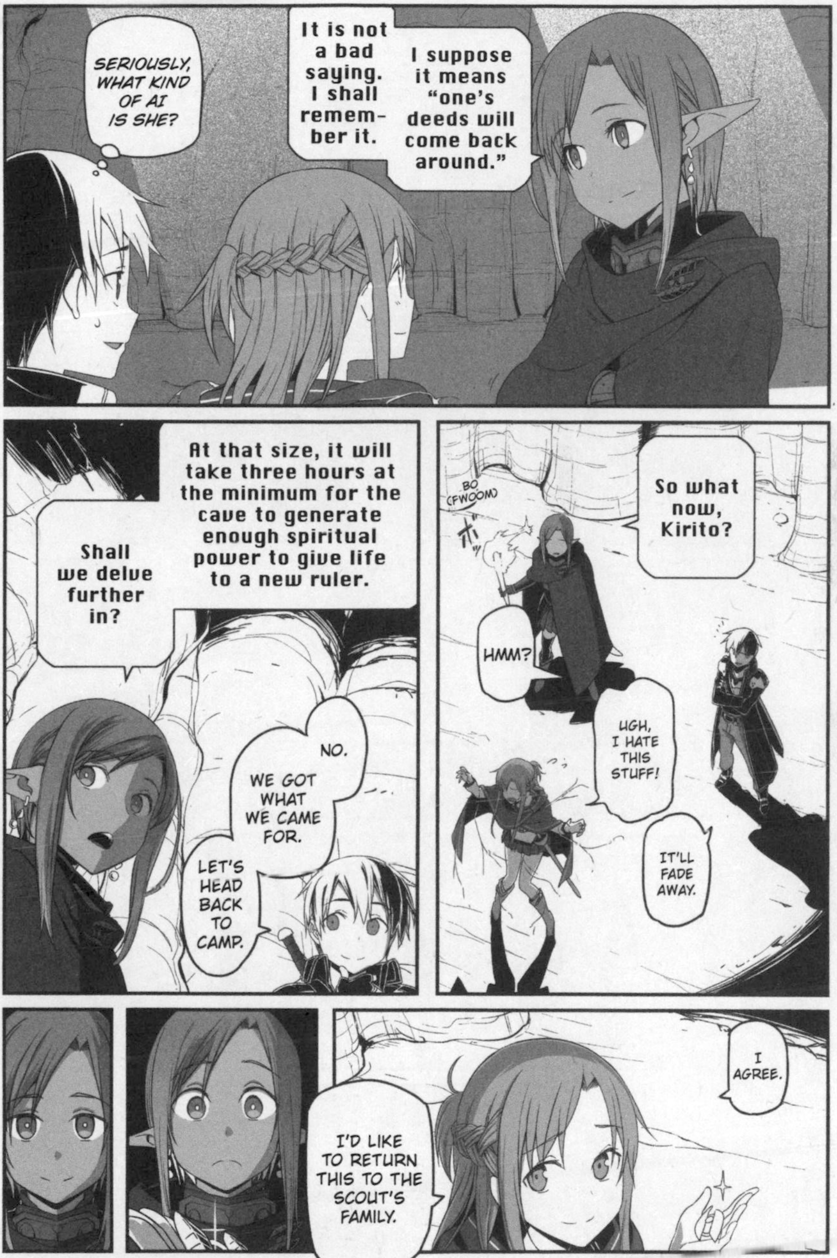
I suppose it means "one's deeds will come back around."
It is not a bad saying. I shall remember it.
SERIOUSLY, WHAT KIND OF AI IS SHE?
So what now, Kirito?
BO (FWOOM)
HMM?
UGH, I HATE THIS STUFF!
IT'LL FADE AWAY.
At that size, it will take three hours at the minimum for the cave to generate enough spiritual power to give life to a new ruler.
Shall we delve further in?
NO.
WE GOT WHAT WE CAME FOR.
LET'S HEAD BACK TO CAMP.
I AGREE.
I'D LIKE TO RETURN THIS TO THE SCOUT'S FAMILY.

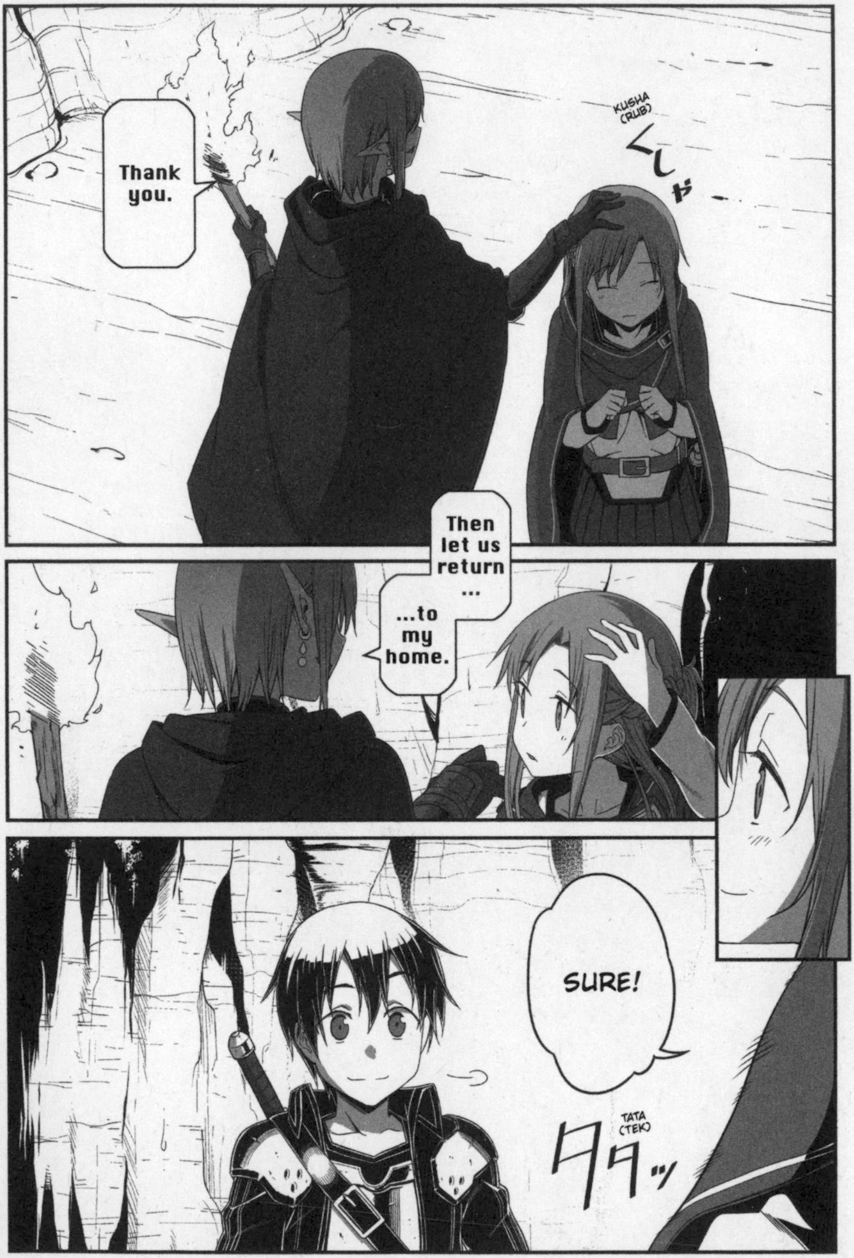
KUSHA (RUB)
くしゃ
Thank you.
Then let us return ...
...to my home.
SURE!
TATA (TEK)
タタッ

#032: Memento

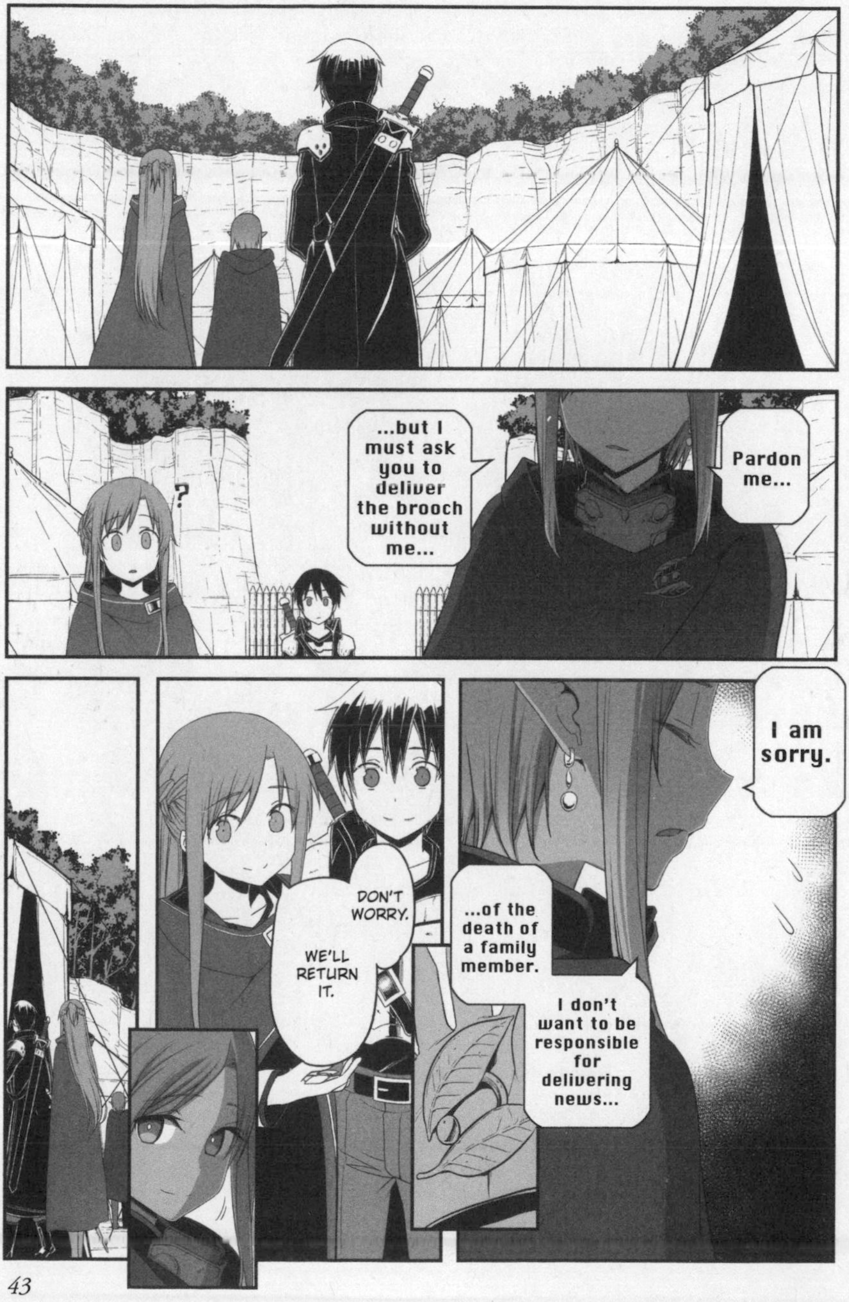

Pardon me...
...but I must ask you to deliver the brooch without me...
?
I am sorry.
I don't want to be responsible for delivering news...
...of the death of a family member.
DON'T WORRY.
WE'LL RETURN IT.

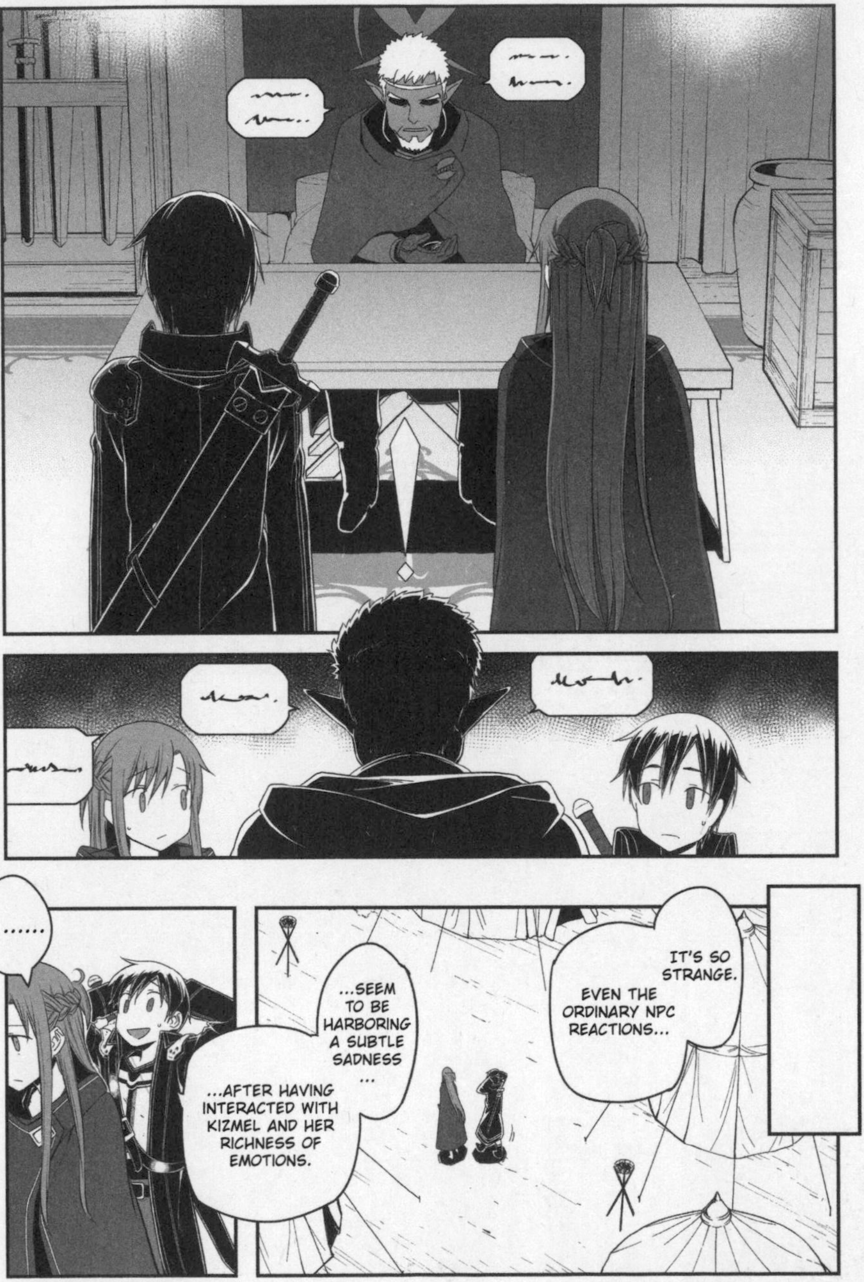
IT'S SO STRANGE.
EVEN THE ORDINARY NPC REACTIONS...
...SEEM TO BE HARBORING A SUBTLE SADNESS ...
...AFTER HAVING INTERACTED WITH KIZMEL AND HER RICHNESS OF EMOTIONS.
......

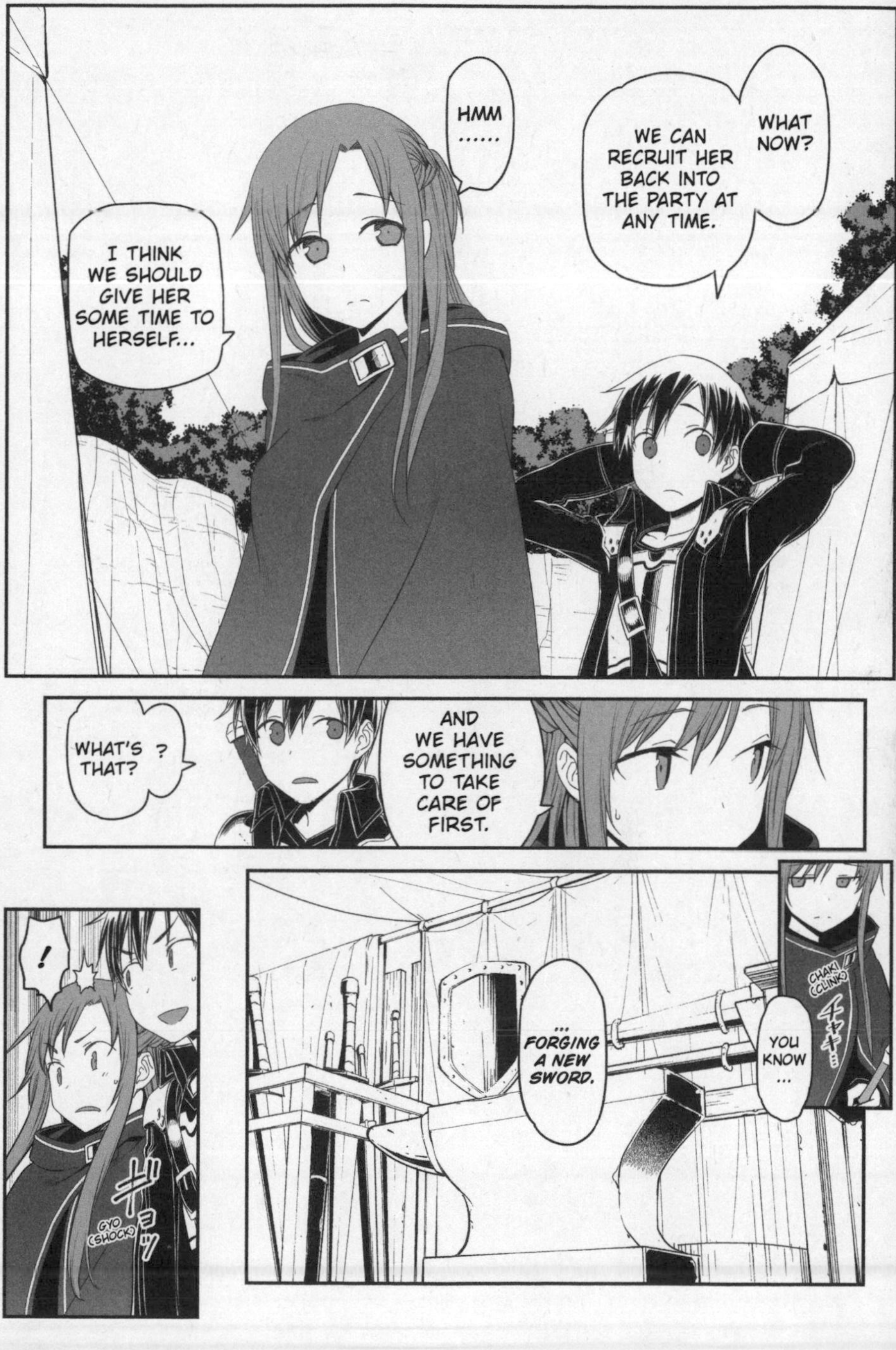
WHAT NOW?
WE CAN RECRUIT HER BACK INTO THE PARTY AT ANY TIME.
HMM ......
I THINK WE SHOULD GIVE HER SOME TIME TO HERSELF...
AND WE HAVE SOMETHING TO TAKE CARE OF FIRST.
WHAT'S THAT? ?
CHAKI (CLINK)
チャキ
YOU KNOW ...
... FORGING A NEW SWORD.
!
ギョッ
GYO (SHOCK)

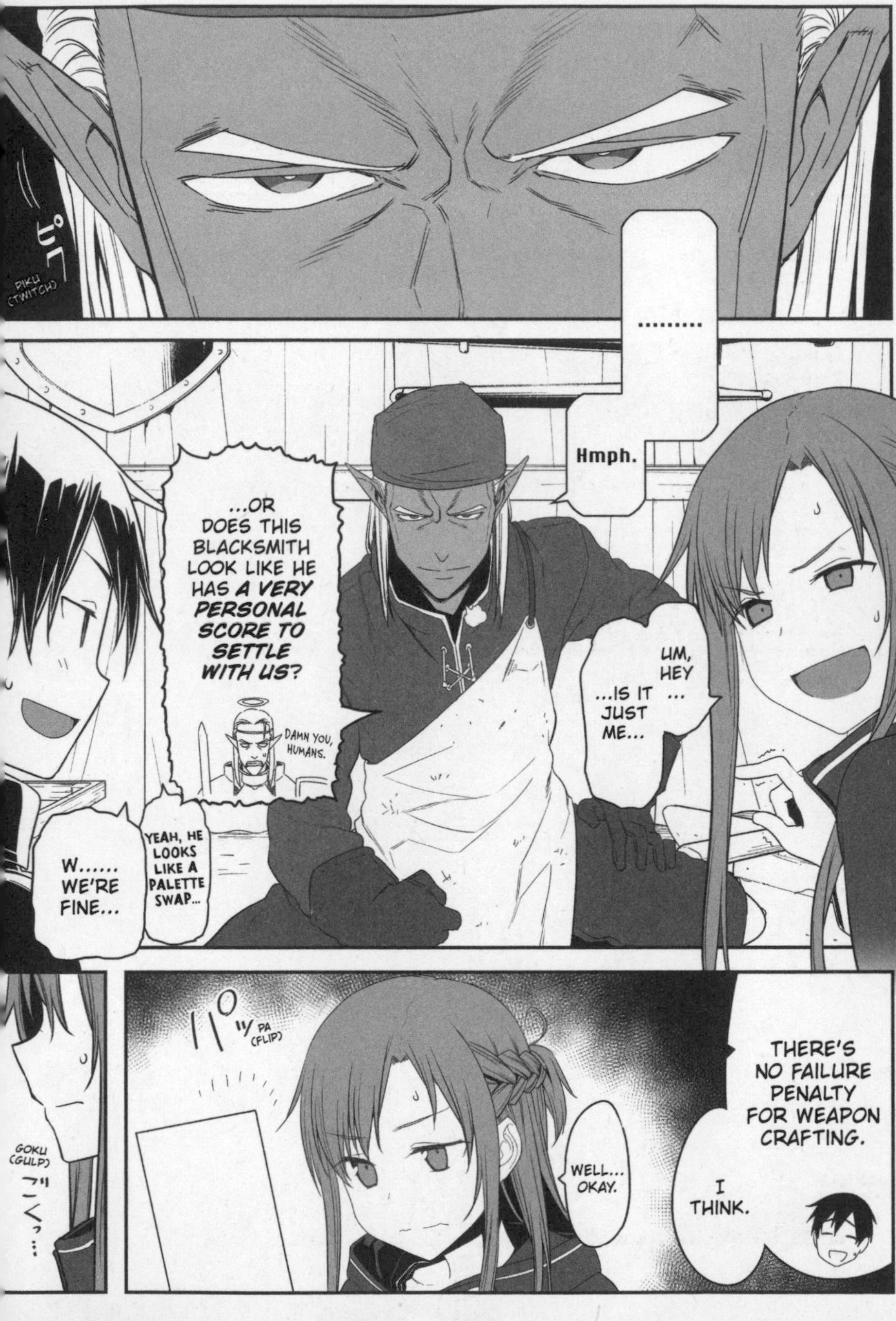
....
ぴく
PIKU (TWITCH)
Hmph.
UM, HEY ... ...IS IT JUST ME...
...OR DOES THIS BLACKSMITH LOOK LIKE HE HAS A VERY PERSONAL SCORE TO SETTLE WITH US?
DAMN YOU, HUMANS.
YEAH, HE LOOKS LIKE A PALETTE SWAP...
W...... WE'RE FINE...
THERE'S NO FAILURE PENALTY FOR WEAPON CRAFTING.
I THINK.
WELL... OKAY.
パッ
PA (FLIP)
GOKU (GULP)
ごくっ…

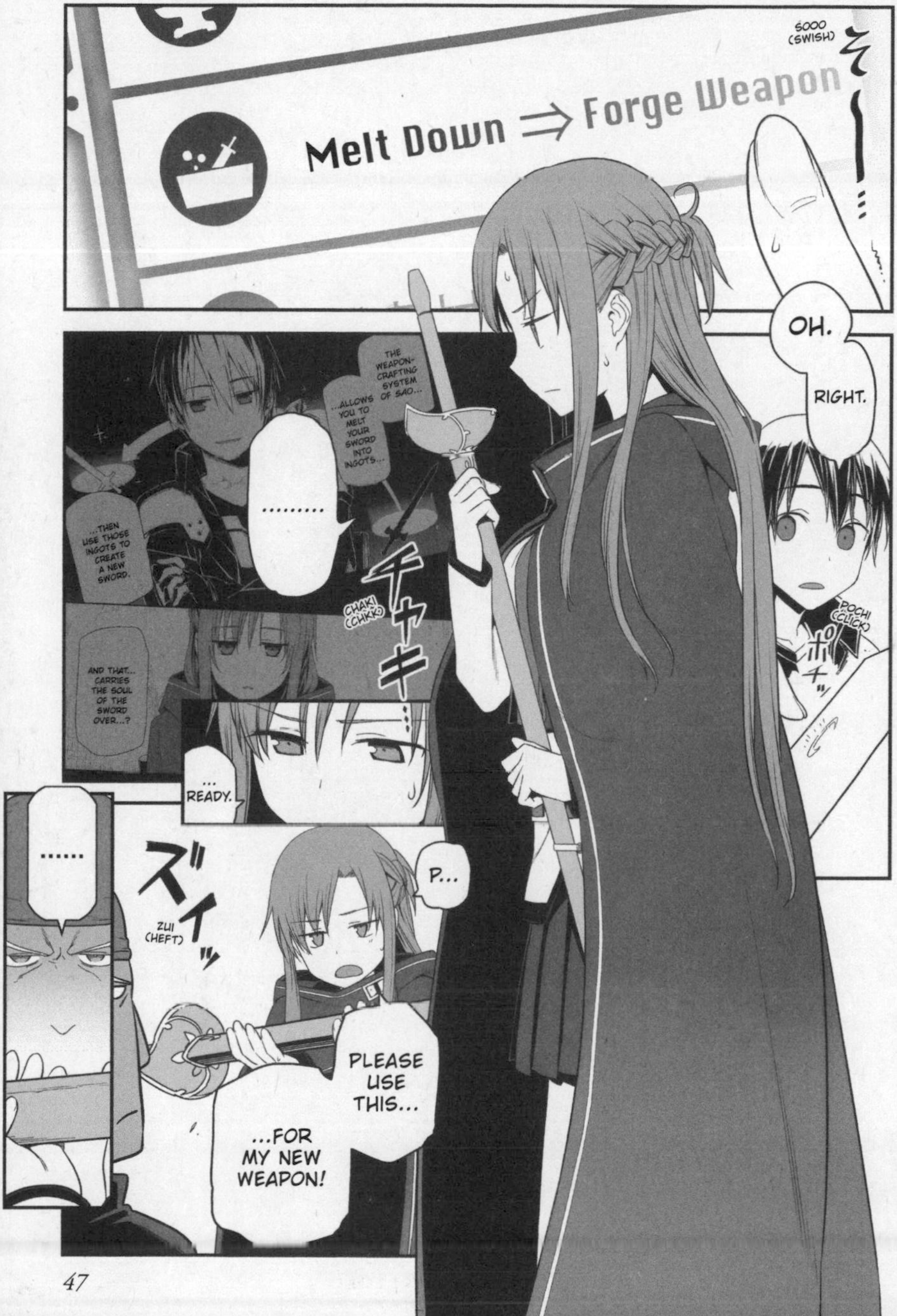
Melt Down ⇒ Forge Weapon
SOOO (SWISH)
OH.
RIGHT.
POCHI (CLICK)
THE WEAPON-CRAFTING SYSTEM OF SAO...
...ALLOWS YOU TO MELT YOUR SWORD INTO INGOTS...
....
...THEN USE THOSE INGOTS TO CREATE A NEW SWORD.
CHAKI (CHKK)
AND THAT... CARRIES THE SOUL OF THE SWORD OVER...?
...READY.
P...
ZUI (HEFT)
......
PLEASE USE THIS...
...FOR MY NEW WEAPON!

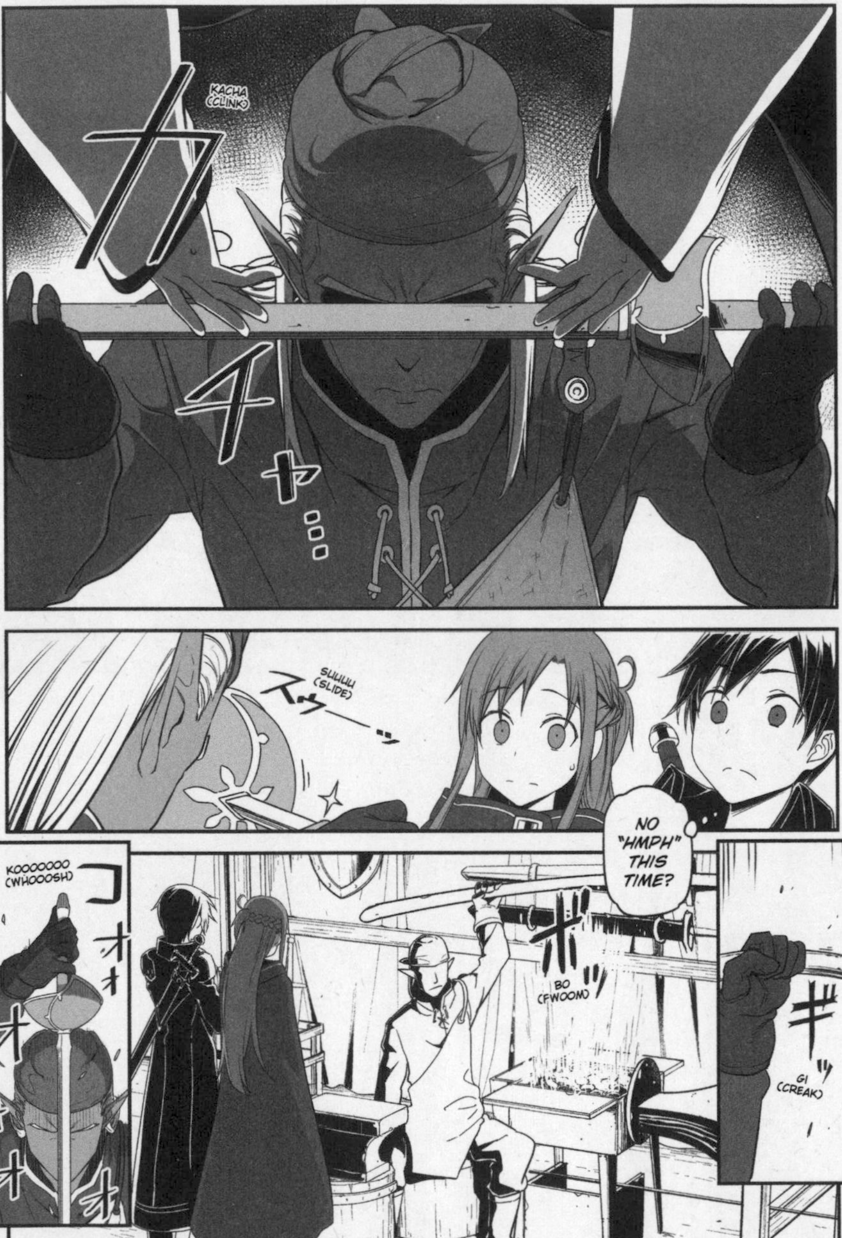
KACHA (CLINK)
SUUUU (SLIDE)
NO "HMPH" THIS TIME?
GI (CREAK)
BO (FWOOM)
KOOOOOOO (WHOOOSH)

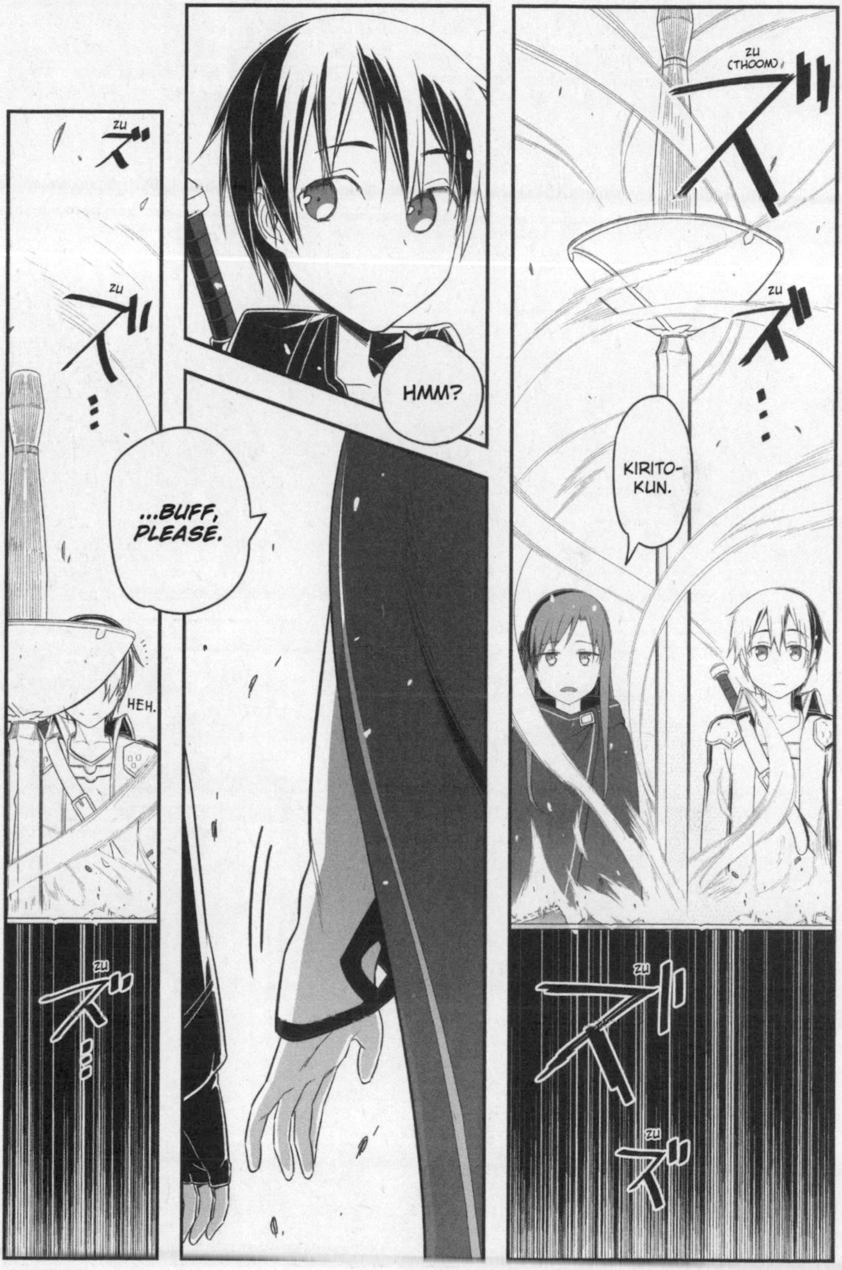
ZU (THOOM)
ZU
KIRITO-KUN.
ZU
ZU
HMM?
...BUFF, PLEASE.
ZU
ZU
HEH.
ZU

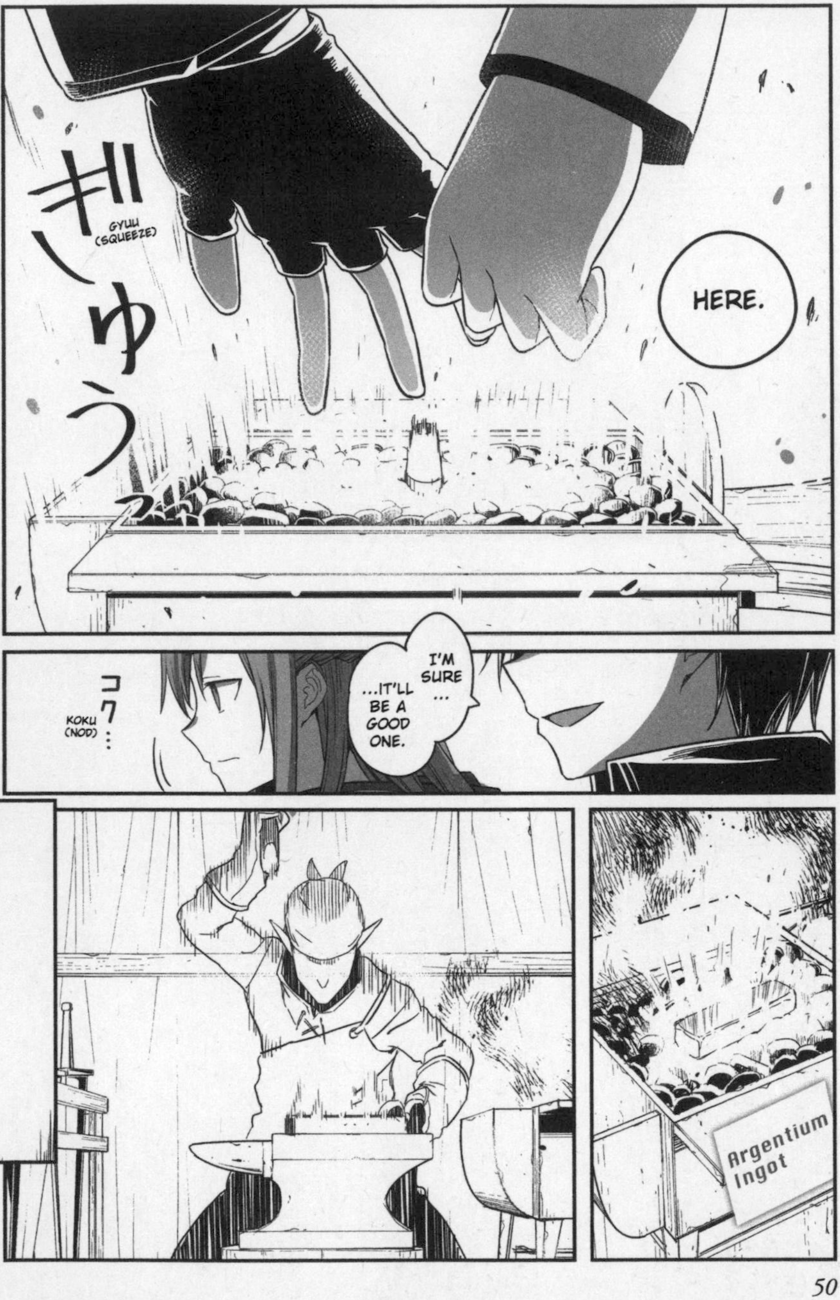
HERE.
ぎゅう
GYUU (SQUEEZE)
I'M SURE ... ...IT'LL BE A GOOD ONE.
コク…
KOKU (NOD)
Argentium Ingot

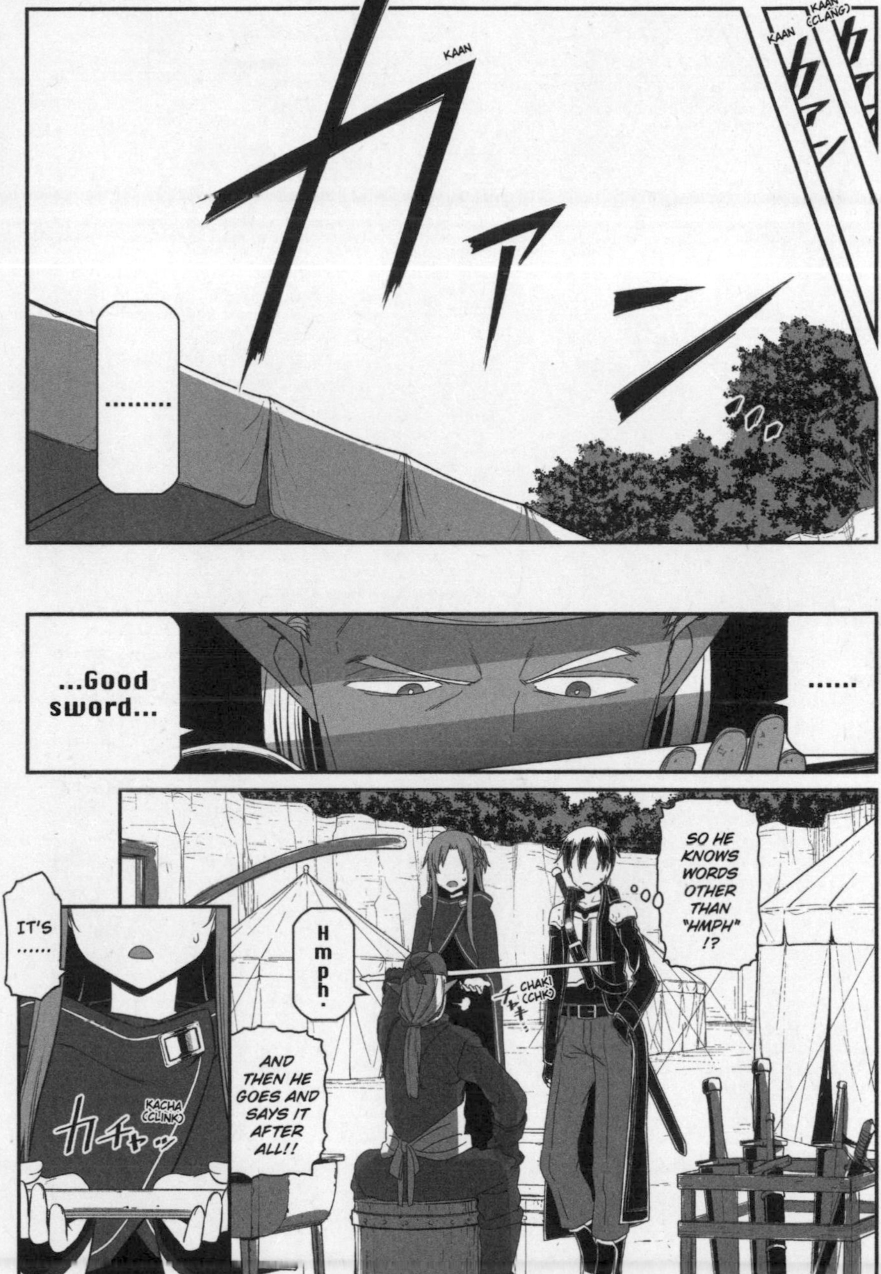
KAAN (CLANG)
KAAN
KAAN
....
......
...Good sword...
SO HE KNOWS WORDS OTHER THAN "HMPH" !?
CHAKI (CHK)
Hmph.
AND THEN HE GOES AND SAYS IT AFTER ALL!!
IT'S ......
KACHA (CLINK)

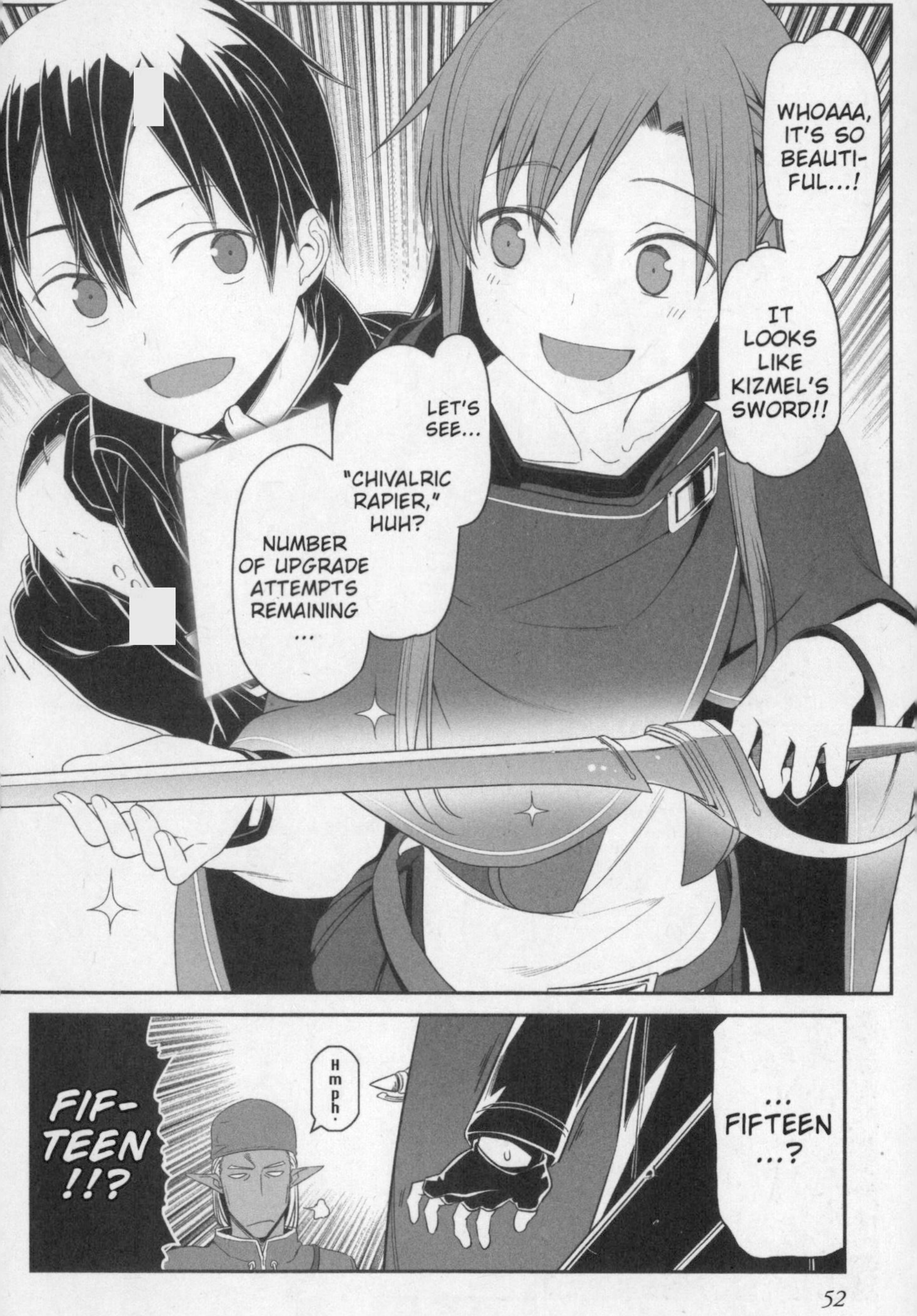
WHOAAA, IT'S SO BEAUTI-FUL...!
IT LOOKS LIKE KIZMEL'S SWORD!!
LET'S SEE...
"CHIVALRIC RAPIER," HUH?
NUMBER OF UPGRADE ATTEMPTS REMAINING ...
... FIFTEEN ...?
Hmph.
FIF-TEEN !!?

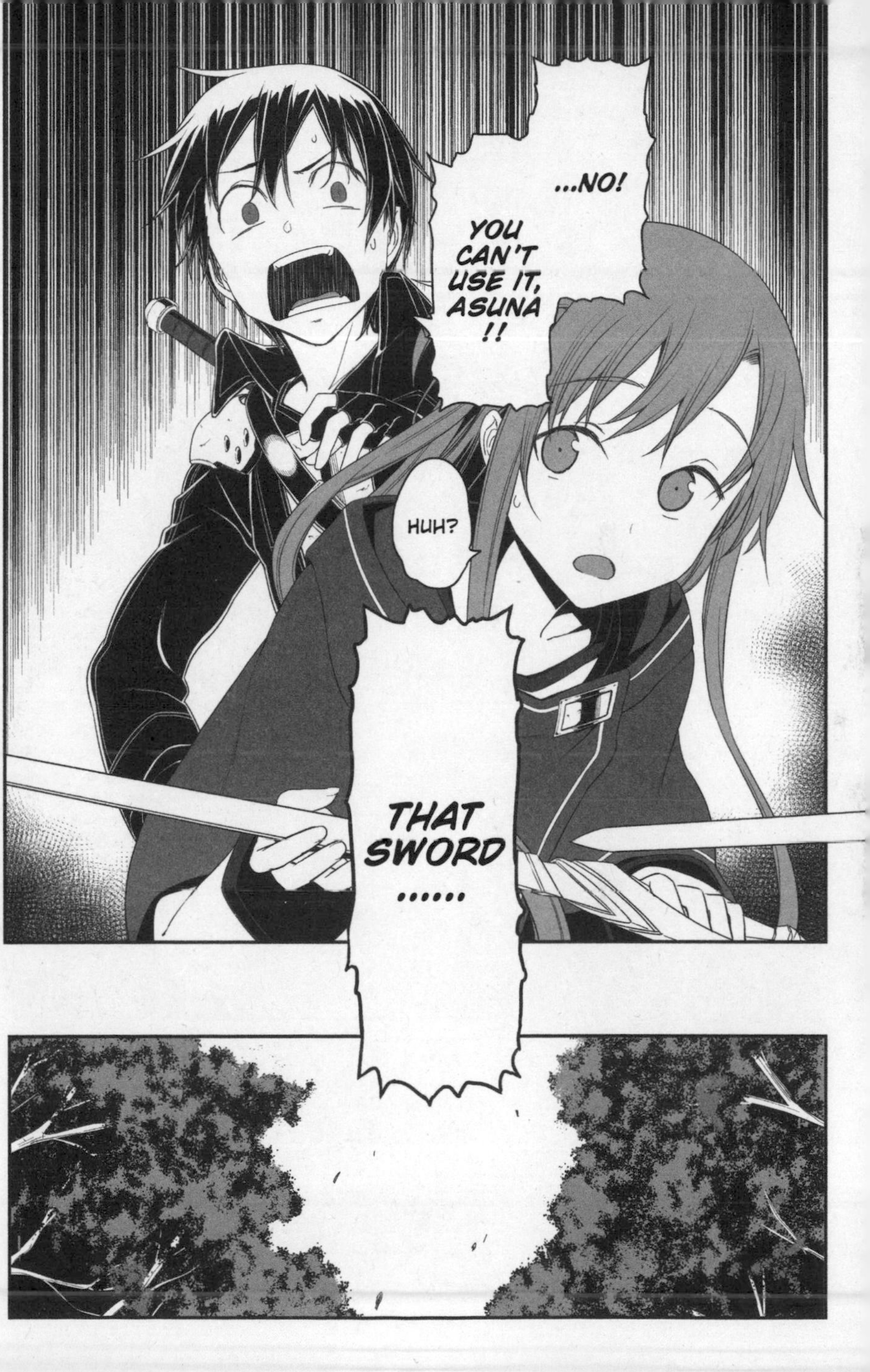
...NO!
YOU CAN'T USE IT, ASUNA!!
HUH?
THAT SWORD ......

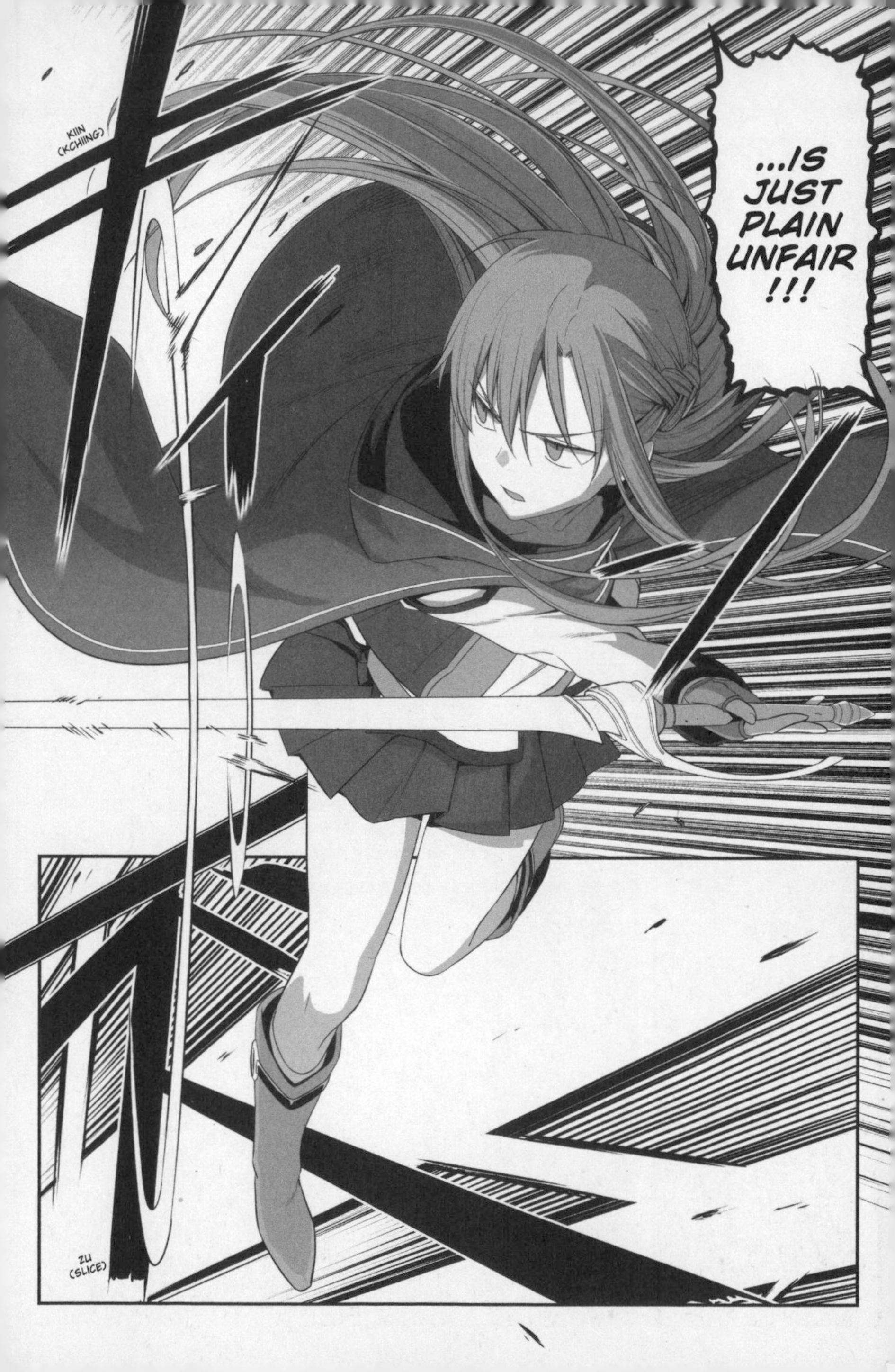
...IS JUST PLAIN UNFAIR!!!
KIIN (KCHIING)
ZU (SLICE)

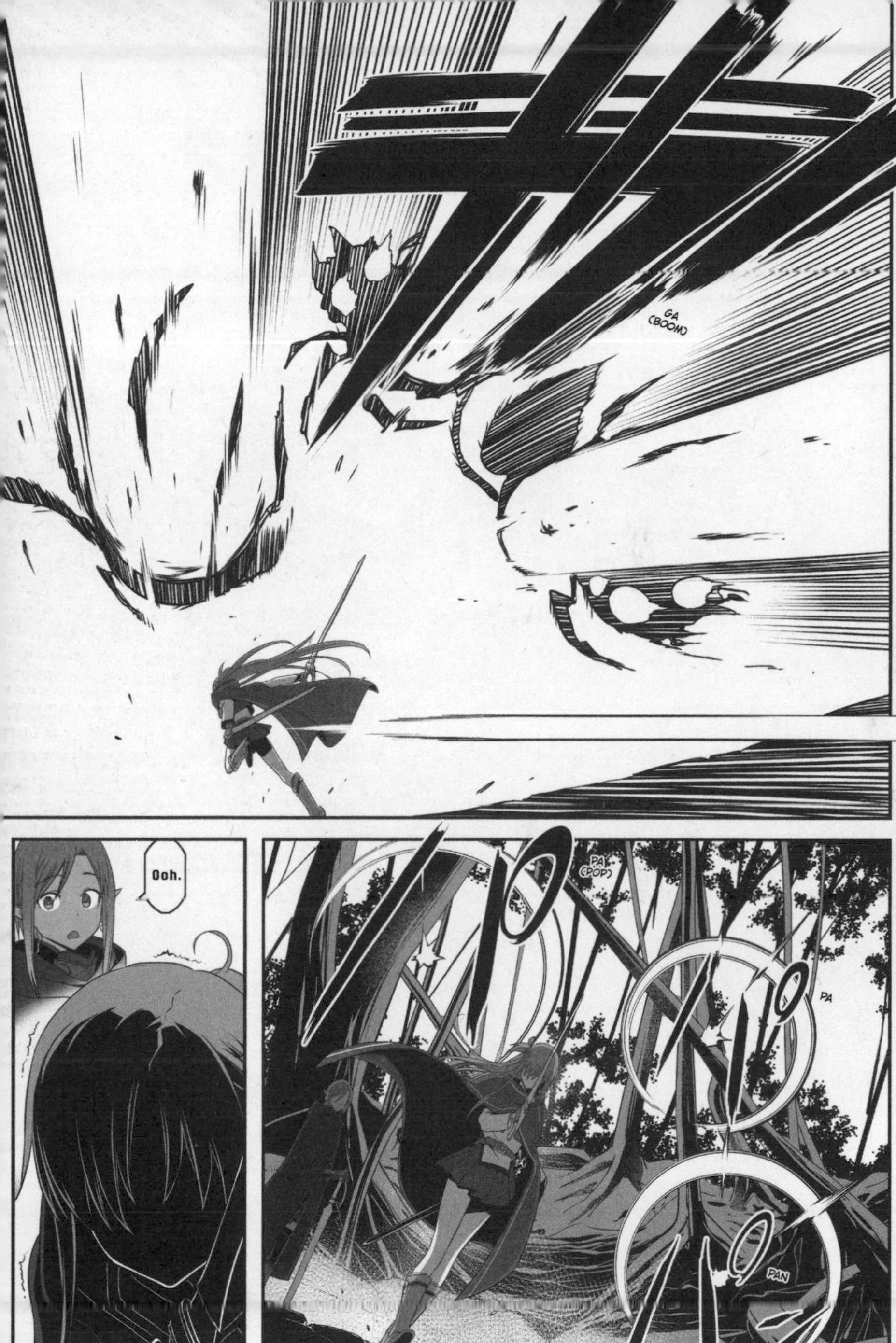
GA
(BOOM)
PA
(POP)
PA
PAN
Ooh.

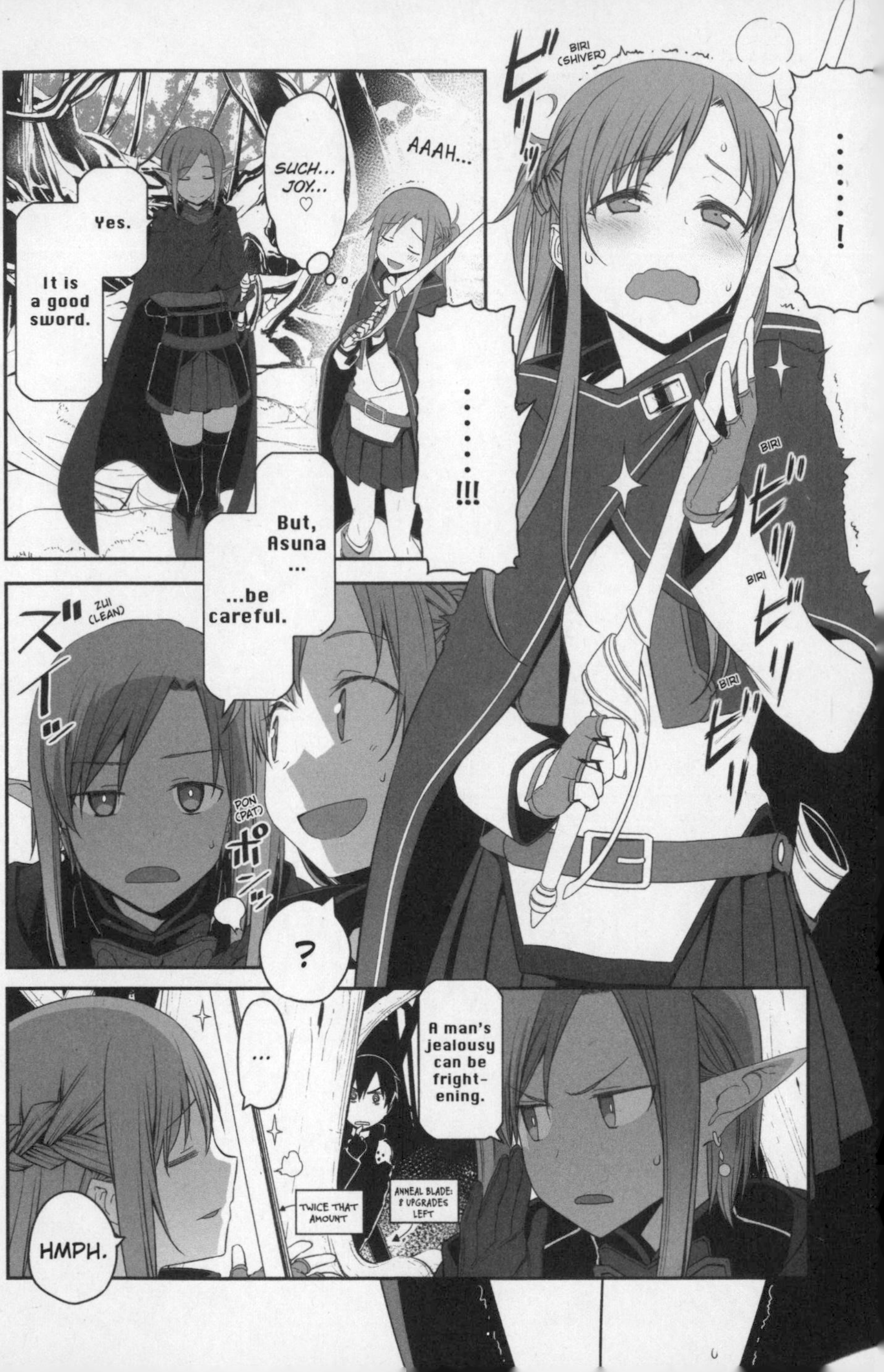
BIRI (SHIVER)
......!
BIRI
BIRI
BIRI
AAAH...
SUCH... JOY... ♡
Yes.
It is a good sword.
......!!!
But, Asuna ... ...be careful.
ZUI (LEAN)
PON (PAT)
?
A man's jealousy can be frightening.
...
ANNEAL BLADE: 8 UPGRADES LEFT
TWICE THAT AMOUNT
HMPH.

#033: Zumfut

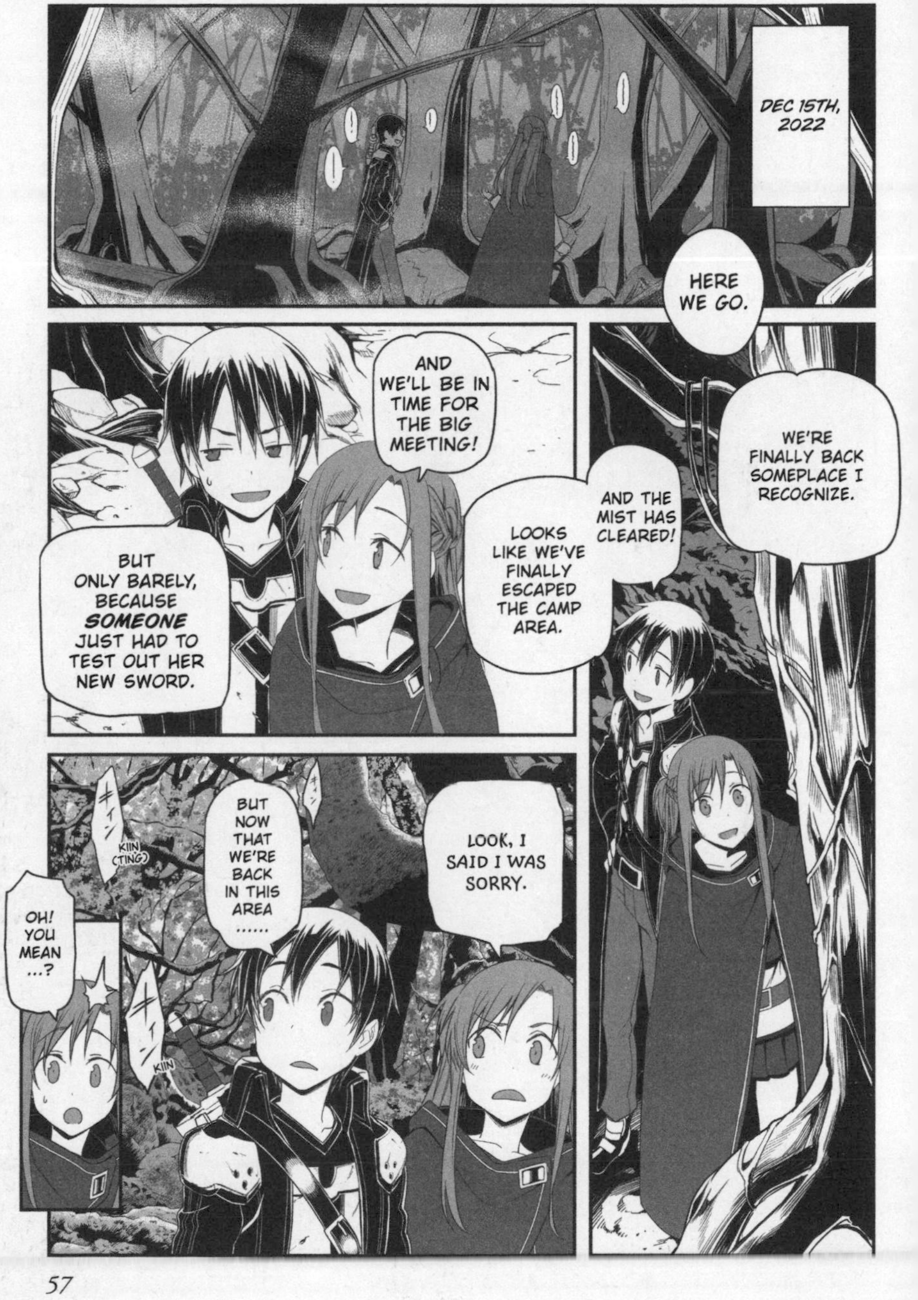
DEC 15TH, 2022
!
!
!
!
!
!
HERE WE GO.
WE'RE FINALLY BACK SOMEPLACE I RECOGNIZE.
AND THE MIST HAS CLEARED!
LOOKS LIKE WE'VE FINALLY ESCAPED THE CAMP AREA.
AND WE'LL BE IN TIME FOR THE BIG MEETING!
BUT ONLY BARELY, BECAUSE **SOMEONE** JUST HAD TO TEST OUT HER NEW SWORD.
LOOK, I SAID I WAS SORRY.
BUT NOW THAT WE'RE BACK IN THIS AREA ......
KIIN (TING)
OH! YOU MEAN ...?
KIIN

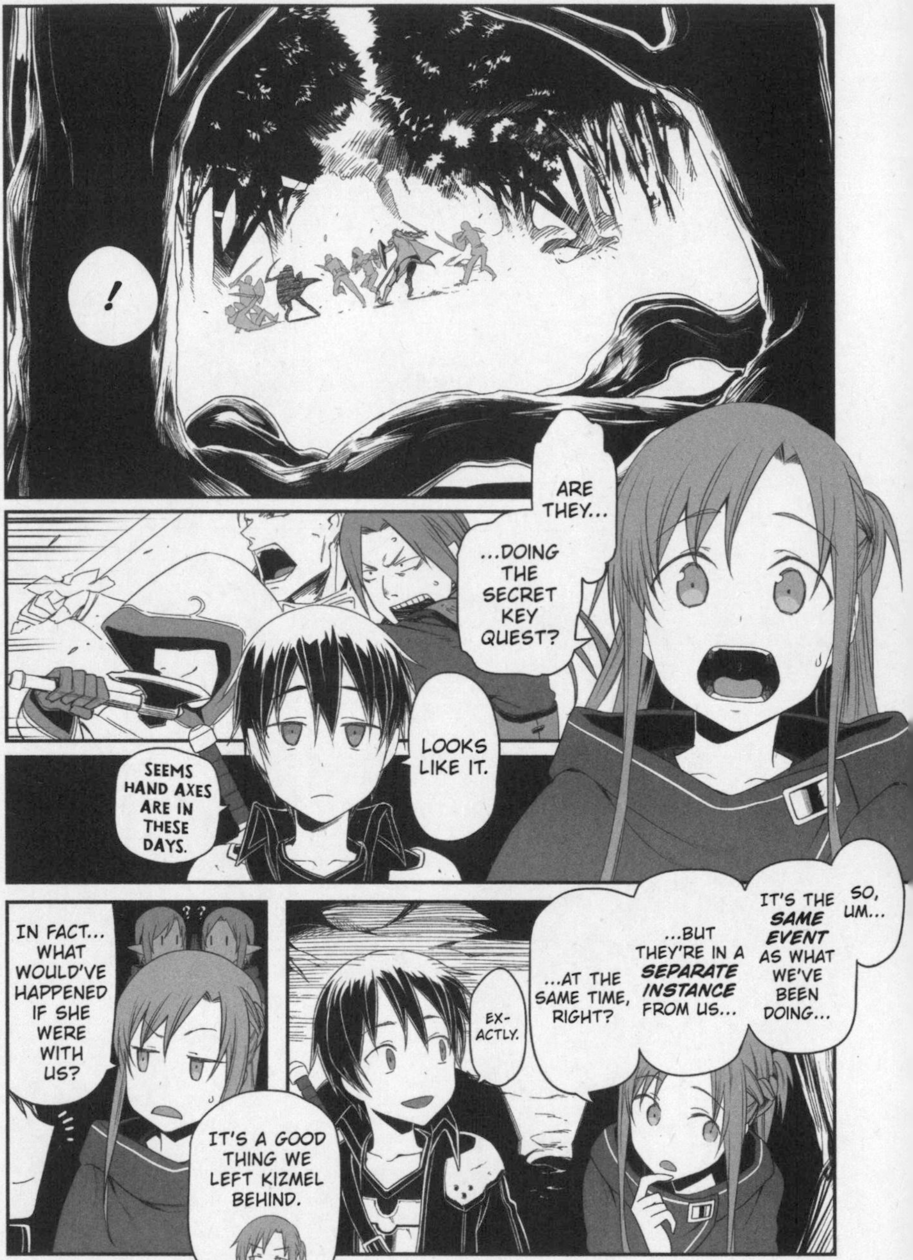
!
ARE THEY...
...DOING THE SECRET KEY QUEST?
LOOKS LIKE IT.
SEEMS HAND AXES ARE IN THESE DAYS.
SO, UM...
IT'S THE *SAME EVENT* AS WHAT WE'VE BEEN DOING...
...BUT THEY'RE IN A *SEPARATE INSTANCE* FROM US...
...AT THE SAME TIME, RIGHT?
EX-ACTLY.
IT'S A GOOD THING WE LEFT KIZMEL BEHIND.
IN FACT... WHAT WOULD'VE HAPPENED IF SHE WERE WITH US?

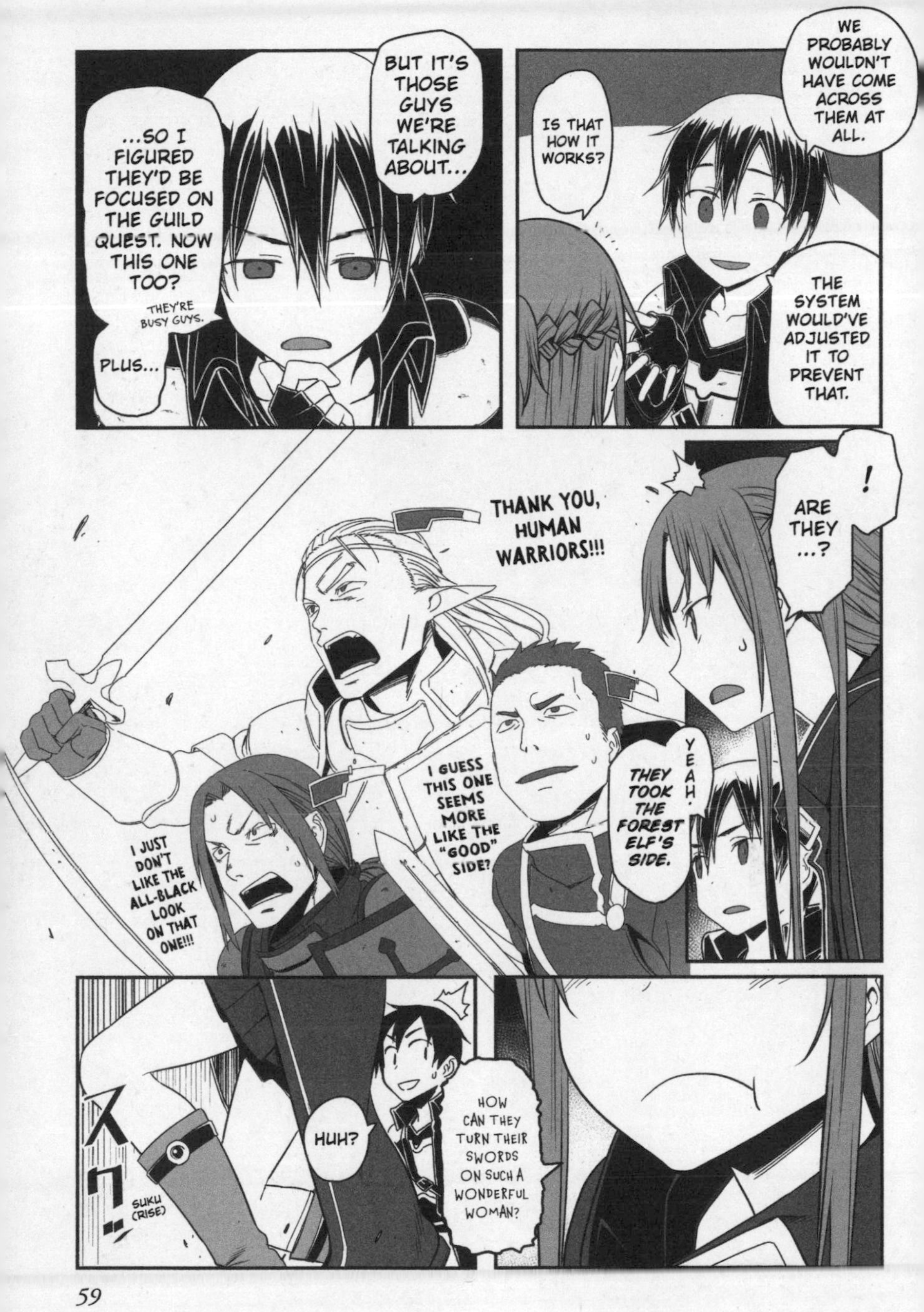

WE PROBABLY WOULDN'T HAVE COME ACROSS THEM AT ALL.
IS THAT HOW IT WORKS?
THE SYSTEM WOULD'VE ADJUSTED IT TO PREVENT THAT.
BUT IT'S THOSE GUYS WE'RE TALKING ABOUT...
...SO I FIGURED THEY'D BE FOCUSED ON THE GUILD QUEST. NOW THIS ONE TOO?
THEY'RE BUSY GUYS.
PLUS...
!
ARE THEY ...?
YEAH.
THEY TOOK THE FOREST ELF'S SIDE.
THANK YOU, HUMAN WARRIORS!!!
I GUESS THIS ONE SEEMS MORE LIKE THE "GOOD" SIDE?
I JUST DON'T LIKE THE ALL-BLACK LOOK ON THAT ONE!!!
HOW CAN THEY TURN THEIR SWORDS ON SUCH A WONDERFUL WOMAN?
HUH?
SUKU (RISE)

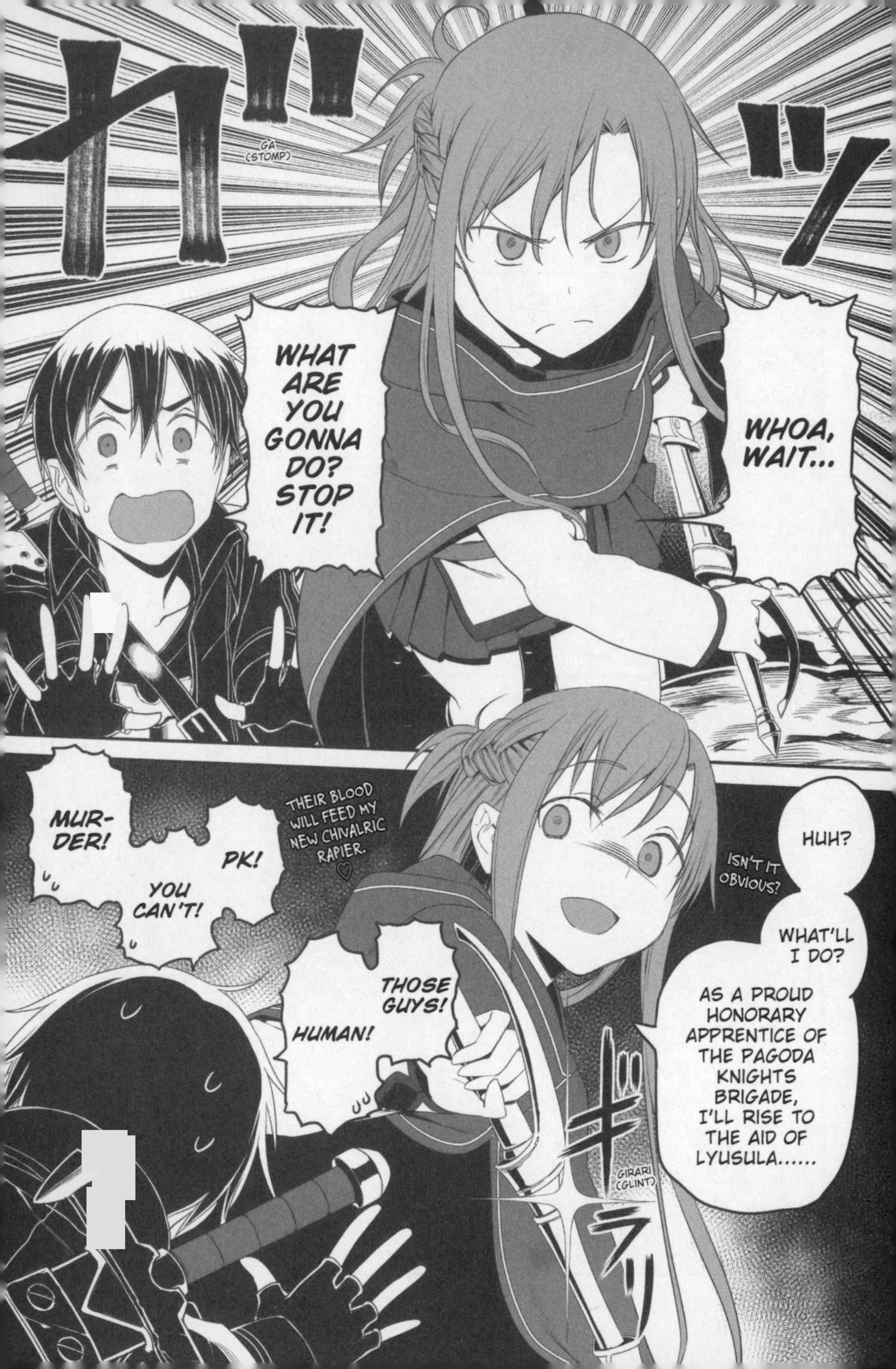
GA (STOMP)
WHOA, WAIT...
WHAT ARE YOU GONNA DO? STOP IT!
HUH?
WHAT'LL I DO?
ISN'T IT OBVIOUS?
AS A PROUD HONORARY APPRENTICE OF THE PAGODA KNIGHTS BRIGADE, I'LL RISE TO THE AID OF LYUSULA......
GIRARI (GLINT)
THEIR BLOOD WILL FEED MY NEW CHIVALRIC RAPIER. ♡
THOSE GUYS!
HUMAN!
MUR-DER!
PK!
YOU CAN'T!

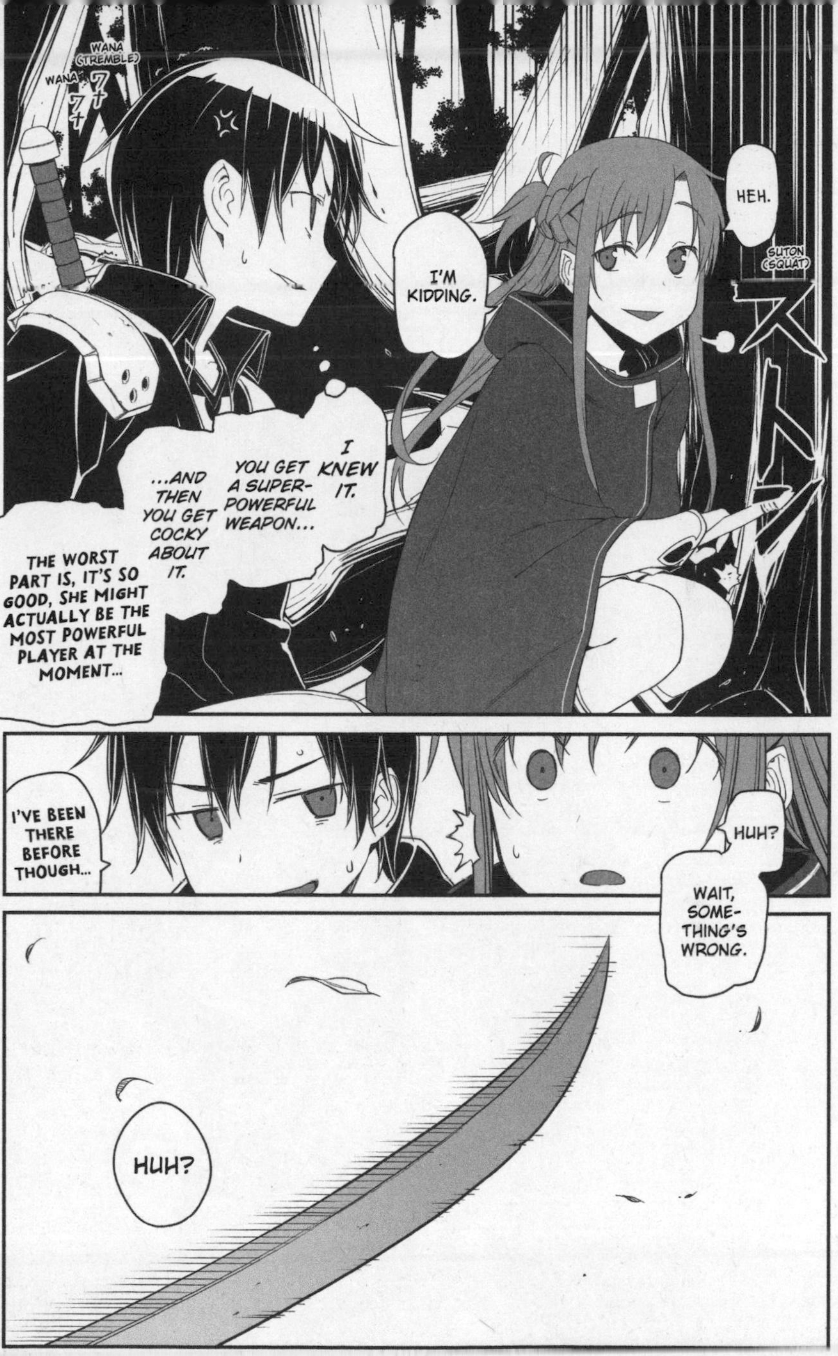
HEH.
SUTON (SQUAT)
I'M KIDDING.
WANA WANA (TREMBLE)
I KNEW IT. YOU GET A SUPER-POWERFUL WEAPON... ...AND THEN YOU GET COCKY ABOUT IT.
THE WORST PART IS, IT'S SO GOOD, SHE MIGHT ACTUALLY BE THE MOST POWERFUL PLAYER AT THE MOMENT...
HUH?
I'VE BEEN THERE BEFORE THOUGH...
WAIT, SOMETHING'S WRONG.
HUH?

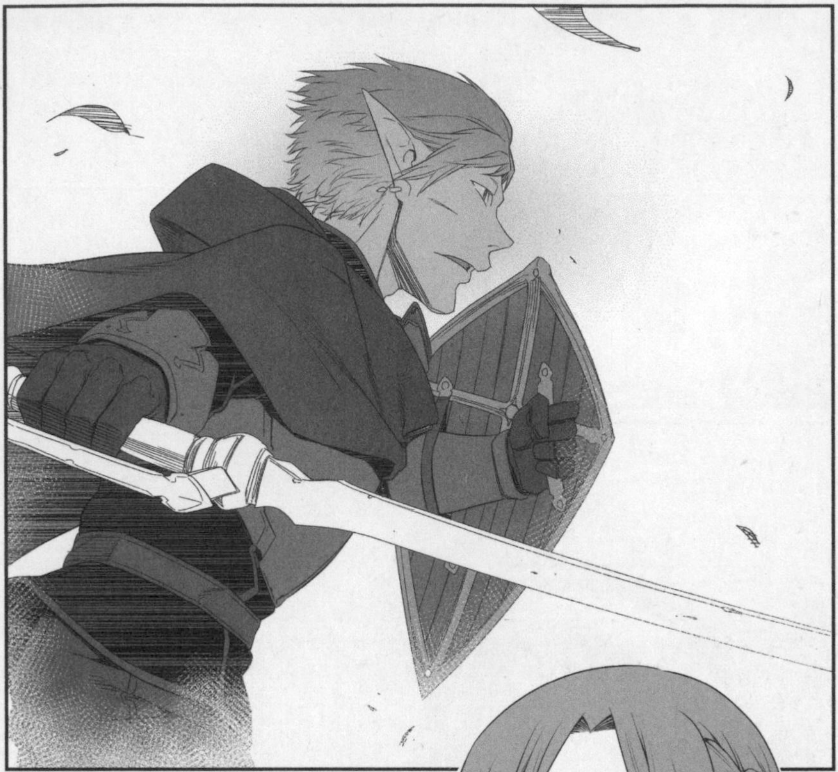

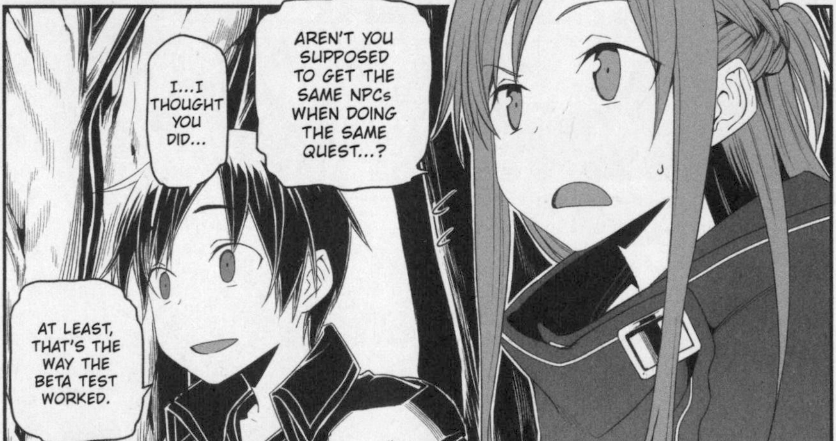
AREN'T YOU SUPPOSED TO GET THE SAME NPCs WHEN DOING THE SAME QUEST...?
I...I THOUGHT YOU DID...
AT LEAST, THAT'S THE WAY THE BETA TEST WORKED.

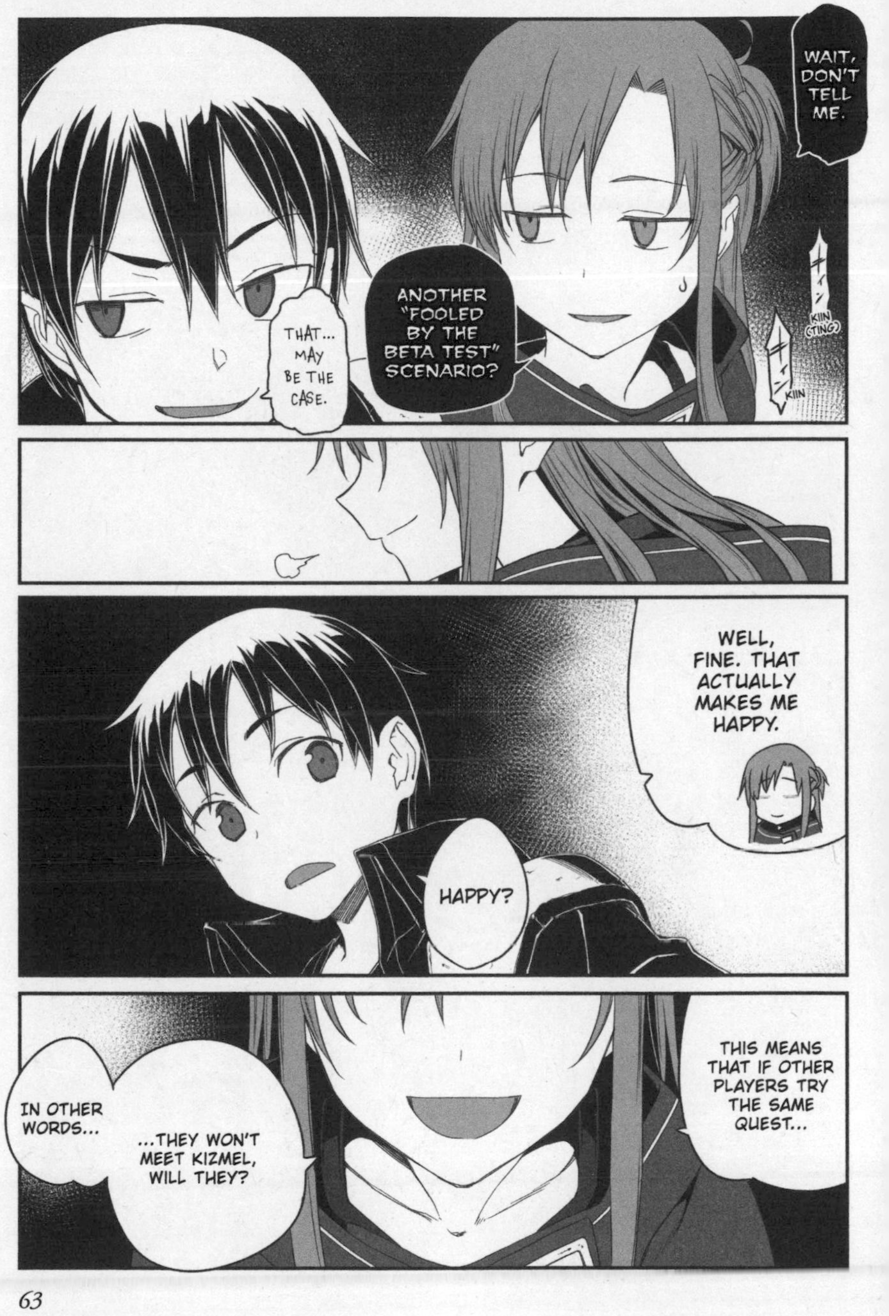
WAIT, DON'T TELL ME.
KIIN (TING)
KIIN
ANOTHER "FOOLED BY THE BETA TEST" SCENARIO?
THAT... MAY BE THE CASE.
WELL, FINE. THAT ACTUALLY MAKES ME HAPPY.
HAPPY?
THIS MEANS THAT IF OTHER PLAYERS TRY THE SAME QUEST...
IN OTHER WORDS...
...THEY WON'T MEET KIZMEL, WILL THEY?

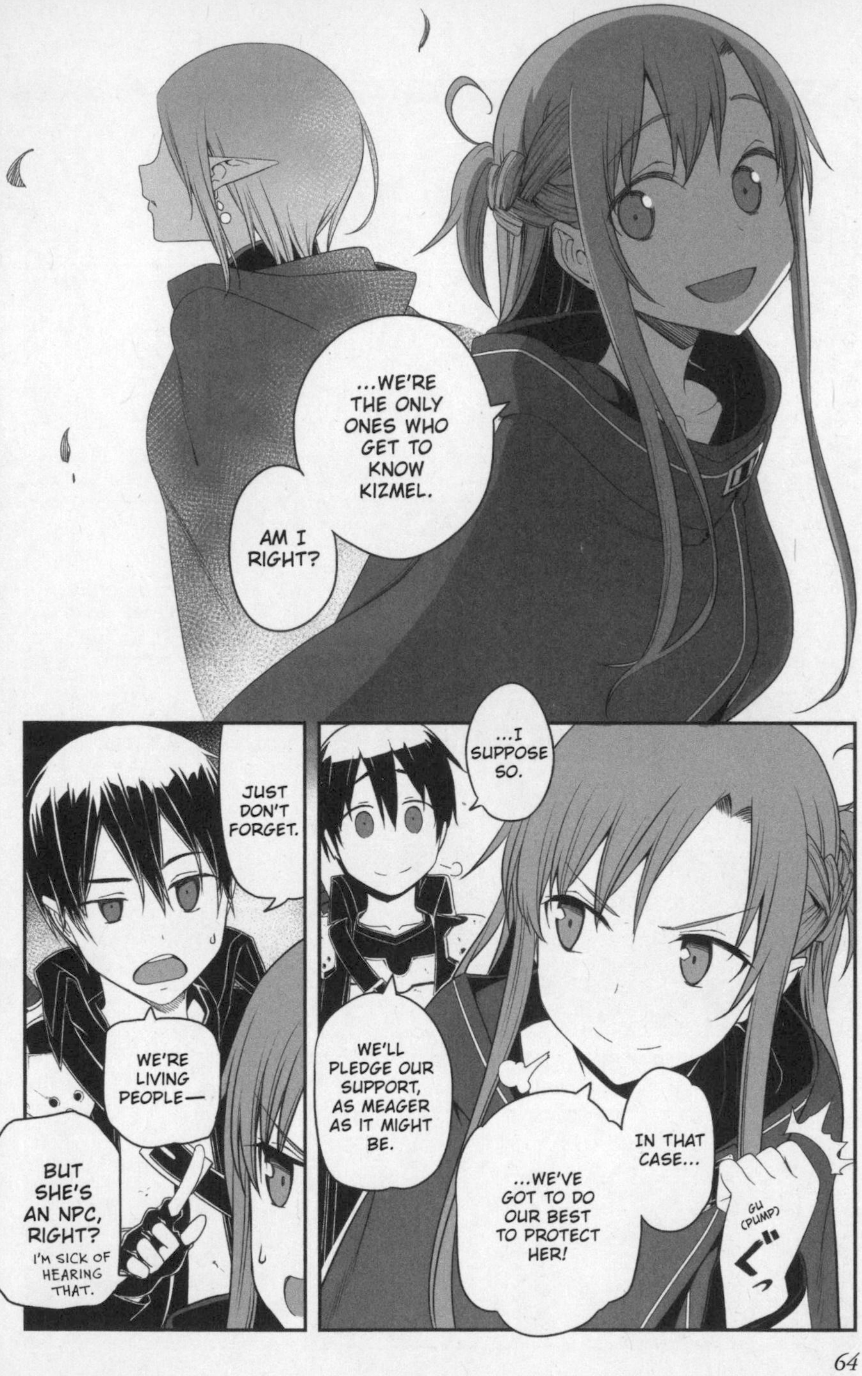
...WE'RE THE ONLY ONES WHO GET TO KNOW KIZMEL.
AM I RIGHT?
...I SUPPOSE SO.
IN THAT CASE...
...WE'VE GOT TO DO OUR BEST TO PROTECT HER!
GU (PUMP)
WE'LL PLEDGE OUR SUPPORT, AS MEAGER AS IT MIGHT BE.
JUST DON'T FORGET.
WE'RE LIVING PEOPLE—
BUT SHE'S AN NPC, RIGHT?
I'M SICK OF HEARING THAT.

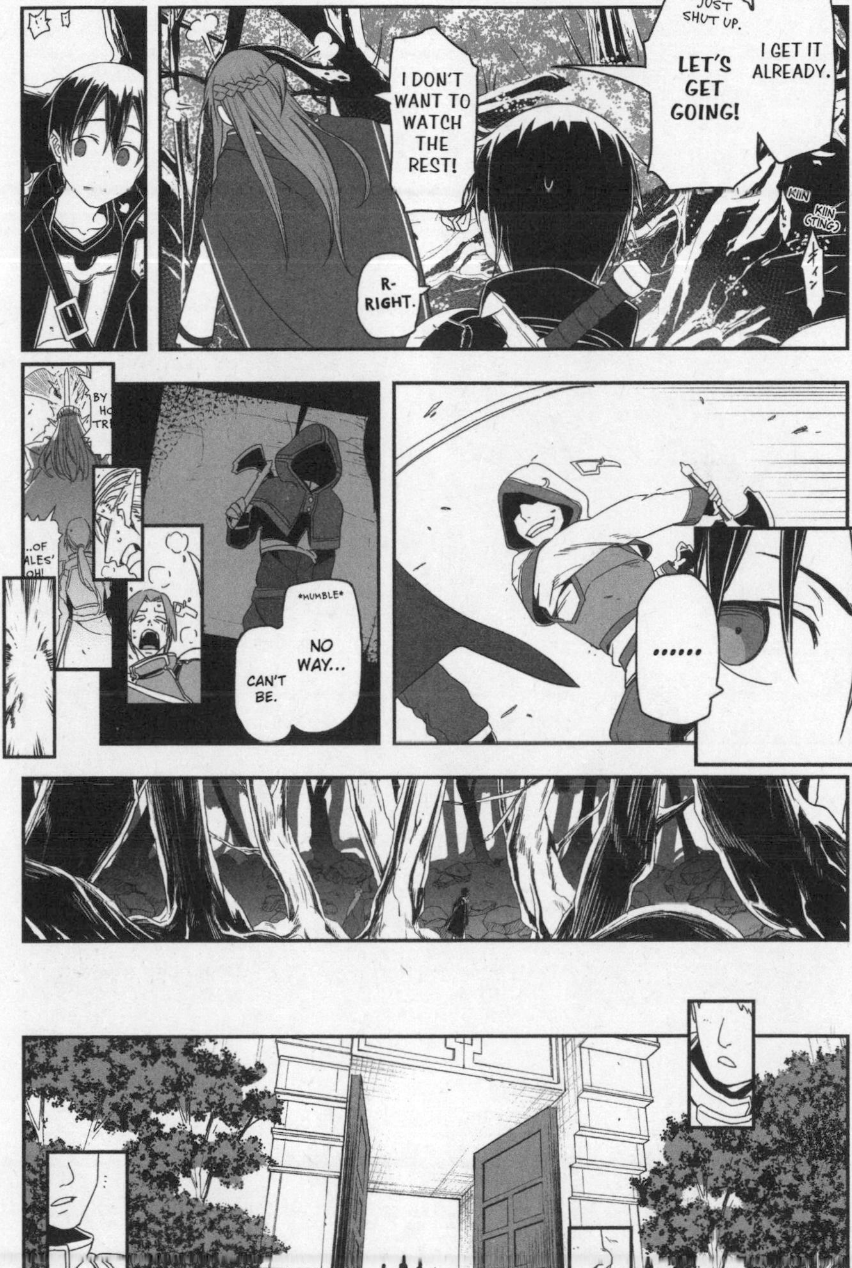
JUST SHUT UP.
I GET IT ALREADY.
LET'S GET GOING!
I DON'T WANT TO WATCH THE REST!
KIIN KIIN (TING)
キィン
R-RIGHT.
......
HUMBLE
NO WAY...
CAN'T BE.

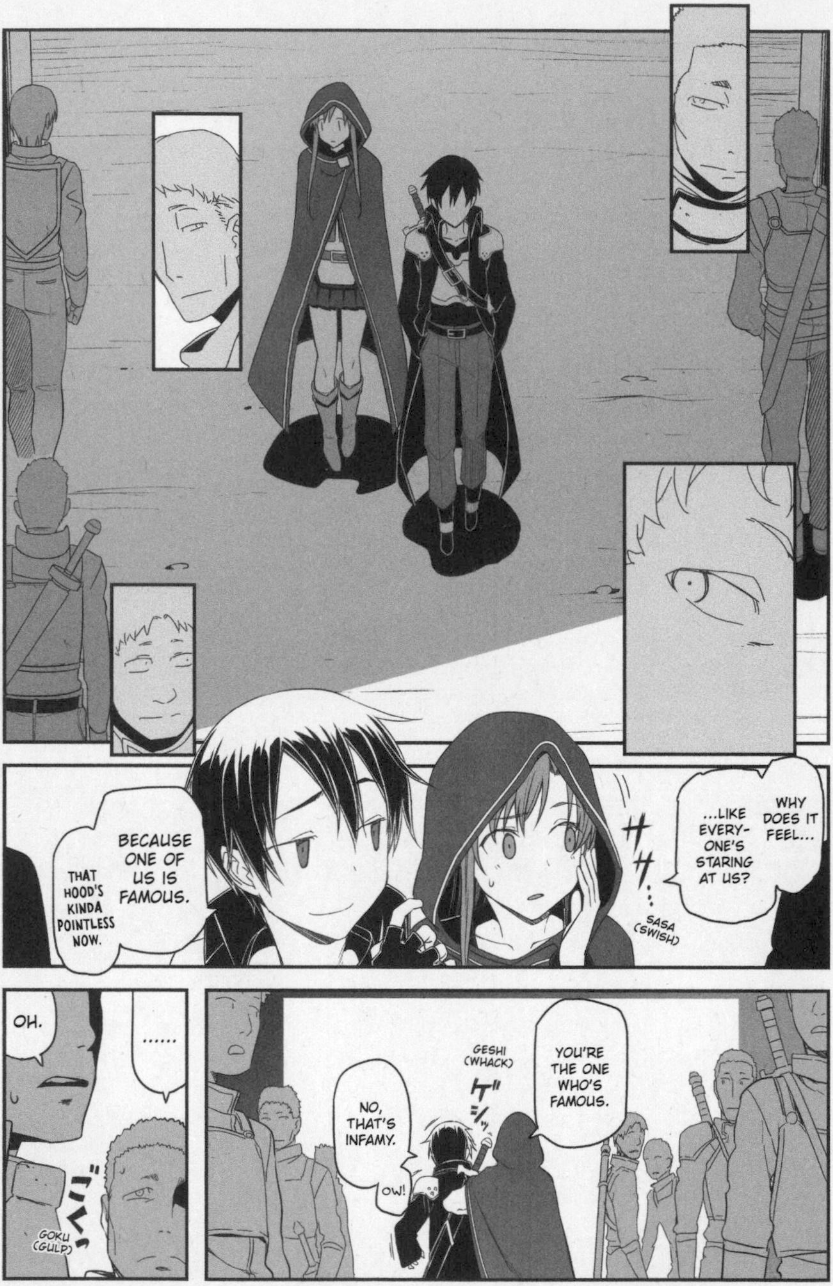
WHY DOES IT FEEL...
...LIKE EVERY-ONE'S STARING AT US?
SASA (SWISH)
BECAUSE ONE OF US IS FAMOUS.
THAT HOOD'S KINDA POINTLESS NOW.
YOU'RE THE ONE WHO'S FAMOUS.
GESHI (WHACK)
NO, THAT'S INFAMY.
OW!
......
OH.
GOKU (GULP)

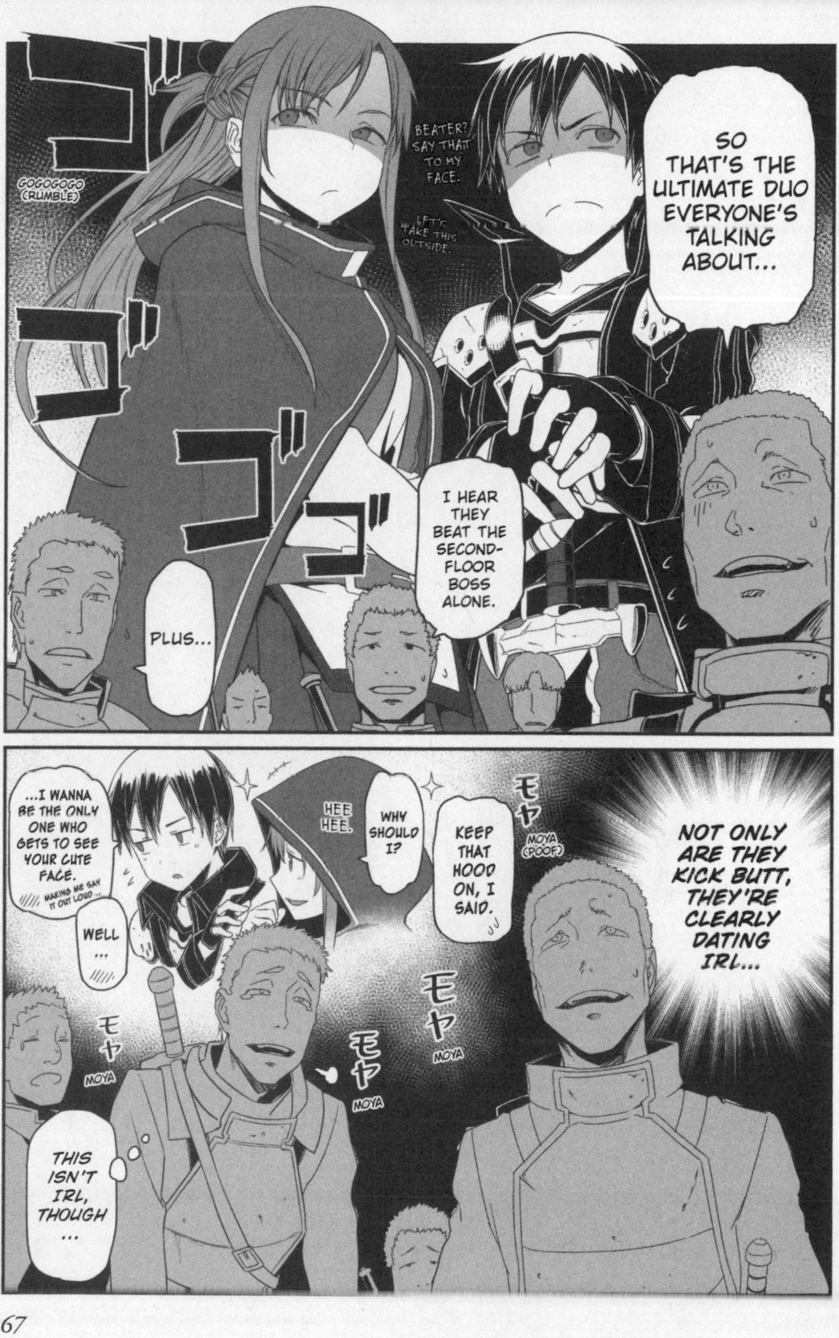
SO THAT'S THE ULTIMATE DUO EVERYONE'S TALKING ABOUT...
BEATER? SAY THAT TO MY FACE.
LET'S TAKE THIS OUTSIDE.
ゴゴゴゴ
GOGOGOGO (RUMBLE)
I HEAR THEY BEAT THE SECOND-FLOOR BOSS ALONE.
PLUS...
NOT ONLY ARE THEY KICK BUTT, THEY'RE CLEARLY DATING IRL...
モヤ
MOYA (POOF)
KEEP THAT HOOD ON, I SAID.
WHY SHOULD I?
HEE HEE.
...I WANNA BE THE ONLY ONE WHO GETS TO SEE YOUR CUTE FACE.
MAKING ME SAY IT OUT LOUD...
WELL...
モヤ
MOYA
モヤ
MOYA
モヤ
MOYA
THIS ISN'T IRL, THOUGH...

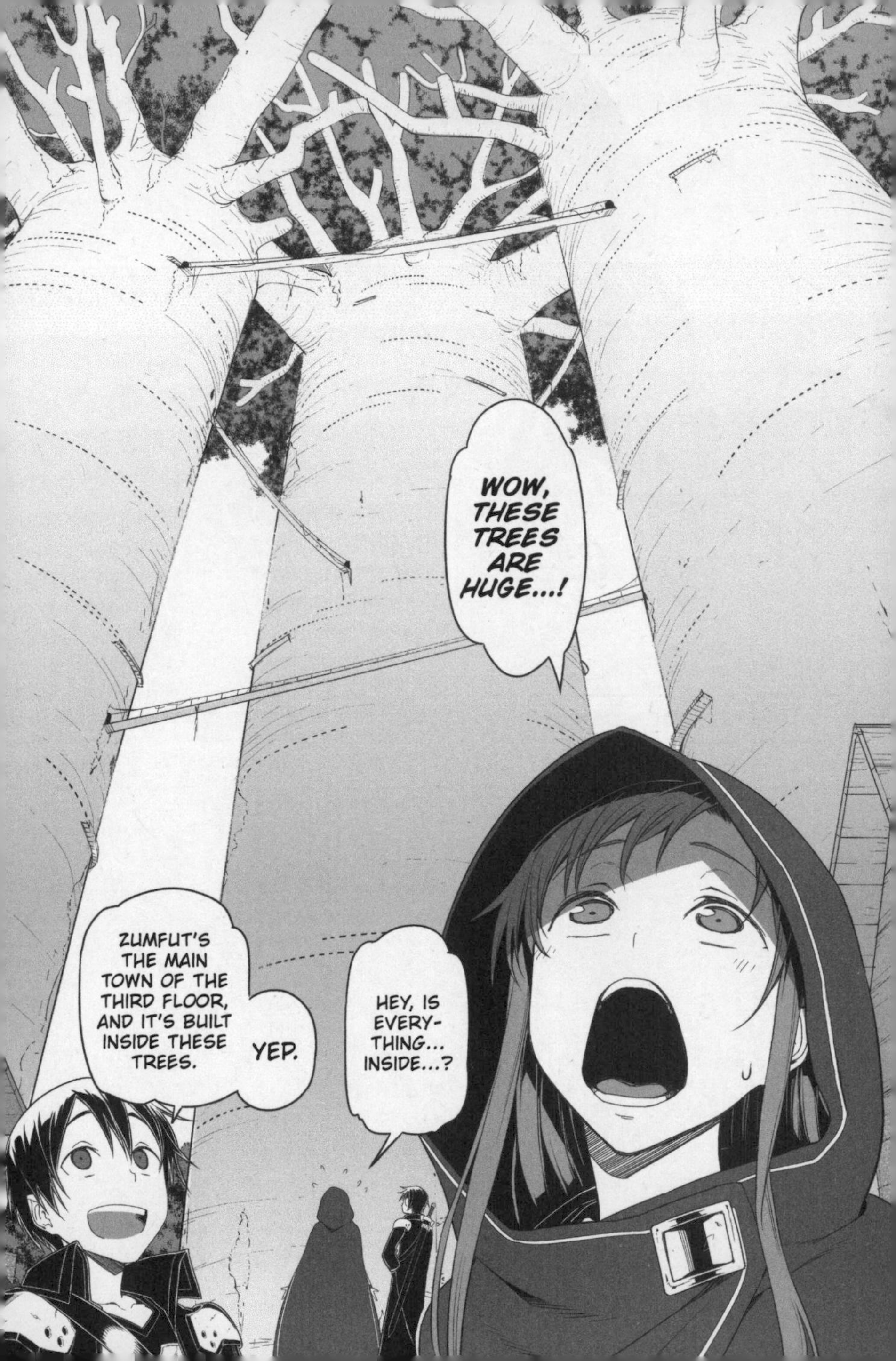
WOW, THESE TREES ARE HUGE...!
HEY, IS EVERY-THING... INSIDE...?
YEP.
ZUMFUT'S THE MAIN TOWN OF THE THIRD FLOOR, AND IT'S BUILT INSIDE THESE TREES.

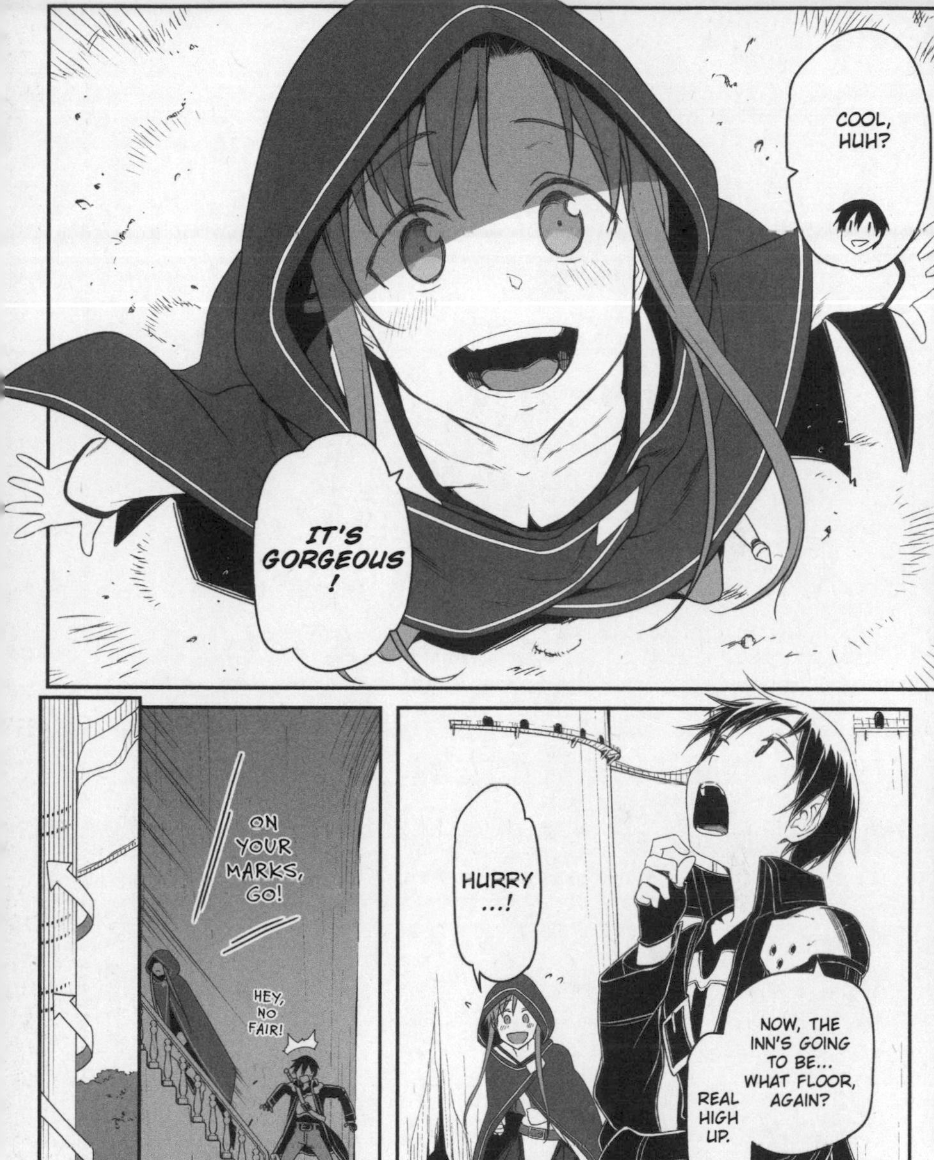
COOL, HUH?
IT'S GORGEOUS!
NOW, THE INN'S GOING TO BE... WHAT FLOOR, AGAIN?
REAL HIGH UP.
HURRY...!
ON YOUR MARKS, GO!
HEY, NO FAIR!

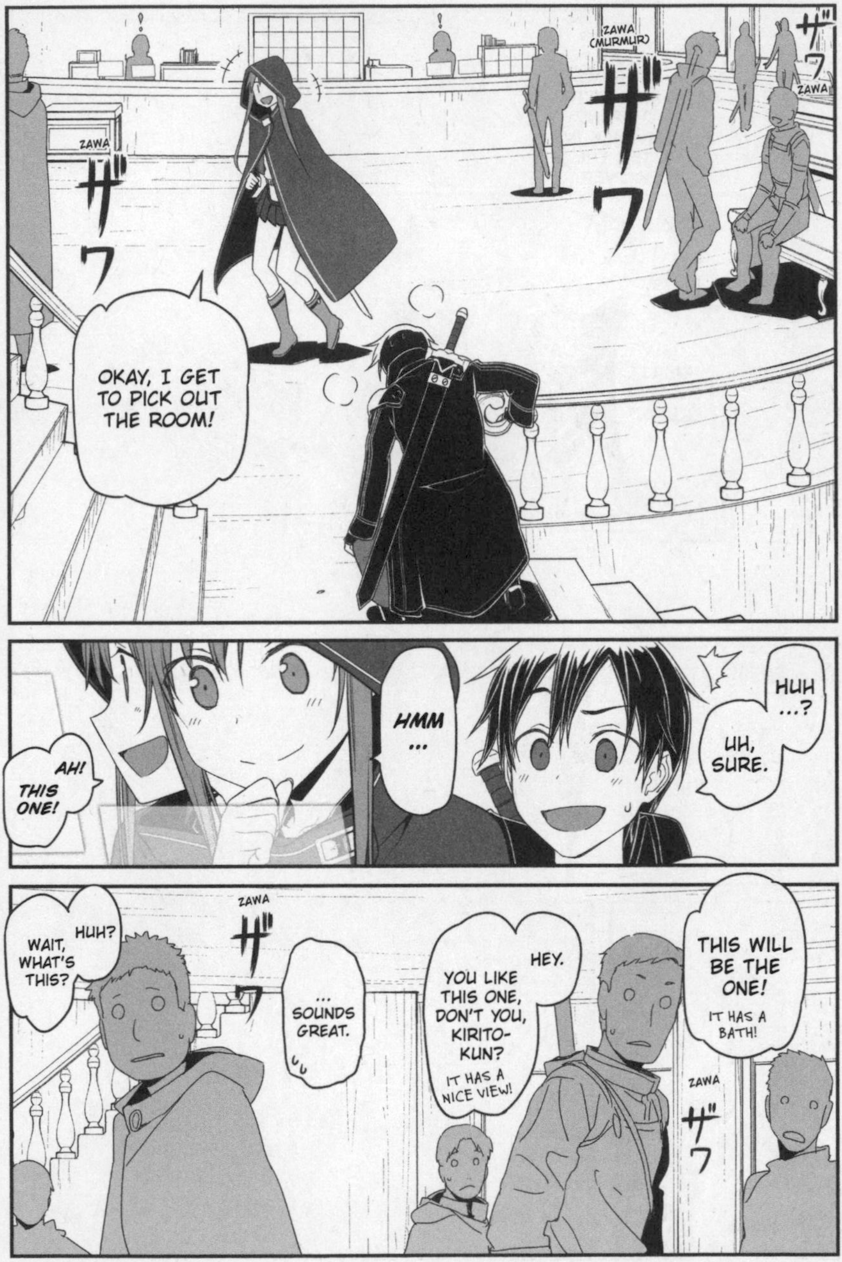
ZAWA (MURMUR)
ザワ
ZAWA
ザワ
ZAWA
ザワ
OKAY, I GET TO PICK OUT THE ROOM!
HUH ...?
UH, SURE.
HMM ...
AH! THIS ONE!
THIS WILL BE THE ONE!
IT HAS A BATH!
ZAWA
ザワ
HEY.
YOU LIKE THIS ONE, DON'T YOU, KIRITO-KUN?
IT HAS A NICE VIEW!
... SOUNDS GREAT.
ZAWA
ザワ
HUH?
WAIT, WHAT'S THIS?

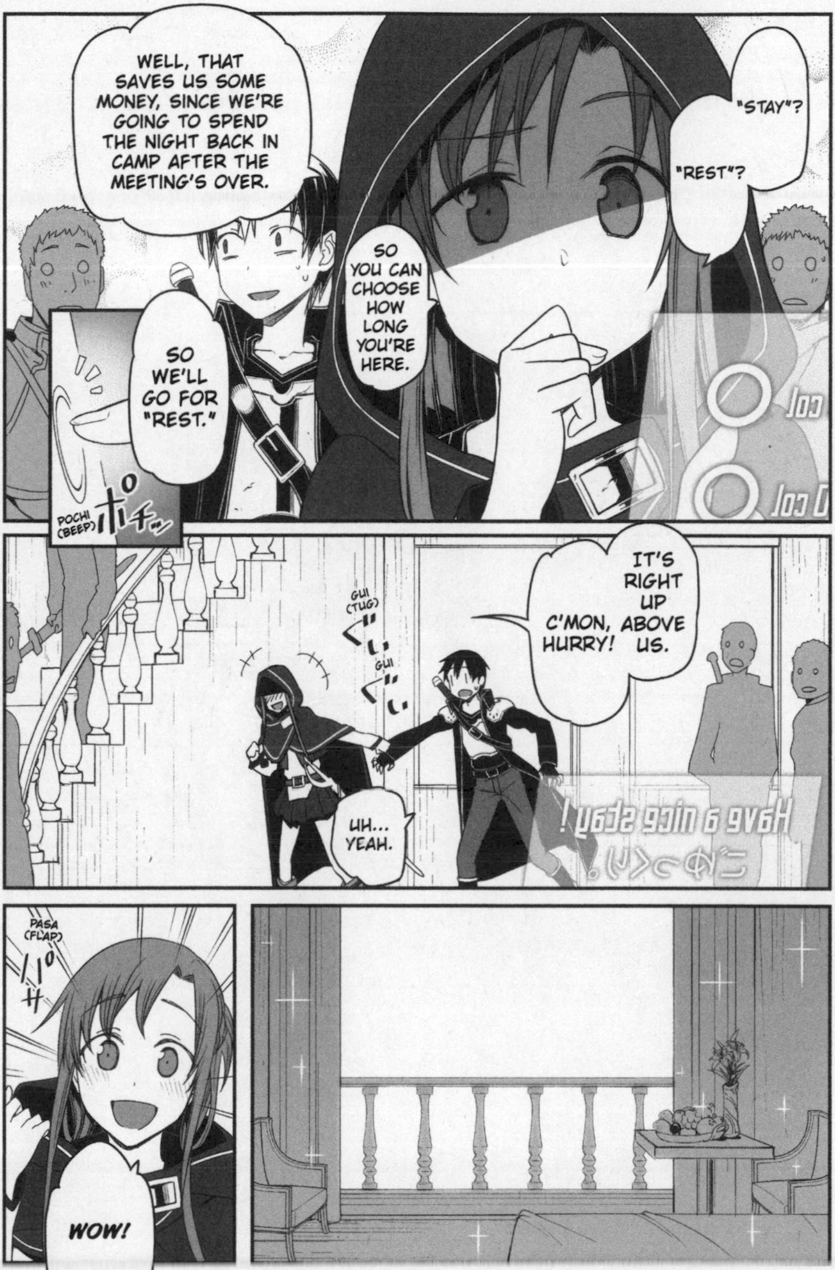
"STAY"?
"REST"?
SO YOU CAN CHOOSE HOW LONG YOU'RE HERE.
WELL, THAT SAVES US SOME MONEY, SINCE WE'RE GOING TO SPEND THE NIGHT BACK IN CAMP AFTER THE MEETING'S OVER.
SO WE'LL GO FOR "REST."
POCHI (BEEP)
IT'S RIGHT UP ABOVE US.
C'MON, HURRY!
GUI (TUG)
GUI
UH... YEAH.
PASA (FLAP)
WOW!

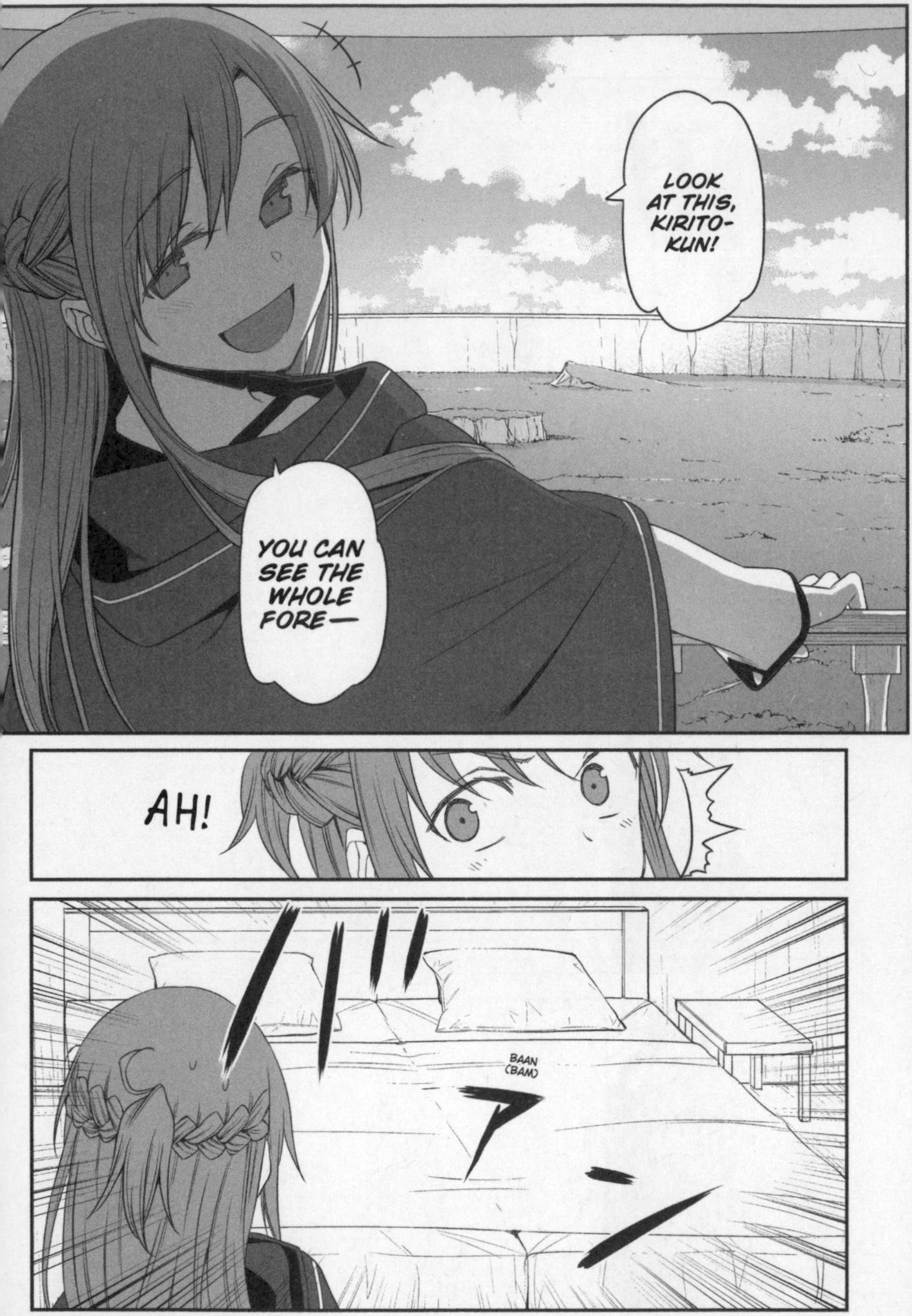
LOOK AT THIS, KIRITO-KUN!
YOU CAN SEE THE WHOLE FORE—
AH!
BAAN (BAM)

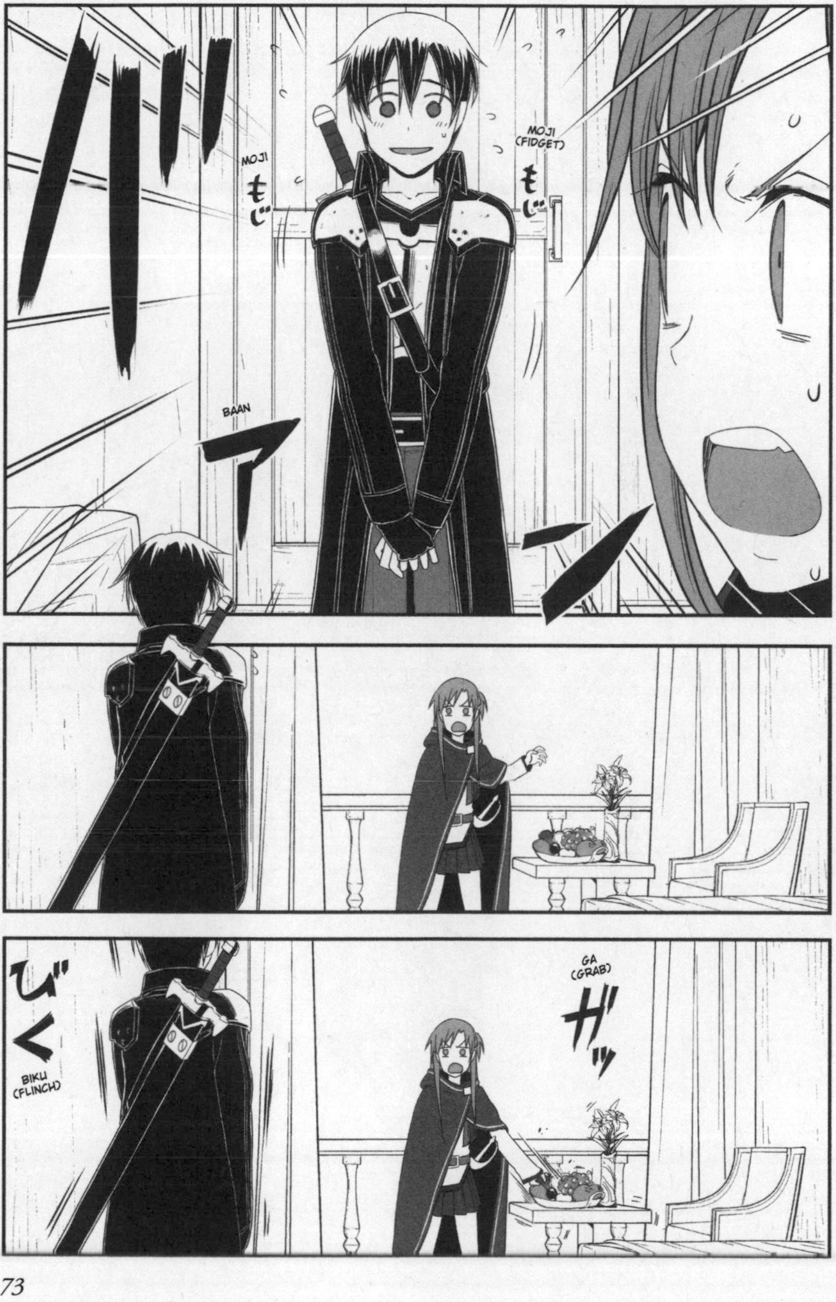
MOJI (FIDGET)
もじ
MOJI
もじ
BAAN
GA (GRAB)
ガッ
BIKU (FLINCH)
びく

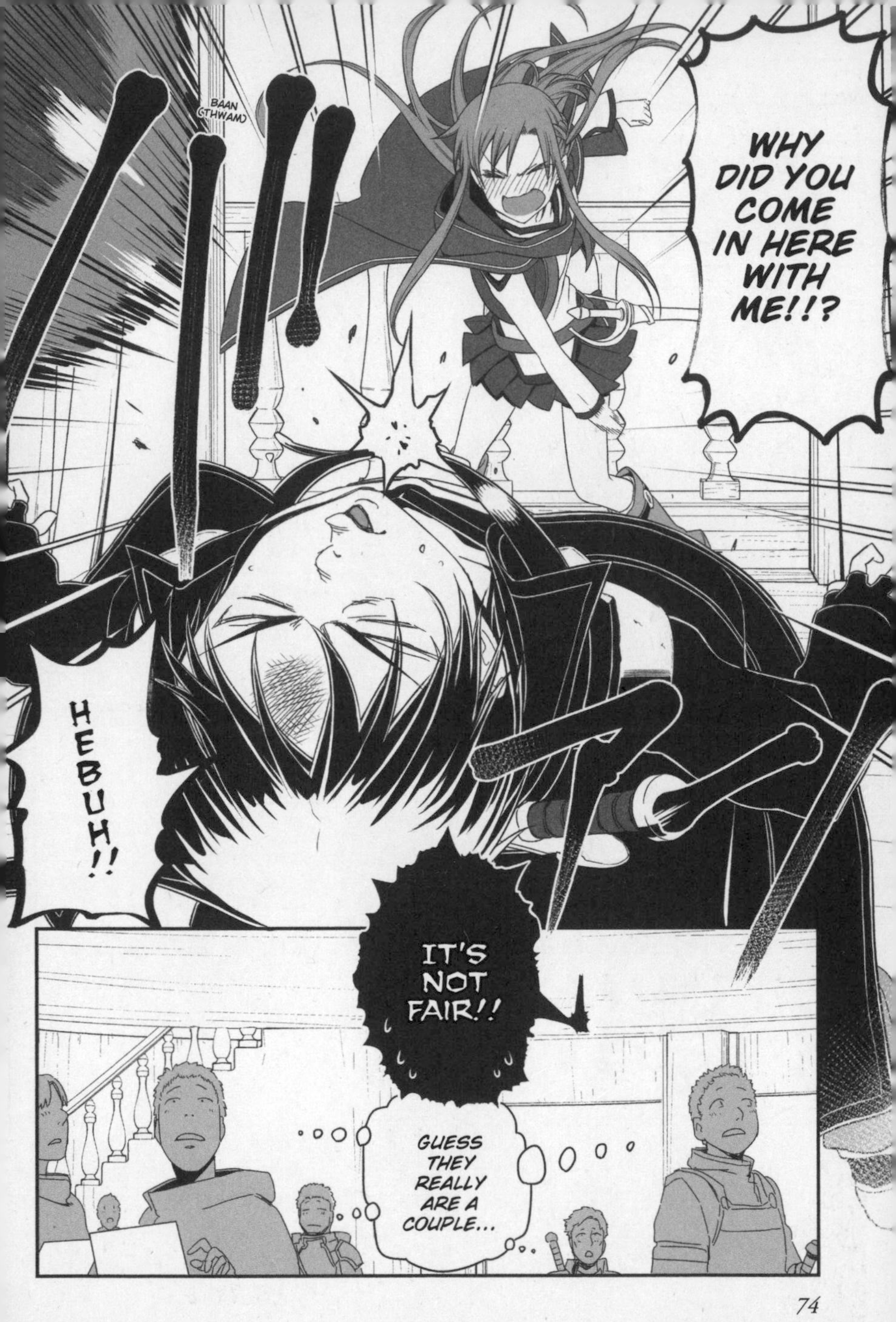
WHY DID YOU COME IN HERE WITH ME!!?
BAAN (THWAM)
HEBUH!!
IT'S NOT FAIR!!
GUESS THEY REALLY ARE A COUPLE...

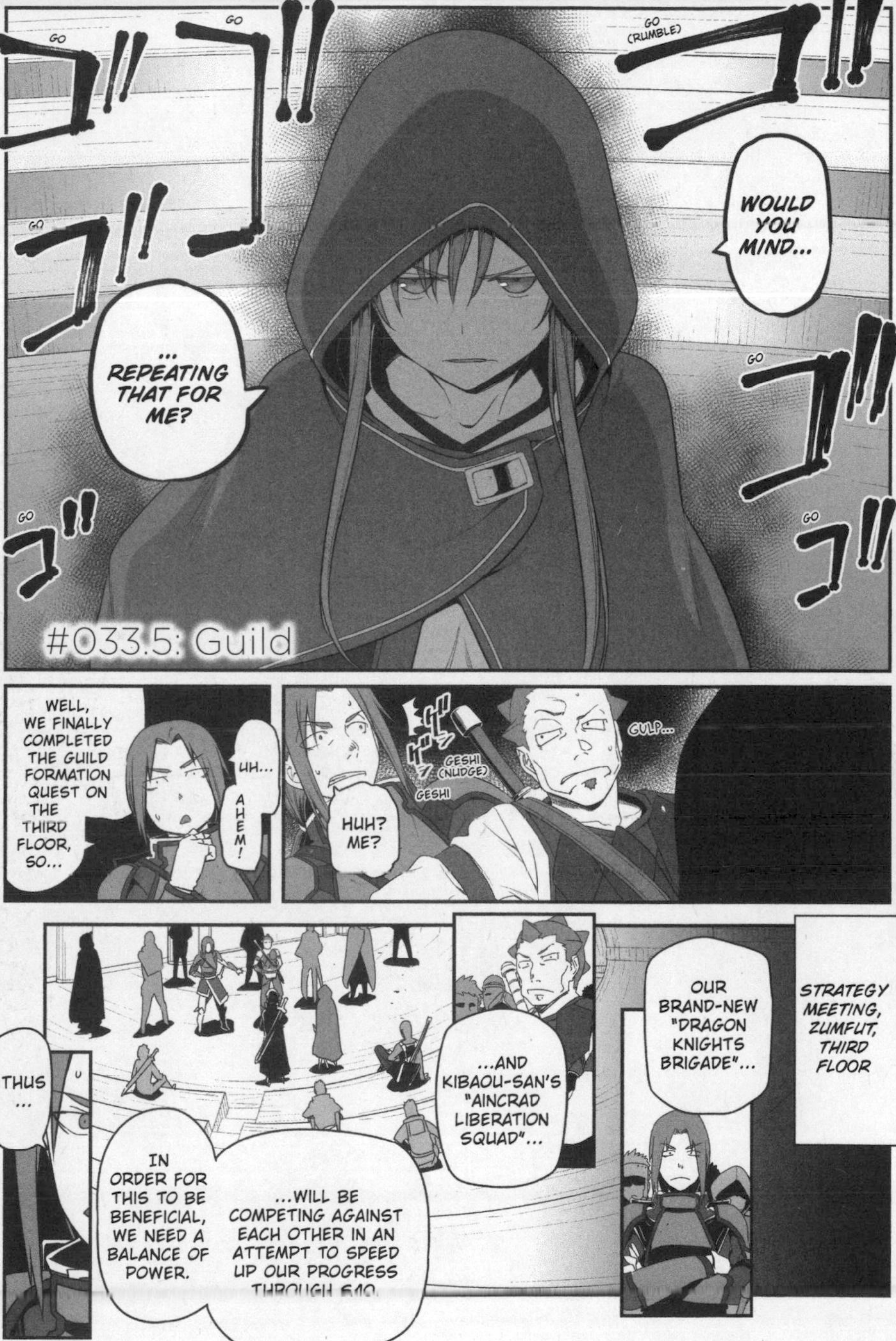
GO (RUMBLE)
GO
GO
GO
WOULD YOU MIND...
...REPEATING THAT FOR ME?
GO
GO
GO
#033.5: Guild
GULP...
GESHI (NUDGE)
GESHI
HUH? ME?
WELL, WE FINALLY COMPLETED THE GUILD FORMATION QUEST ON THE THIRD FLOOR, SO...
UH...
AHEM!
STRATEGY MEETING, ZUMFUT, THIRD FLOOR
OUR BRAND-NEW "DRAGON KNIGHTS BRIGADE"...
...AND KIBAOU-SAN'S "AINCRAD LIBERATION SQUAD"...
...WILL BE COMPETING AGAINST EACH OTHER IN AN ATTEMPT TO SPEED UP OUR PROGRESS THROUGH SAO.
THUS...
U
IN ORDER FOR THIS TO BE BENEFICIAL, WE NEED A BALANCE OF POWER.

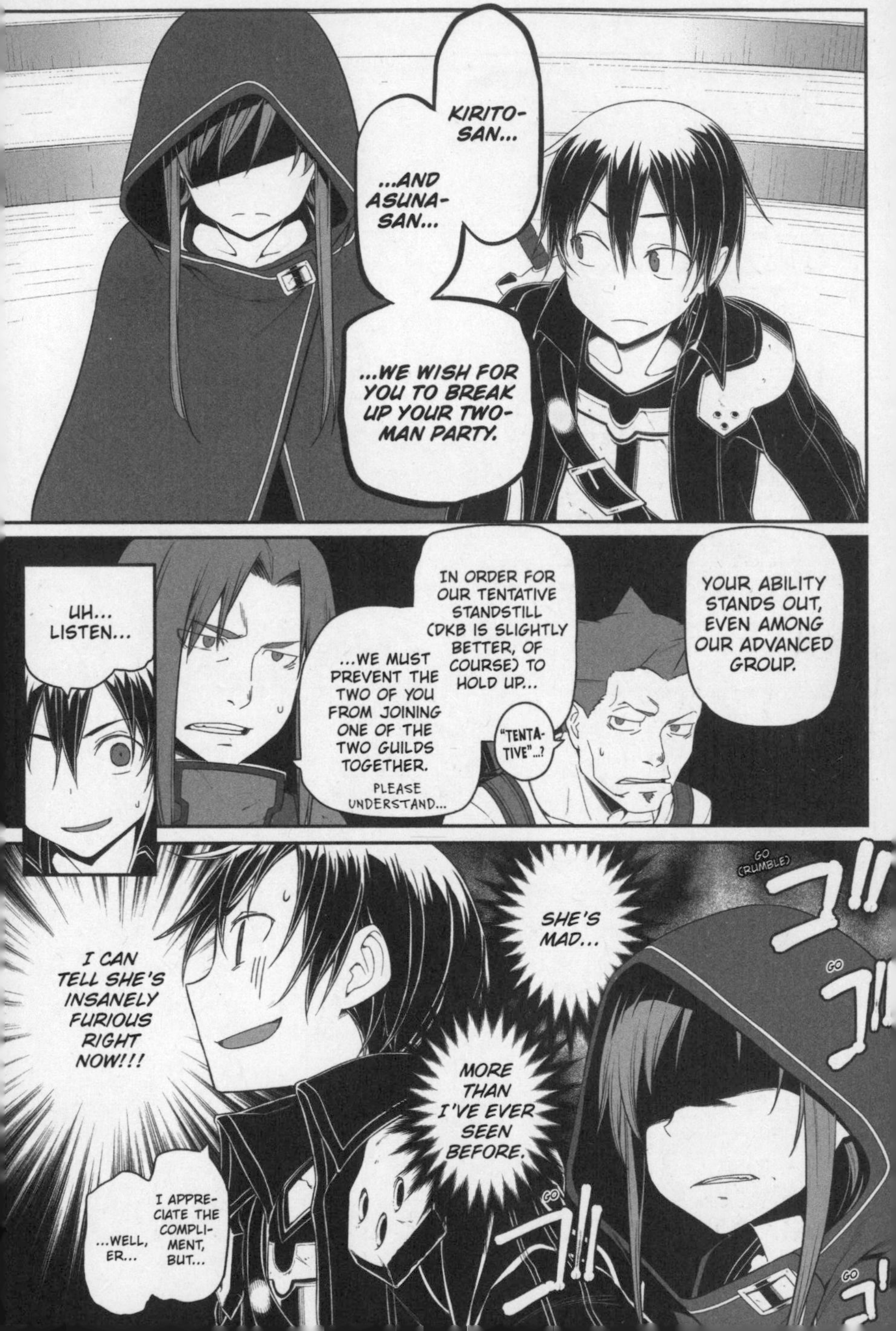
KIRITO-SAN...
...AND ASUNA-SAN...
...WE WISH FOR YOU TO BREAK UP YOUR TWO-MAN PARTY.
YOUR ABILITY STANDS OUT, EVEN AMONG OUR ADVANCED GROUP.
IN ORDER FOR OUR TENTATIVE STANDSTILL (DKB IS SLIGHTLY BETTER, OF COURSE) TO HOLD UP...
"TENTATIVE"...?
...WE MUST PREVENT THE TWO OF YOU FROM JOINING ONE OF THE TWO GUILDS TOGETHER.
PLEASE UNDERSTAND...
UH... LISTEN...
GO (RUMBLE)
ゴ!!
GO
ゴ!!
SHE'S MAD...
I CAN TELL SHE'S INSANELY FURIOUS RIGHT NOW!!!
MORE THAN I'VE EVER SEEN BEFORE.
GO
ゴ!!
GO
ゴ!
I APPRECIATE THE COMPLIMENT, BUT...
...WELL, ER...

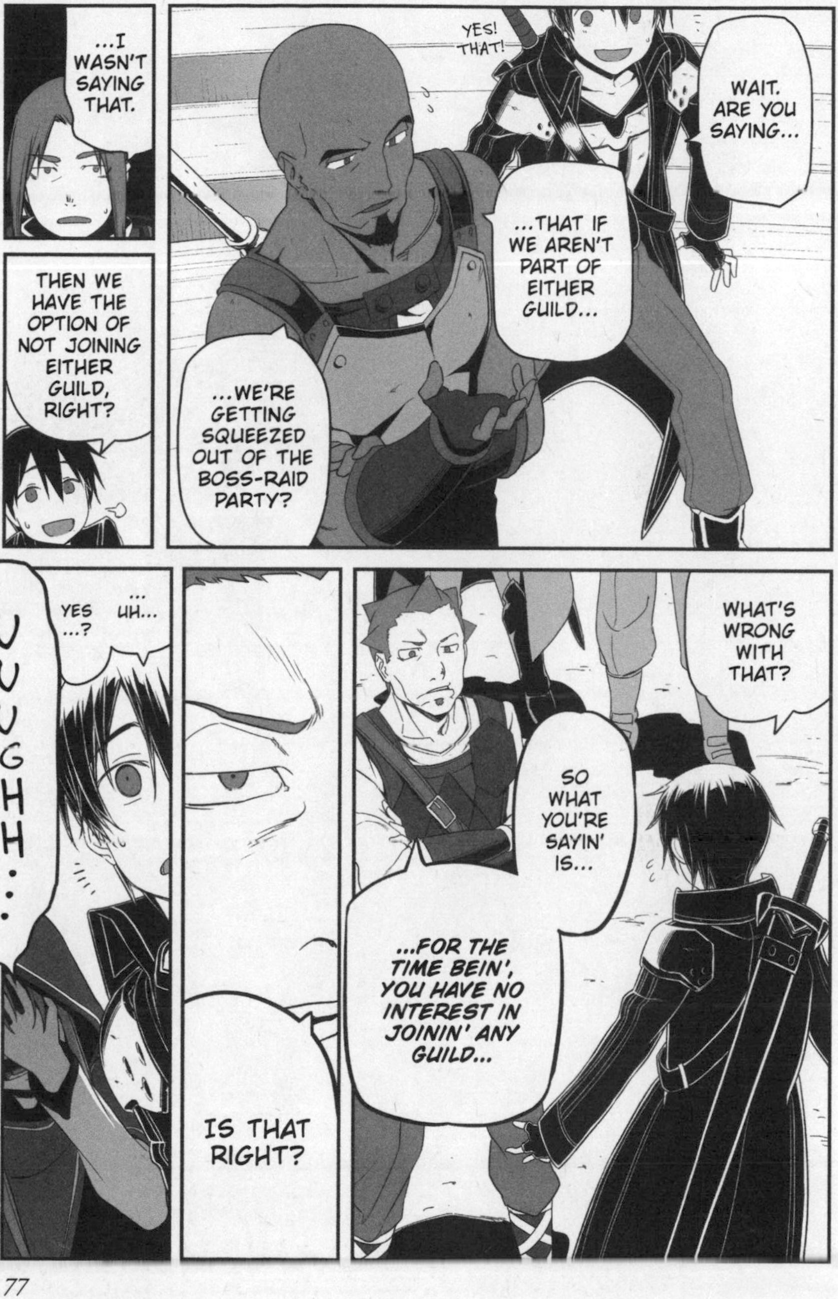
WAIT. ARE YOU SAYING...
YES! THAT!
...THAT IF WE AREN'T PART OF EITHER GUILD...
...WE'RE GETTING SQUEEZED OUT OF THE BOSS-RAID PARTY?
...I WASN'T SAYING THAT.
THEN WE HAVE THE OPTION OF NOT JOINING EITHER GUILD, RIGHT?
WHAT'S WRONG WITH THAT?
SO WHAT YOU'RE SAYIN' IS...
...FOR THE TIME BEIN', YOU HAVE NO INTEREST IN JOININ' ANY GUILD...
IS THAT RIGHT?
...UH...
YES...?
UUUGH...

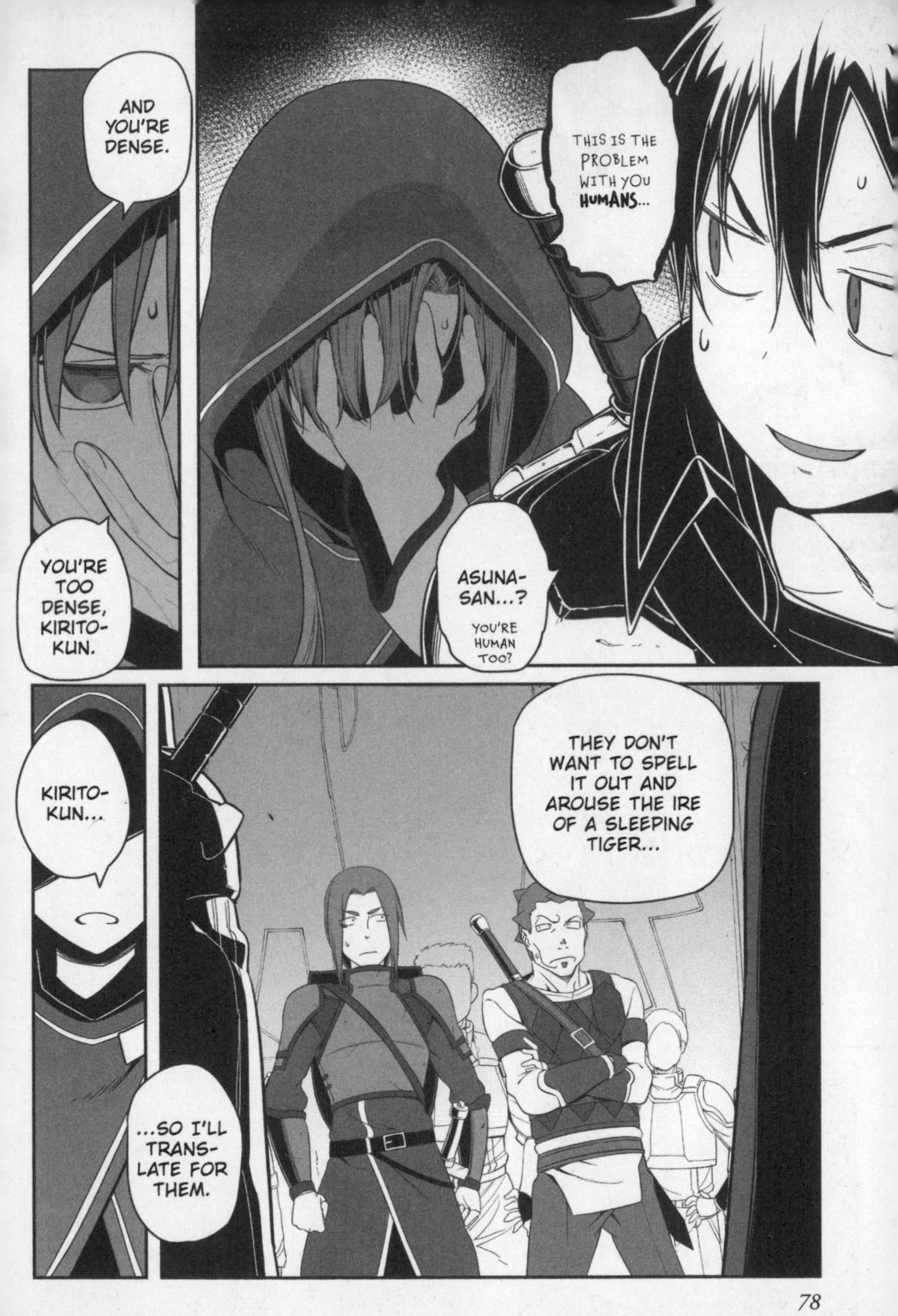
THIS IS THE PROBLEM WITH YOU **HUMANS**...
ASUNA-SAN...?
YOU'RE HUMAN TOO?
YOU'RE TOO DENSE, KIRITO-KUN.
AND YOU'RE DENSE.
THEY DON'T WANT TO SPELL IT OUT AND AROUSE THE IRE OF A SLEEPING TIGER...
KIRITO-KUN...
...SO I'LL TRANS-LATE FOR THEM.

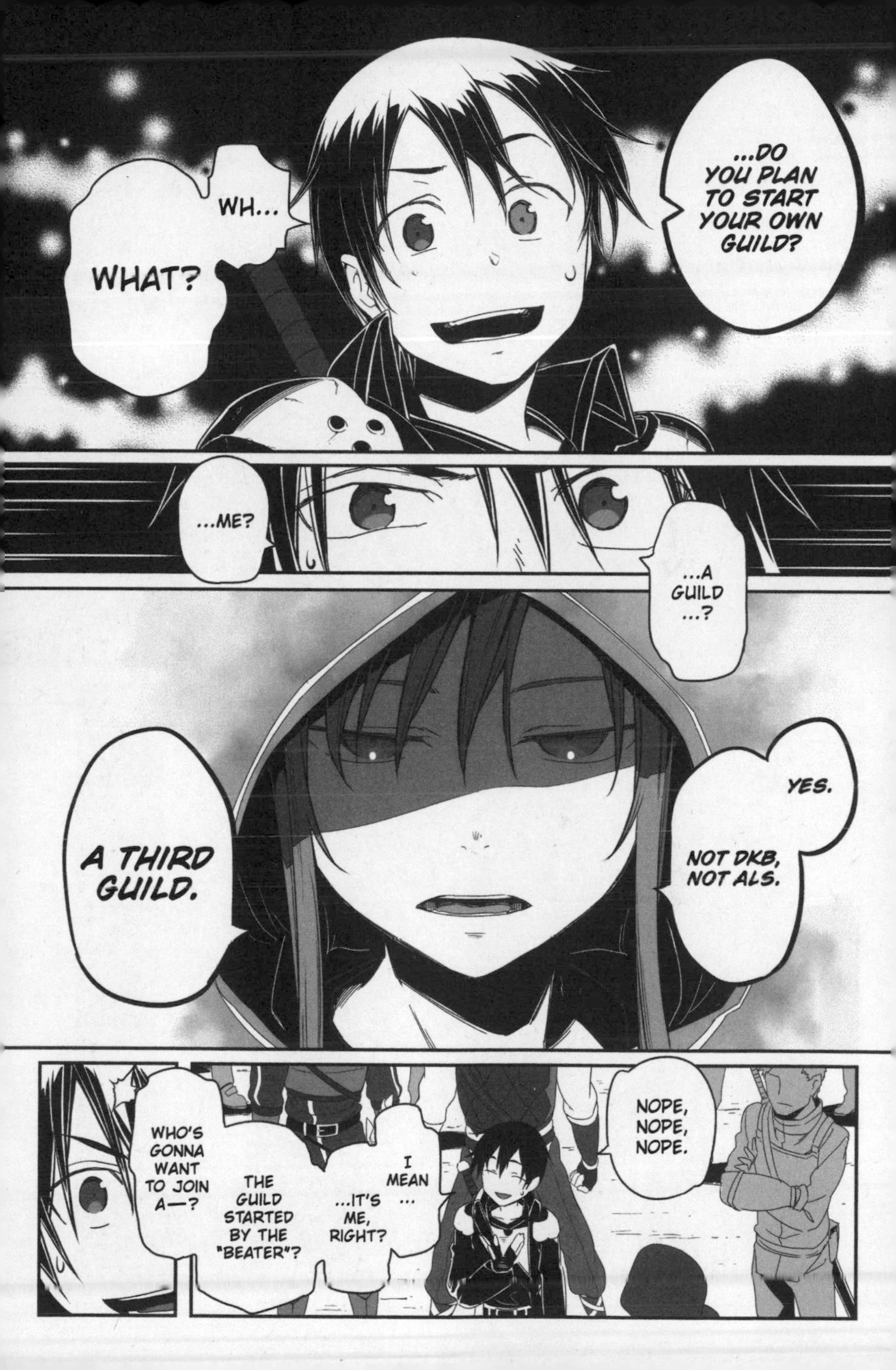
...DO YOU PLAN TO START YOUR OWN GUILD?
WH...
WHAT?
...ME?
...A GUILD ...?
YES.
NOT DKB, NOT ALS.
A THIRD GUILD.
NOPE, NOPE, NOPE.
I MEAN ...
...IT'S ME, RIGHT?
WHO'S GONNA WANT TO JOIN A—?
THE GUILD STARTED BY THE "BEATER"?

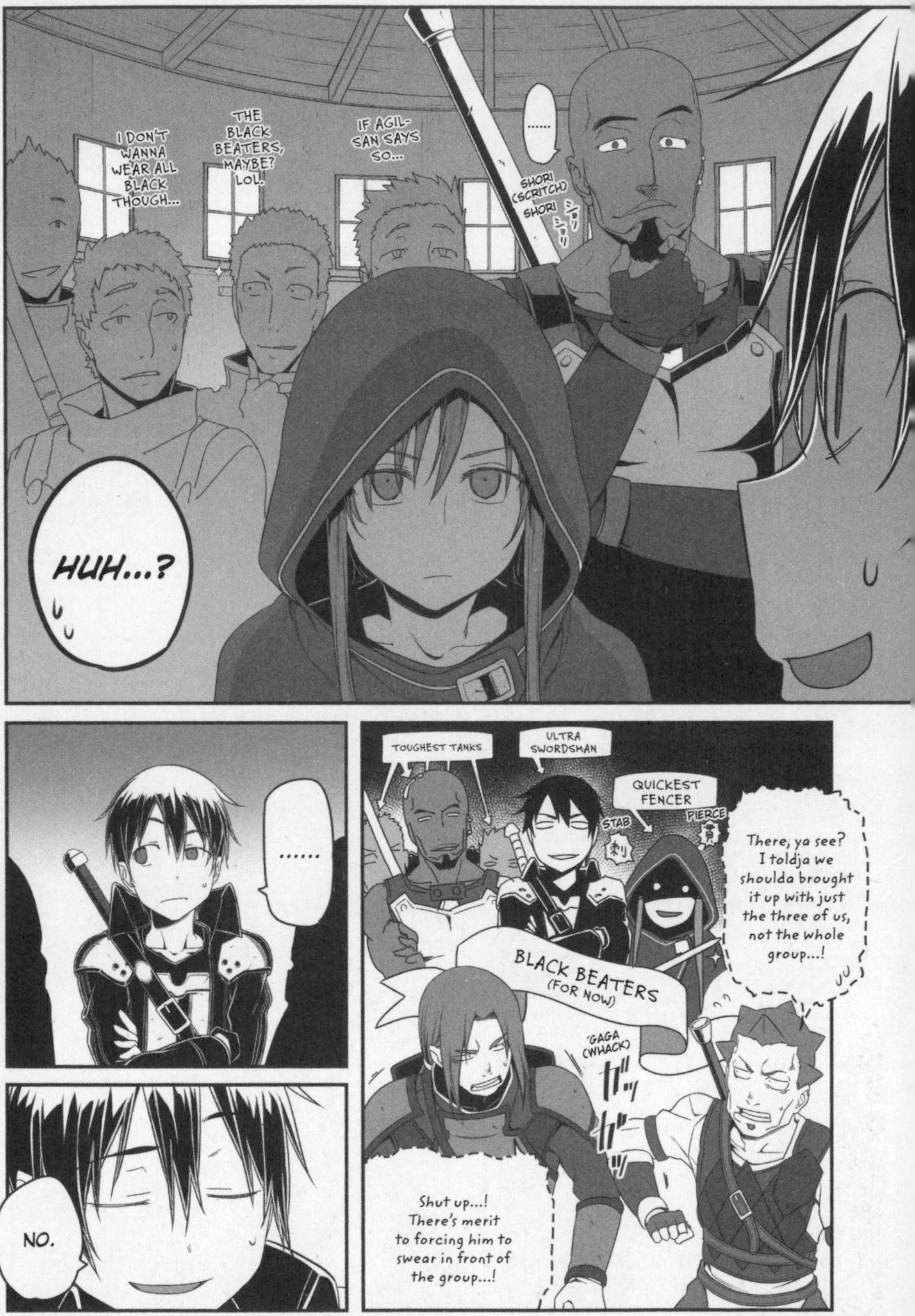
......
SHORI (SCRITCH) SHORI
IF AGIL-SAN SAYS SO...
THE BLACK BEATERS, MAYBE? LOL.
I DON'T WANNA WEAR ALL BLACK THOUGH...
HUH...?
There, ya see? I toldja we shoulda brought it up with just the three of us, not the whole group...!
PIERCE
QUICKEST FENCER
STAB
ULTRA SWORDSMAN
TOUGHEST TANKS
BLACK BEATERS (FOR NOW)
GAGA (WHACK)
Shut up...! There's merit to forcing him to swear in front of the group...!
......
NO.

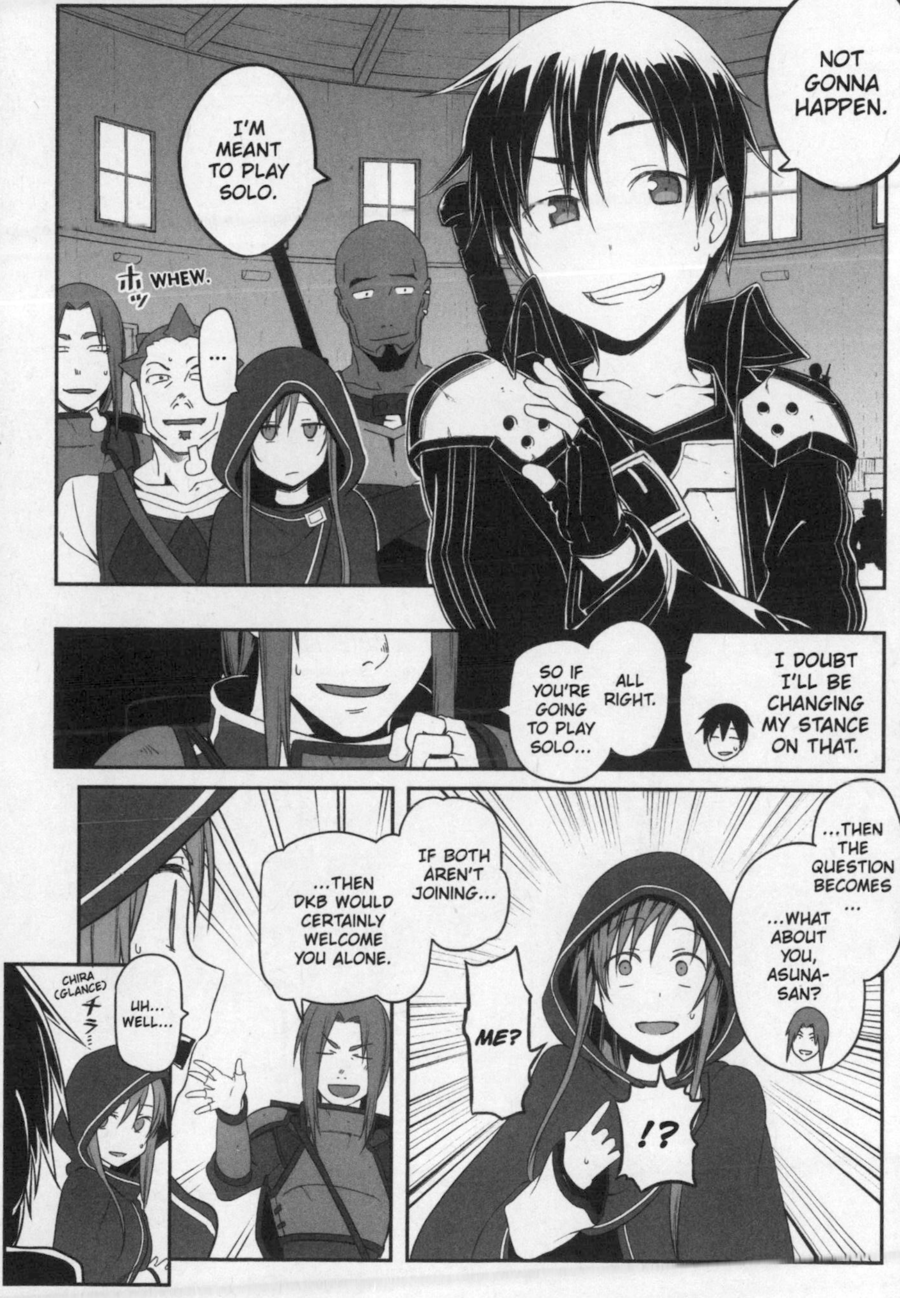
NOT GONNA HAPPEN.
I'M MEANT TO PLAY SOLO.
ホッ WHEW.
...
I DOUBT I'LL BE CHANGING MY STANCE ON THAT.
ALL RIGHT.
SO IF YOU'RE GOING TO PLAY SOLO...
...THEN THE QUESTION BECOMES...
...WHAT ABOUT YOU, ASUNA-SAN?
!?
ME?
IF BOTH AREN'T JOINING...
...THEN DKB WOULD CERTAINLY WELCOME YOU ALONE.
CHIRA (GLANCE)
UH... WELL...

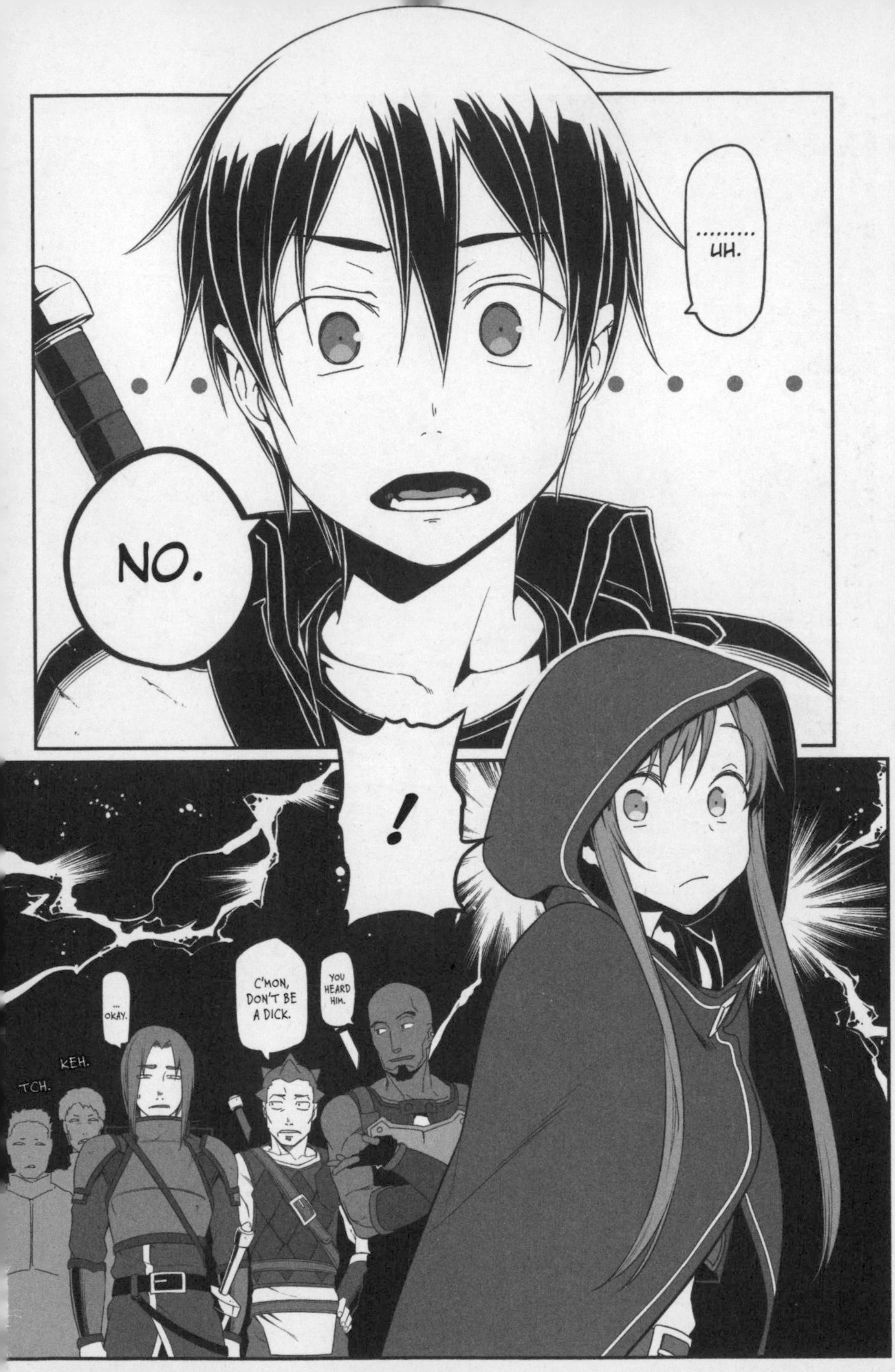
..........UH.
NO.
!
YOU HEARD HIM.
C'MON, DON'T BE A DICK.
...OKAY.
KEH.
TCH.

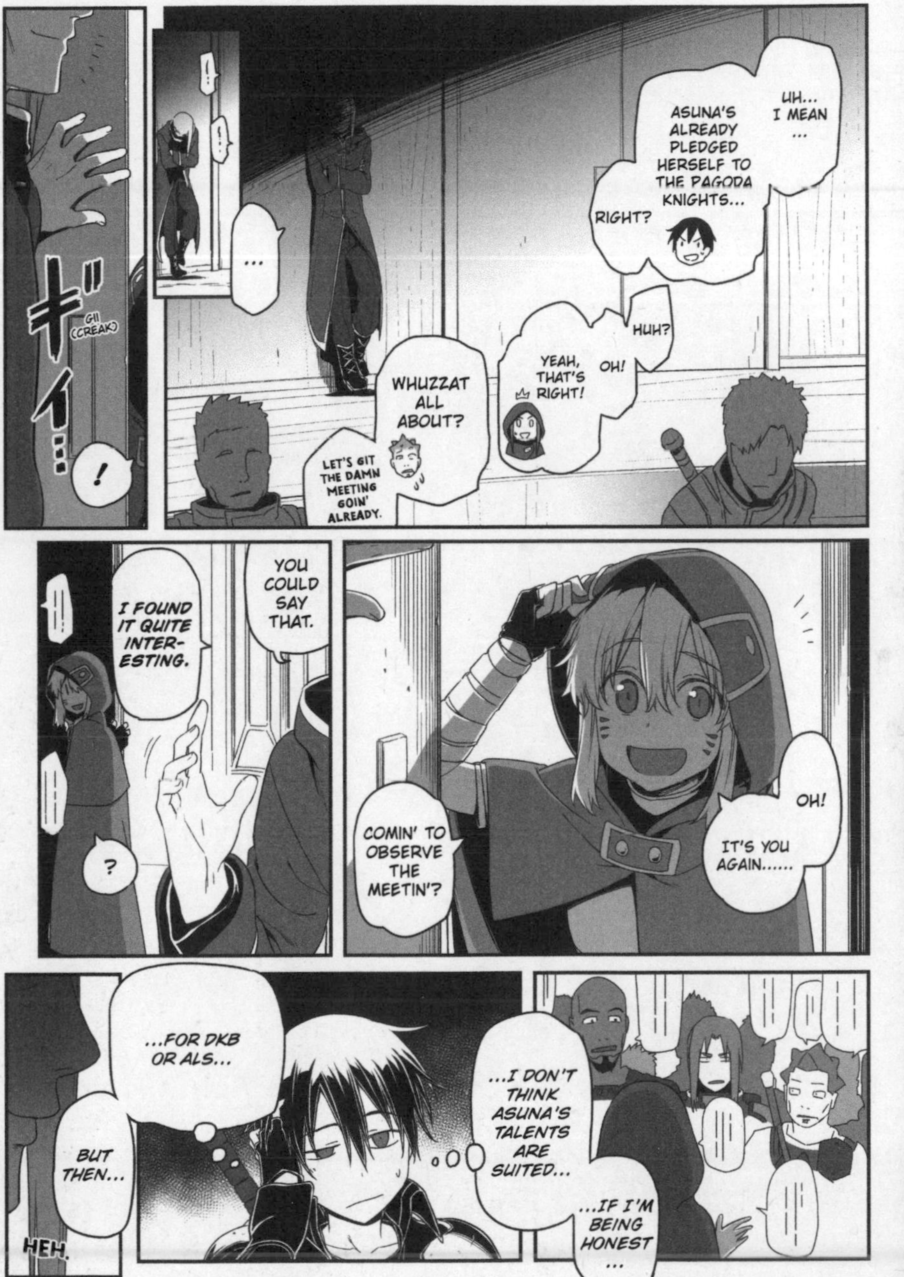
UH... I MEAN ...
ASUNA'S ALREADY PLEDGED HERSELF TO THE PAGODA KNIGHTS...
RIGHT?
HUH?
OH!
YEAH, THAT'S RIGHT!
WHUZZAT ALL ABOUT?
LET'S GIT THE DAMN MEETING GOIN' ALREADY.
!
!...
...
ギイ
GII (CREAK)
!
OH!
IT'S YOU AGAIN......
COMIN' TO OBSERVE THE MEETIN'?
YOU COULD SAY THAT.
I FOUND IT QUITE INTERESTING.
!!
!!
?
...I DON'T THINK ASUNA'S TALENTS ARE SUITED...
...IF I'M BEING HONEST ...
!!
!!
...FOR DKB OR ALS...
BUT THEN...
HEH.

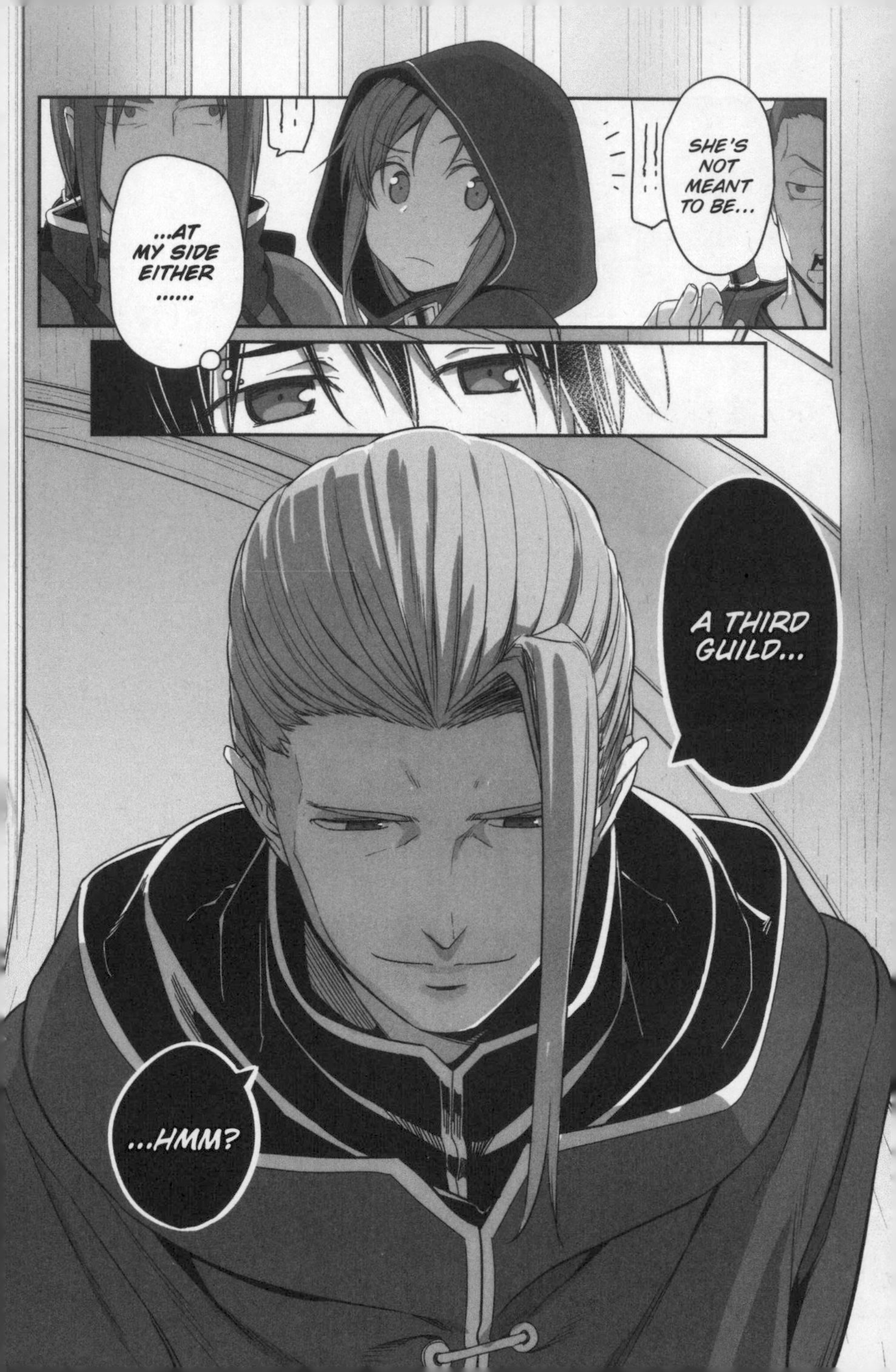
SHE'S NOT MEANT TO BE...
...AT MY SIDE EITHER ......
A THIRD GUILD...
...HMM?

#034: Mission II

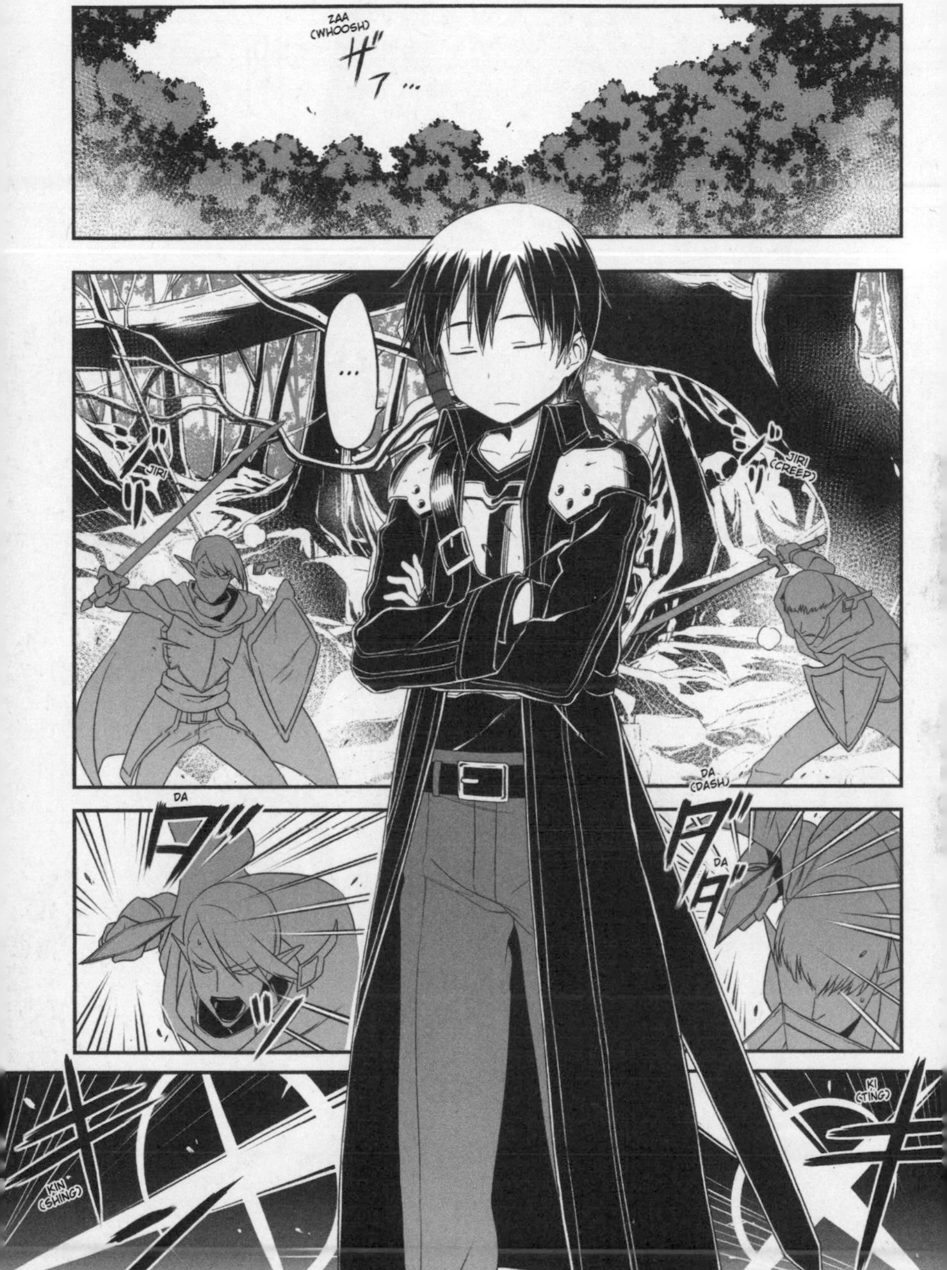

ZAA (WHOOSH)
ザァ…
JIRI (CREEP)
…
JIRI
DA (DASH)
DA
DA
KI (TING)
KIN (SHING)

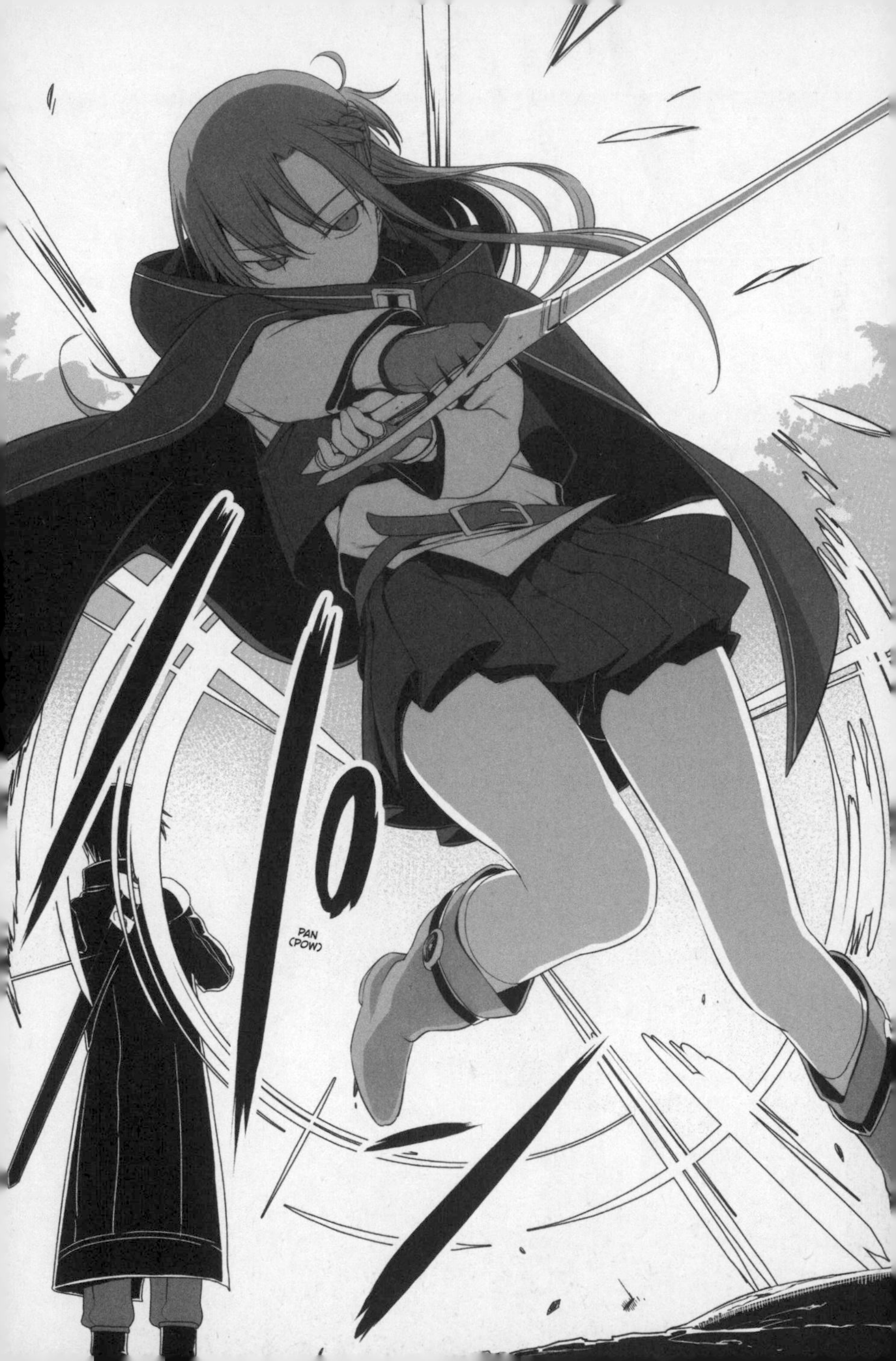
PAN
(POW)

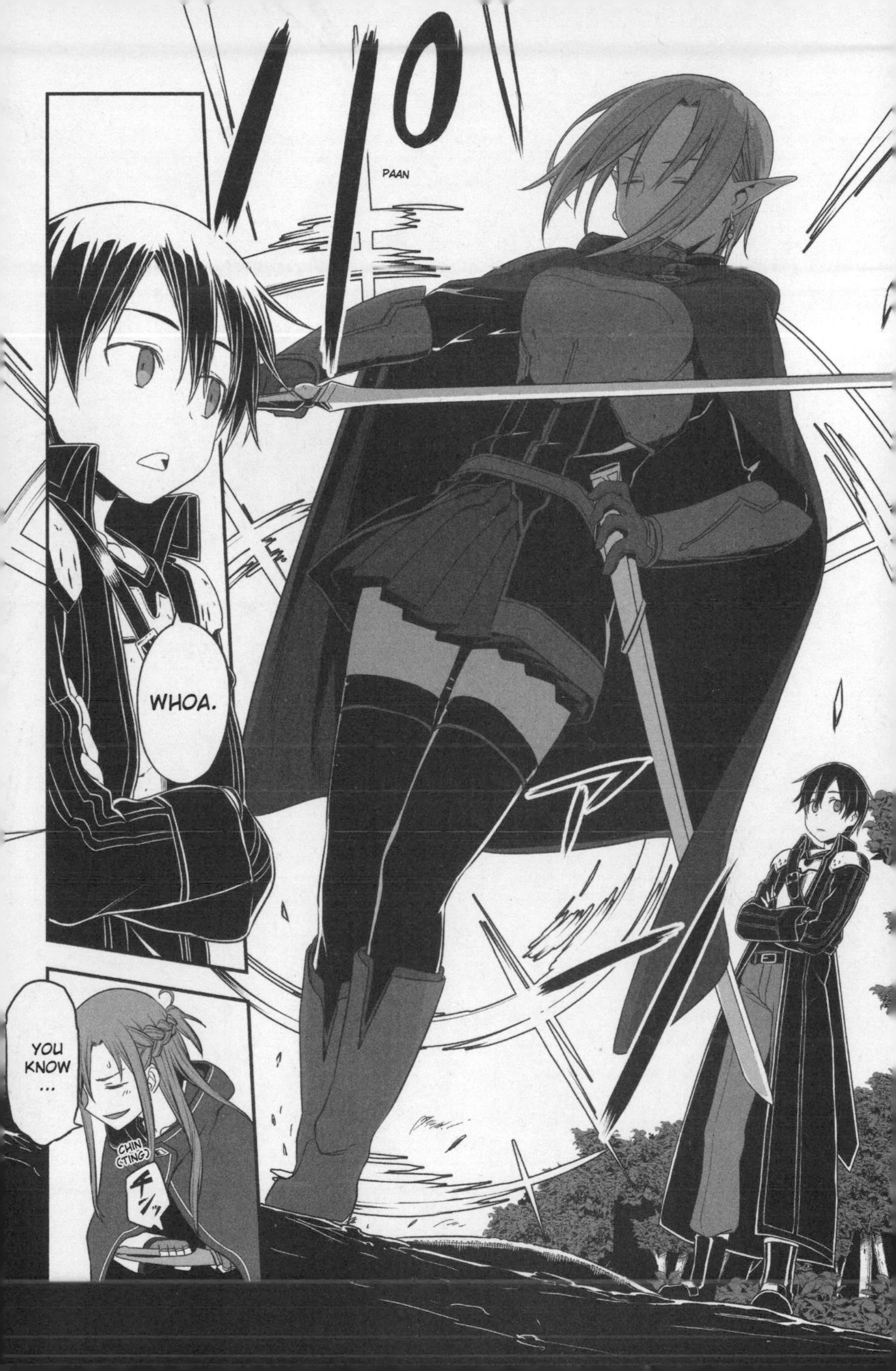
PAAN
WHOA.
YOU KNOW ...
CHIN (TING)
チンッ

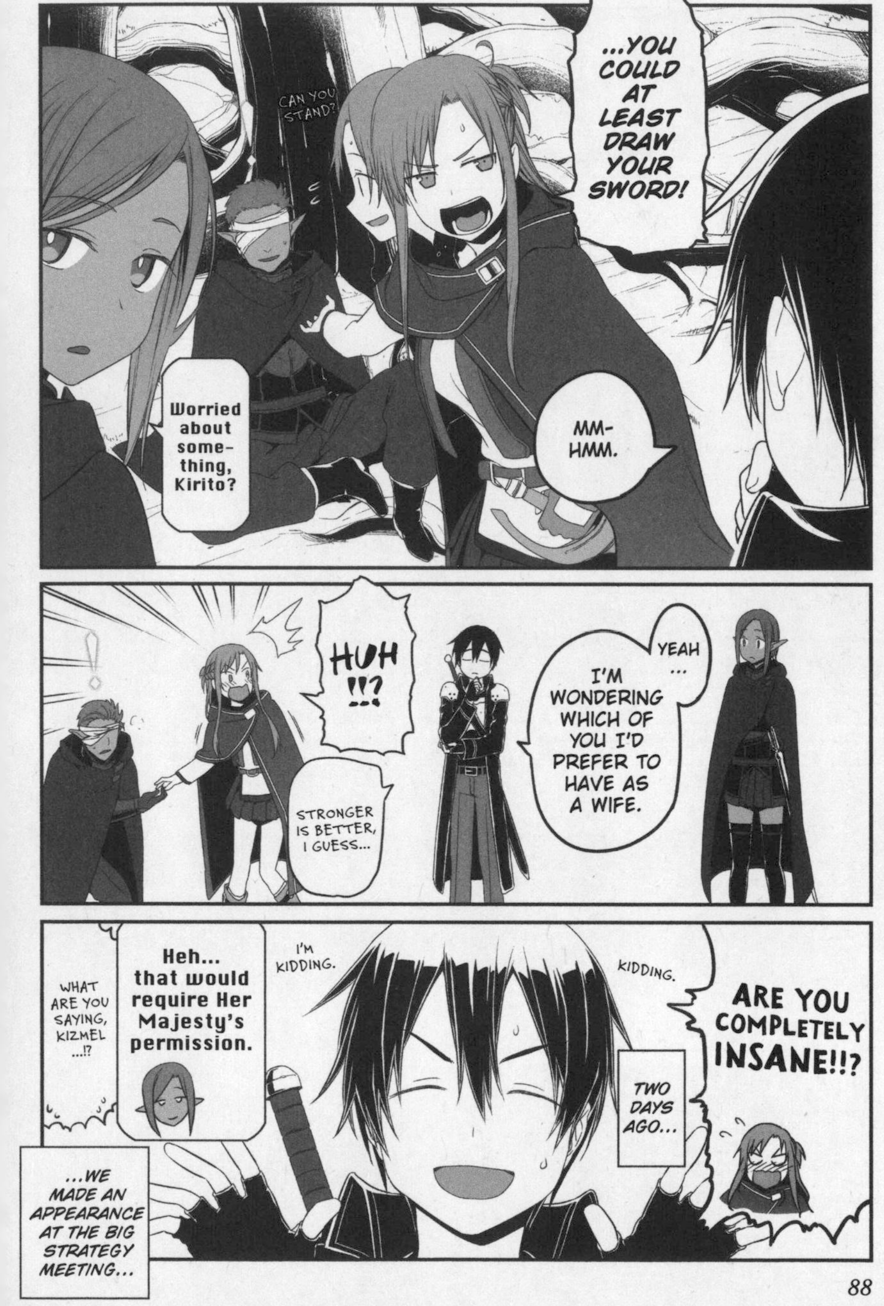
...YOU COULD AT LEAST DRAW YOUR SWORD!
CAN YOU STAND?
MM-HMM.
Worried about some-thing, Kirito?
YEAH...
I'M WONDERING WHICH OF YOU I'D PREFER TO HAVE AS A WIFE.
HUH!!?
STRONGER IS BETTER, I GUESS...
ARE YOU COMPLETELY INSANE!!?
KIDDING.
TWO DAYS AGO...
I'M KIDDING.
Heh... that would require Her Majesty's permission.
WHAT ARE YOU SAYING, KIZMEL ...!?
...WE MADE AN APPEARANCE AT THE BIG STRATEGY MEETING...

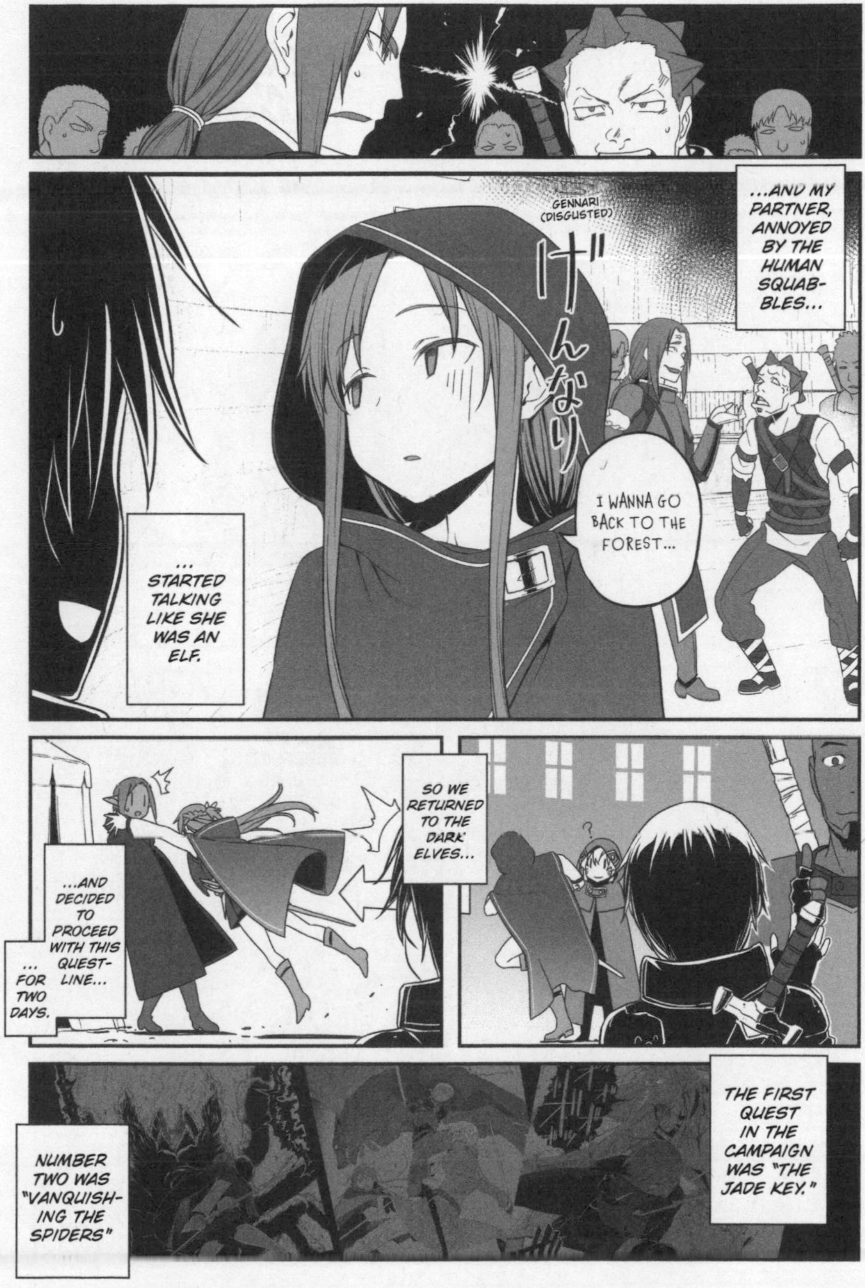
...AND MY PARTNER, ANNOYED BY THE HUMAN SQUABBLES...
GENNARI (DISGUSTED)
げんなり
I WANNA GO BACK TO THE FOREST...
...STARTED TALKING LIKE SHE WAS AN ELF.
SO WE RETURNED TO THE DARK ELVES...
...AND DECIDED TO PROCEED WITH THIS QUEST-LINE...
...FOR TWO DAYS.
THE FIRST QUEST IN THE CAMPAIGN WAS "THE JADE KEY."
NUMBER TWO WAS "VANQUISHING THE SPIDERS"

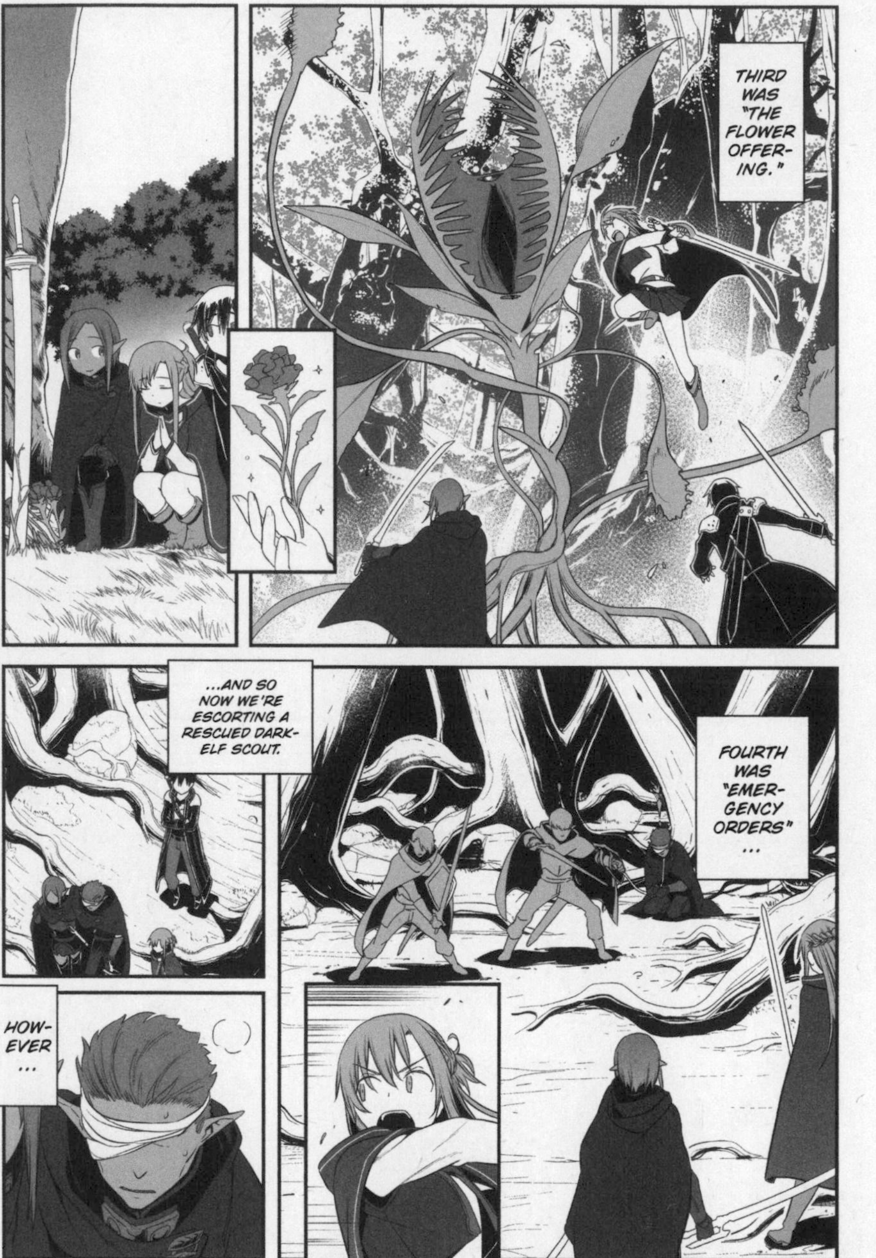
THIRD WAS "THE FLOWER OFFER-ING."
FOURTH WAS "EMER-GENCY ORDERS" ...
...AND SO NOW WE'RE ESCORTING A RESCUED DARK-ELF SCOUT.
HOW-EVER ...

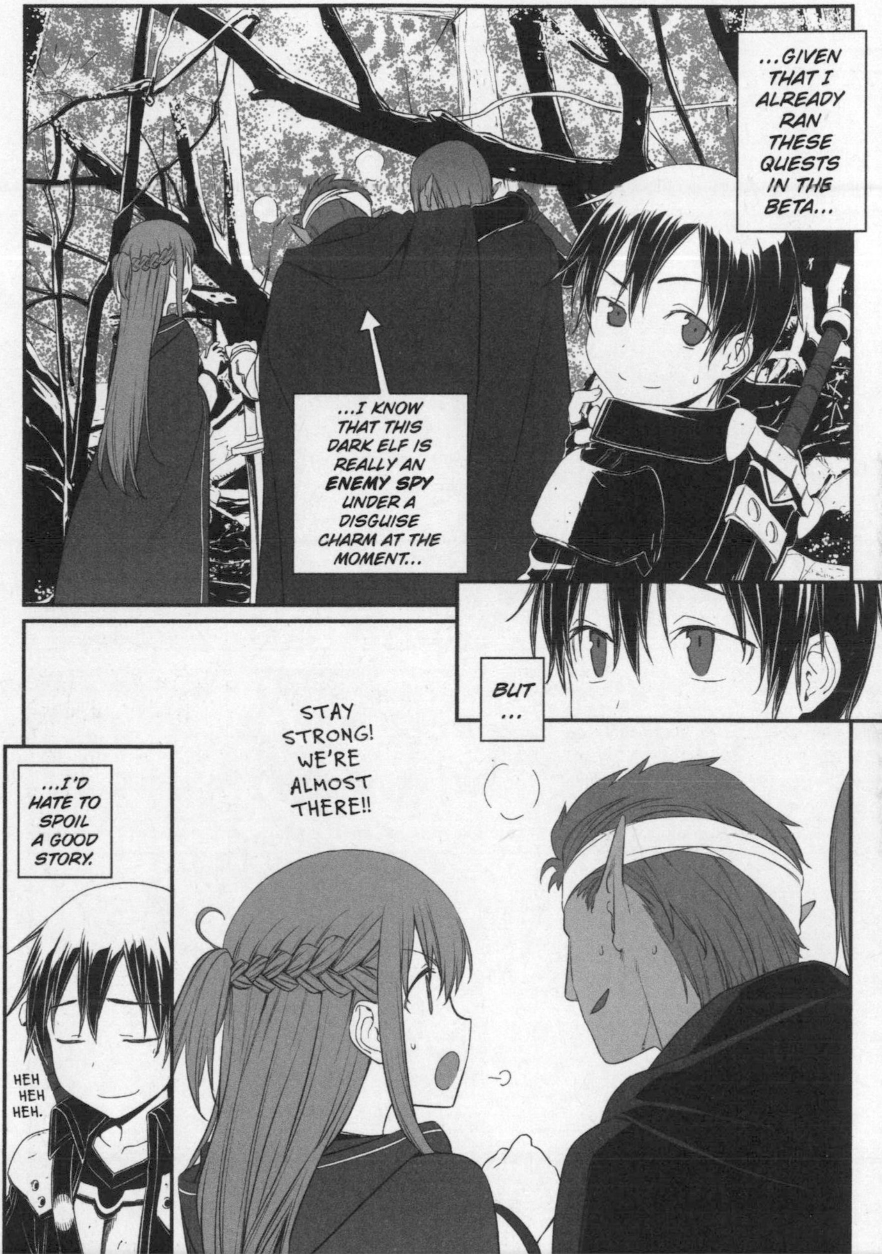
...GIVEN THAT I ALREADY RAN THESE QUESTS IN THE BETA...
...I KNOW THAT THIS DARK ELF IS REALLY AN **ENEMY SPY** UNDER A DISGUISE CHARM AT THE MOMENT...
BUT ...
STAY STRONG! WE'RE ALMOST THERE!!
...I'D HATE TO SPOIL A GOOD STORY.
HEH HEH HEH.

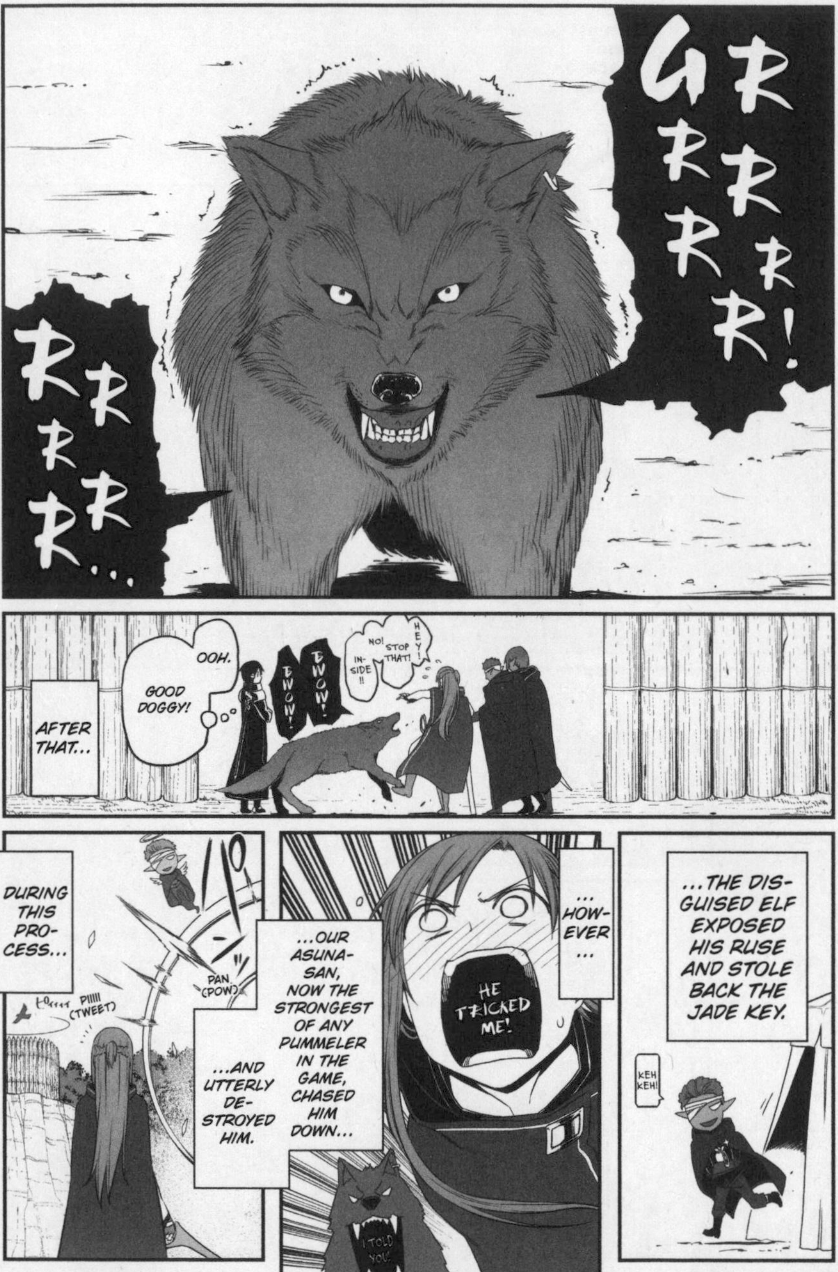
GRRRRRRR!
RRRRR...
HEY! STOP THAT!
NO! INSIDE!!
BWOW!
BWOW!
OOH. GOOD DOGGY!
AFTER THAT...
...THE DISGUISED ELF EXPOSED HIS RUSE AND STOLE BACK THE JADE KEY.
KEH KEH!
...HOWEVER...
HE TRICKED ME!
...OUR ASUNA-SAN, NOW THE STRONGEST OF ANY PUMMELER IN THE GAME, CHASED HIM DOWN...
I TOLD YOU!
DURING THIS PROCESS...
PAN (POW)
PIIIII (TWEET)
...AND UTTERLY DESTROYED HIM.

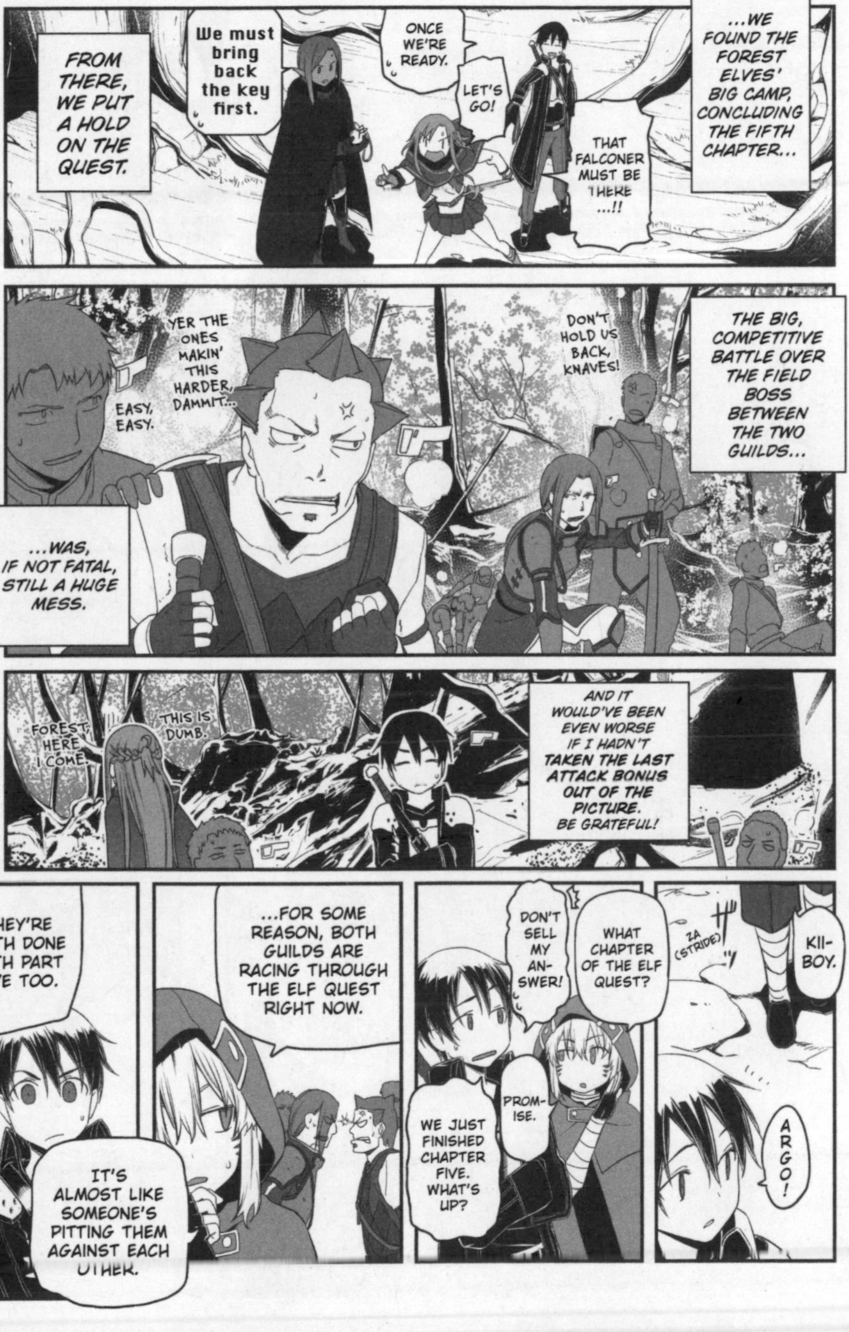
...WE FOUND THE FOREST ELVES' BIG CAMP, CONCLUDING THE FIFTH CHAPTER...
THAT FALCONER MUST BE THERE ...!!
LET'S GO!
ONCE WE'RE READY.
We must bring back the key first.
FROM THERE, WE PUT A HOLD ON THE QUEST.
THE BIG, COMPETITIVE BATTLE OVER THE FIELD BOSS BETWEEN THE TWO GUILDS...
DON'T HOLD US BACK, KNAVES!
YER THE ONES MAKIN' THIS HARDER, DAMMIT...
EASY, EASY.
...WAS, IF NOT FATAL, STILL A HUGE MESS.
AND IT WOULD'VE BEEN EVEN WORSE IF I HADN'T TAKEN THE LAST ATTACK BONUS OUT OF THE PICTURE. BE GRATEFUL!
THIS IS DUMB.
FOREST, HERE I COME.
KII-BOY.
ZA (STRIDE)
ARGO!
WHAT CHAPTER OF THE ELF QUEST?
DON'T SELL MY ANSWER!
PROMISE.
WE JUST FINISHED CHAPTER FIVE. WHAT'S UP?
...FOR SOME REASON, BOTH GUILDS ARE RACING THROUGH THE ELF QUEST RIGHT NOW.
THEY'RE BOTH DONE WITH PART FIVE TOO.
IT'S ALMOST LIKE SOMEONE'S PITTING THEM AGAINST EACH OTHER.

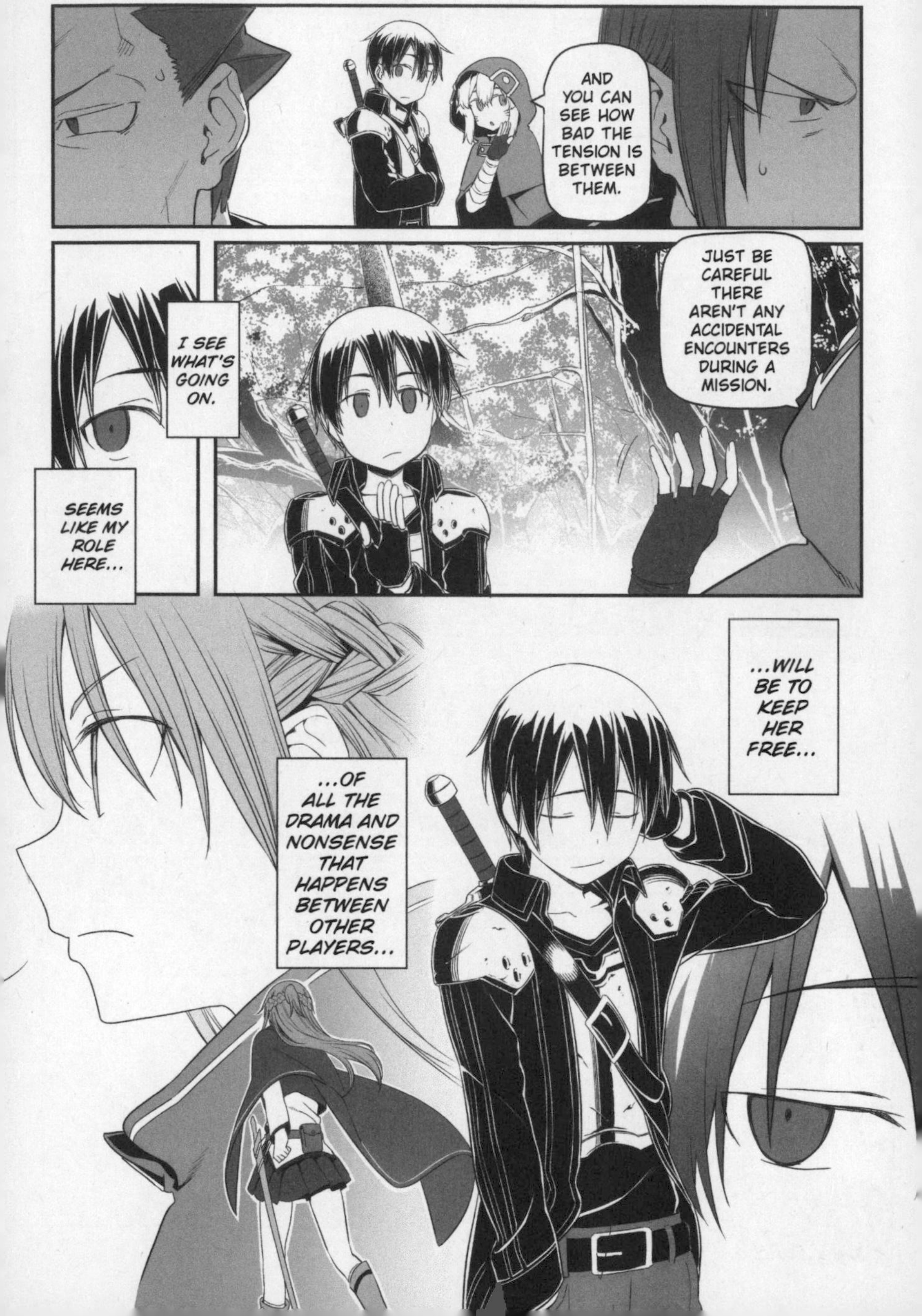
AND YOU CAN SEE HOW BAD THE TENSION IS BETWEEN THEM.
JUST BE CAREFUL THERE AREN'T ANY ACCIDENTAL ENCOUNTERS DURING A MISSION.
I SEE WHAT'S GOING ON.
SEEMS LIKE MY ROLE HERE...
...WILL BE TO KEEP HER FREE...
...OF ALL THE DRAMA AND NONSENSE THAT HAPPENS BETWEEN OTHER PLAYERS...

#035: Trap

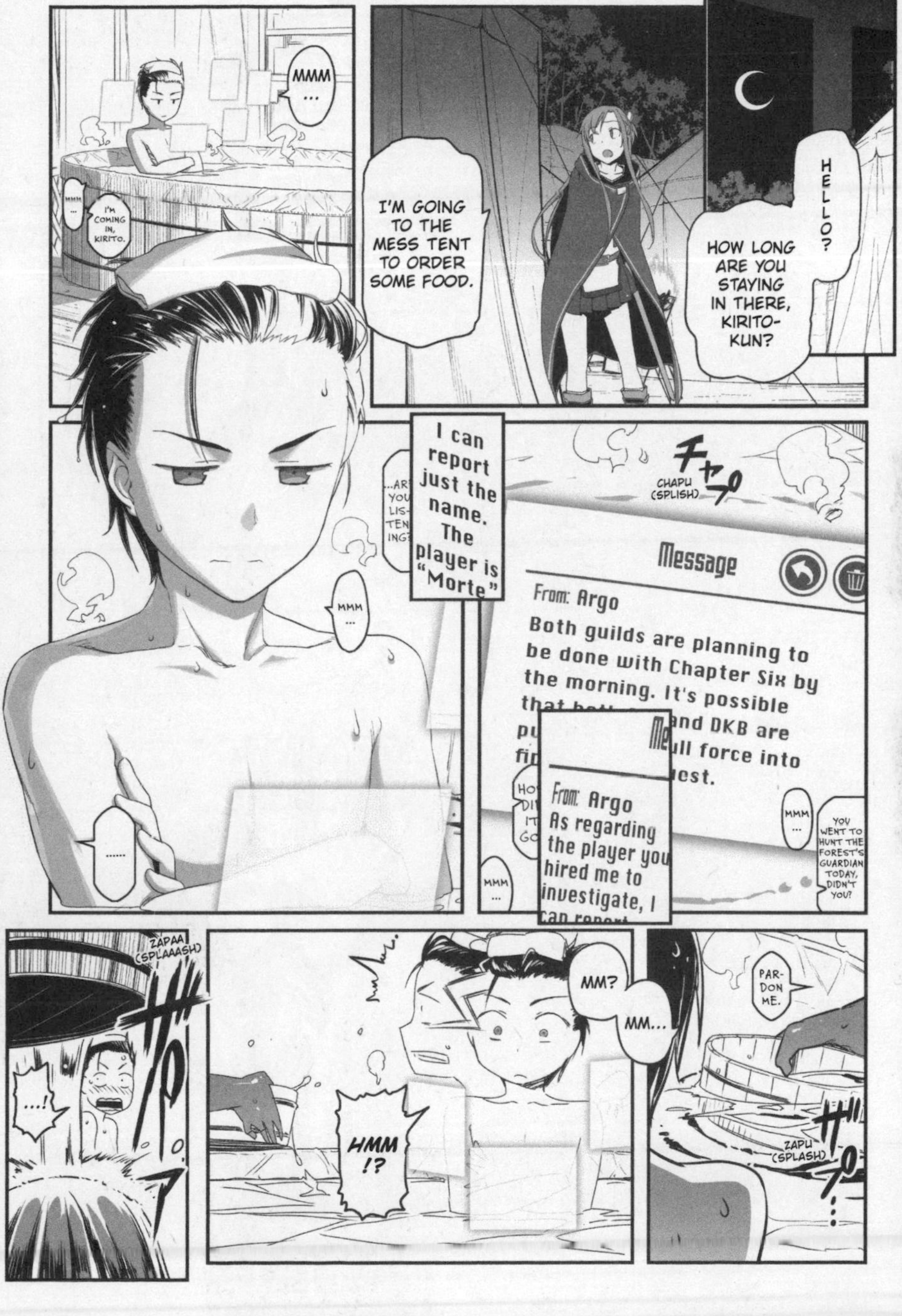
HELLO?
HOW LONG ARE YOU STAYING IN THERE, KIRITO-KUN?
I'M GOING TO THE MESS TENT TO ORDER SOME FOOD.
MMM ...
I'M COMING IN, KIRITO.
MMM ...
チャプ
CHAPU (SPLISH)
Message
From: Argo
Both guilds are planning to be done with Chapter Six by the morning. It's possible
that bo
and DKB are
pu
ull force into
fi
est.
YOU WENT TO HUNT THE FOREST'S GUARDIAN TODAY, DIDN'T YOU?
MMM ...
MMM ...
Me
From: Argo
As regarding the player you hired me to investigate, I can report
I can report just the name. The player is "Morte"
...AR YOU LIS-TEN ING?
MMM ...
......
PARDON ME.
ZAPU (SPLASH)
MM?
MM...
HMM !?
ZAPAA (SPLAAASH)
...!

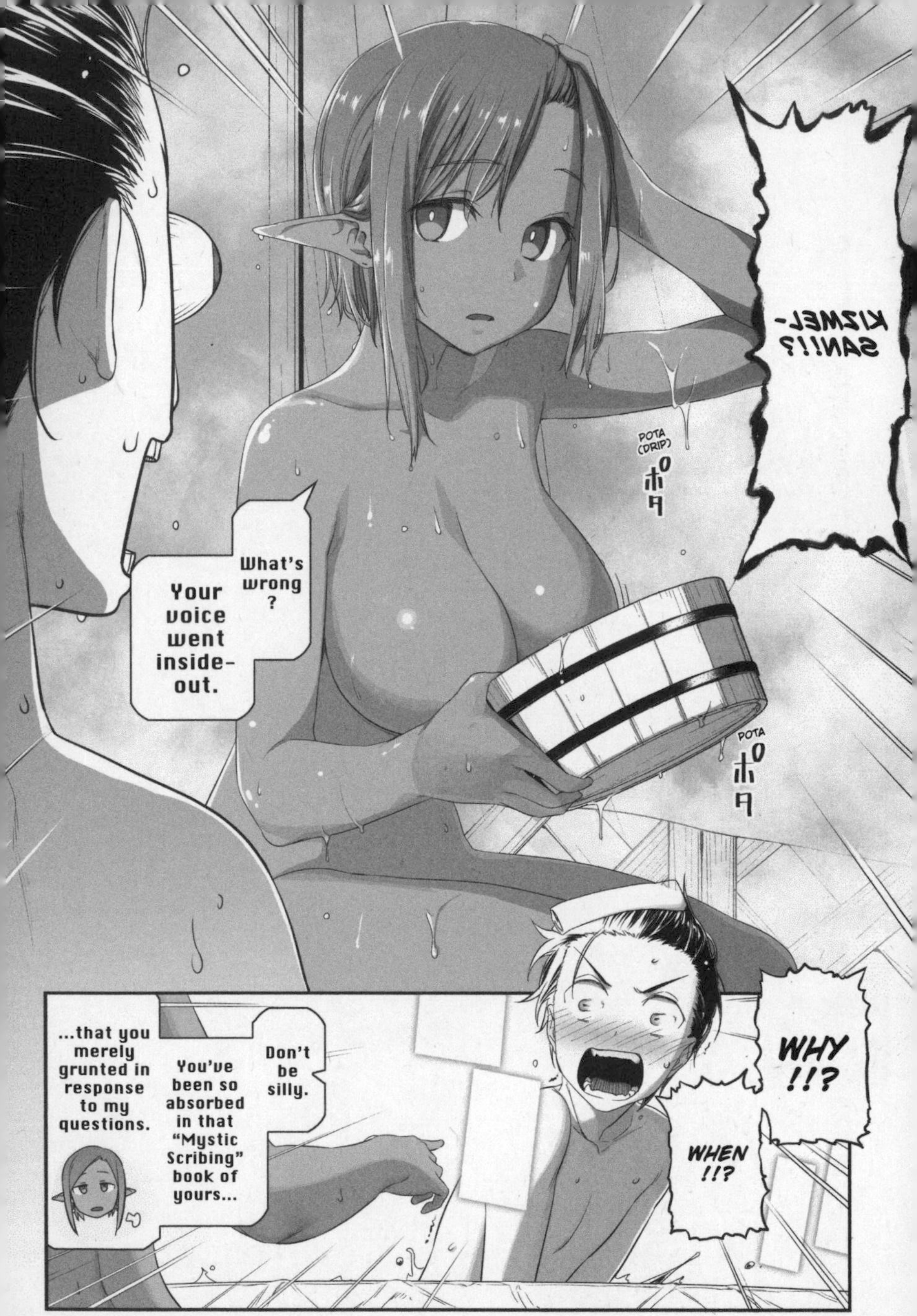
KIZMEL-SAN!!?
POTA (DRIP)
ポタ
What's wrong?
Your voice went inside-out.
POTA
ポタ
WHY!!?
WHEN!!?
Don't be silly.
You've been so absorbed in that "Mystic Scribing" book of yours...
...that you merely grunted in response to my questions.

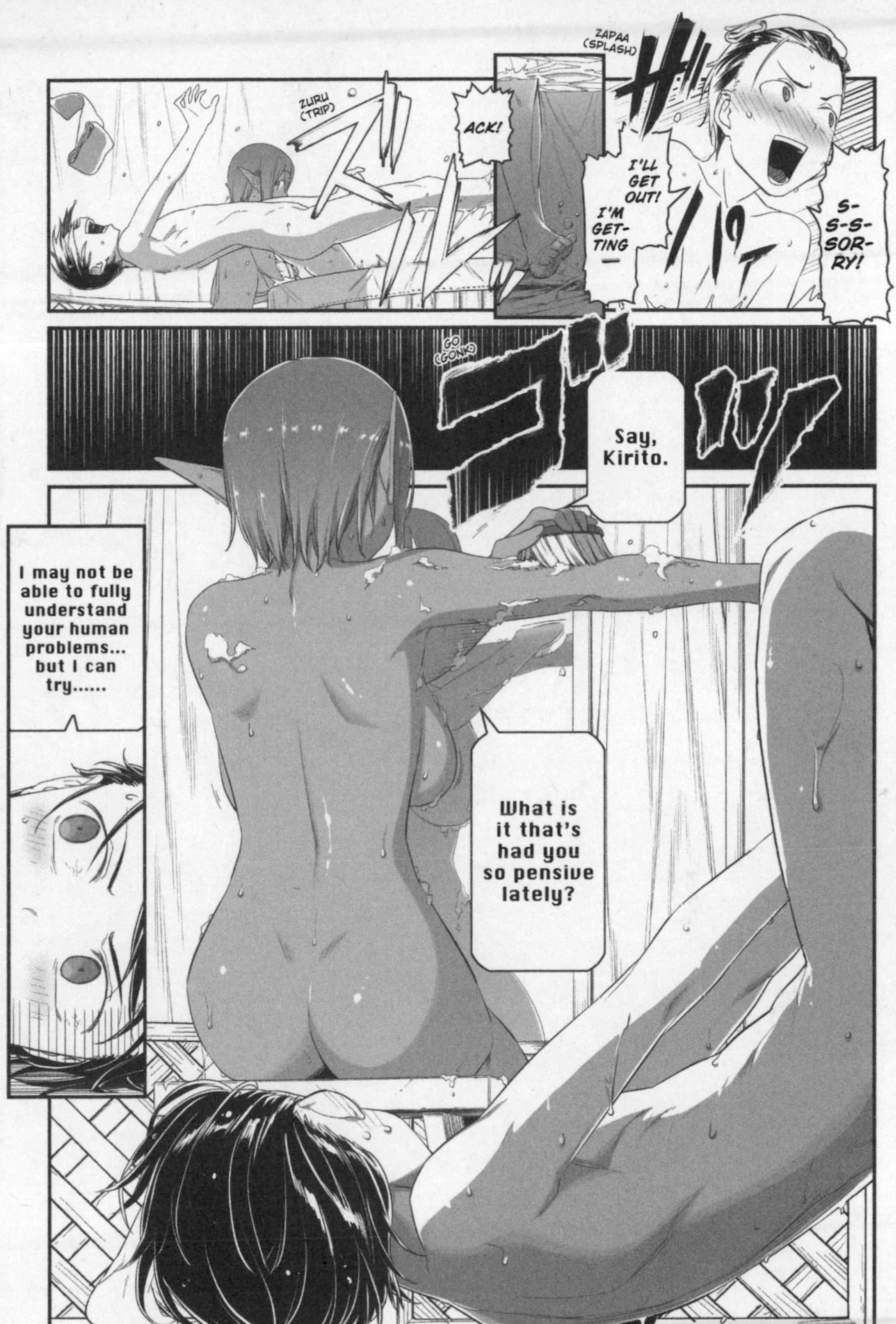
ZAPAA (SPLASH)
S-S-S-SORRY!
I'LL GET OUT!
I'M GETTING—
ACK!
ZURU (TRIP)
GO (GONK)
Say, Kirito.
What is it that's had you so pensive lately?
I may not be able to fully understand your human problems... but I can try......

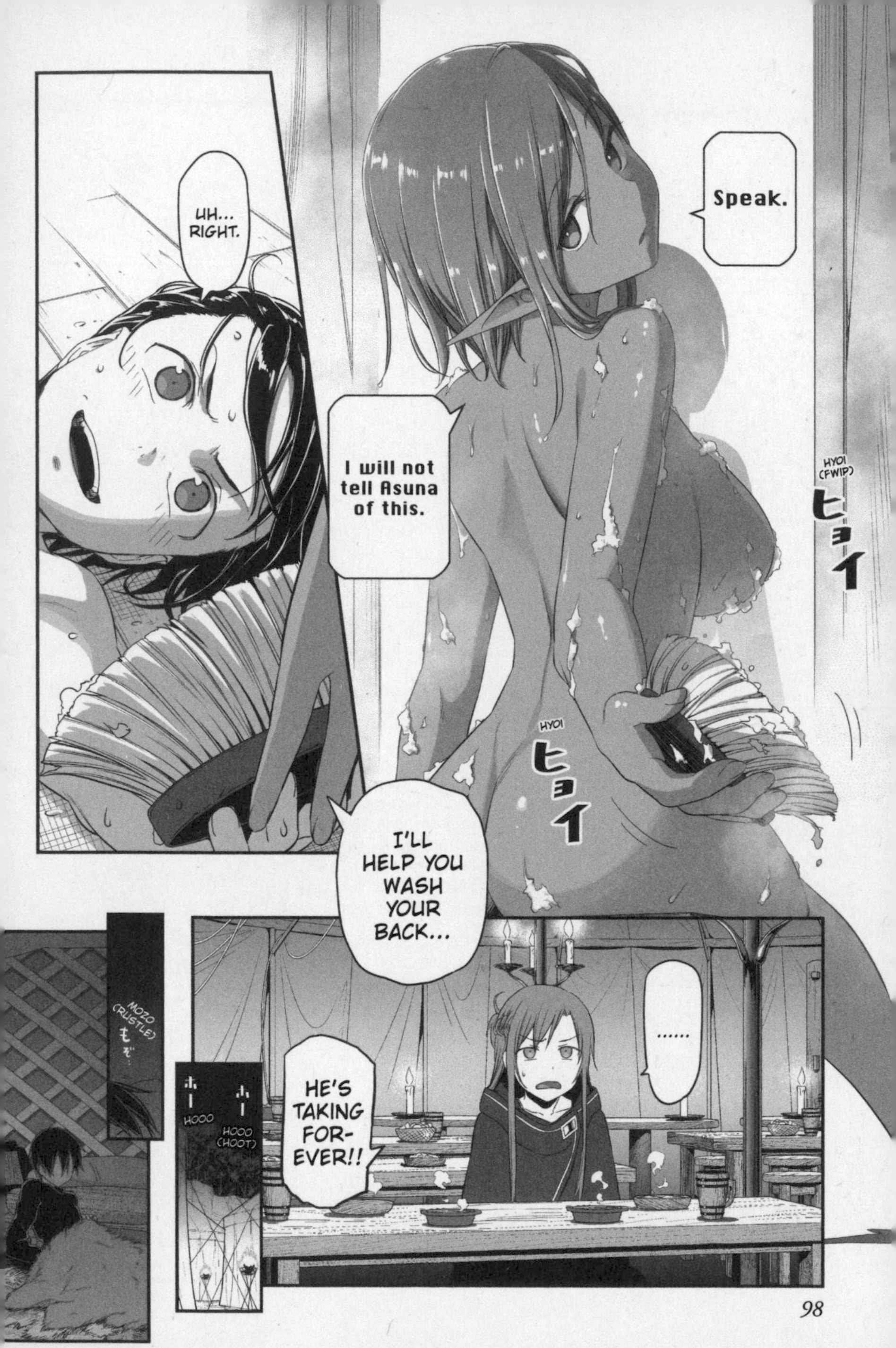
Speak.
HYOI (FWIP)
ヒョイ
I will not tell Asuna of this.
HYOI
ヒョイ
I'LL HELP YOU WASH YOUR BACK...
UH... RIGHT.
......
HE'S TAKING FOR-EVER!!
ホー
HOOO
ホー
HOOO (HOOT)
MOZO (RUSTLE)
もぞ…

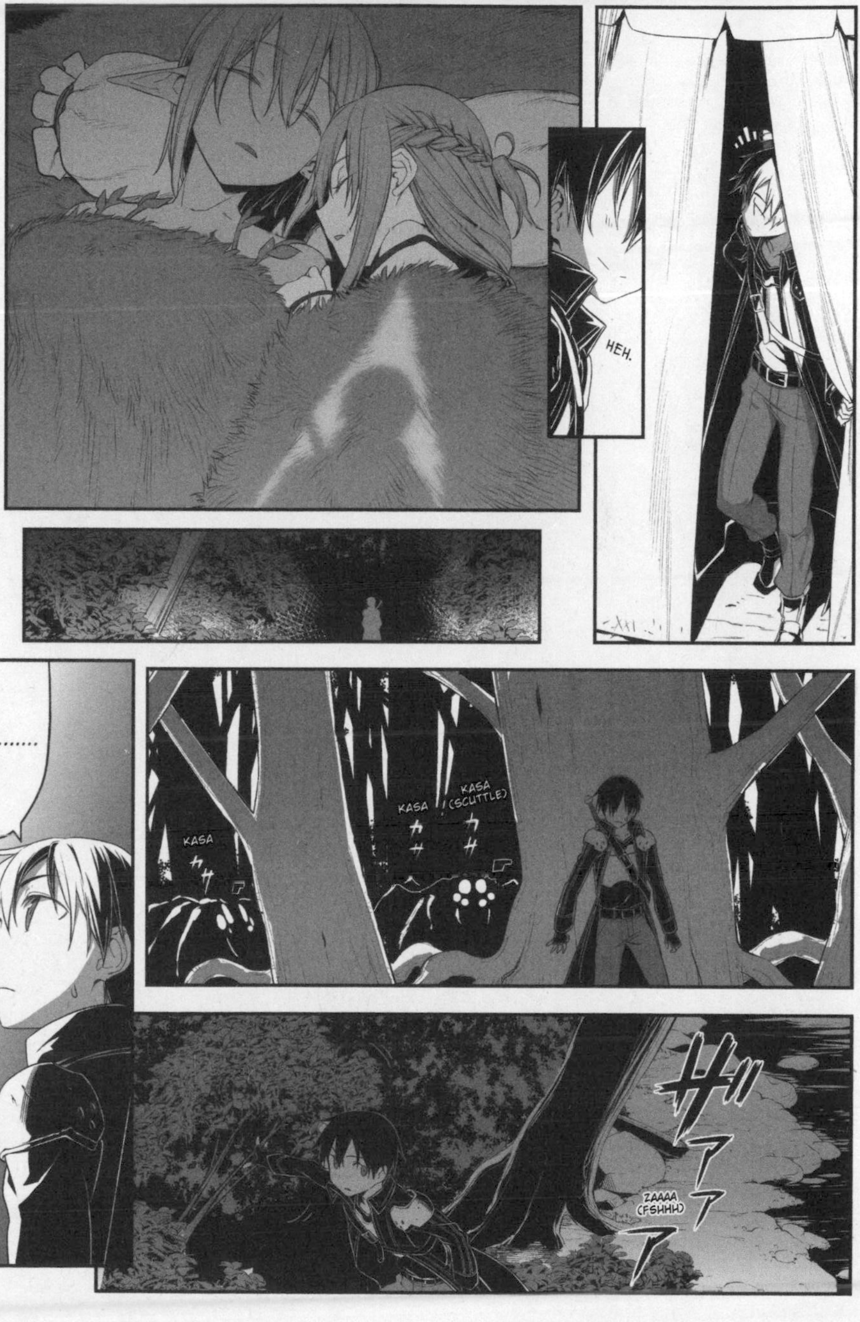
HEH.
KASA (SCUTTLE)
KASA
KASA
ZAAAA (FSHHH)
....

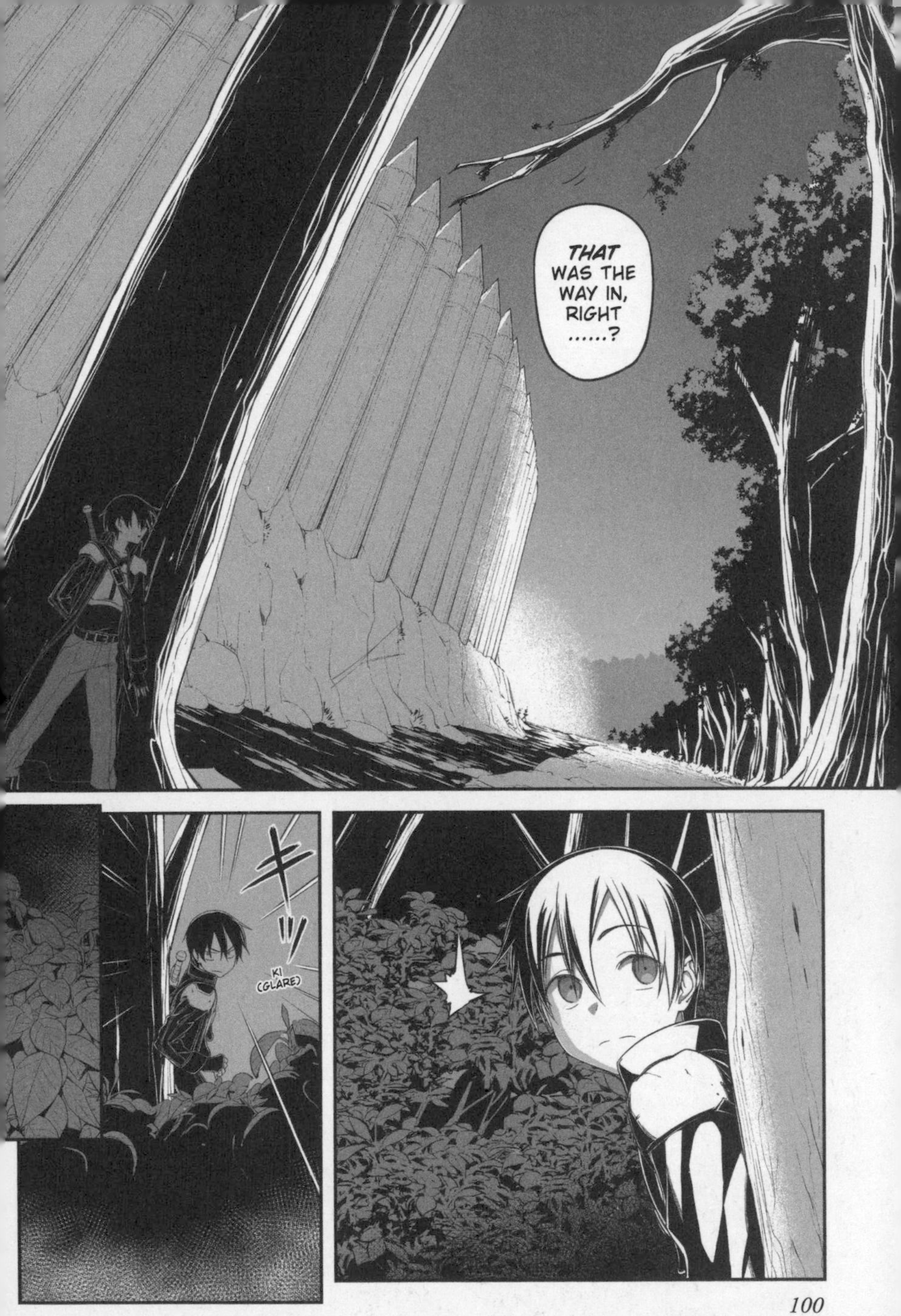
THAT WAS THE WAY IN, RIGHT ......?
キッ
KI (GLARE)

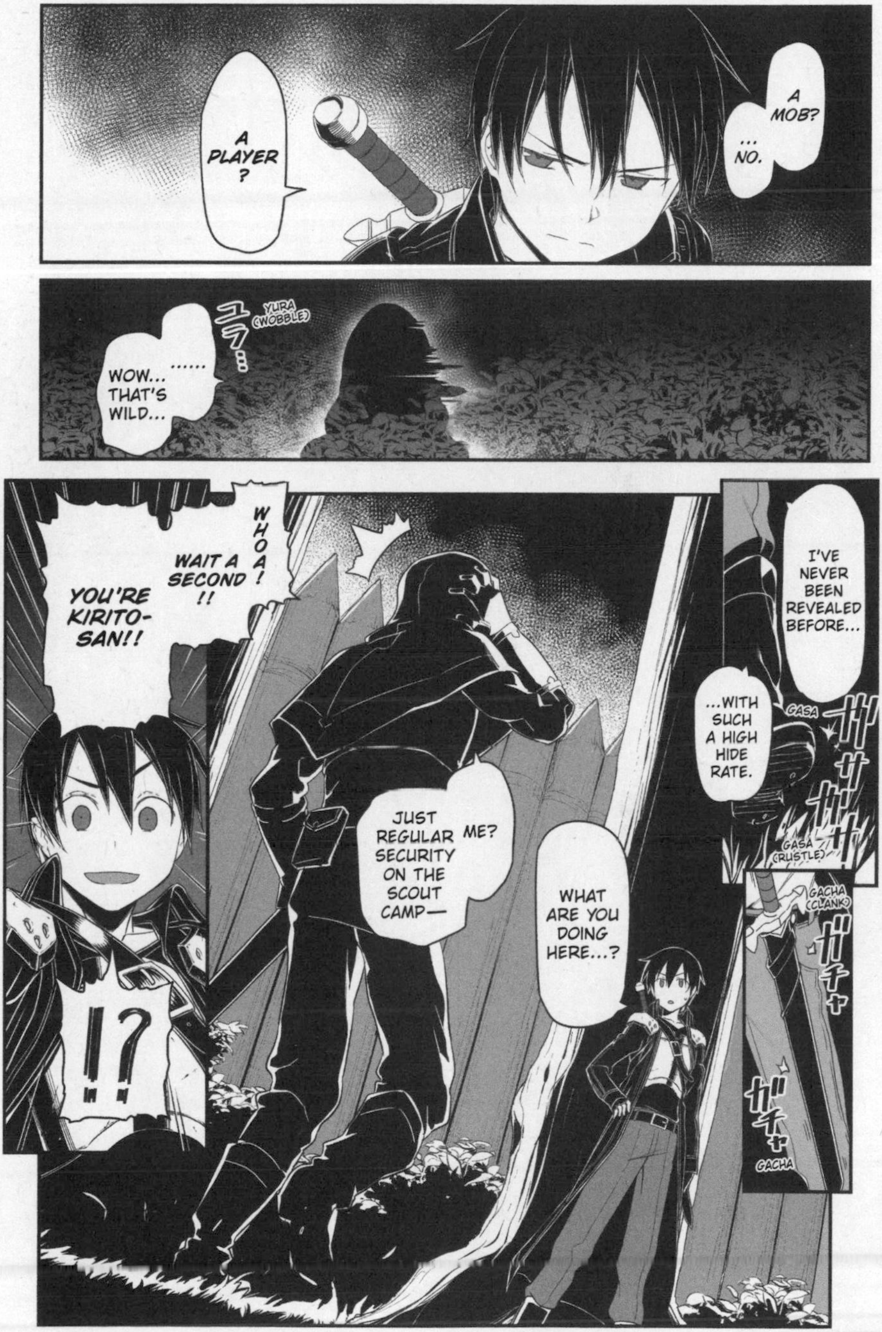
A MOB?
... NO.
A PLAYER ?
ユラ…
YURA (WOBBLE)
......
WOW... THAT'S WILD...
I'VE NEVER BEEN REVEALED BEFORE...
...WITH SUCH A HIGH HIDE RATE.
ガサガサ
GASA
GASA (RUSTLE)
ガチャ
GACHA (CLANK)
ガチャ
GACHA
WHAT ARE YOU DOING HERE...?
ME?
JUST REGULAR SECURITY ON THE SCOUT CAMP—
WHOA!
WAIT A SECOND!!
YOU'RE KIRITO-SAN!!
!?

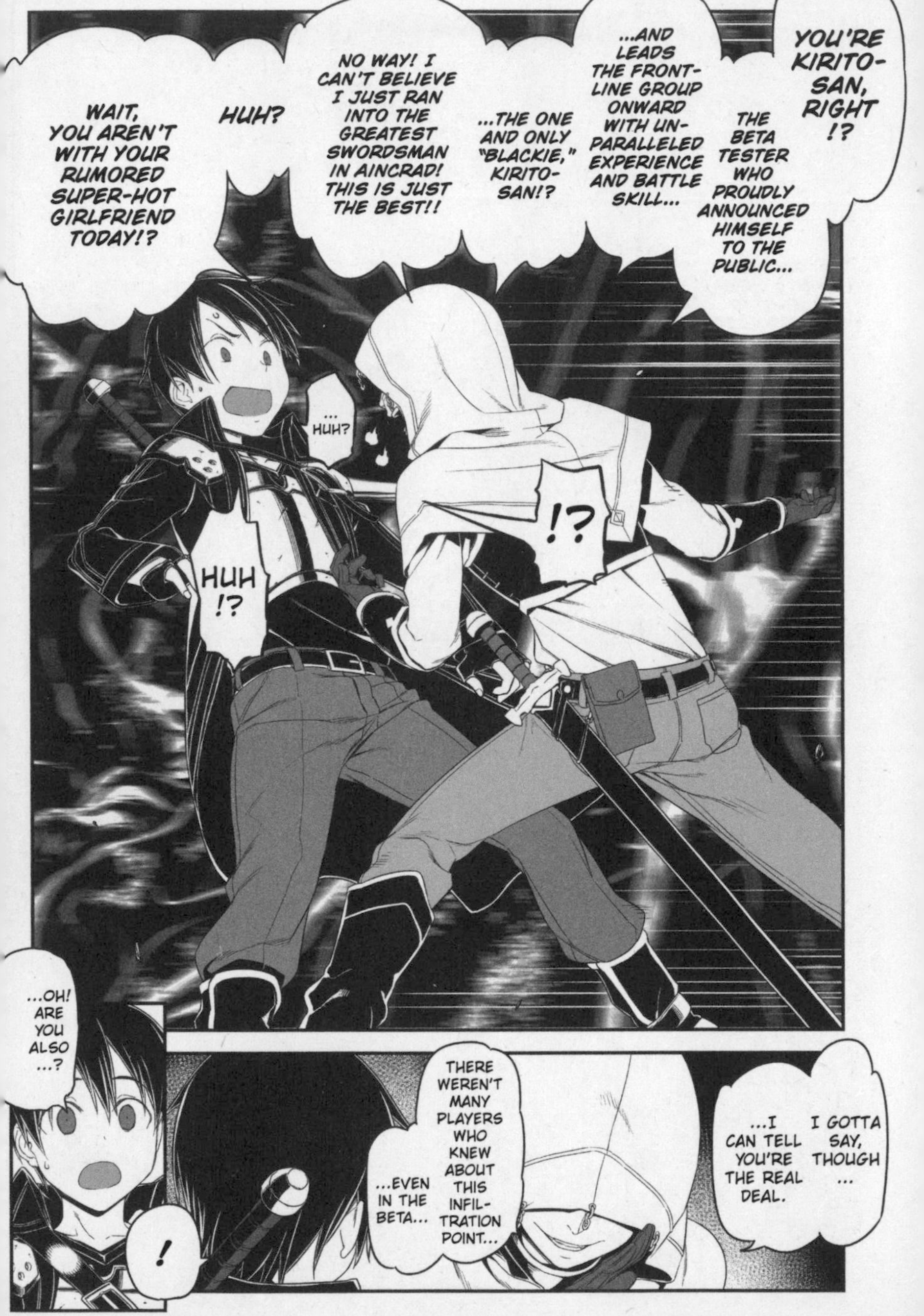
YOU'RE KIRITO-SAN, RIGHT!?
THE BETA TESTER WHO PROUDLY ANNOUNCED HIMSELF TO THE PUBLIC...
...AND LEADS THE FRONT-LINE GROUP ONWARD WITH UN-PARALLELED EXPERIENCE AND BATTLE SKILL...
...THE ONE AND ONLY "BLACKIE," KIRITO-SAN!?
NO WAY! I CAN'T BELIEVE I JUST RAN INTO THE GREATEST SWORDSMAN IN AINCRAD! THIS IS JUST THE BEST!!
HUH?
WAIT, YOU AREN'T WITH YOUR RUMORED SUPER-HOT GIRLFRIEND TODAY!?
!?
... HUH?
HUH !?
I GOTTA SAY, THOUGH ...
...I CAN TELL YOU'RE THE REAL DEAL.
THERE WEREN'T MANY PLAYERS WHO KNEW ABOUT THIS INFILTRATION POINT...
...EVEN IN THE BETA...
!
...OH! ARE YOU ALSO ...?

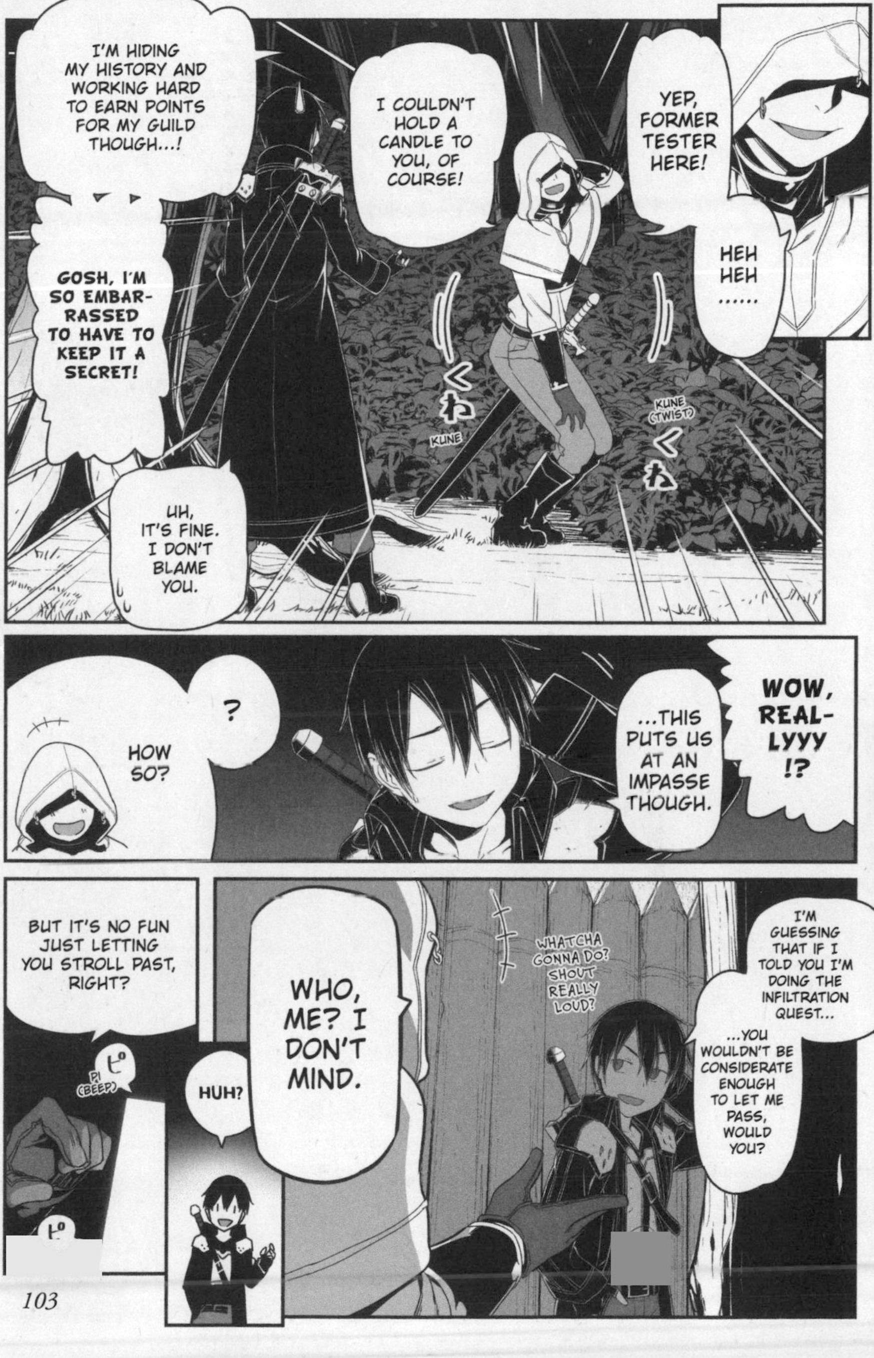
YEP, FORMER TESTER HERE!
HEH HEH ......
I COULDN'T HOLD A CANDLE TO YOU, OF COURSE!
くね
KUNE (TWIST)
くね
KUNE
I'M HIDING MY HISTORY AND WORKING HARD TO EARN POINTS FOR MY GUILD THOUGH...!
GOSH, I'M SO EMBARRASSED TO HAVE TO KEEP IT A SECRET!
UH, IT'S FINE. I DON'T BLAME YOU.
WOW, REAL-LYYY!?
...THIS PUTS US AT AN IMPASSE THOUGH.
?
HOW SO?
I'M GUESSING THAT IF I TOLD YOU I'M DOING THE INFILTRATION QUEST...
...YOU WOULDN'T BE CONSIDERATE ENOUGH TO LET ME PASS, WOULD YOU?
WHATCHA GONNA DO? SHOUT REALLY LOUD?
WHO, ME? I DON'T MIND.
BUT IT'S NO FUN JUST LETTING YOU STROLL PAST, RIGHT?
ピ
PI (BEEP)
HUH?
ピ

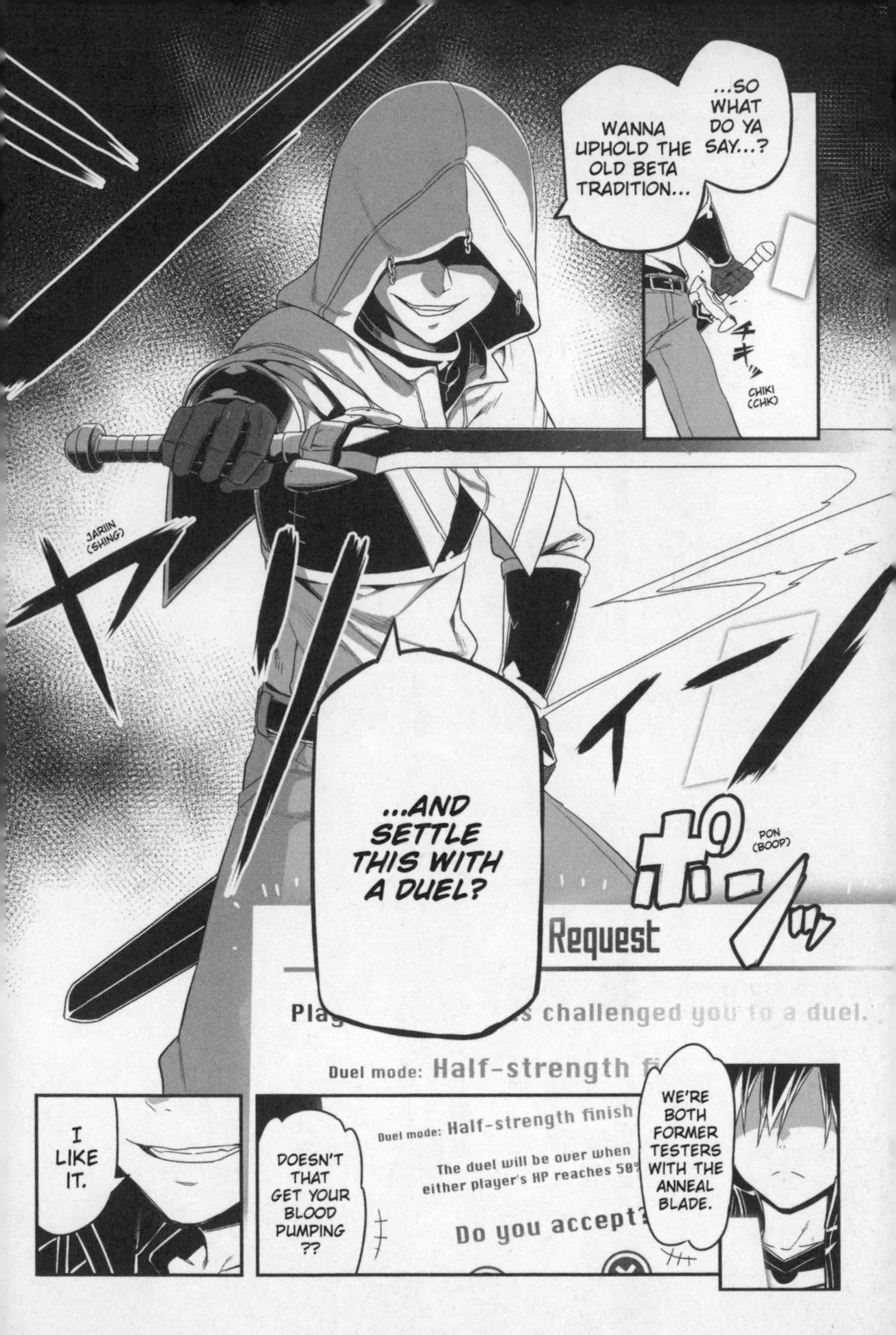
...SO WHAT DO YA SAY...?
WANNA UPHOLD THE OLD BETA TRADITION...
チキッ
CHIKI (CHK)
JARIIN (SHING)
...AND SETTLE THIS WITH A DUEL?
PON (BOOP)
Request
Play... ...s challenged you to a duel.
Duel mode: Half-strength fi...
WE'RE BOTH FORMER TESTERS WITH THE ANNEAL BLADE.
Duel mode: Half-strength finish
The duel will be over when either player's HP reaches 50%
Do you accept?
DOESN'T THAT GET YOUR BLOOD PUMPING??
I LIKE IT.

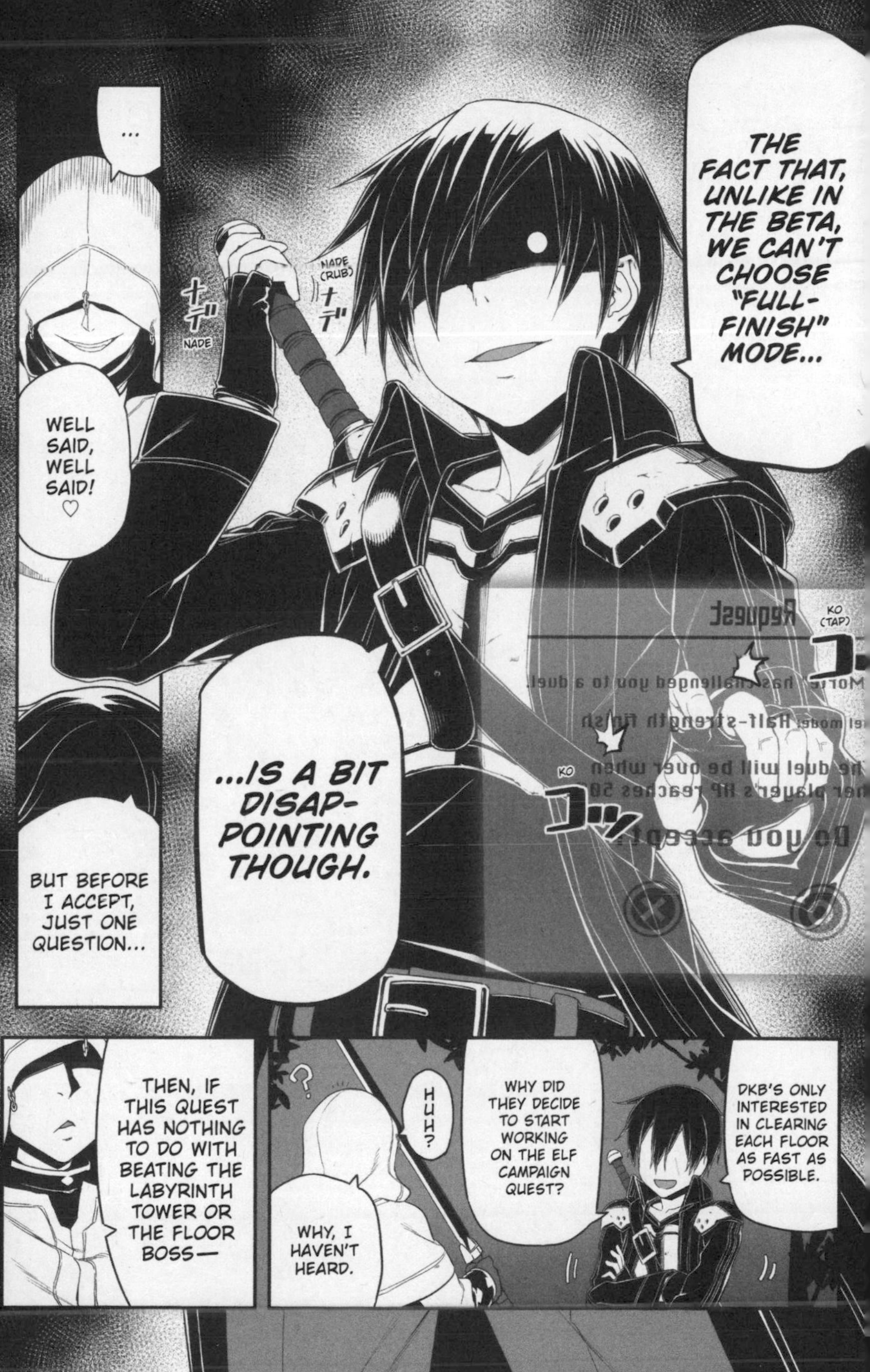

THE FACT THAT, UNLIKE IN THE BETA, WE CAN'T CHOOSE "FULL-FINISH" MODE...
NADE (RUB)
NADE
...IS A BIT DISAP-POINTING THOUGH.
KO (TAP)
KO
...
WELL SAID, WELL SAID! ♡
BUT BEFORE I ACCEPT, JUST ONE QUESTION...
DKB'S ONLY INTERESTED IN CLEARING EACH FLOOR AS FAST AS POSSIBLE.
WHY DID THEY DECIDE TO START WORKING ON THE ELF CAMPAIGN QUEST?
HUH?
WHY, I HAVEN'T HEARD.
THEN, IF THIS QUEST HAS NOTHING TO DO WITH BEATING THE LABYRINTH TOWER OR THE FLOOR BOSS—

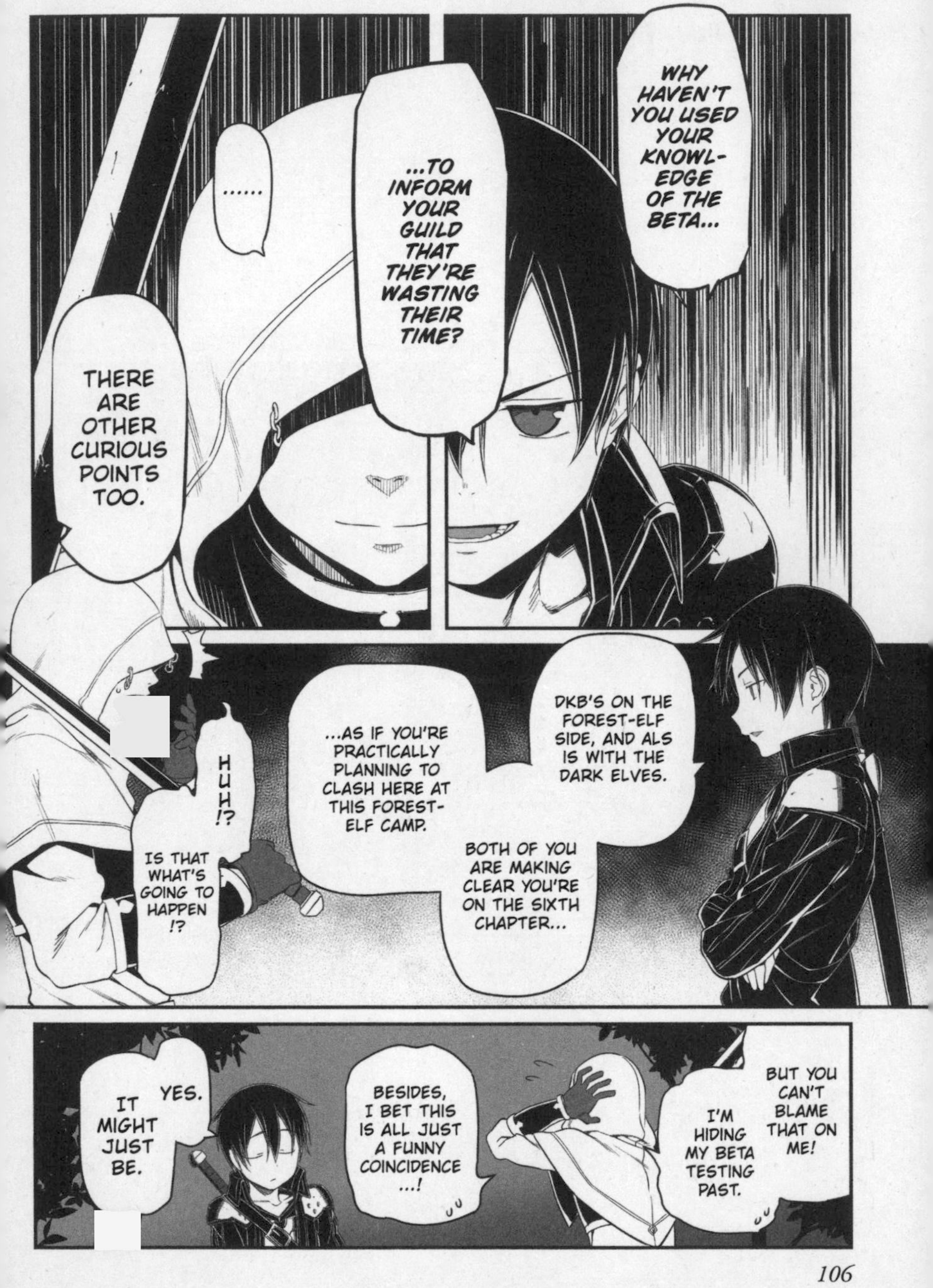
WHY HAVEN'T YOU USED YOUR KNOWL-EDGE OF THE BETA...
...TO INFORM YOUR GUILD THAT THEY'RE WASTING THEIR TIME?
......
THERE ARE OTHER CURIOUS POINTS TOO.
DKB'S ON THE FOREST-ELF SIDE, AND ALS IS WITH THE DARK ELVES.
BOTH OF YOU ARE MAKING CLEAR YOU'RE ON THE SIXTH CHAPTER...
...AS IF YOU'RE PRACTICALLY PLANNING TO CLASH HERE AT THIS FOREST-ELF CAMP.
HUH!?
IS THAT WHAT'S GOING TO HAPPEN!?
BUT YOU CAN'T BLAME THAT ON ME!
I'M HIDING MY BETA TESTING PAST.
BESIDES, I BET THIS IS ALL JUST A FUNNY COINCIDENCE...!
YES.
IT MIGHT JUST BE.

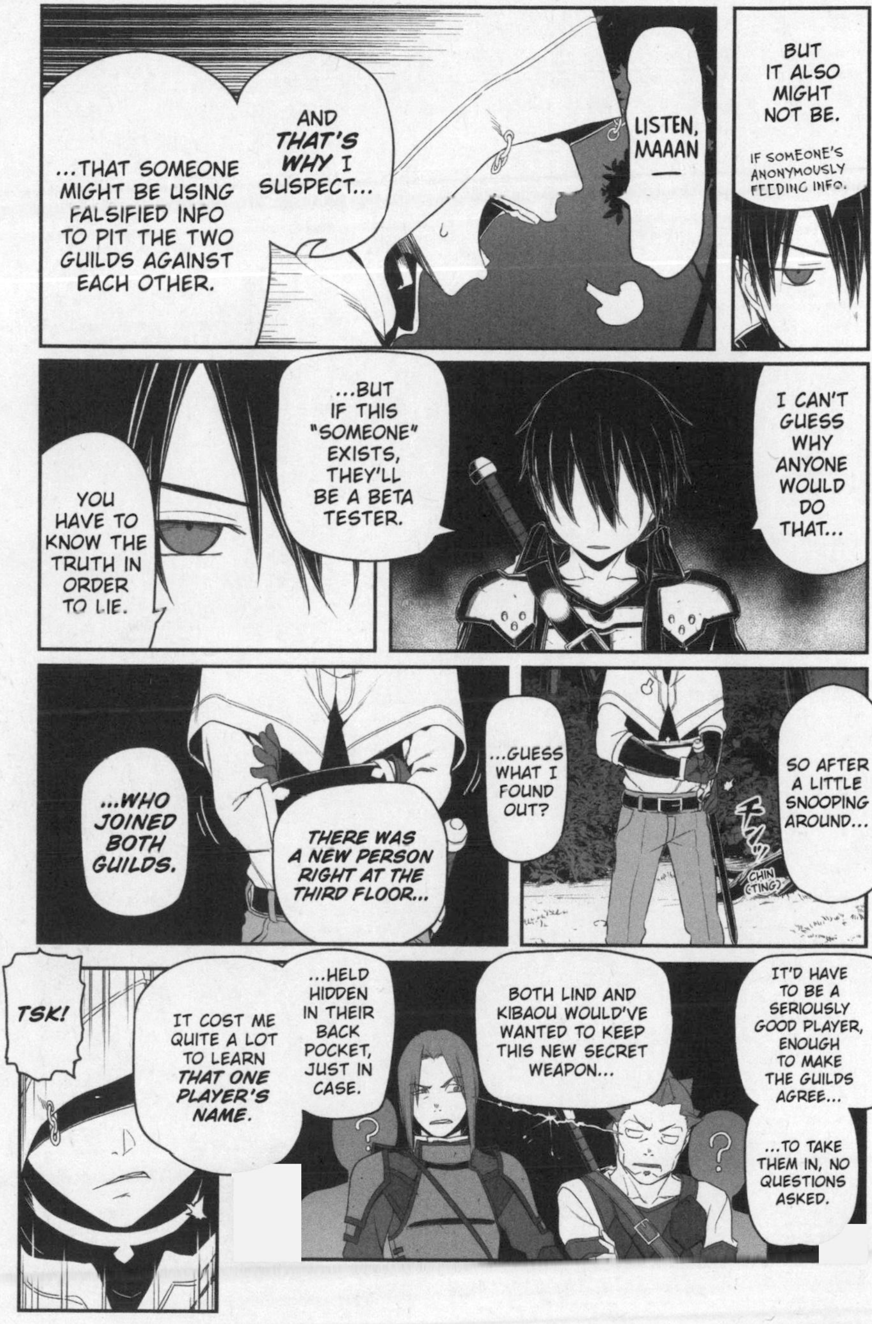
BUT IT ALSO MIGHT NOT BE.
IF SOMEONE'S ANONYMOUSLY FEEDING INFO.
LISTEN, MAAAN—
AND THAT'S WHY I SUSPECT...
...THAT SOMEONE MIGHT BE USING FALSIFIED INFO TO PIT THE TWO GUILDS AGAINST EACH OTHER.
I CAN'T GUESS WHY ANYONE WOULD DO THAT...
...BUT IF THIS "SOMEONE" EXISTS, THEY'LL BE A BETA TESTER.
YOU HAVE TO KNOW THE TRUTH IN ORDER TO LIE.
SO AFTER A LITTLE SNOOPING AROUND...
CHIN (TING)
...GUESS WHAT I FOUND OUT?
THERE WAS A NEW PERSON RIGHT AT THE THIRD FLOOR...
...WHO JOINED BOTH GUILDS.
IT'D HAVE TO BE A SERIOUSLY GOOD PLAYER, ENOUGH TO MAKE THE GUILDS AGREE...
...TO TAKE THEM IN, NO QUESTIONS ASKED.
BOTH LIND AND KIBAOU WOULD'VE WANTED TO KEEP THIS NEW SECRET WEAPON...
...HELD HIDDEN IN THEIR BACK POCKET, JUST IN CASE.
?
?
IT COST ME QUITE A LOT TO LEARN THAT ONE PLAYER'S NAME.
TSK!

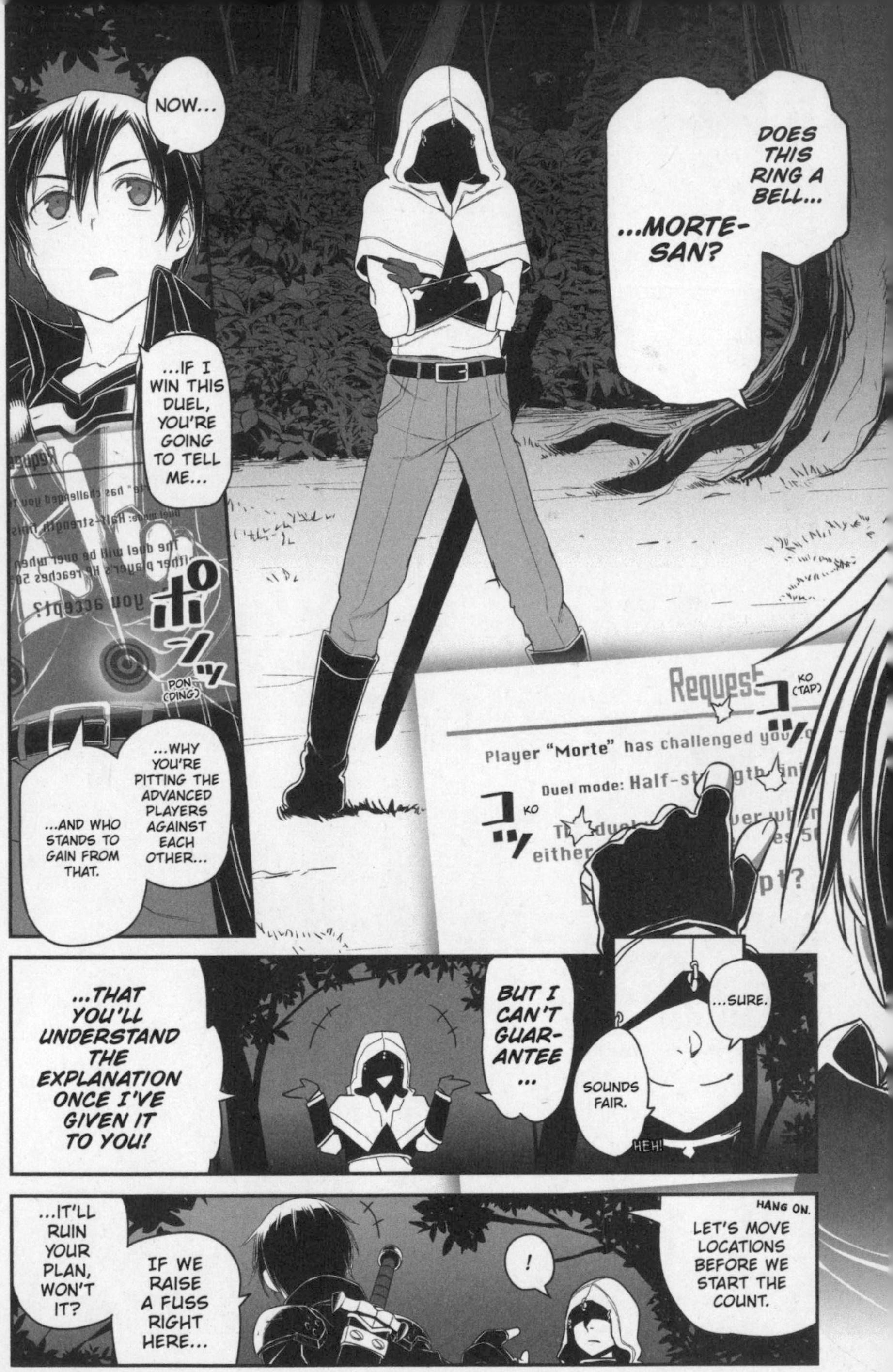
DOES THIS RING A BELL...
...MORTE-SAN?
Request
KO (TAP)
Player “Morte” has challenged
KO
NOW...
...IF I WIN THIS DUEL, YOU'RE GOING TO TELL ME...
PON (DING)
...WHY YOU'RE PITTING THE ADVANCED PLAYERS AGAINST EACH OTHER...
...AND WHO STANDS TO GAIN FROM THAT.
...SURE.
SOUNDS FAIR.
HEH!
BUT I CAN'T GUARANTEE...
...THAT YOU'LL UNDERSTAND THE EXPLANATION ONCE I'VE GIVEN IT TO YOU!
HANG ON.
LET'S MOVE LOCATIONS BEFORE WE START THE COUNT.
!
IF WE RAISE A FUSS RIGHT HERE...
...IT'LL RUIN YOUR PLAN, WON'T IT?

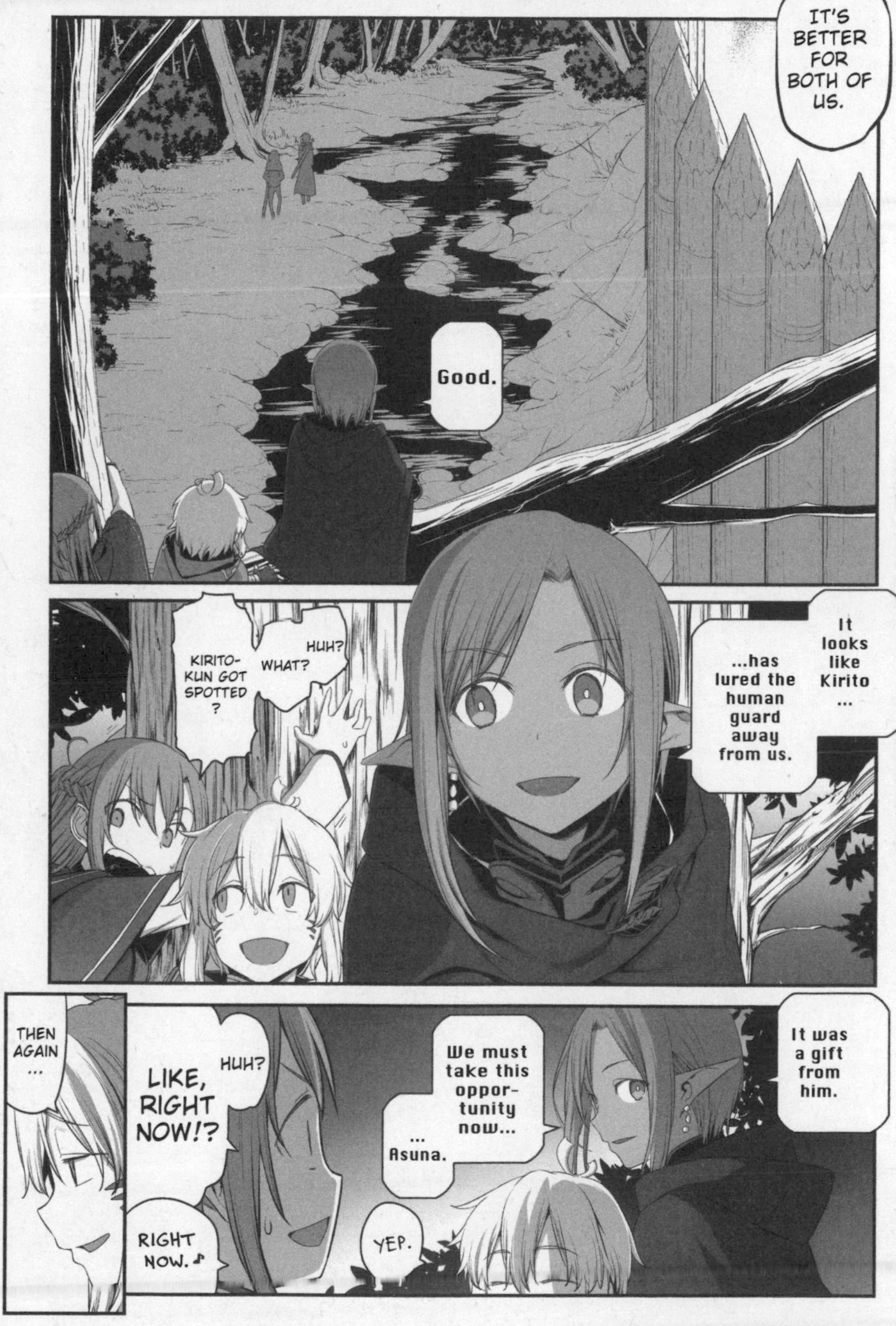
IT'S BETTER FOR BOTH OF US.
Good.
It looks like Kirito ...
...has lured the human guard away from us.
HUH? WHAT?
KIRITO-KUN GOT SPOTTED?
It was a gift from him.
We must take this opportunity now...
... Asuna.
YEP.
HUH?
LIKE, RIGHT NOW!?
RIGHT NOW. ♪
THEN AGAIN ...

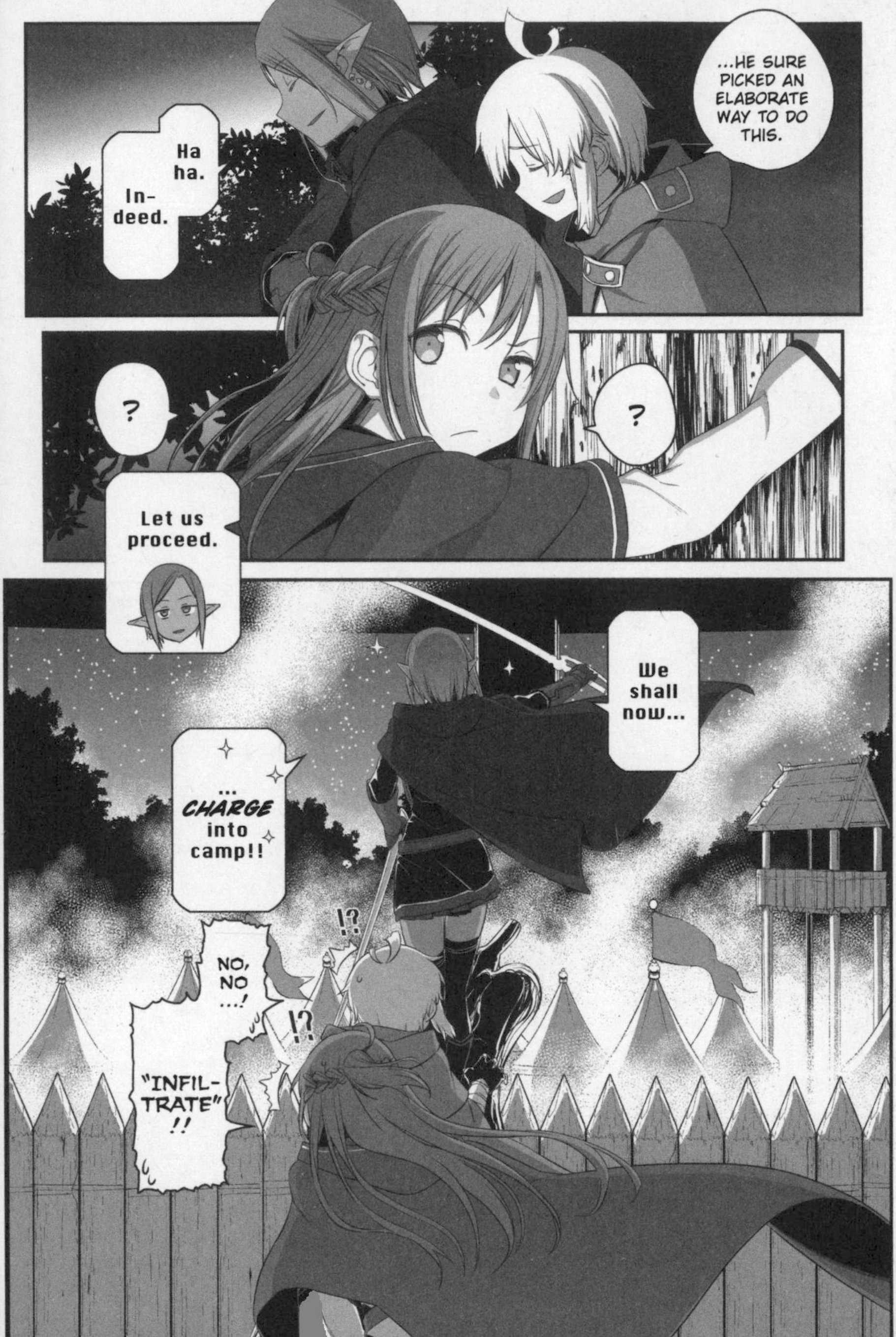
...HE SURE PICKED AN ELABORATE WAY TO DO THIS.
Ha ha. In-deed.
?
?
Let us proceed.
We shall now...
...CHARGE into camp!!
!?
NO, NO ...!
!?
"INFIL-TRATE"!!

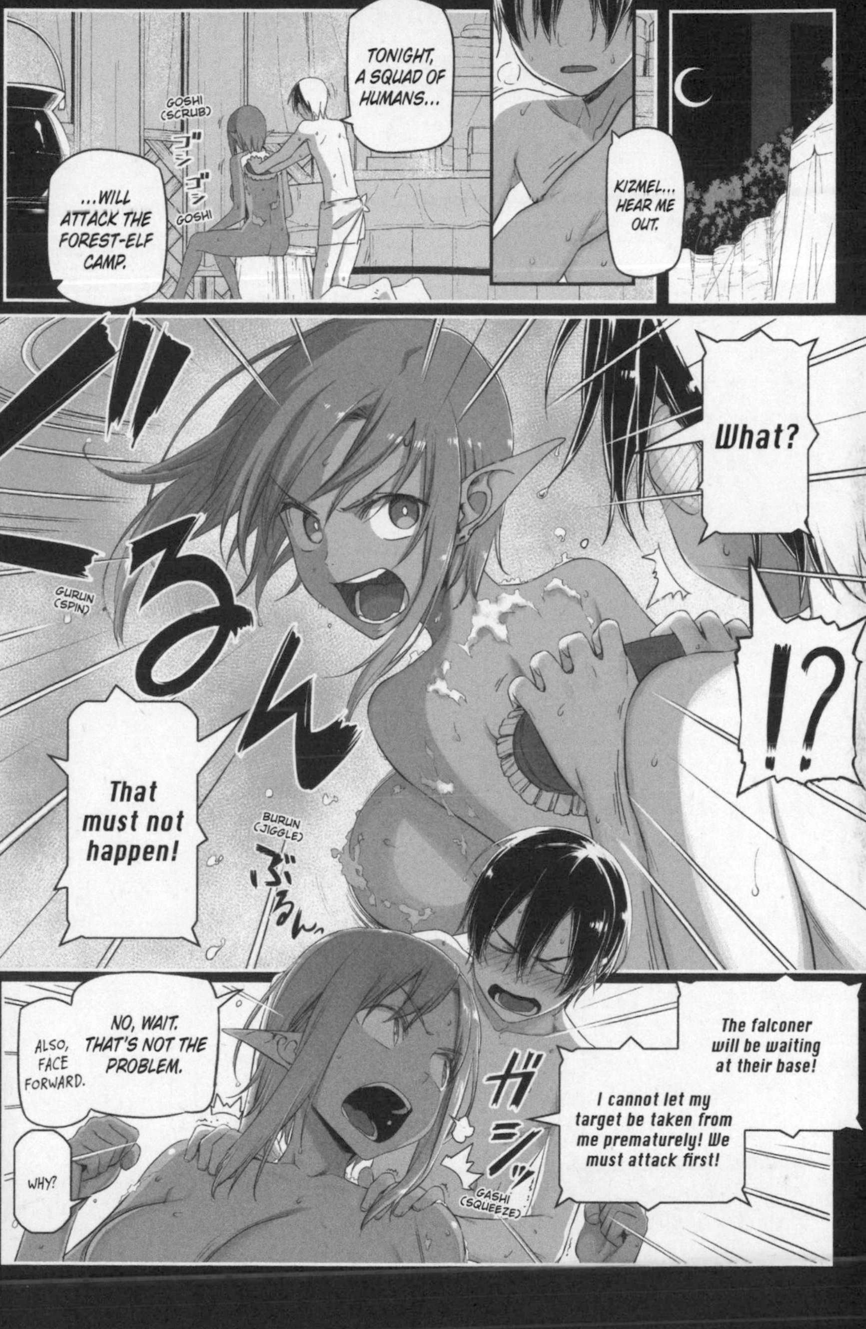
KIZMEL... HEAR ME OUT.
TONIGHT, A SQUAD OF HUMANS...
GOSHI (SCRUB)
ゴシ ゴシ
GOSHI
...WILL ATTACK THE FOREST-ELF CAMP.
What?
!?
ぐるん
GURUN (SPIN)
That must not happen!
BURUN (JIGGLE)
ぶるん
The falconer will be waiting at their base!
I cannot let my target be taken from me prematurely! We must attack first!
ガシッ
GASHI (SQUEEZE)
NO, WAIT. THAT'S NOT THE PROBLEM.
ALSO, FACE FORWARD.
WHY?

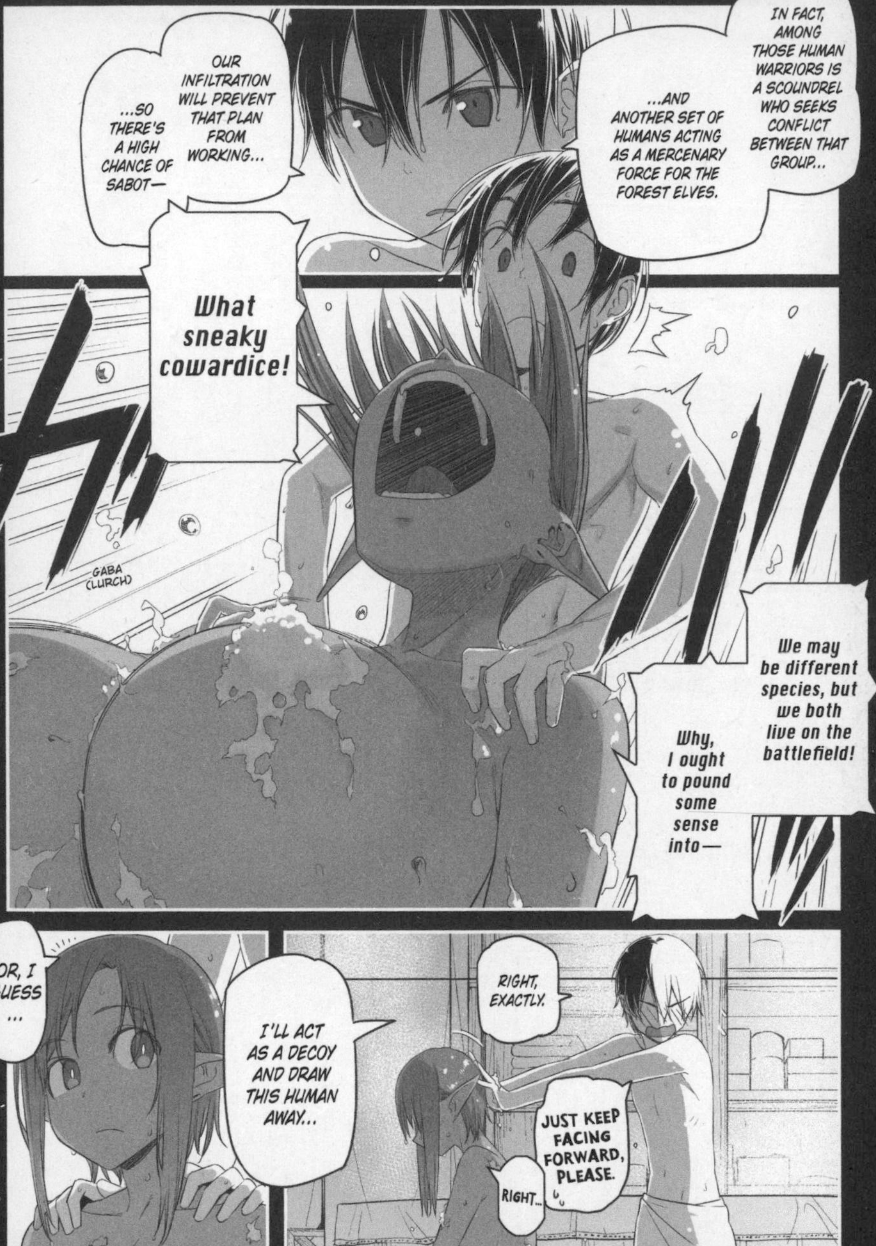
IN FACT, AMONG THOSE HUMAN WARRIORS IS A SCOUNDREL WHO SEEKS CONFLICT BETWEEN THAT GROUP...
...AND ANOTHER SET OF HUMANS ACTING AS A MERCENARY FORCE FOR THE FOREST ELVES.
OUR INFILTRATION WILL PREVENT THAT PLAN FROM WORKING...
...SO THERE'S A HIGH CHANCE OF SABOT—
What sneaky cowardice!
We may be different species, but we both live on the battlefield!
Why, I ought to pound some sense into—
GABA (LURCH)
RIGHT, EXACTLY.
I'LL ACT AS A DECOY AND DRAW THIS HUMAN AWAY...
JUST KEEP FACING FORWARD, PLEASE.
RIGHT...
OR, I GUESS ...

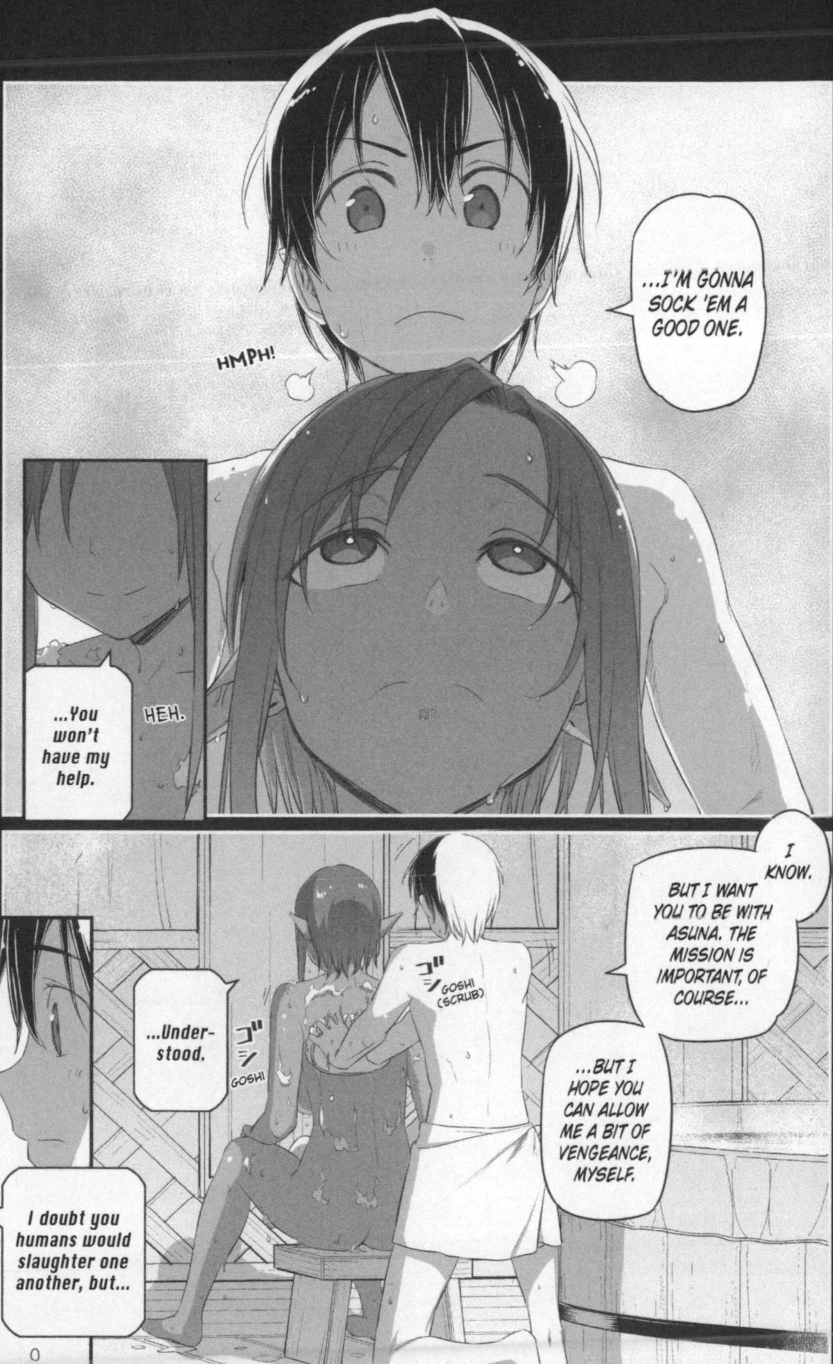
...I'M GONNA SOCK 'EM A GOOD ONE.
HMPH!
HEH.
...You won't have my help.
I KNOW.
BUT I WANT YOU TO BE WITH ASUNA. THE MISSION IS IMPORTANT, OF COURSE...
...BUT I HOPE YOU CAN ALLOW ME A BIT OF VENGEANCE, MYSELF.
ゴシ GOSHI (SCRUB)
ゴシ GOSHI
...Under-stood.
I doubt you humans would slaughter one another, but...

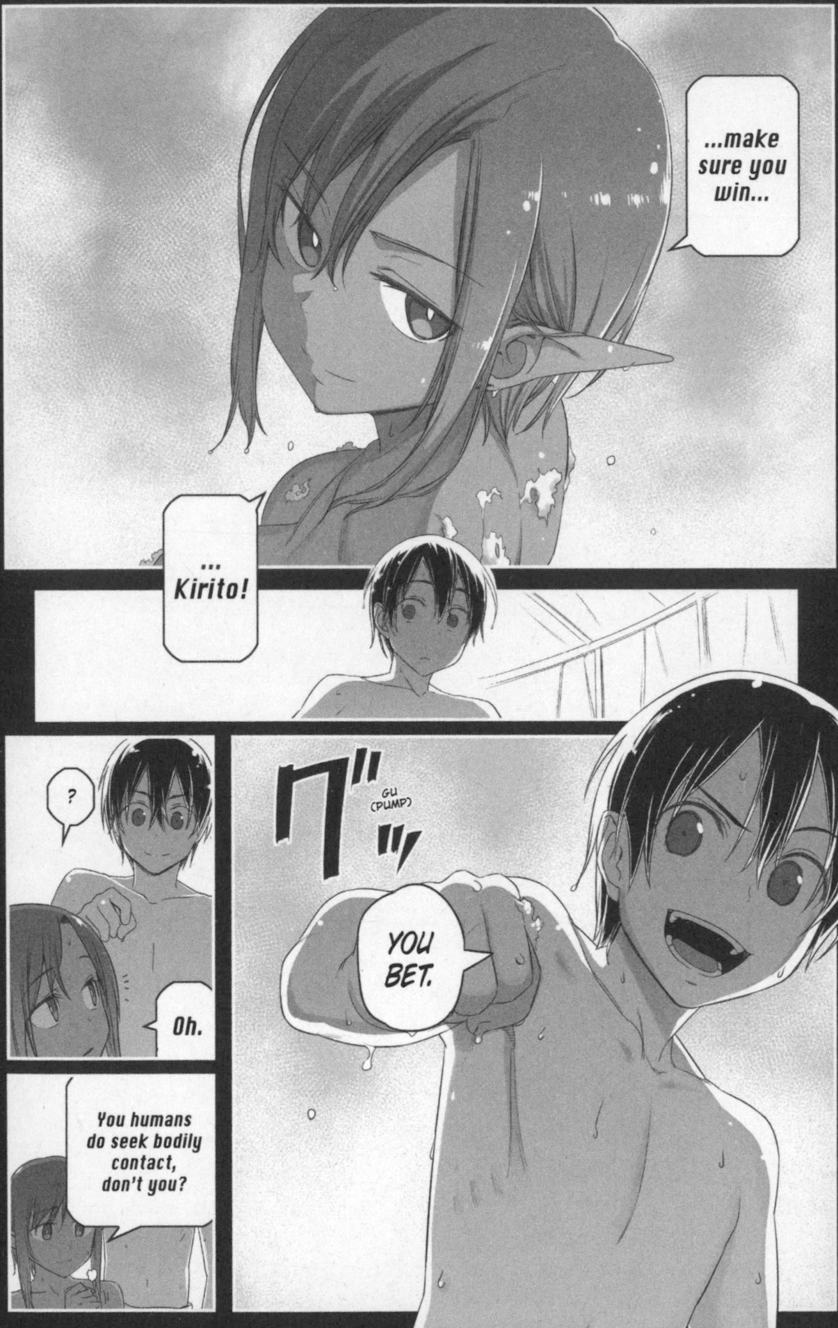
...make sure you win...
... Kirito!
GU (PUMP)
YOU BET.
?
Oh.
You humans do seek bodily contact, don't you?

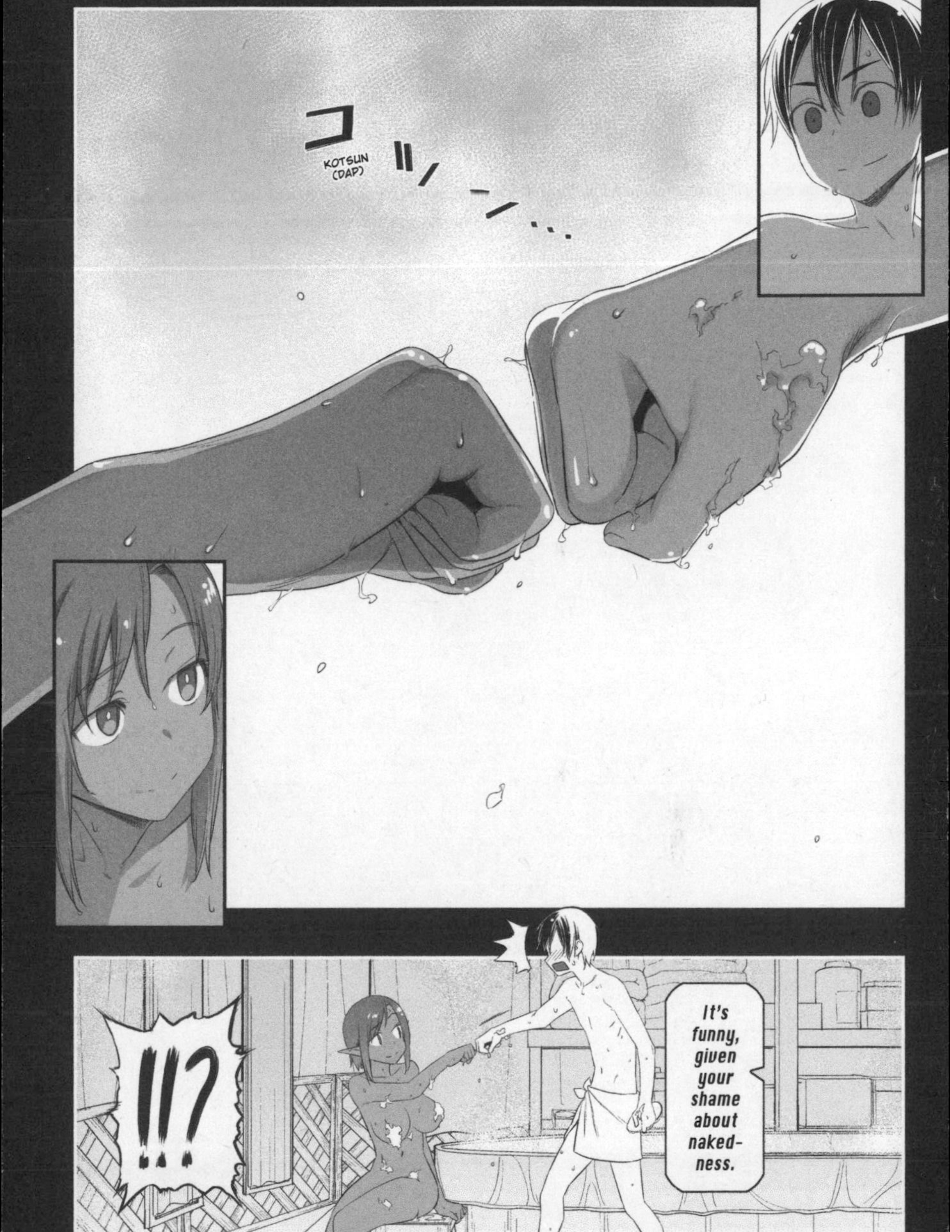
コツン…
KOTSUN (DAP)
It's funny, given your shame about naked-ness.
!!?

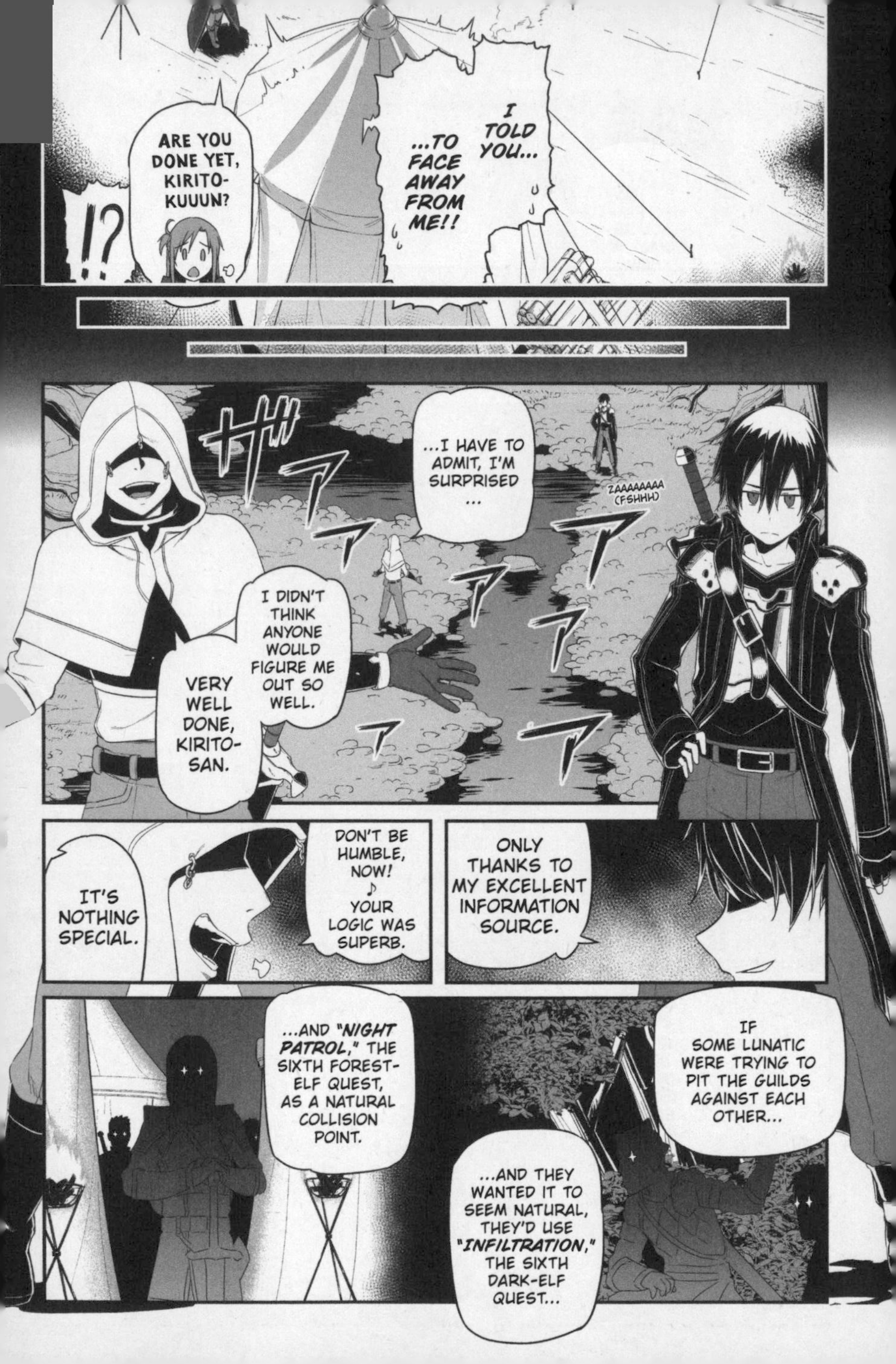
I TOLD YOU...
...TO FACE AWAY FROM ME!!
ARE YOU DONE YET, KIRITO-KUUUN?
!?
ZAAAAAAAA (FSHHH)
...I HAVE TO ADMIT, I'M SURPRISED ...
I DIDN'T THINK ANYONE WOULD FIGURE ME OUT SO WELL.
VERY WELL DONE, KIRITO-SAN.
ONLY THANKS TO MY EXCELLENT INFORMATION SOURCE.
DON'T BE HUMBLE, NOW! ♪ YOUR LOGIC WAS SUPERB.
IT'S NOTHING SPECIAL.
IF SOME LUNATIC WERE TRYING TO PIT THE GUILDS AGAINST EACH OTHER...
...AND THEY WANTED IT TO SEEM NATURAL, THEY'D USE "*INFILTRATION*," THE SIXTH DARK-ELF QUEST...
...AND "*NIGHT PATROL*," THE SIXTH FOREST-ELF QUEST, AS A NATURAL COLLISION POINT.

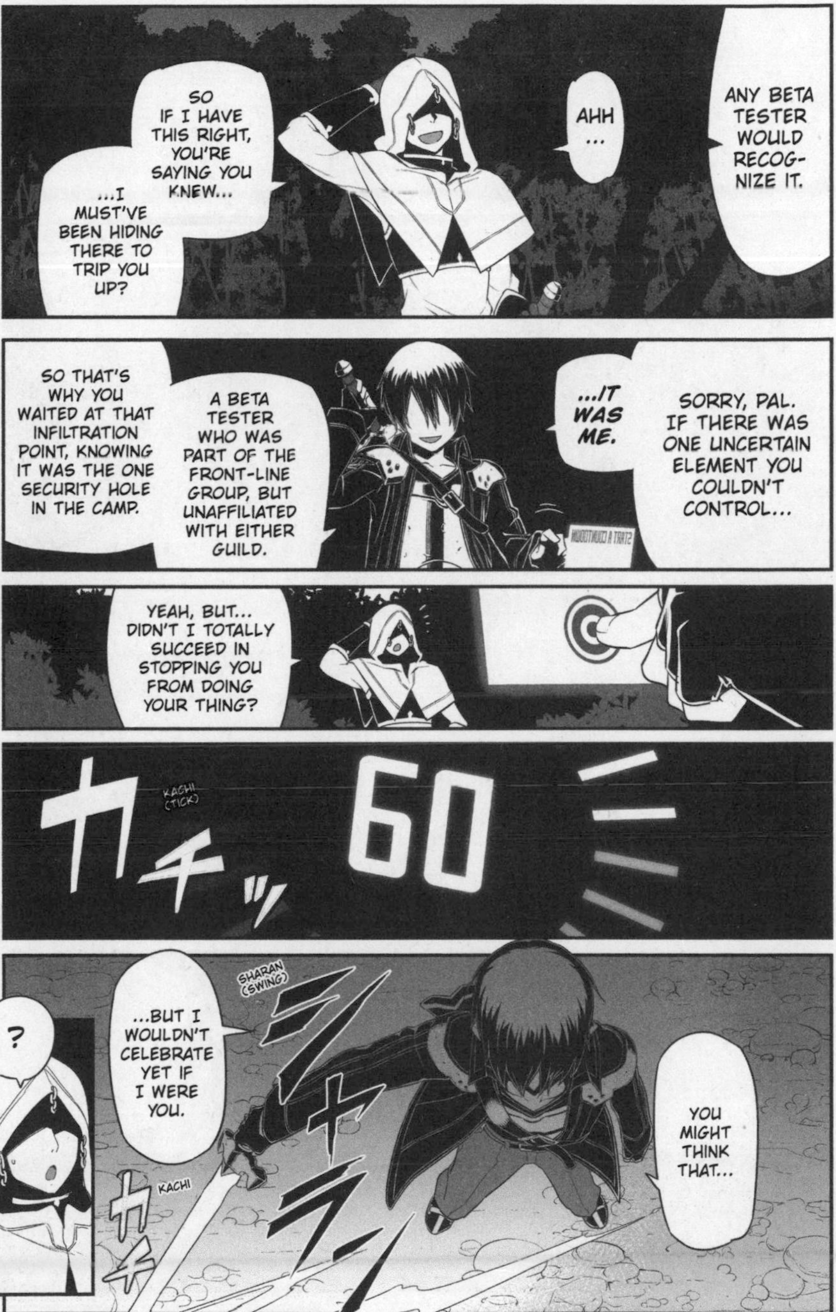
ANY BETA TESTER WOULD RECOGNIZE IT.
AHH...
SO IF I HAVE THIS RIGHT, YOU'RE SAYING YOU KNEW...
...I MUST'VE BEEN HIDING THERE TO TRIP YOU UP?
SORRY, PAL. IF THERE WAS ONE UNCERTAIN ELEMENT YOU COULDN'T CONTROL...
...IT WAS ME.
START A COUNTDOWN
A BETA TESTER WHO WAS PART OF THE FRONT-LINE GROUP, BUT UNAFFILIATED WITH EITHER GUILD.
SO THAT'S WHY YOU WAITED AT THAT INFILTRATION POINT, KNOWING IT WAS THE ONE SECURITY HOLE IN THE CAMP.
YEAH, BUT... DIDN'T I TOTALLY SUCCEED IN STOPPING YOU FROM DOING YOUR THING?
60
KACHI (TICK)
YOU MIGHT THINK THAT...
SHARAN (SWING)
...BUT I WOULDN'T CELEBRATE YET IF I WERE YOU.
KACHI
?

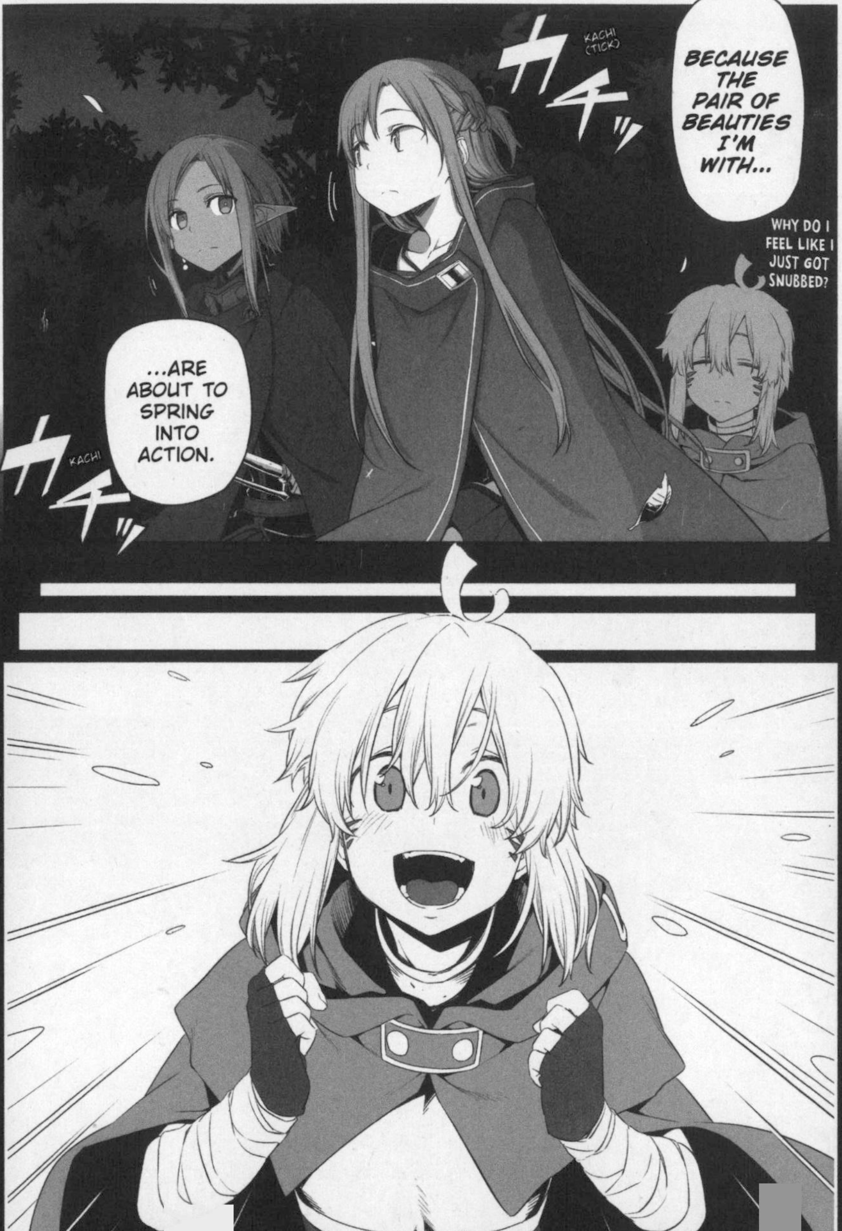
BECAUSE THE PAIR OF BEAUTIES I'M WITH...
KACHI (TICK)
カチッ
WHY DO I FEEL LIKE I JUST GOT SNUBBED?
...ARE ABOUT TO SPRING INTO ACTION.
KACHI
カチッ

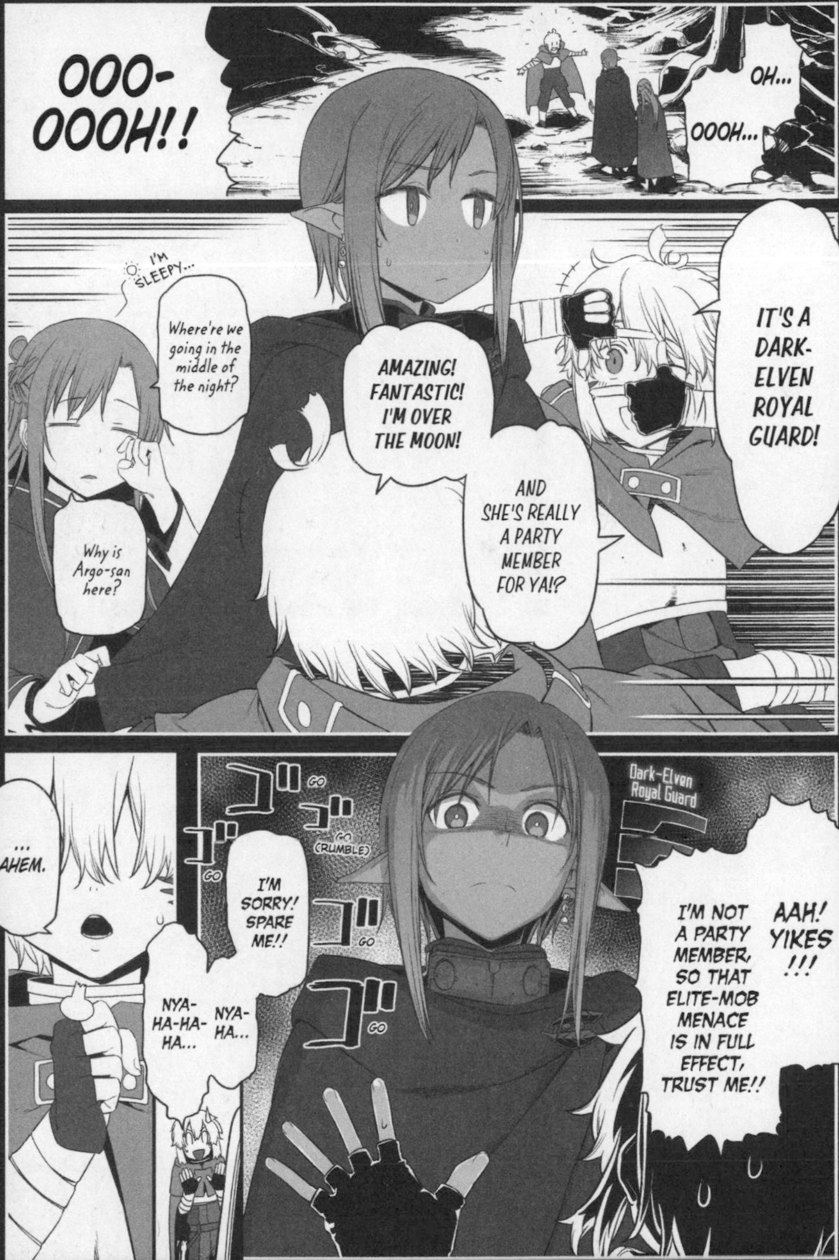
OH...
OOOH...
OOO-OOOH!!
IT'S A DARK-ELVEN ROYAL GUARD!
AND SHE'S REALLY A PARTY MEMBER FOR YA!?
AMAZING! FANTASTIC! I'M OVER THE MOON!
I'M SLEEPY...
Where're we going in the middle of the night?
Why is Argo-san here?
Dark-Elven Royal Guard
GO GO GO GO GO GO (RUMBLE)
AAH! YIKES!!!
I'M NOT A PARTY MEMBER, SO THAT ELITE-MOB MENACE IS IN FULL EFFECT, TRUST ME!!
I'M SORRY! SPARE ME!!
NYA-HA-HA-HA...
NYA-HA...
... AHEM.

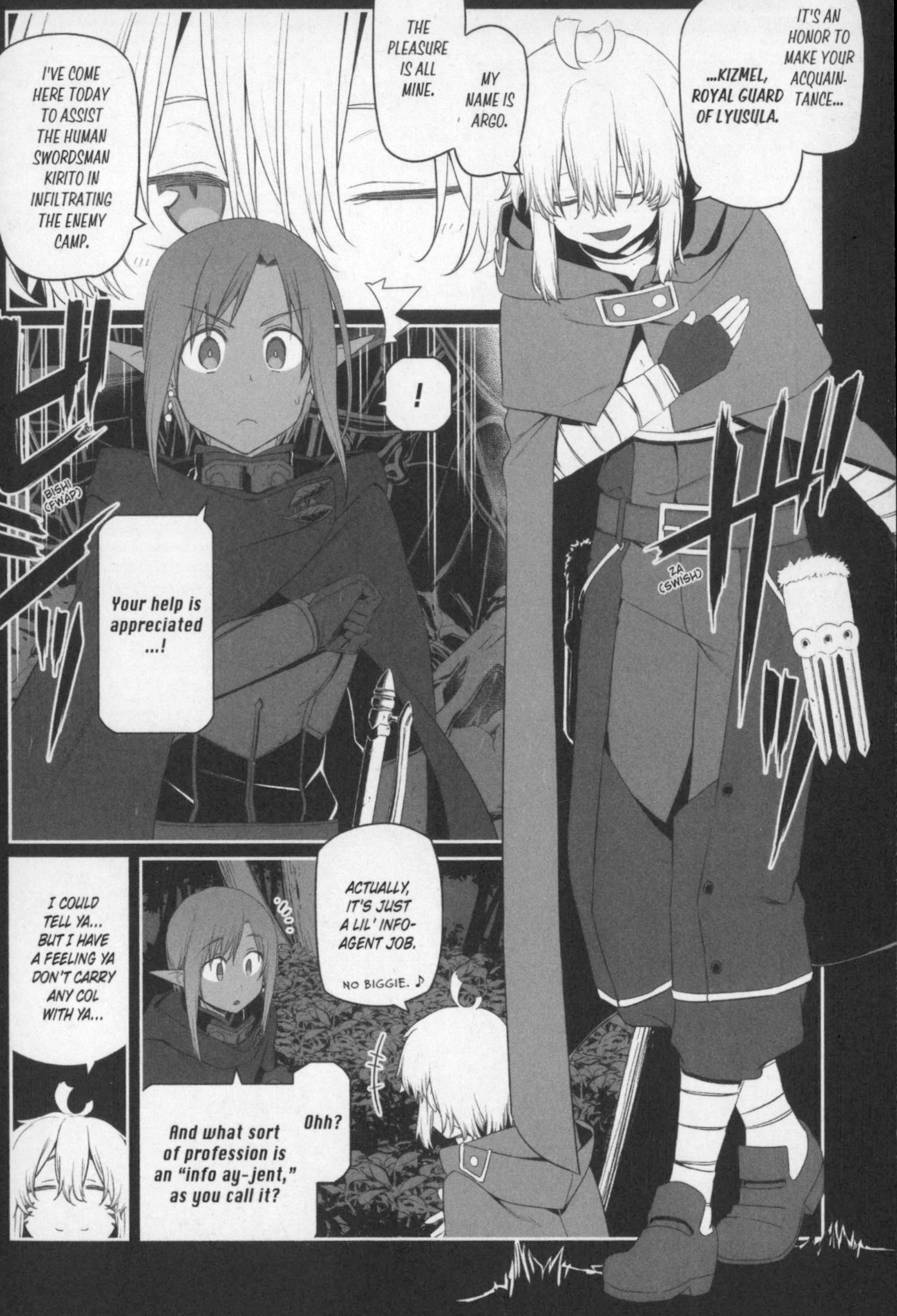
IT'S AN HONOR TO MAKE YOUR ACQUAINTANCE...
...KIZMEL, ROYAL GUARD OF LYUSULA.
THE PLEASURE IS ALL MINE.
MY NAME IS ARGO.
I'VE COME HERE TODAY TO ASSIST THE HUMAN SWORDSMAN KIRITO IN INFILTRATING THE ENEMY CAMP.
ZA (SWISH)
!
BISHI (FWAP)
Your help is appreciated ...!
ACTUALLY, IT'S JUST A LIL' INFO-AGENT JOB.
NO BIGGIE. ♪
Ohh?
And what sort of profession is an "info ay-jent," as you call it?
I COULD TELL YA... BUT I HAVE A FEELING YA DON'T CARRY ANY COL WITH YA...

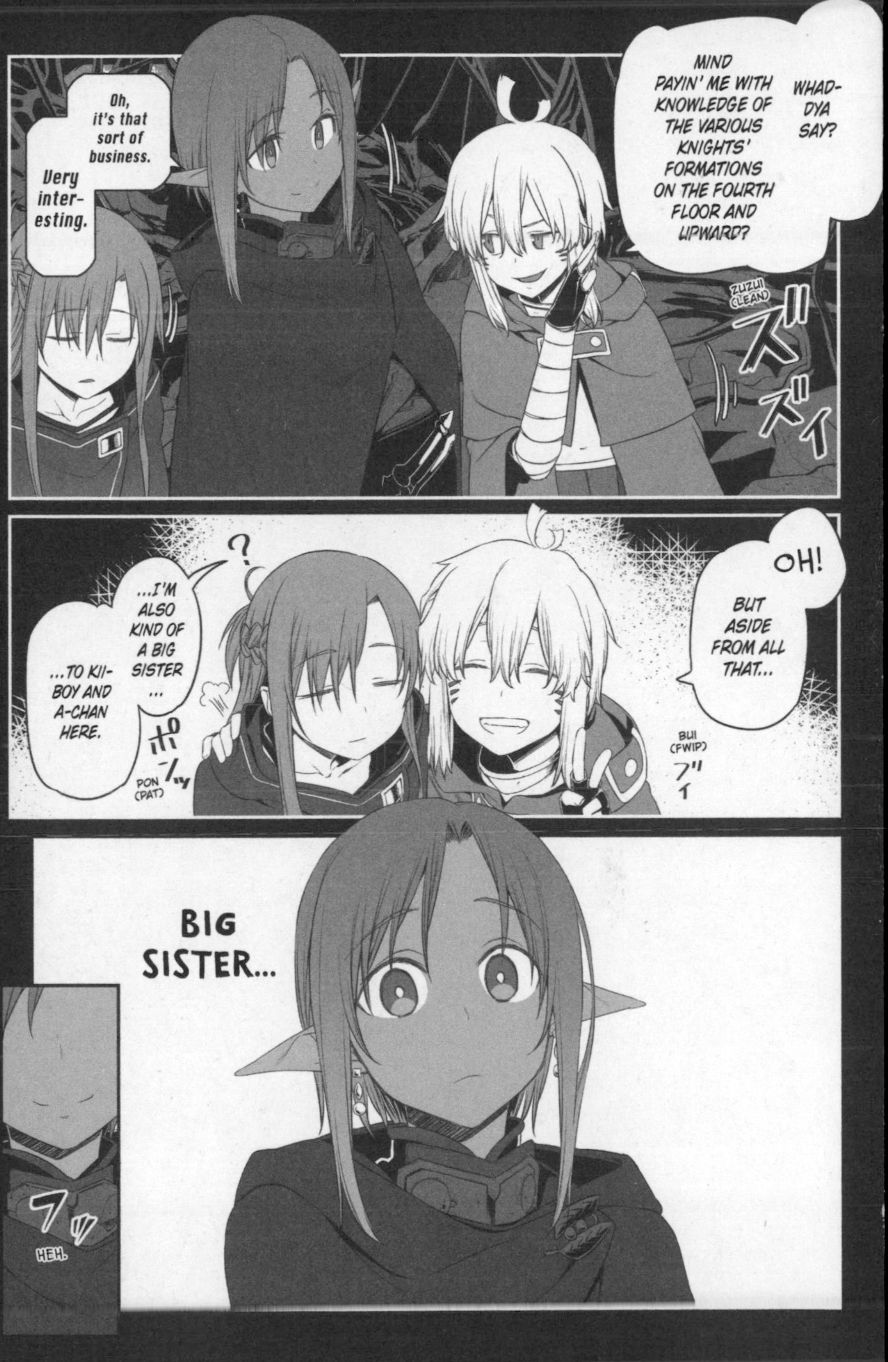
WHAD-DYA SAY?
MIND PAYIN' ME WITH KNOWLEDGE OF THE VARIOUS KNIGHTS' FORMATIONS ON THE FOURTH FLOOR AND UPWARD?
Oh, it's that sort of business.
Very inter-esting.
ZUZUI (LEAN)
OH!
BUT ASIDE FROM ALL THAT...
BUI (FWIP)
...I'M ALSO KIND OF A BIG SISTER ...
...TO KII-BOY AND A-CHAN HERE.
PON (PAT)
BIG SISTER...
HEH.

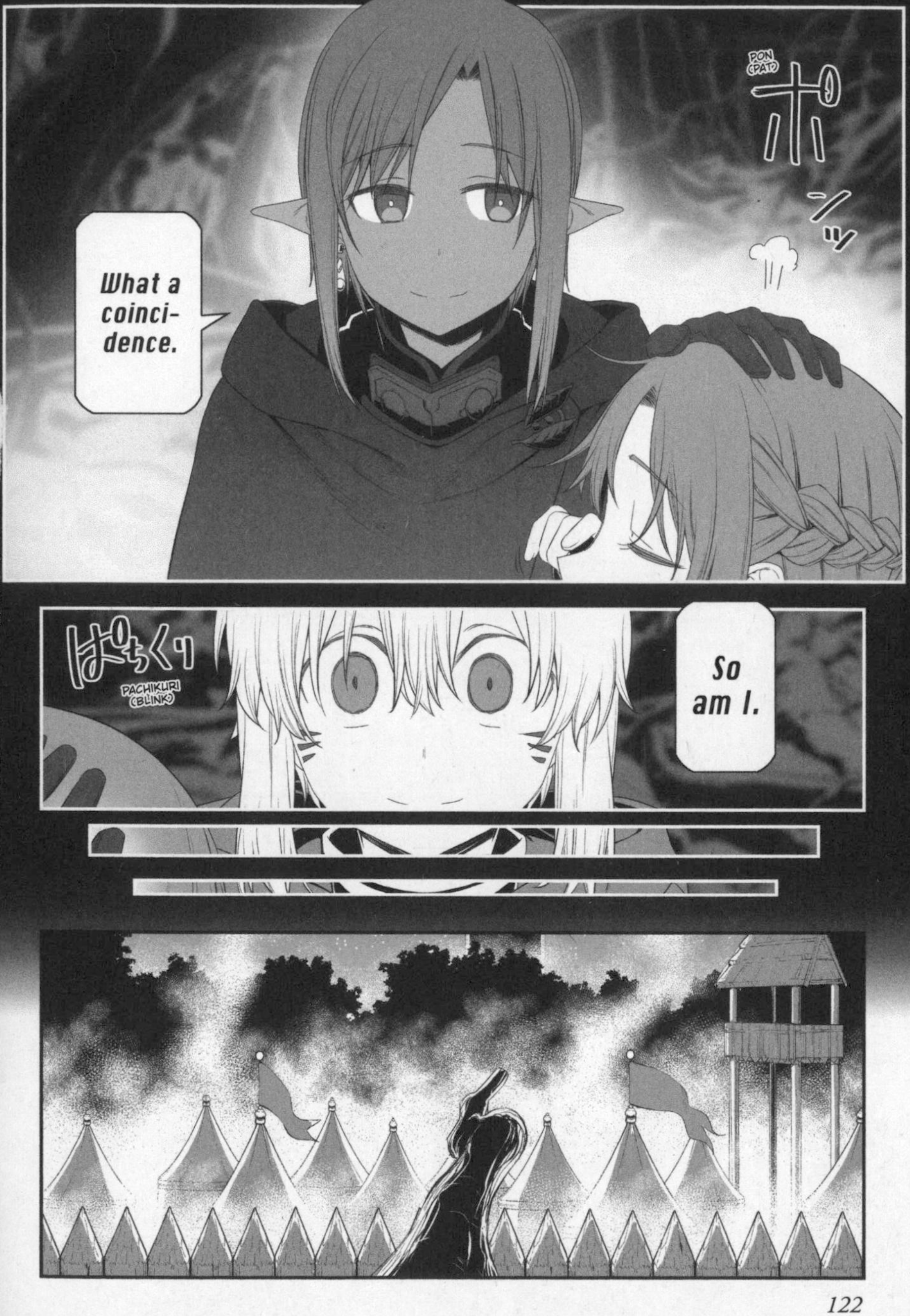
ポンッ
PON (PAT)
What a coinci-dence.
So am I.
ぱちくり
PACHIKURI (BLINK)

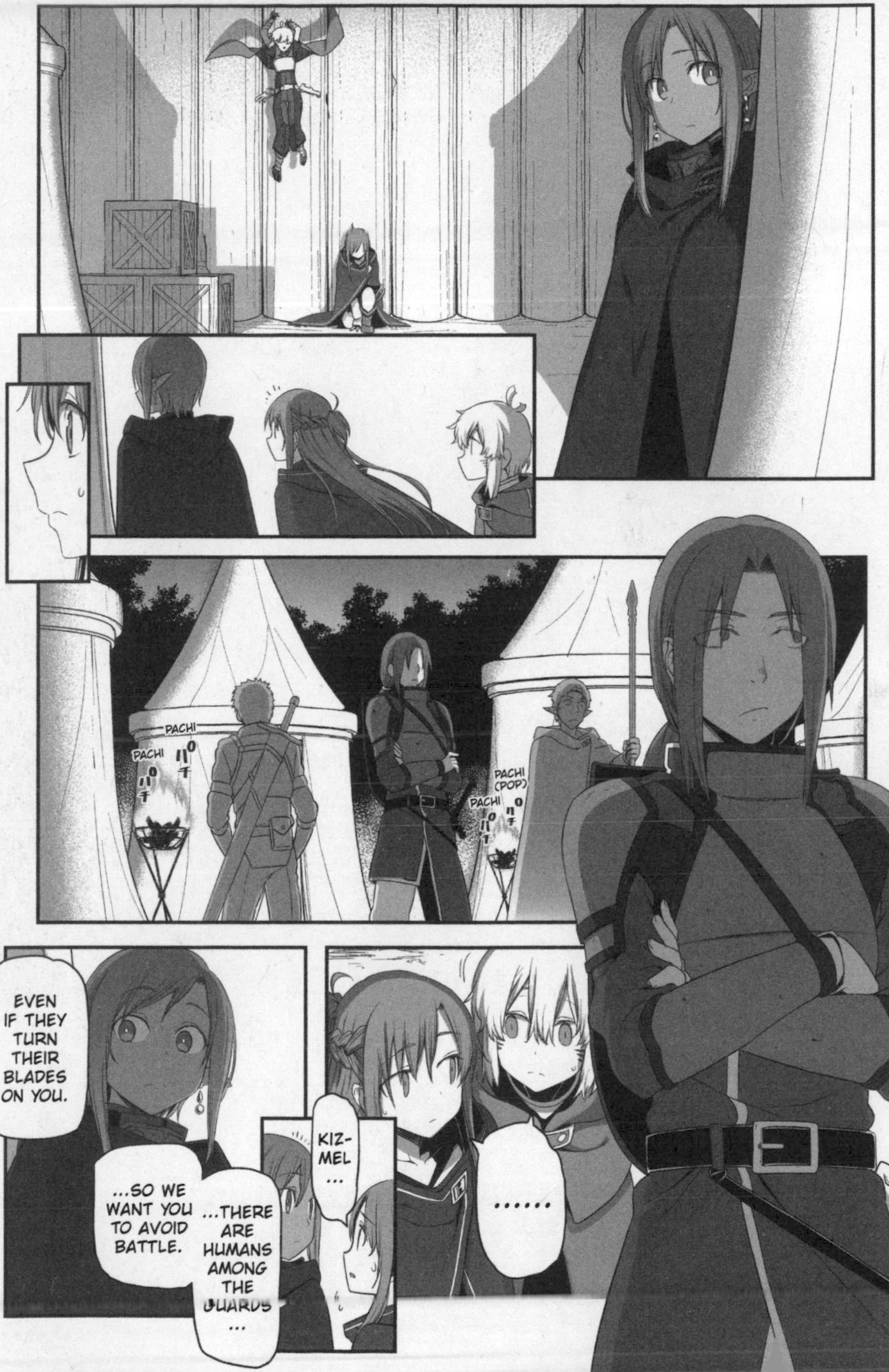
PACHI (POP)
PACHI
PACHI
PACHI
KIZMEL...
......
...THERE ARE HUMANS AMONG THE GUARDS...
...SO WE WANT YOU TO AVOID BATTLE.
EVEN IF THEY TURN THEIR BLADES ON YOU.

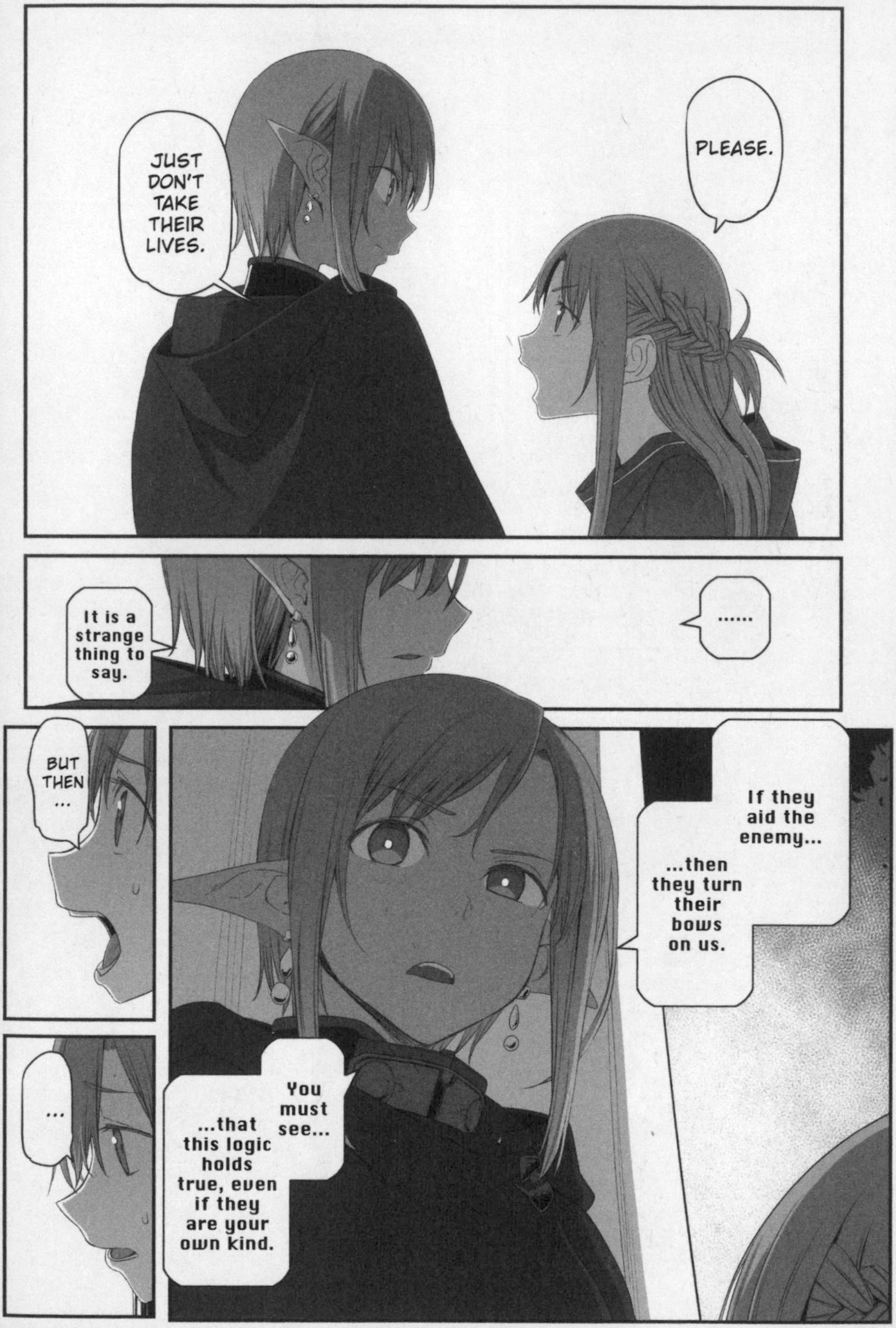
PLEASE.
JUST DON'T TAKE THEIR LIVES.
......
It is a strange thing to say.
If they aid the enemy...
...then they turn their bows on us.
BUT THEN ...
You must see...
...that this logic holds true, even if they are your own kind.
...

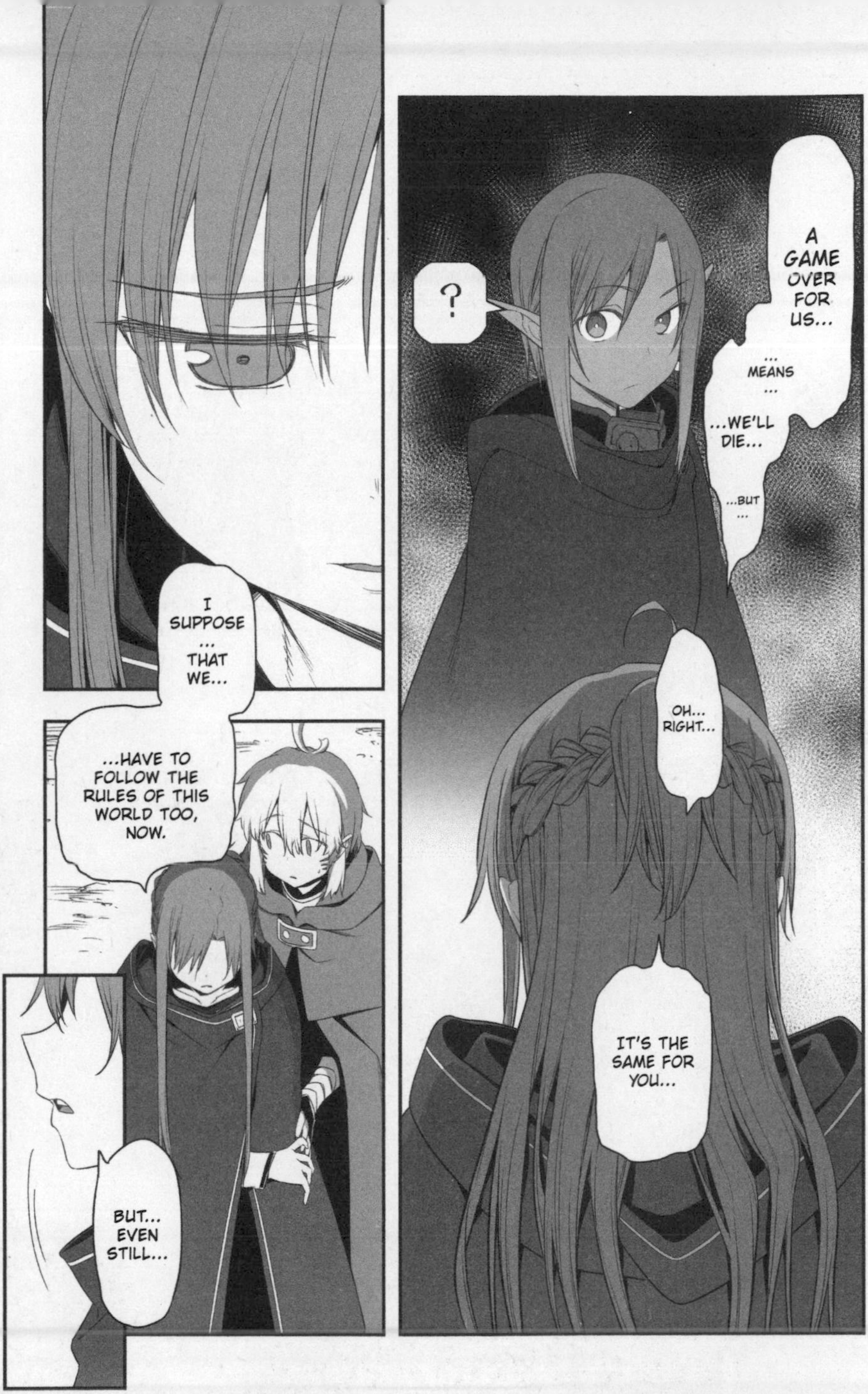
A GAME OVER FOR US...
...MEANS...
...WE'LL DIE...
...BUT...
?
OH... RIGHT...
IT'S THE SAME FOR YOU...
I SUPPOSE... THAT WE...
...HAVE TO FOLLOW THE RULES OF THIS WORLD TOO, NOW.
BUT... EVEN STILL...

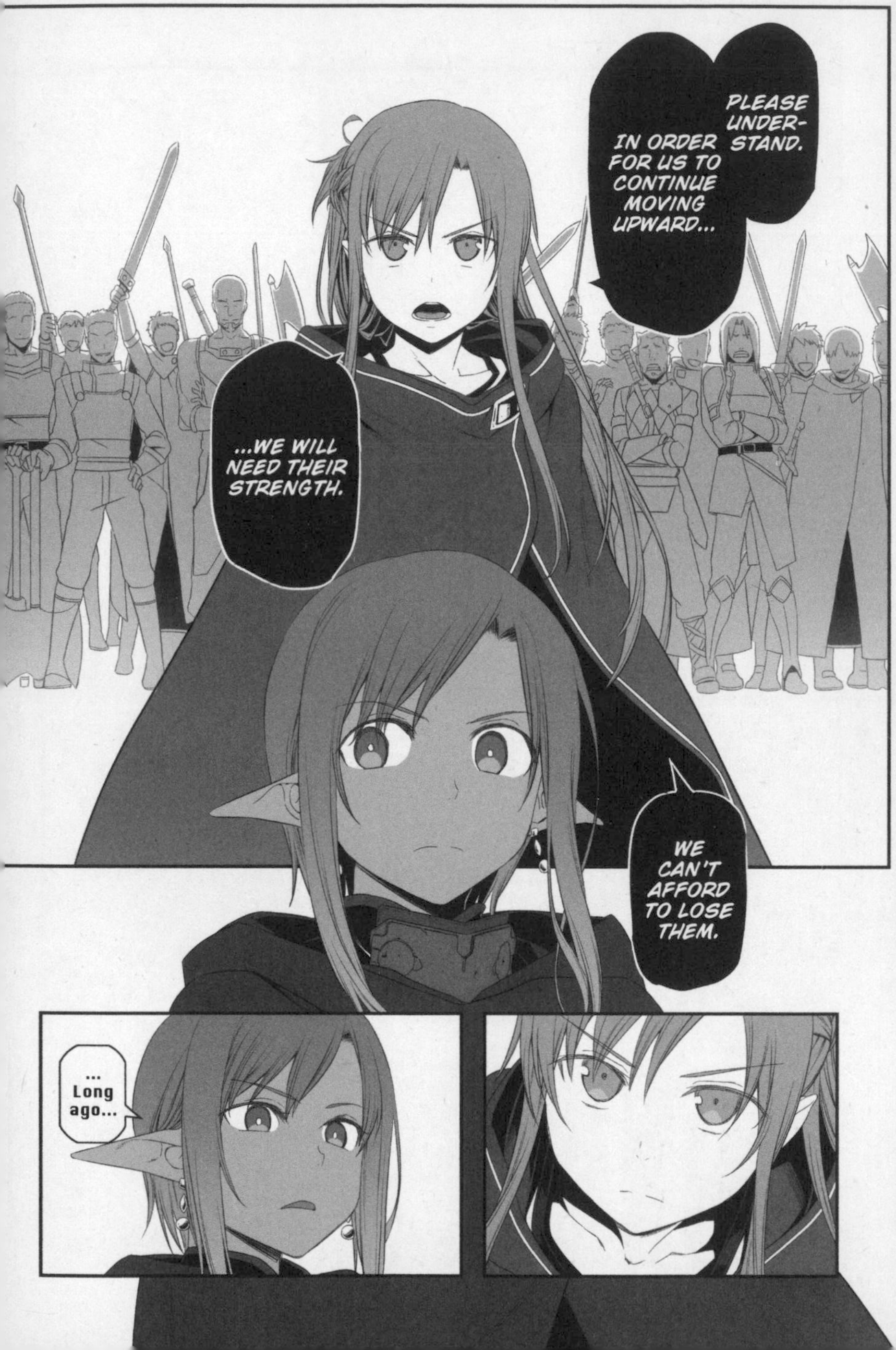
PLEASE UNDER- STAND.
IN ORDER FOR US TO CONTINUE MOVING UPWARD...
...WE WILL NEED THEIR STRENGTH.
WE CAN'T AFFORD TO LOSE THEM.
... Long ago...

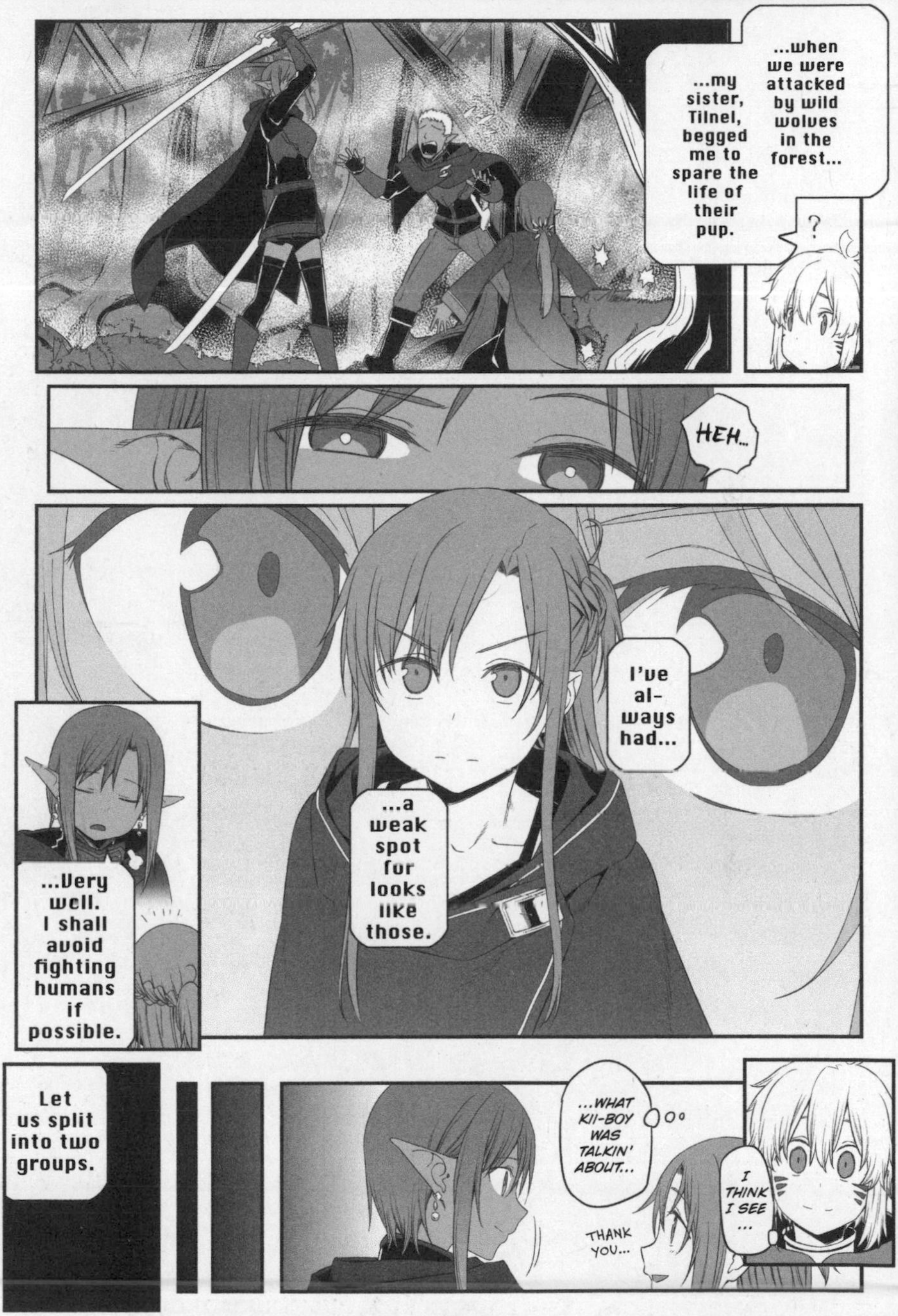

...when we were attacked by wild wolves in the forest...
...my sister, Tilnel, begged me to spare the life of their pup.
?
HEH...
I've al-ways had...
...a weak spot for looks like those.
...Very well. I shall avoid fighting humans if possible.
I THINK I SEE ...
...WHAT KII-BOY WAS TALKIN' ABOUT...
THANK YOU...
Let us split into two groups.

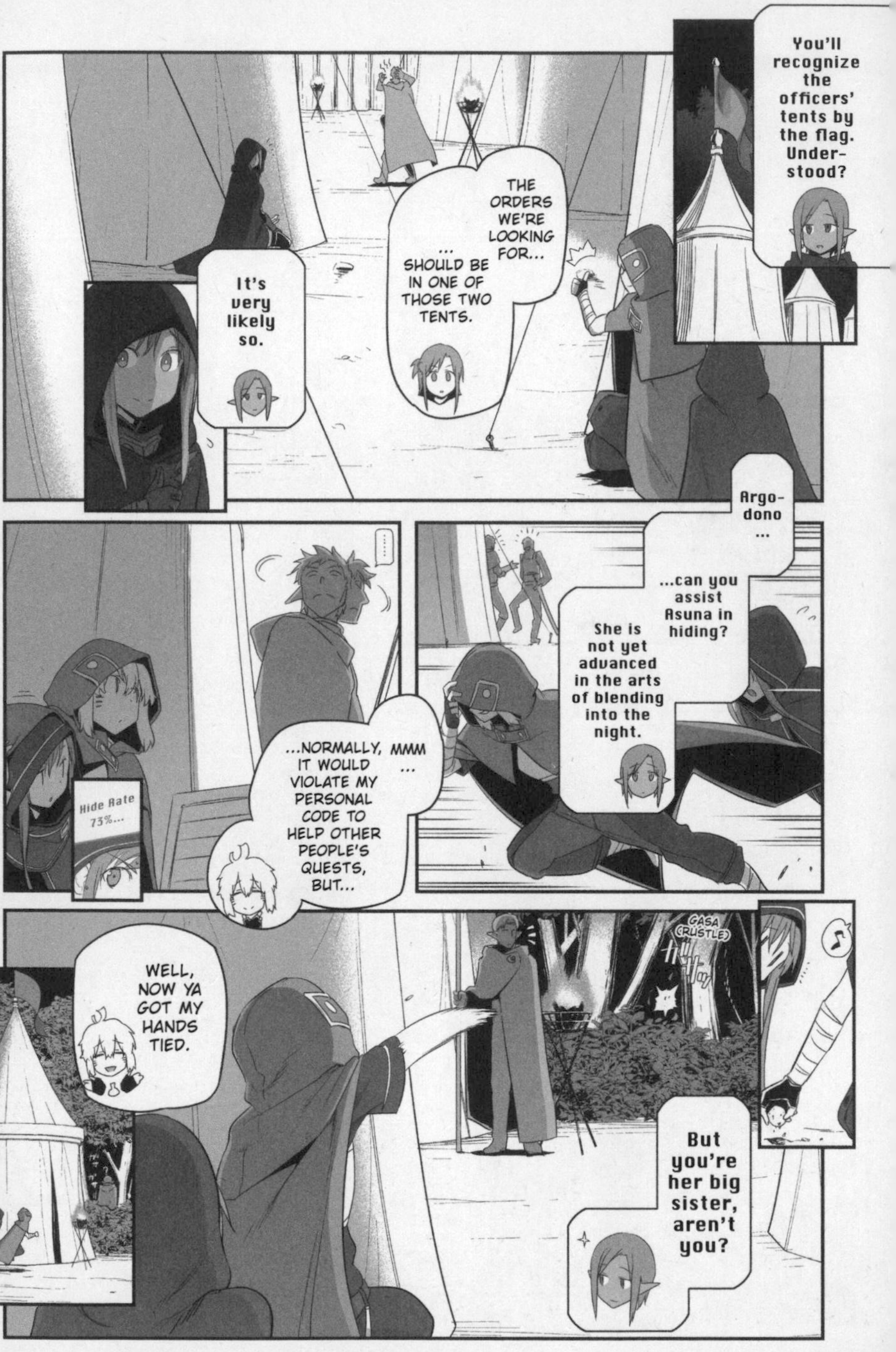

You'll recognize the officers' tents by the flag. Understood?
THE ORDERS WE'RE LOOKING FOR... ...SHOULD BE IN ONE OF THOSE TWO TENTS.
It's very likely so.
Argo-dono...
...can you assist Asuna in hiding?
She is not yet advanced in the arts of blending into the night.
......
...NORMALLY, MMM... IT WOULD VIOLATE MY PERSONAL CODE TO HELP OTHER PEOPLE'S QUESTS, BUT...
Hide Rate 73%...
♪
But you're her big sister, aren't you?
GASA (RUSTLE)
WELL, NOW YA GOT MY HANDS TIED.

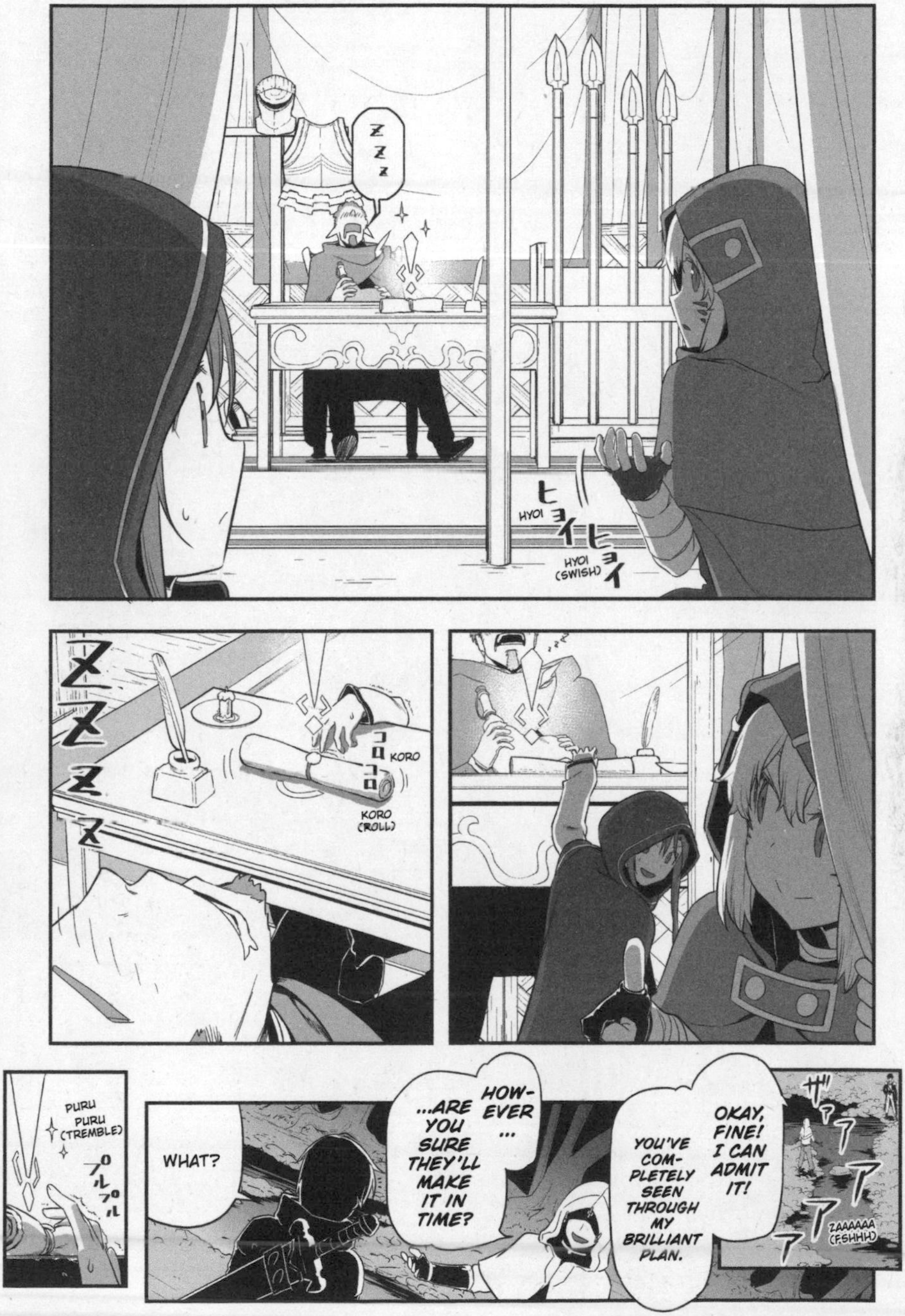
Z Z Z
ヒョイヒョイ
HYOI HYOI (SWISH)
Z Z Z Z Z
コロコロ
KORO KORO (ROLL)
ザァァァ
ZAAAAAA (F-SHHH)
OKAY, FINE! I CAN ADMIT IT!
YOU'VE COMPLETELY SEEN THROUGH MY BRILLIANT PLAN.
HOWEVER...
...ARE YOU SURE THEY'LL MAKE IT IN TIME?
WHAT?
プルプル
PURU PURU (TREMBLE)

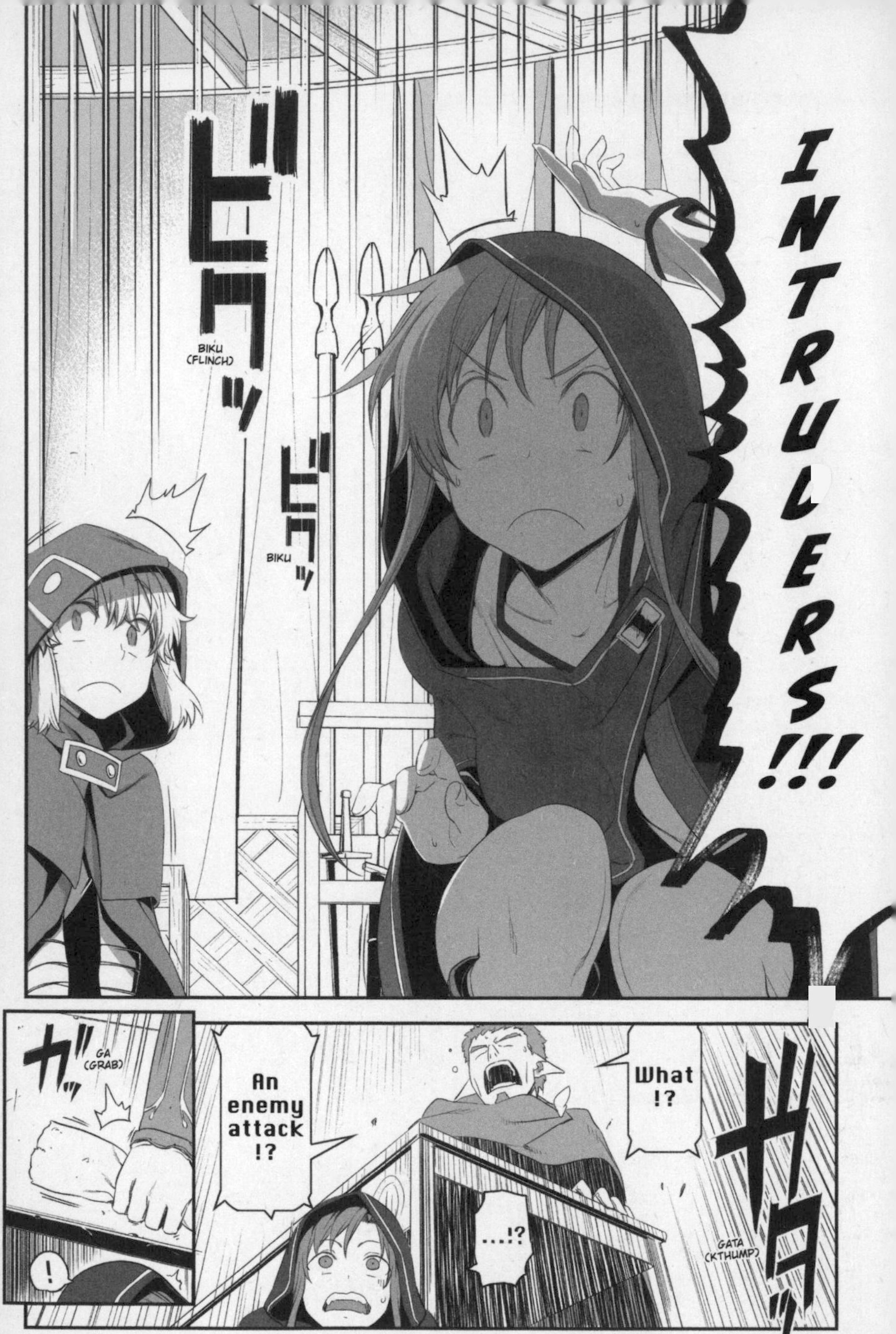
INTRUDERS!!!
BIKU (FLINCH)
BIKU
GATA (KTHUMP)
What !?
An enemy attack !?
...!?
GA (GRAB)
!

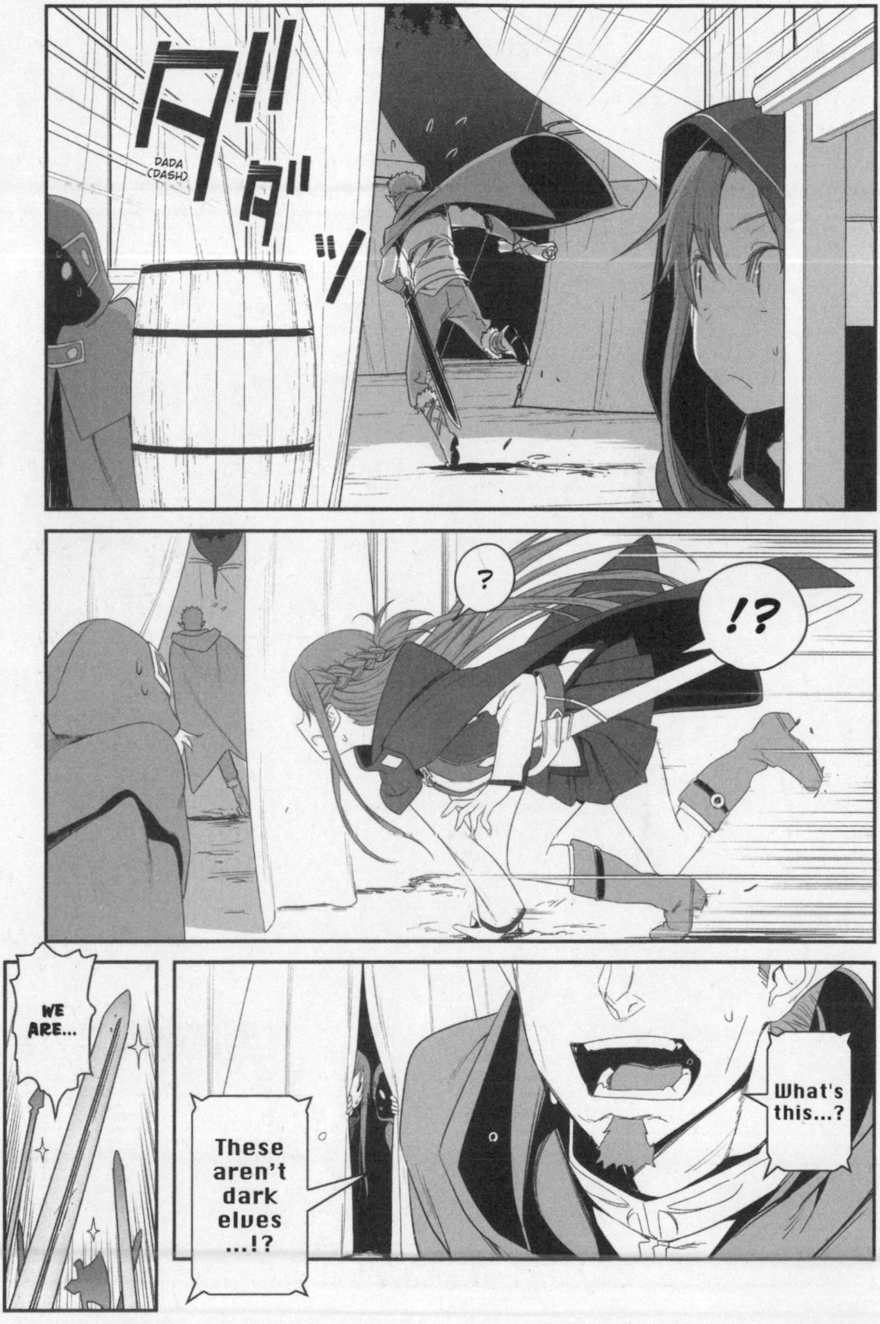
DADA (DASH)
!?
?
What's this...?
These aren't dark elves ...!?
WE ARE...

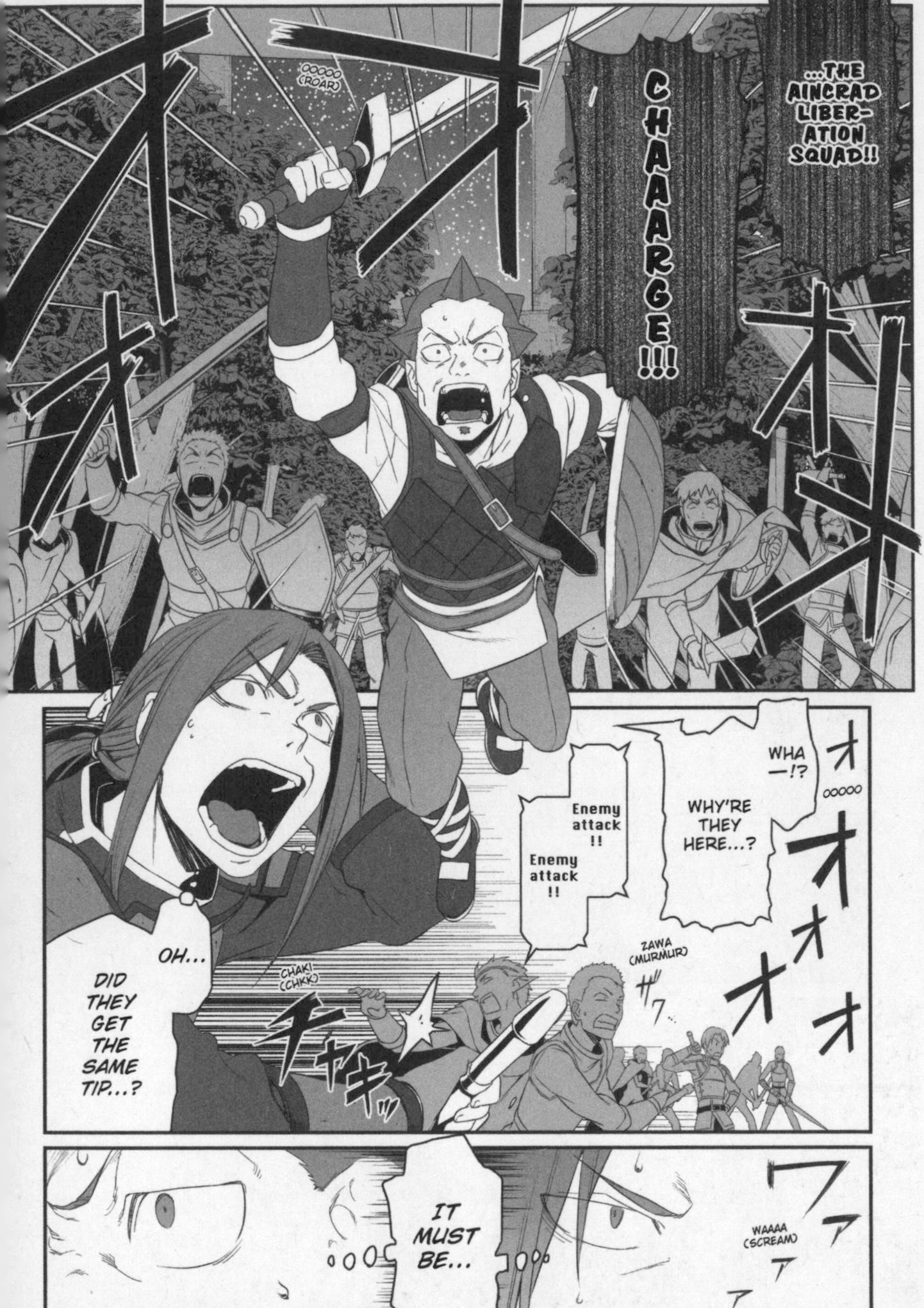
...THE AINCRAD LIBERATION SQUAD!!
CHAAARGE!!!
OOOOO (ROAR)
WHA—!?
OOOOO
WHY'RE THEY HERE...?
Enemy attack!! Enemy attack!!
ZAWA (MURMUR)
CHAKI (CHKK)
OH... DID THEY GET THE SAME TIP...?
WAAAA (SCREAM)
IT MUST BE...

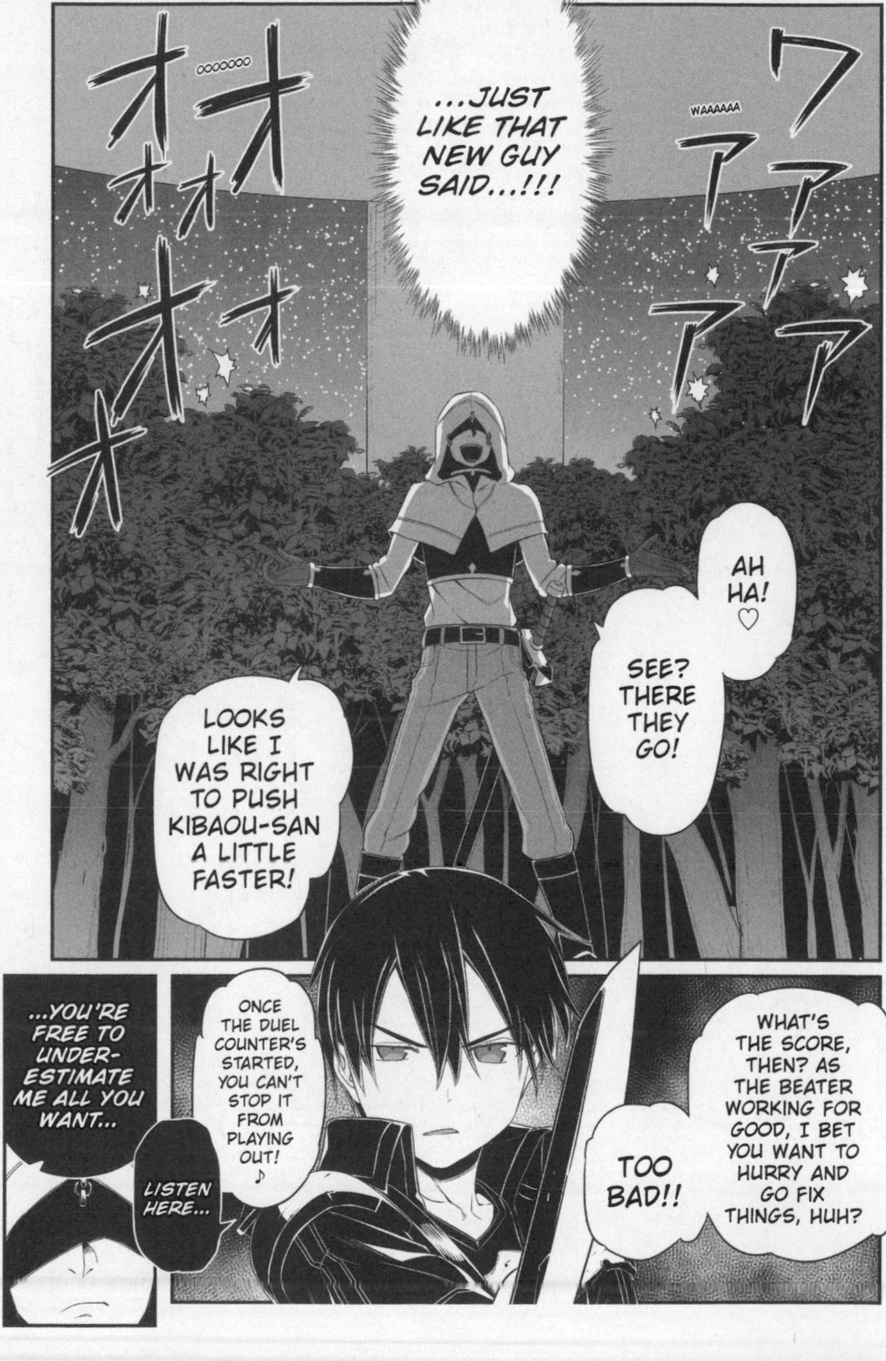
WAAAAAA
...JUST LIKE THAT NEW GUY SAID...!!!
OOOOOOO
AH HA! ♡
SEE? THERE THEY GO!
LOOKS LIKE I WAS RIGHT TO PUSH KIBAOU-SAN A LITTLE FASTER!
WHAT'S THE SCORE, THEN? AS THE BEATER WORKING FOR GOOD, I BET YOU WANT TO HURRY AND GO FIX THINGS, HUH?
TOO BAD!!
ONCE THE DUEL COUNTER'S STARTED, YOU CAN'T STOP IT FROM PLAYING OUT! ♪
LISTEN HERE...
...YOU'RE FREE TO UNDER-ESTIMATE ME ALL YOU WANT...

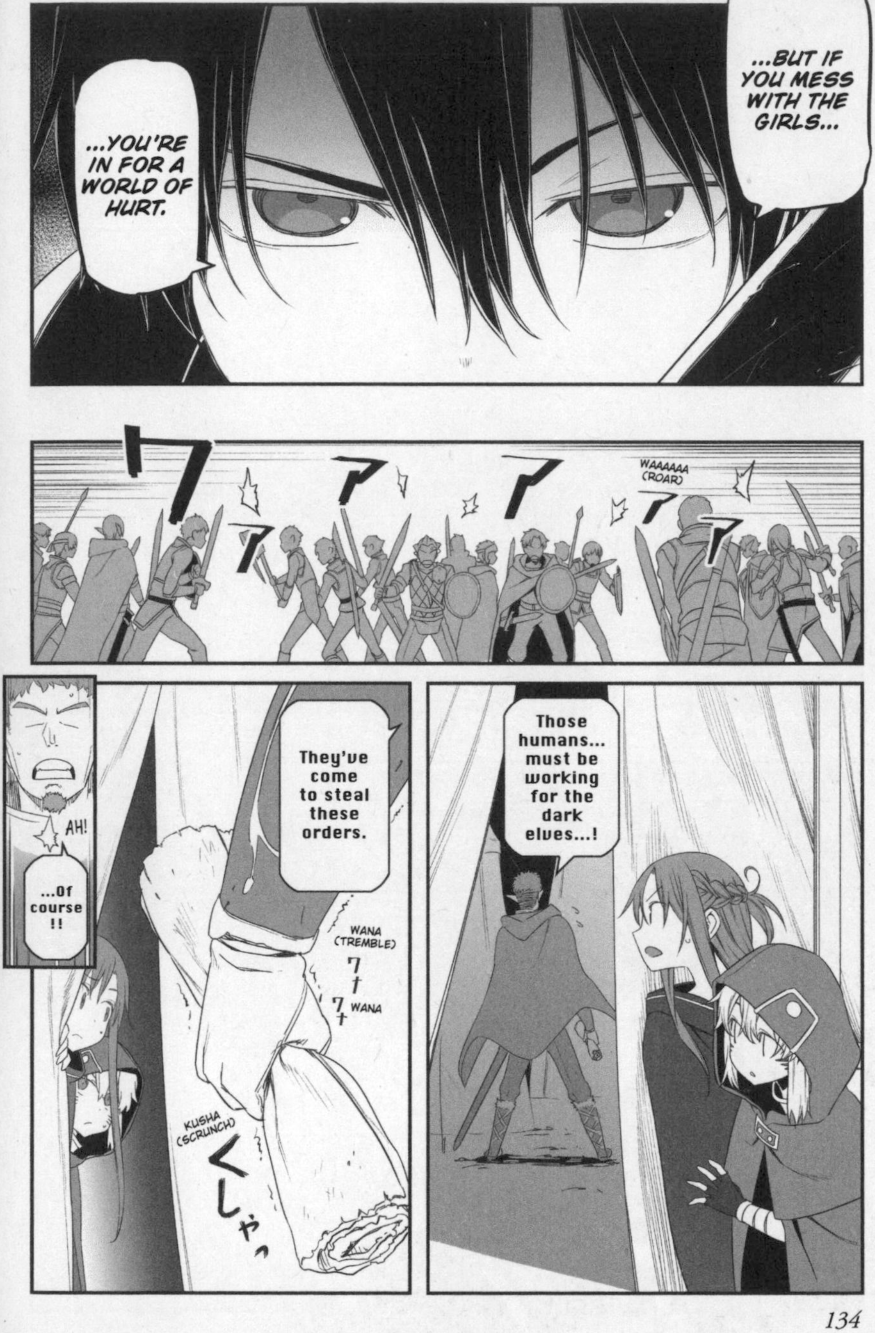
...BUT IF YOU MESS WITH THE GIRLS...
...YOU'RE IN FOR A WORLD OF HURT.
WAAAAAA (ROAR)
Those humans... must be working for the dark elves...!
They've come to steal these orders.
WANA (TREMBLE)
ワナ
ワナ
WANA
KUSHA (SCRUNCH)
くしゃっ
AH!
...Of course!!

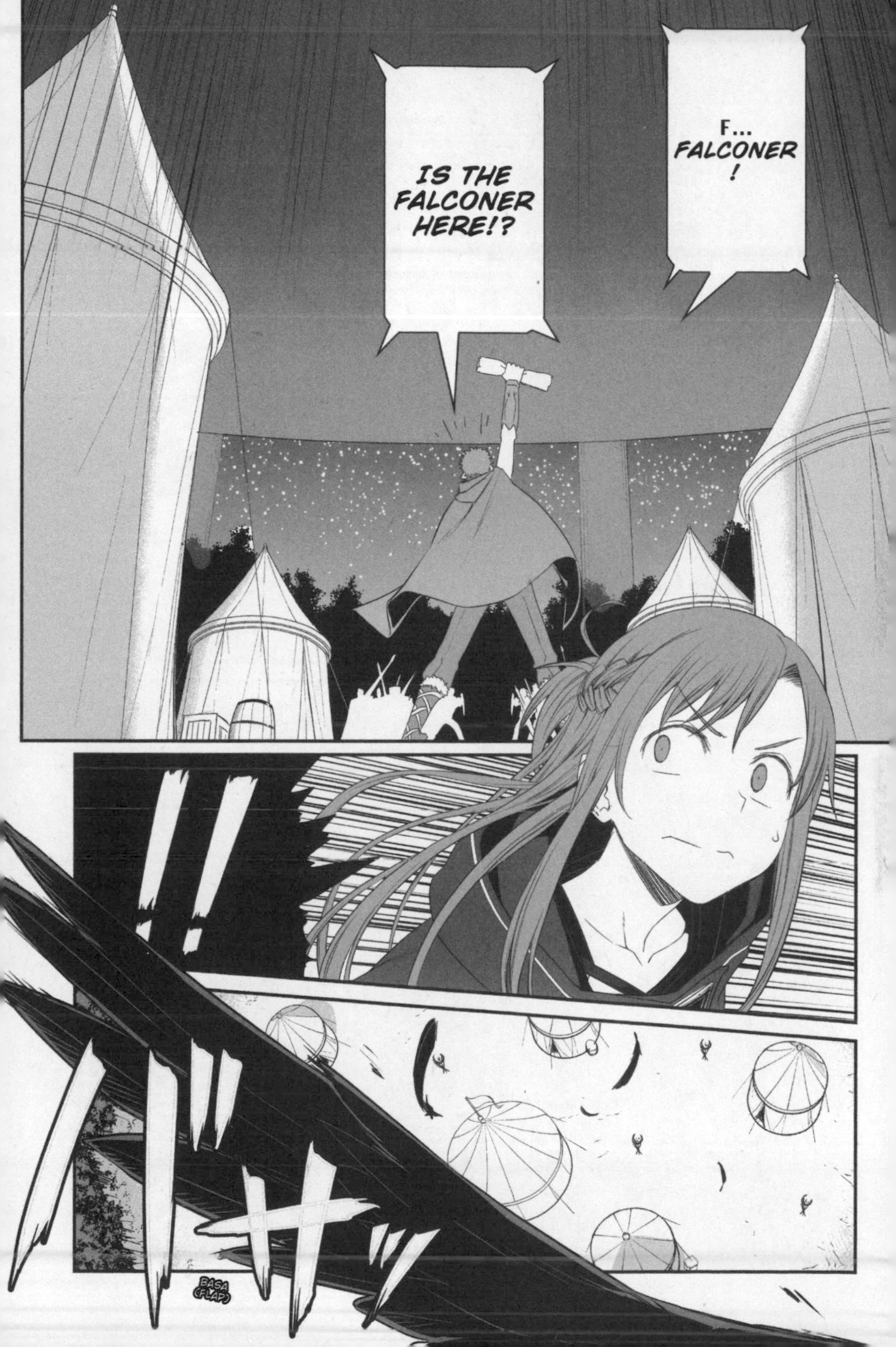
F... FALCONER!
IS THE FALCONER HERE!?
!!
BASA (FLAP)

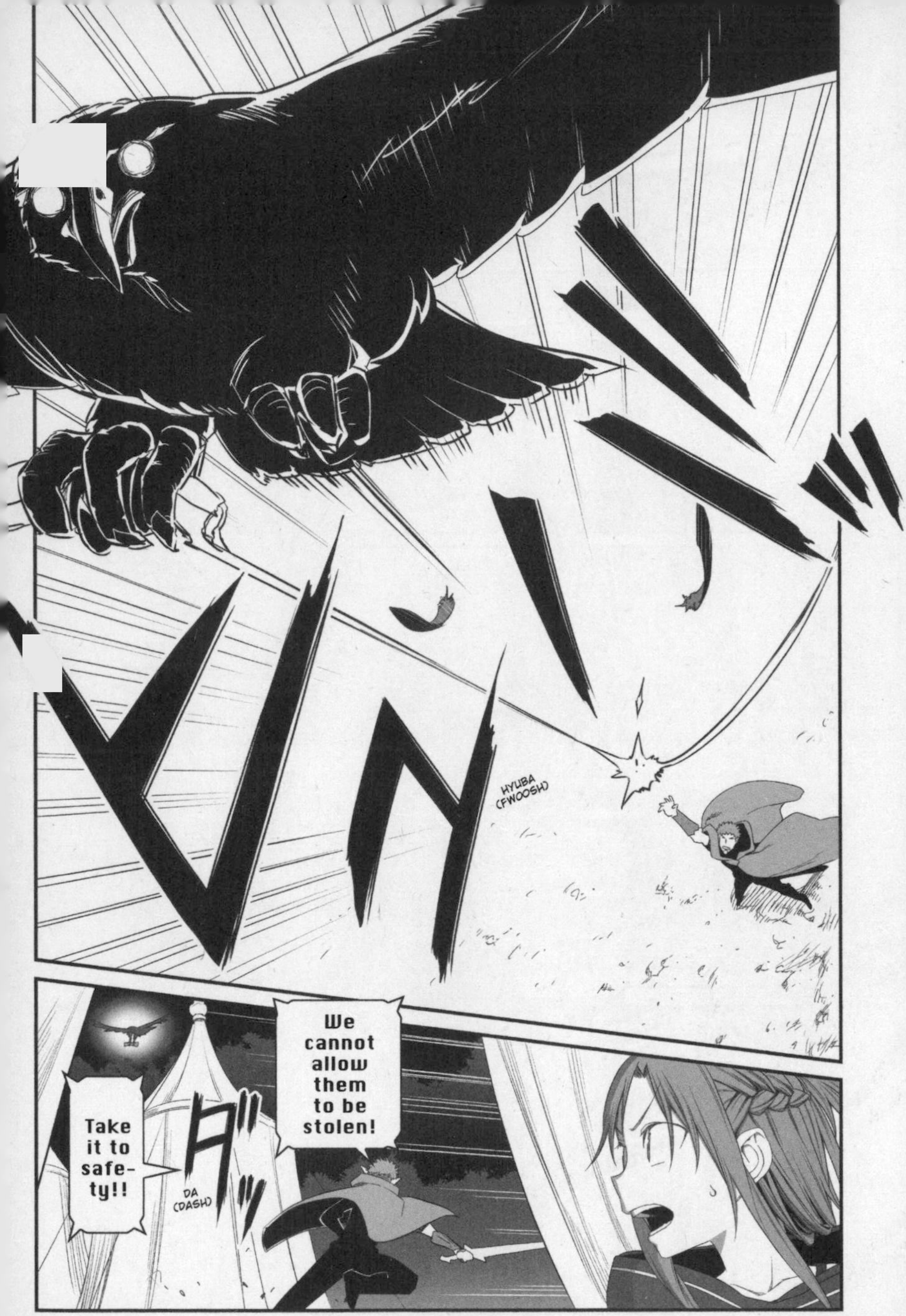
HYUBA (FWOOSH)
We cannot allow them to be stolen!
Take it to safety!!
DA (DASH)

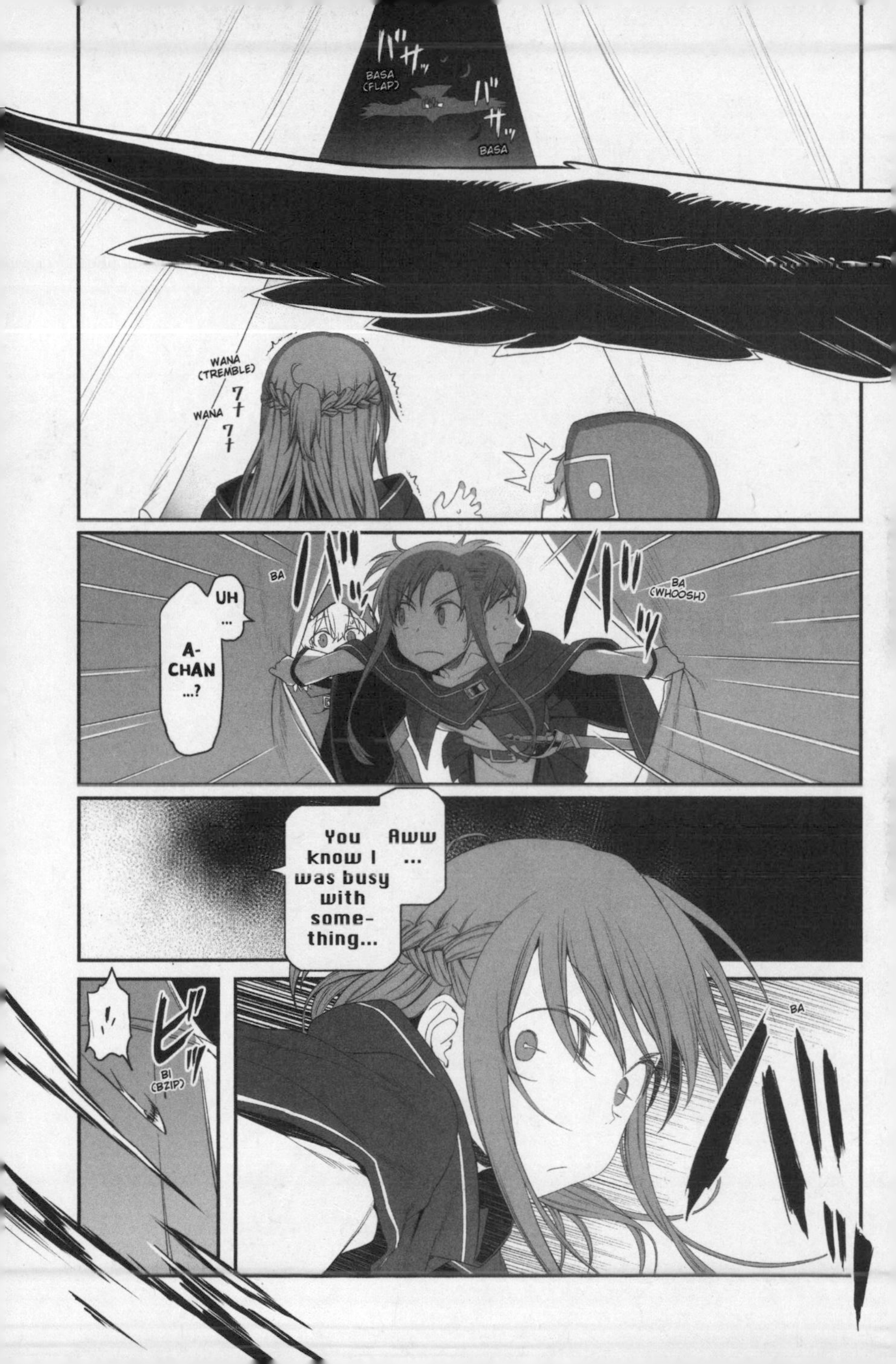

バサッ
BASA (FLAP)
バサッ
BASA
WANA (TREMBLE)
ワナ
WANA
ワナ
BA (WHOOSH)
BA
UH ... A-CHAN ...?
Aww ... You know I was busy with something...
BA
!
BI (BZIP)

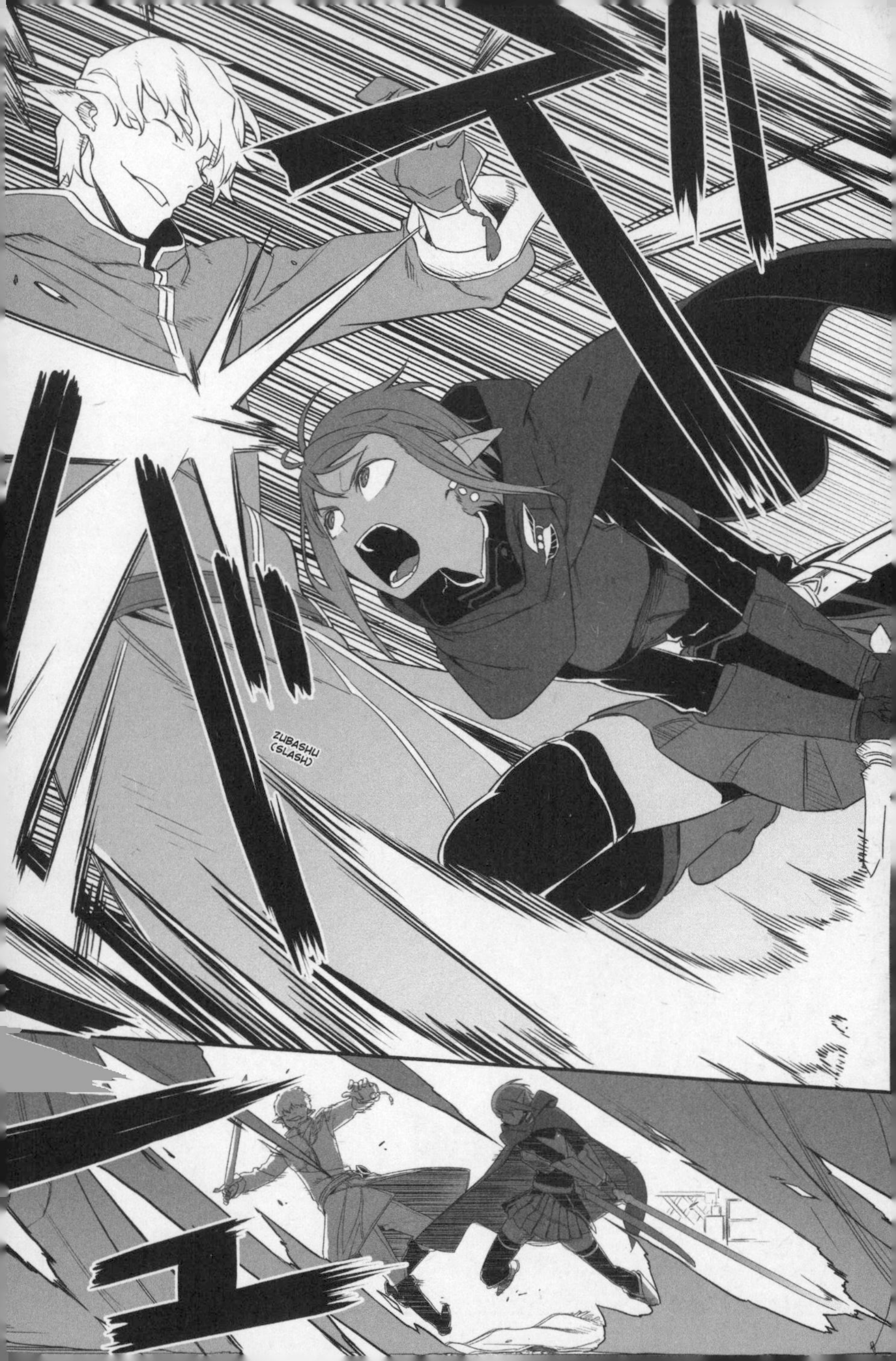
ZUBASHU
(SLASH)

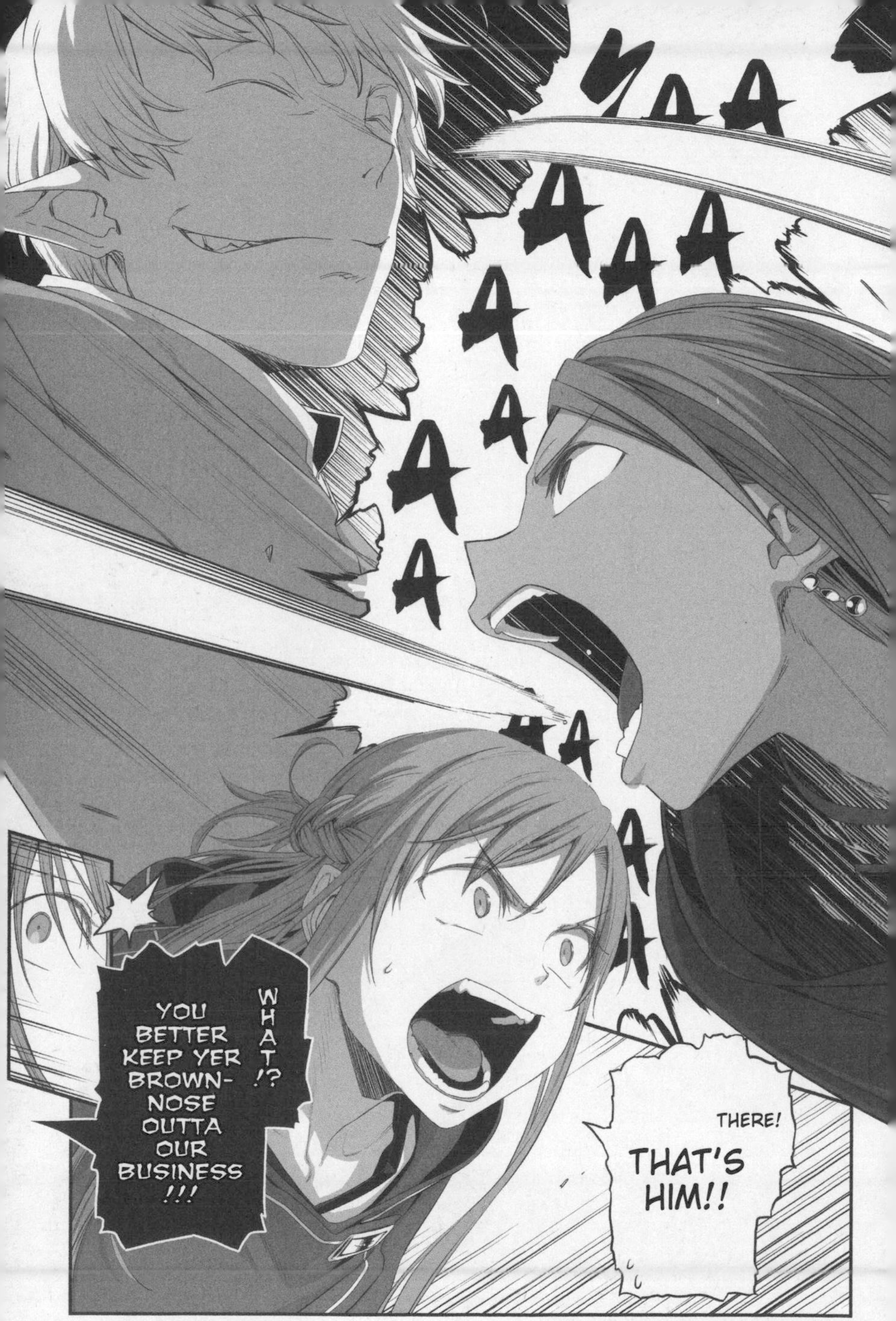
THERE!
THAT'S HIM!!
WHAT!?
YOU BETTER KEEP YER BROWN-NOSE OUTTA OUR BUSINESS!!!

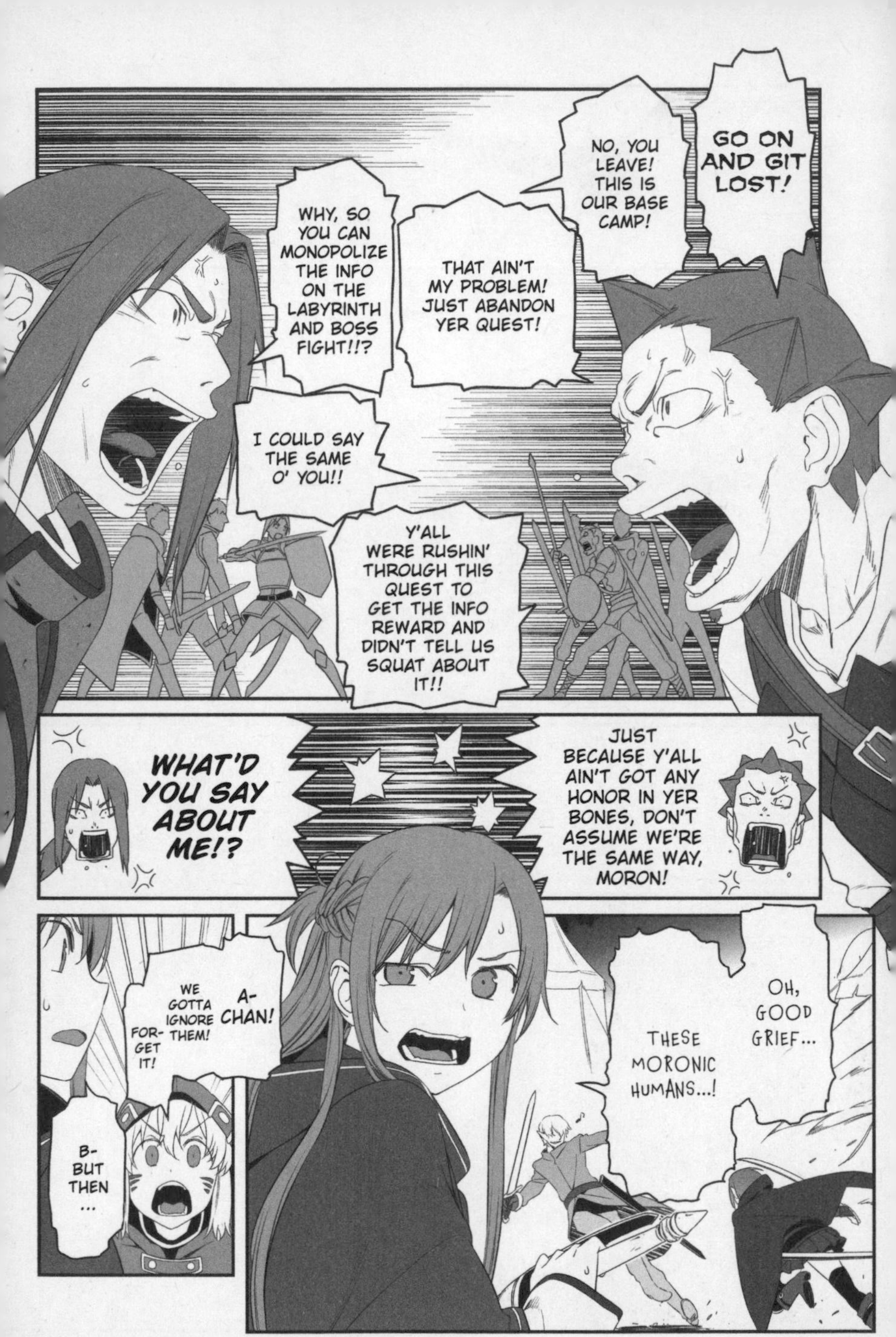
GO ON AND GIT LOST!
NO, YOU LEAVE! THIS IS OUR BASE CAMP!
THAT AIN'T MY PROBLEM! JUST ABANDON YER QUEST!
WHY, SO YOU CAN MONOPOLIZE THE INFO ON THE LABYRINTH AND BOSS FIGHT!!?
I COULD SAY THE SAME O' YOU!!
Y'ALL WERE RUSHIN' THROUGH THIS QUEST TO GET THE INFO REWARD AND DIDN'T TELL US SQUAT ABOUT IT!!
JUST BECAUSE Y'ALL AIN'T GOT ANY HONOR IN YER BONES, DON'T ASSUME WE'RE THE SAME WAY, MORON!
WHAT'D YOU SAY ABOUT ME!?
OH, GOOD GRIEF...
THESE MORONIC HUMANS...!
A-CHAN!
WE GOTTA IGNORE THEM!
FOR-GET IT!
B-BUT THEN...

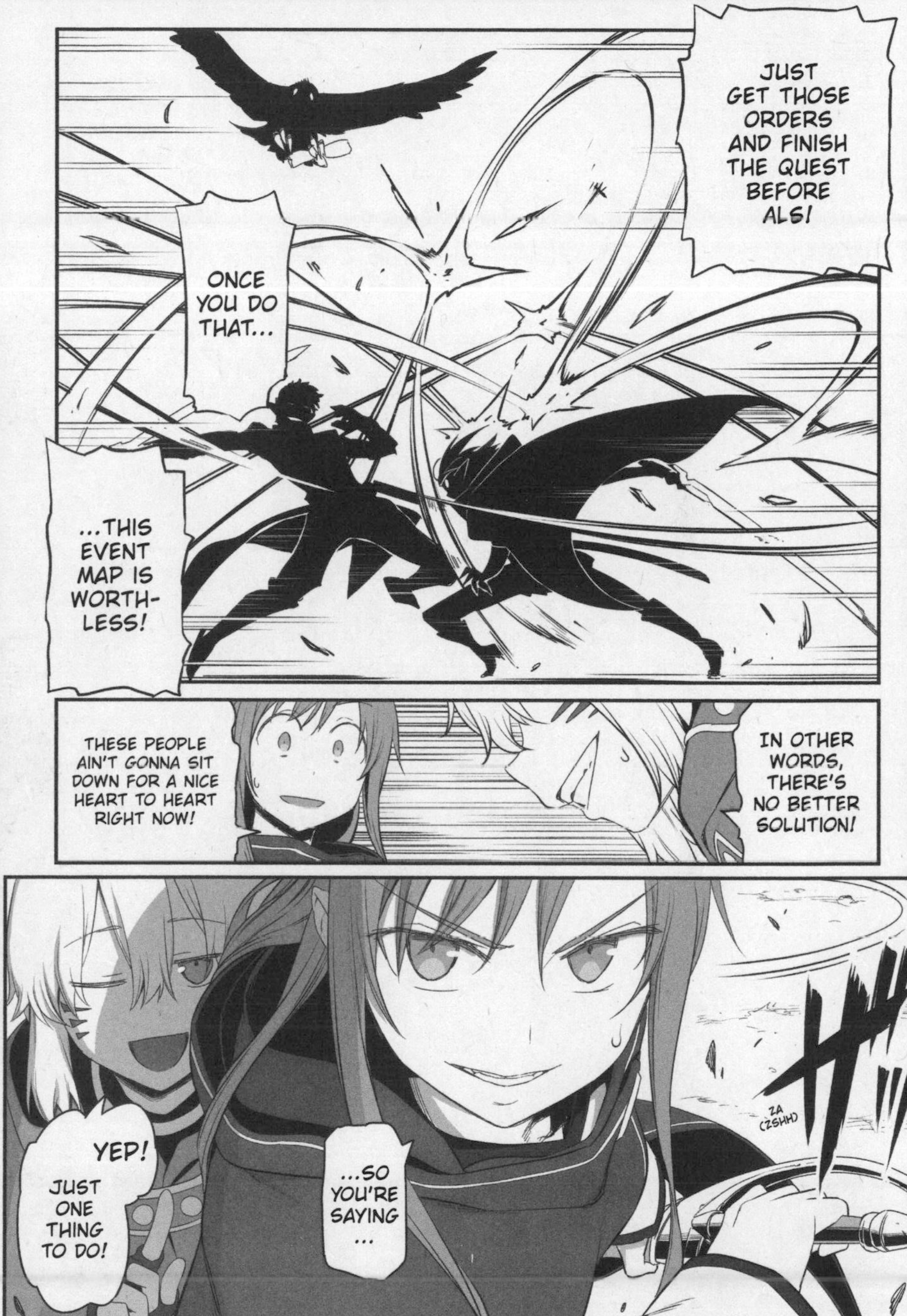
JUST GET THOSE ORDERS AND FINISH THE QUEST BEFORE ALS!
ONCE YOU DO THAT...
...THIS EVENT MAP IS WORTHLESS!
IN OTHER WORDS, THERE'S NO BETTER SOLUTION!
THESE PEOPLE AIN'T GONNA SIT DOWN FOR A NICE HEART TO HEART RIGHT NOW!
ZA (ZSHH)
...SO YOU'RE SAYING...
YEP!
JUST ONE THING TO DO!

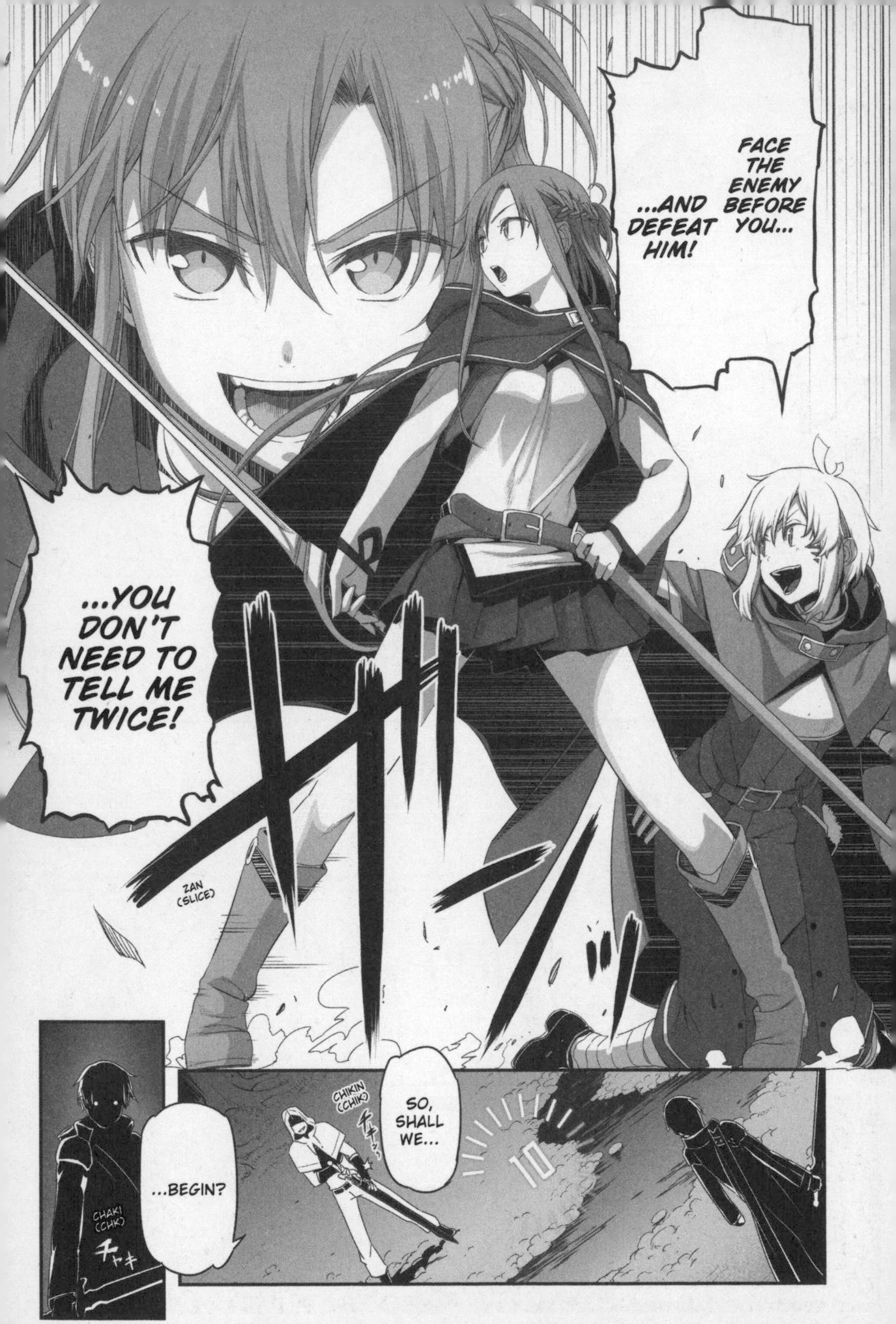
FACE THE ENEMY BEFORE YOU...
...AND DEFEAT HIM!
...YOU DON'T NEED TO TELL ME TWICE!
ZAN (SLICE)
SO, SHALL WE...
CHIKIN (CHIK)
10
...BEGIN?
CHAKI (CHK)
チャキ

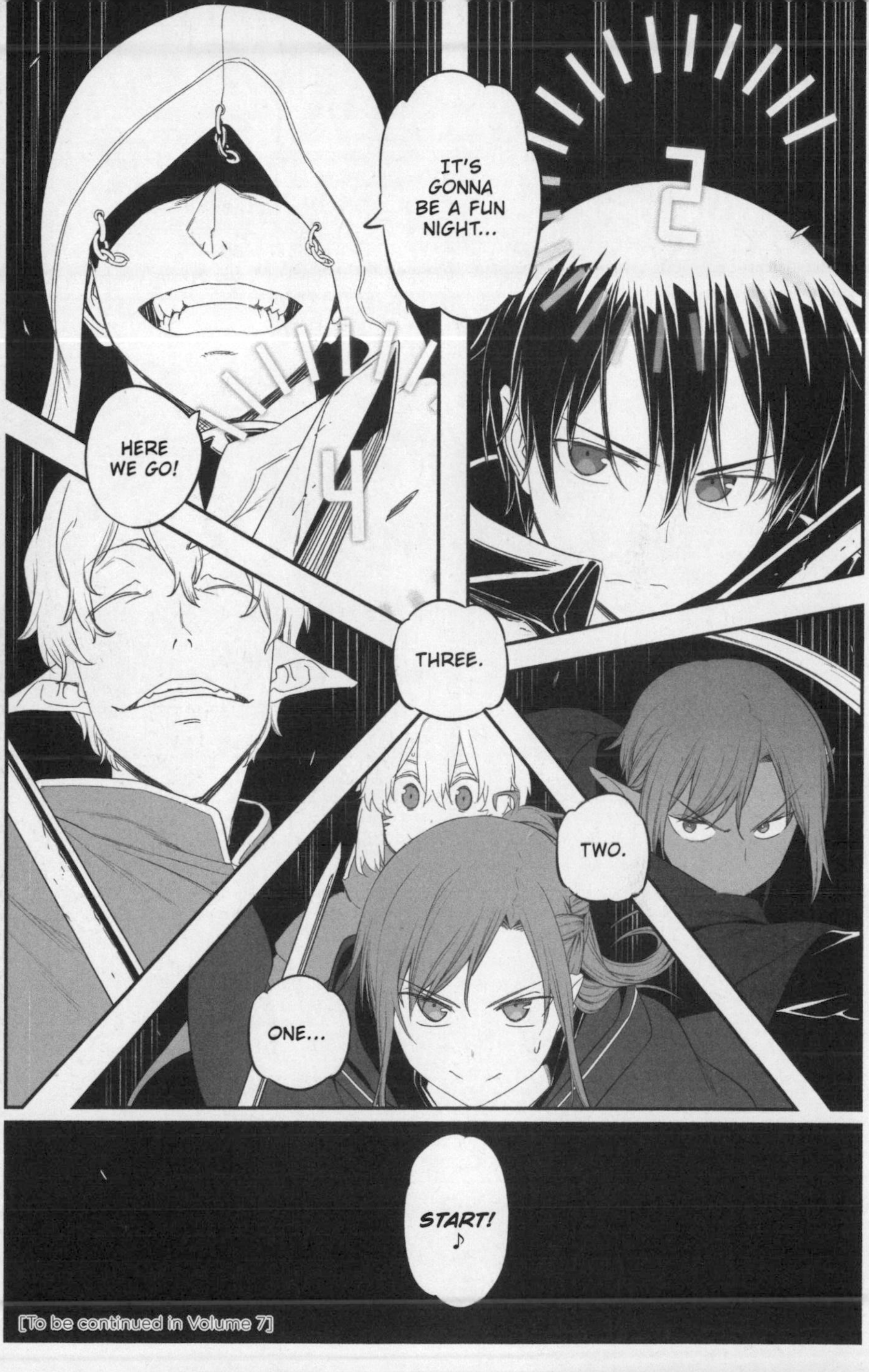
2
IT'S GONNA BE A FUN NIGHT...
4
HERE WE GO!
THREE.
TWO.
ONE...
START! ♪
[To be continued in Volume 7]

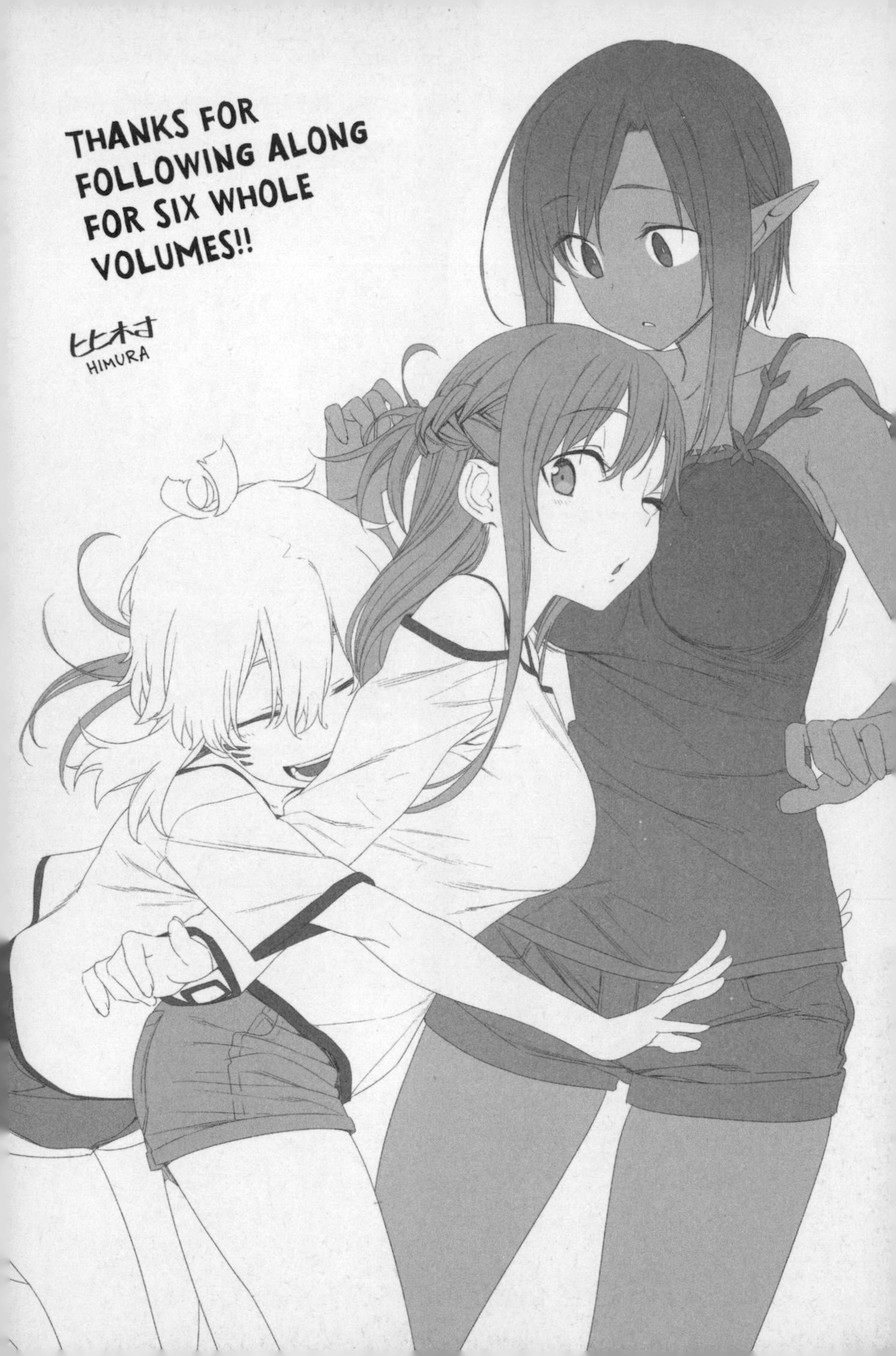
THANKS FOR FOLLOWING ALONG FOR SIX WHOLE VOLUMES!!
ひむら
HIMURA

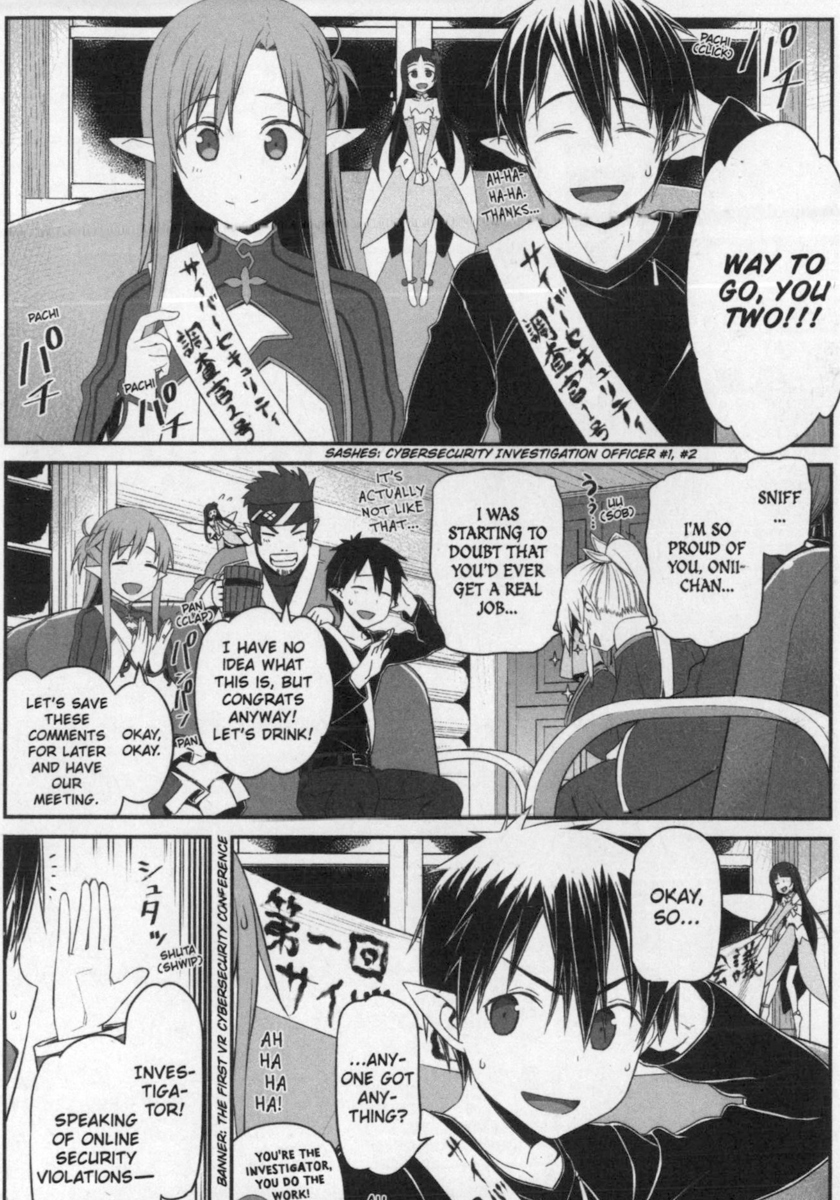
PACHI (CLICK)
WAY TO GO, YOU TWO!!!
AH-HA-HA-HA. THANKS...
PACHI
PACHI
SASHES: CYBERSECURITY INVESTIGATION OFFICER #1, #2
SNIFF ...
I'M SO PROUD OF YOU, ONII-CHAN...
UU (SOB)
I WAS STARTING TO DOUBT THAT YOU'D EVER GET A REAL JOB...
IT'S ACTUALLY NOT LIKE THAT...
I HAVE NO IDEA WHAT THIS IS, BUT CONGRATS ANYWAY! LET'S DRINK!
PAN (CLAP)
PAN
OKAY, OKAY.
LET'S SAVE THESE COMMENTS FOR LATER AND HAVE OUR MEETING.
OKAY, SO...
...ANY-ONE GOT ANY-THING?
AH HA HA HA!
YOU'RE THE INVESTIGATOR, YOU DO THE WORK!
AH HA HA!
BANNER: THE FIRST VR CYBERSECURITY CONFERENCE
SHUTA (SHWIP)
INVES-TIGA-TOR!
SPEAKING OF ONLINE SECURITY VIOLATIONS—

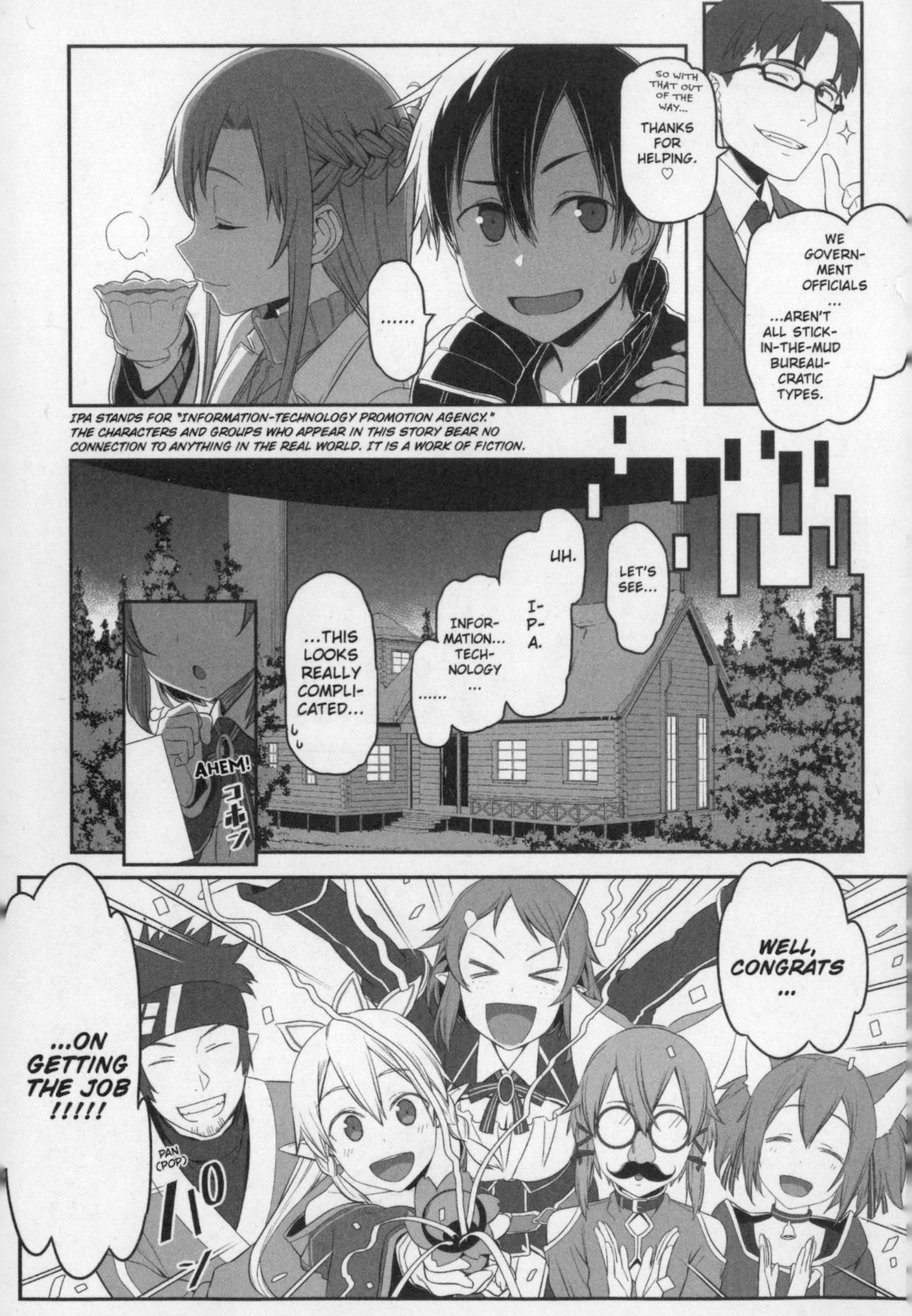
WE GOVERNMENT OFFICIALS ...
...AREN'T ALL STICK-IN-THE-MUD BUREAUCRATIC TYPES.
SO WITH THAT OUT OF THE WAY... THANKS FOR HELPING. ♡
......
IPA STANDS FOR "INFORMATION-TECHNOLOGY PROMOTION AGENCY." THE CHARACTERS AND GROUPS WHO APPEAR IN THIS STORY BEAR NO CONNECTION TO ANYTHING IN THE REAL WORLD. IT IS A WORK OF FICTION.
LET'S SEE...
UH.
I-P-A.
INFORMATION... TECHNOLOGY ...
......
...THIS LOOKS REALLY COMPLICATED...
AHEM!
コホン
WELL, CONGRATS ...
...ON GETTING THE JOB !!!!!
PAN (POP)

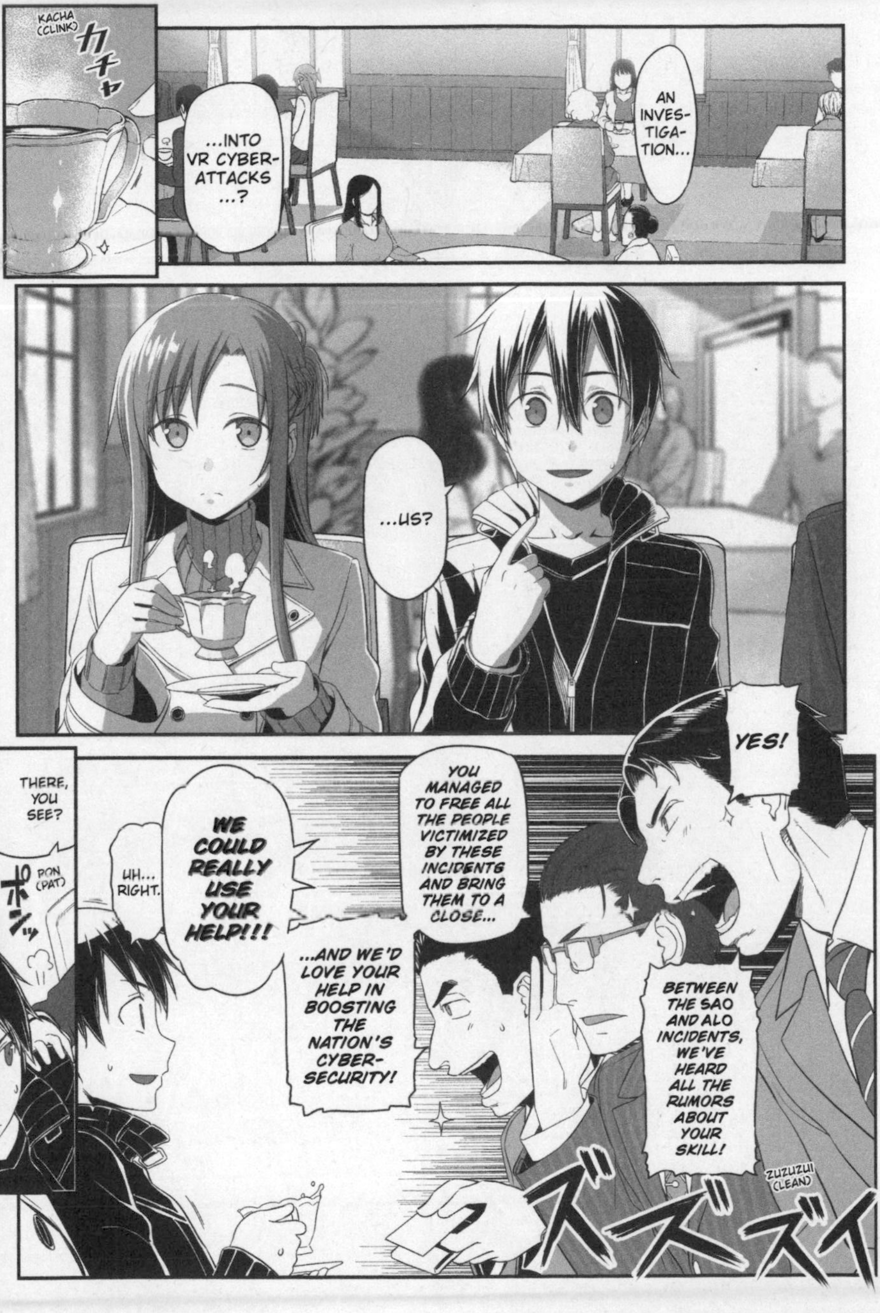
AN INVESTIGATION...
...INTO VR CYBERATTACKS...?
KACHA (CLINK)
...US?
YES!
YOU MANAGED TO FREE ALL THE PEOPLE VICTIMIZED BY THESE INCIDENTS AND BRING THEM TO A CLOSE...
BETWEEN THE SAO AND ALO INCIDENTS, WE'VE HEARD ALL THE RUMORS ABOUT YOUR SKILL!
...AND WE'D LOVE YOUR HELP IN BOOSTING THE NATION'S CYBERSECURITY!
ZUZUZUI (CLEAN)
WE COULD REALLY USE YOUR HELP!!!
UH... RIGHT.
PON (PAT)
THERE, YOU SEE?

Special thanks to...

<Creators>
Reki Kawahara-sensei
abec-sensei

<Art Staff>
Mura-san
Bambi Morino-san
Tsuyoshi Sugimoto-san

<Editor>
Kentarou Ogino-san

<Guest>
Kitsune Tennouji-sensei
(I grew up reading your manga...!)

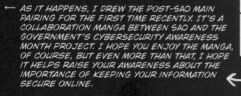

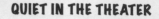

EXTRA 4-PANEL MANGA

QUIET IN THE THEATER

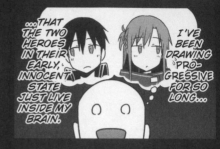

I'VE BEEN DRAWING PRO-GRESSIVE FOR SO LONG...
...THAT THE TWO HEROES IN THEIR EARLY, INNOCENT STATE JUST LIVE INSIDE MY BRAIN.
SO WHEN I WATCH THE MOVIE THAT TAKES PLACE AFTER THEY BEAT SAO...
KIRITO-KUN...
ASUNA...
BACKGROUND: AAAAAAAAAAH!!
NO, NO NO IT'S NOT TRUE!
MY BRAIN ...
WON'T SHUT-UP ABOUT IT.
THIS IS NOT HAPPENING!! WHY ARE YOU LOOKING AT ME LIKE THA STOP GAZING A ME THAT
BIG BOOBIES ...

← AS IT HAPPENS, I DREW THE POST-SAO MAIN PAIRING FOR THE FIRST TIME RECENTLY. IT'S A COLLABORATION MANGA BETWEEN SAO AND THE GOVERNMENT'S CYBERSECURITY AWARENESS MONTH PROJECT. I HOPE YOU ENJOY THE MANGA, OF COURSE, BUT EVEN MORE THAN THAT, I HOPE IT HELPS RAISE YOUR AWARENESS ABOUT THE IMPORTANCE OF KEEPING YOUR INFORMATION SECURE ONLINE.

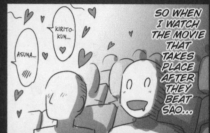

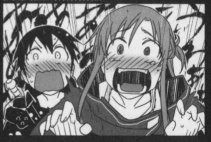

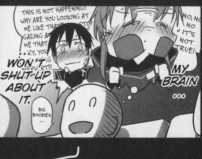

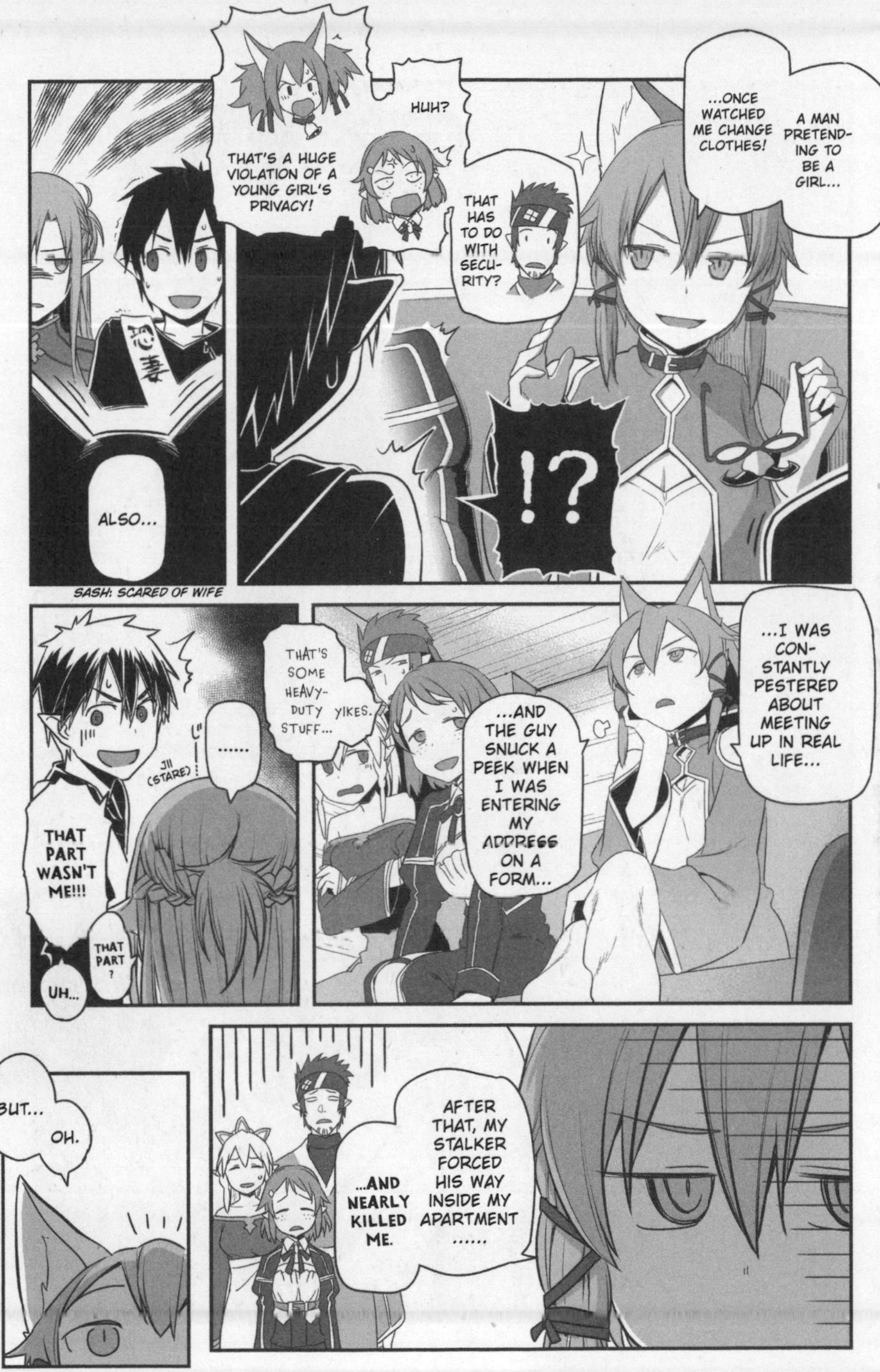
A MAN PRETENDING TO BE A GIRL...
...ONCE WATCHED ME CHANGE CLOTHES!
THAT HAS TO DO WITH SECURITY?
HUH?
THAT'S A HUGE VIOLATION OF A YOUNG GIRL'S PRIVACY!
!?
ALSO...
SASH: SCARED OF WIFE
...I WAS CONSTANTLY PESTERED ABOUT MEETING UP IN REAL LIFE...
...AND THE GUY SNUCK A PEEK WHEN I WAS ENTERING MY ADDRESS ON A FORM...
YIKES.
THAT'S SOME HEAVY-DUTY STUFF...
......
JII (STARE)
THAT PART WASN'T ME!!!
THAT PART?
UH...
AFTER THAT, MY STALKER FORCED HIS WAY INSIDE MY APARTMENT ......
...AND NEARLY KILLED ME.
BUT... OH.

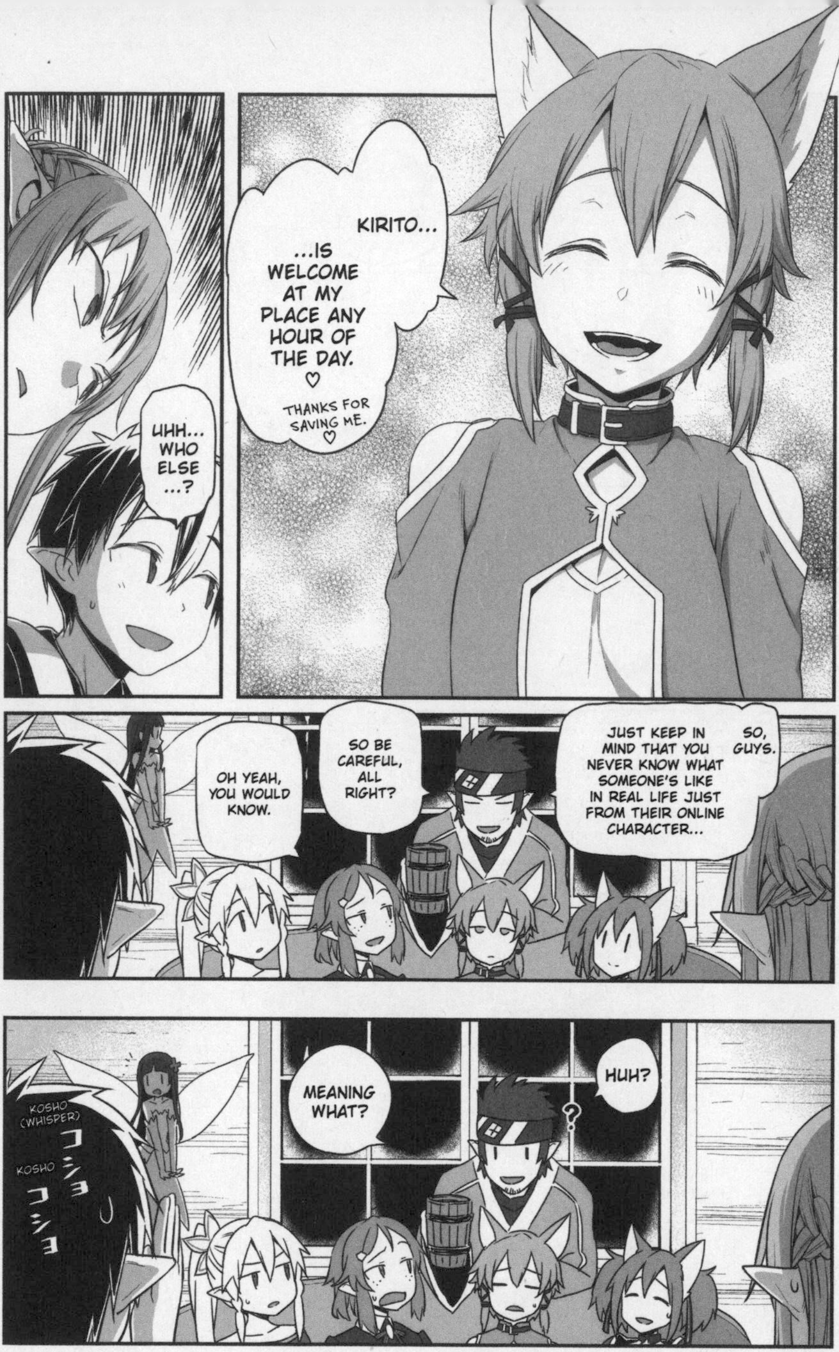
KIRITO...
...IS WELCOME AT MY PLACE ANY HOUR OF THE DAY. ♡
THANKS FOR SAVING ME. ♡
UHH... WHO ELSE ...?
SO, GUYS.
JUST KEEP IN MIND THAT YOU NEVER KNOW WHAT SOMEONE'S LIKE IN REAL LIFE JUST FROM THEIR ONLINE CHARACTER...
SO BE CAREFUL, ALL RIGHT?
OH YEAH, YOU WOULD KNOW.
HUH?
MEANING WHAT?
KOSHO (WHISPER)
コショ
KOSHO
コショ

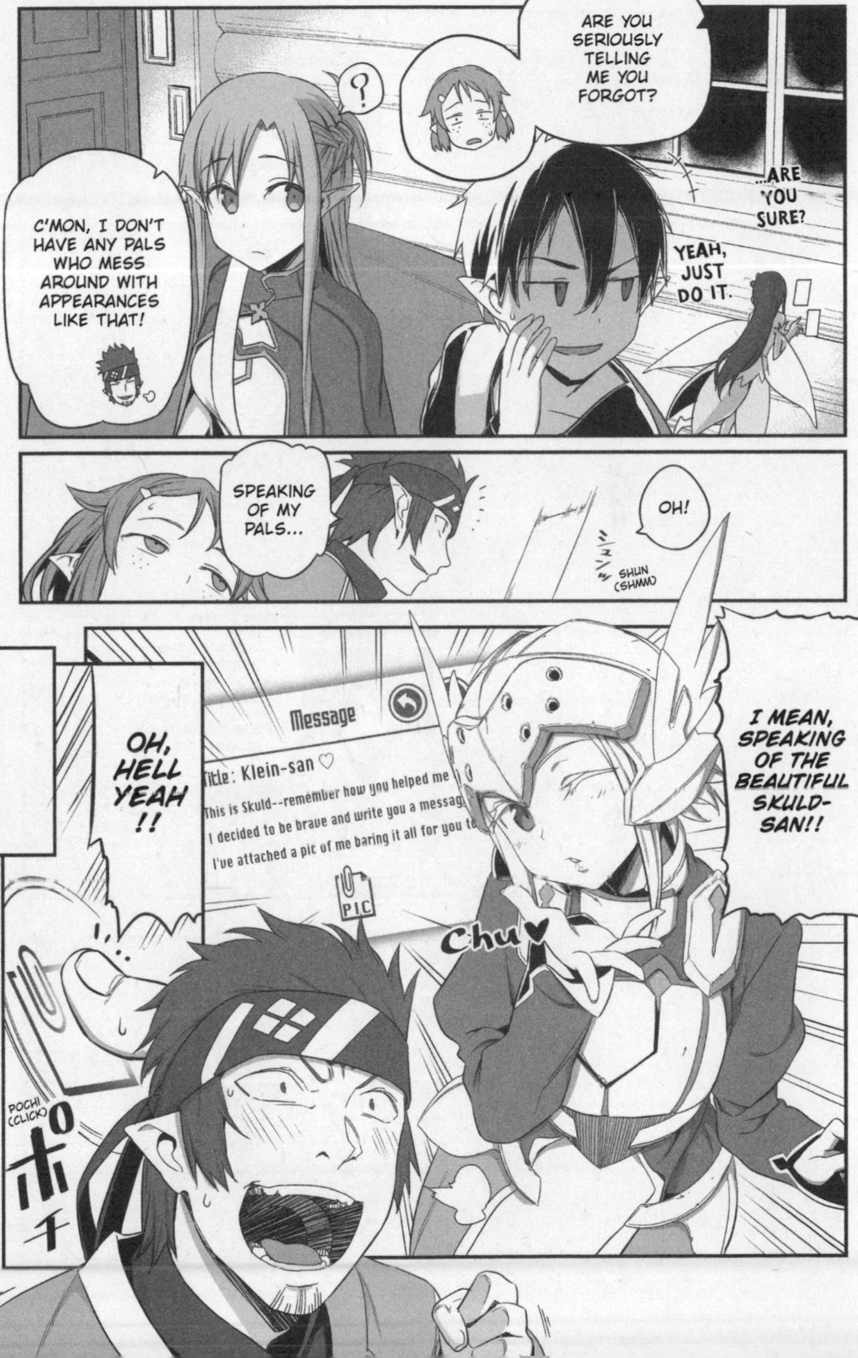
ARE YOU SERIOUSLY TELLING ME YOU FORGOT?
...ARE YOU SURE?
YEAH, JUST DO IT.
?
C'MON, I DON'T HAVE ANY PALS WHO MESS AROUND WITH APPEARANCES LIKE THAT!
OH!
SHUN (SHMM)
SPEAKING OF MY PALS...
I MEAN, SPEAKING OF THE BEAUTIFUL SKULD-SAN!!
Message
Title: Klein-san ♡
This is Skuld--remember how you helped me
I decided to be brave and write you a messag
I've attached a pic of me baring it all for you t
PIC
Chu♥
OH, HELL YEAH!!
POCHI (CLICK)
ポチ

RECENT E-MAIL ATTACKS USE MESSAGE CONTENT THAT IS DESIGNED TO BE INTERESTING TO THE TARGET, ALONG WITH AN ATTACHMENT FILE THAT CONTAINS A VIRUS OR A LINK TO A WEBSITE THAT WILL INFECT THE TARGET'S COMPUTER. PLEASE BE CAREFUL.

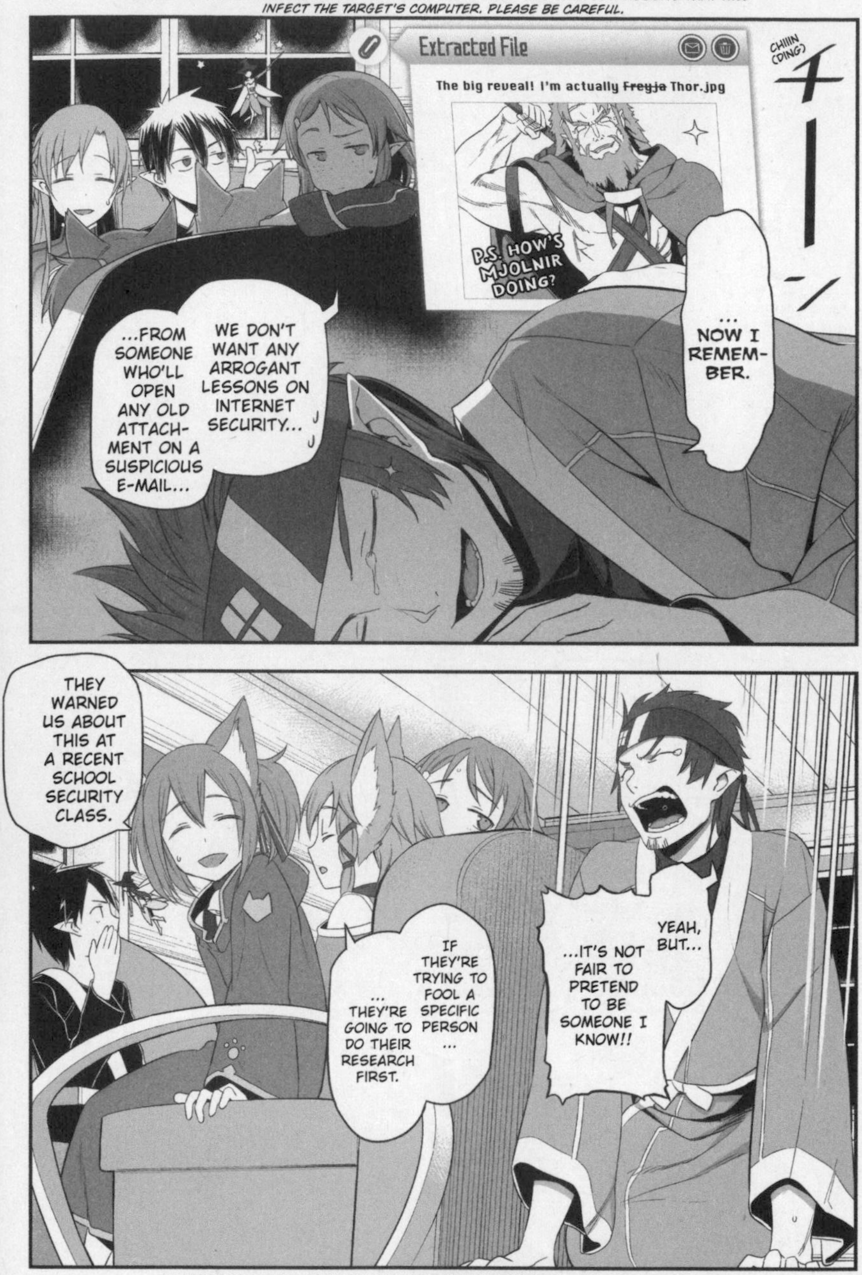
CHIIIN (DING)
Extracted File
The big reveal! I'm actually ~~Freyja~~ Thor.jpg
P.S. HOW'S MJOLNIR DOING?
...NOW I REMEMBER.
WE DON'T WANT ANY ARROGANT LESSONS ON INTERNET SECURITY...
...FROM SOMEONE WHO'LL OPEN ANY OLD ATTACHMENT ON A SUSPICIOUS E-MAIL...
THEY WARNED US ABOUT THIS AT A RECENT SCHOOL SECURITY CLASS.
YEAH, BUT...
...IT'S NOT FAIR TO PRETEND TO BE SOMEONE I KNOW!!
IF THEY'RE TRYING TO FOOL A SPECIFIC PERSON...
...THEY'RE GOING TO DO THEIR RESEARCH FIRST.

IN ORDER TO DEFEND AGAINST VIRUS ATTACKS LIKE THESE, ALWAYS USE AN ANTIVIRUS PROGRAM OR OS TOOL, AND MAKE SURE THAT THE SOFTWARE IS CONFIGURED TO KEEP AN UP-TO-DATE DEFINITION FILE AT ALL TIMES.

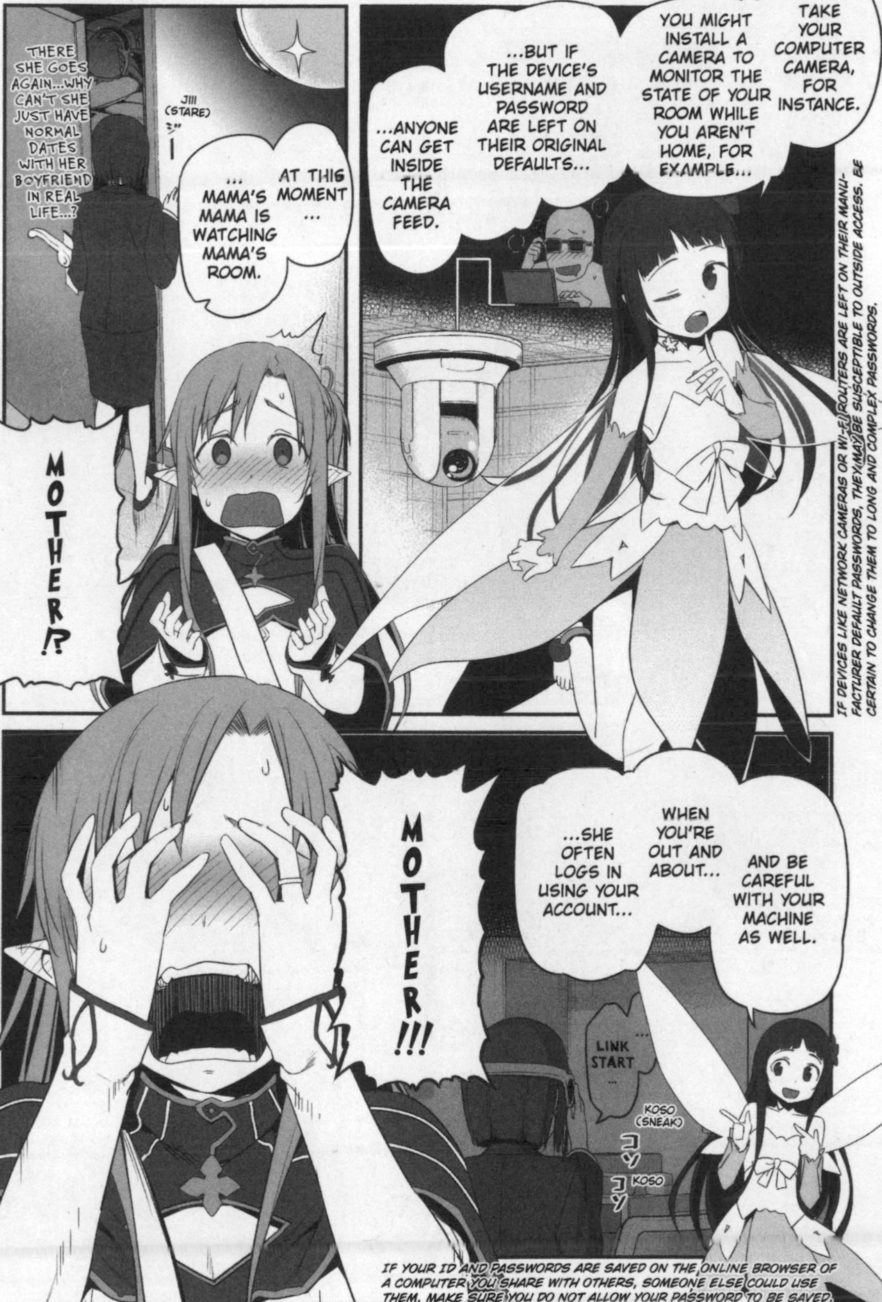
TAKE YOUR COMPUTER CAMERA, FOR INSTANCE.
YOU MIGHT INSTALL A CAMERA TO MONITOR THE STATE OF YOUR ROOM WHILE YOU AREN'T HOME, FOR EXAMPLE...
...BUT IF THE DEVICE'S USERNAME AND PASSWORD ARE LEFT ON THEIR ORIGINAL DEFAULTS...
...ANYONE CAN GET INSIDE THE CAMERA FEED.
IF DEVICES LIKE NETWORK CAMERAS OR WI-FI ROUTERS ARE LEFT ON THEIR MANUFACTURER DEFAULT PASSWORDS, THEY MAY BE SUSCEPTIBLE TO OUTSIDE ACCESS. BE CERTAIN TO CHANGE THEM TO LONG AND COMPLEX PASSWORDS.
AT THIS MOMENT...
...MAMA'S MAMA IS WATCHING MAMA'S ROOM.
JIII (STARE)
THERE SHE GOES AGAIN...WHY CAN'T SHE JUST HAVE NORMAL DATES WITH HER BOYFRIEND IN REAL LIFE...?
MOTHER!?
AND BE CAREFUL WITH YOUR MACHINE AS WELL.
WHEN YOU'RE OUT AND ABOUT...
...SHE OFTEN LOGS IN USING YOUR ACCOUNT...
MOTHER!!!
...LINK START...
KOSO (SNEAK)
KOSO
IF YOUR ID AND PASSWORDS ARE SAVED ON THE ONLINE BROWSER OF A COMPUTER YOU SHARE WITH OTHERS, SOMEONE ELSE COULD USE THEM. MAKE SURE YOU DO NOT ALLOW YOUR PASSWORD TO BE SAVED. AND AGAIN, AVOID EASILY PREDICTABLE PASSWORDS.

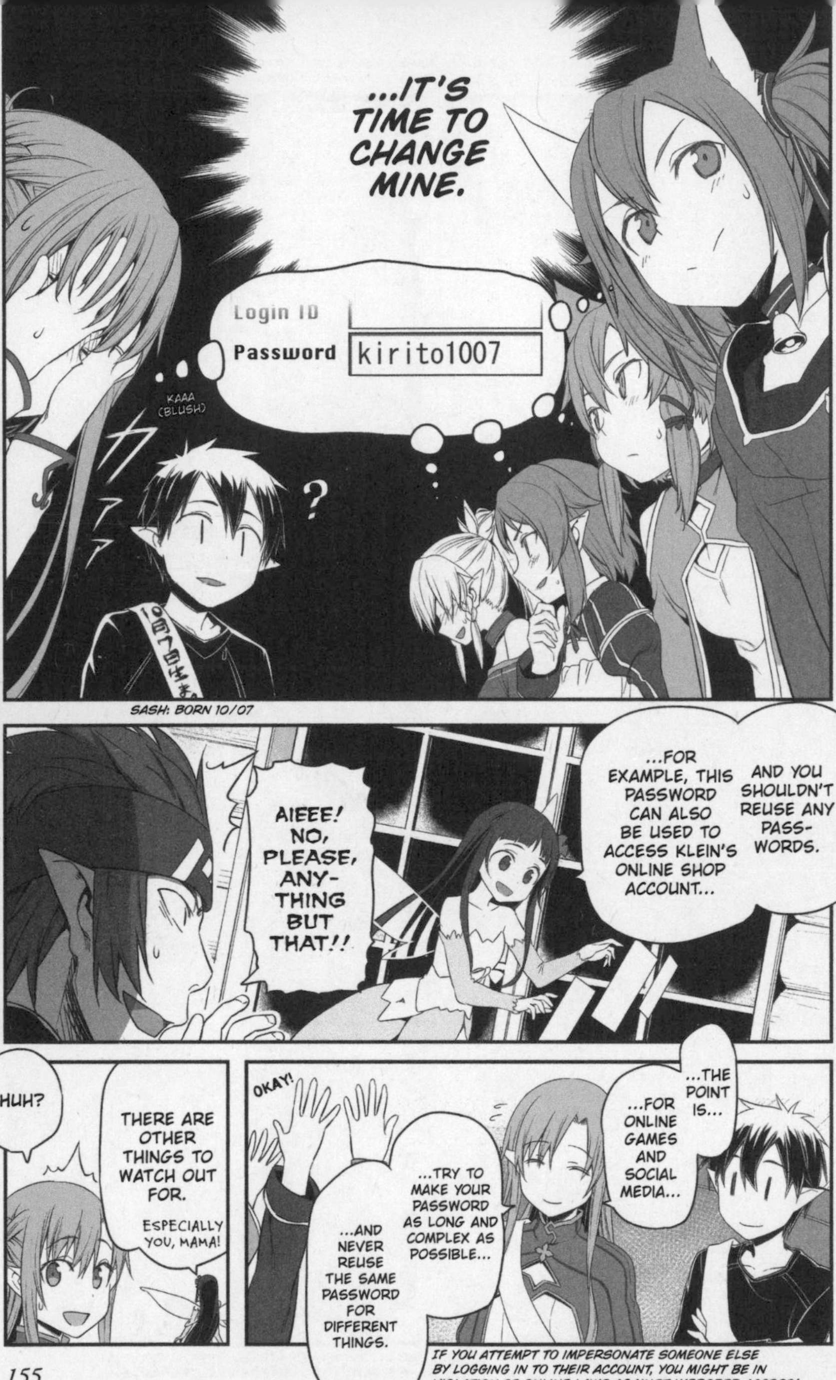
...IT'S TIME TO CHANGE MINE.
Login ID
Password kirito1007
KAAA (BLUSH)
?
SASH: BORN 10/07
AND YOU SHOULDN'T REUSE ANY PASS-WORDS.
...FOR EXAMPLE, THIS PASSWORD CAN ALSO BE USED TO ACCESS KLEIN'S ONLINE SHOP ACCOUNT...
AIEEE! NO, PLEASE, ANY-THING BUT THAT!!
...THE POINT IS...
...FOR ONLINE GAMES AND SOCIAL MEDIA...
...TRY TO MAKE YOUR PASSWORD AS LONG AND COMPLEX AS POSSIBLE...
...AND NEVER REUSE THE SAME PASSWORD FOR DIFFERENT THINGS.
OKAY!
THERE ARE OTHER THINGS TO WATCH OUT FOR.
ESPECIALLY YOU, MAMA!
HUH?

YOU CAN REDUCE YOUR RISK OF HACKING BY MAKING YOUR PASSWORD A COMBINATION OF UPPER AND LOWER CASE LETTERS, NUMBERS, AND SYMBOLS; MAKE IT AS LONG AS POSSIBLE, AND USE A DIFFERENT ONE FOR EACH ACCOUNT. THERE ARE ALSO PROGRAM TOOLS TO HELP YOU MANAGE PASSWORDS.

IF YOU ATTEMPT TO IMPERSONATE SOMEONE ELSE BY LOGGING IN TO THEIR ACCOUNT, YOU MIGHT BE IN VIOLATION OF ONLINE LAWS AGAINST IMPROPER ACCESS!

WHEN USING BLOGS OR SOCIAL MEDIA, ASSUME THAT ANY PERSONAL PROFILE INFORMATION YOU POST, LIKE BIRTHDAYS OR PET NAMES... (CONT. BELOW)

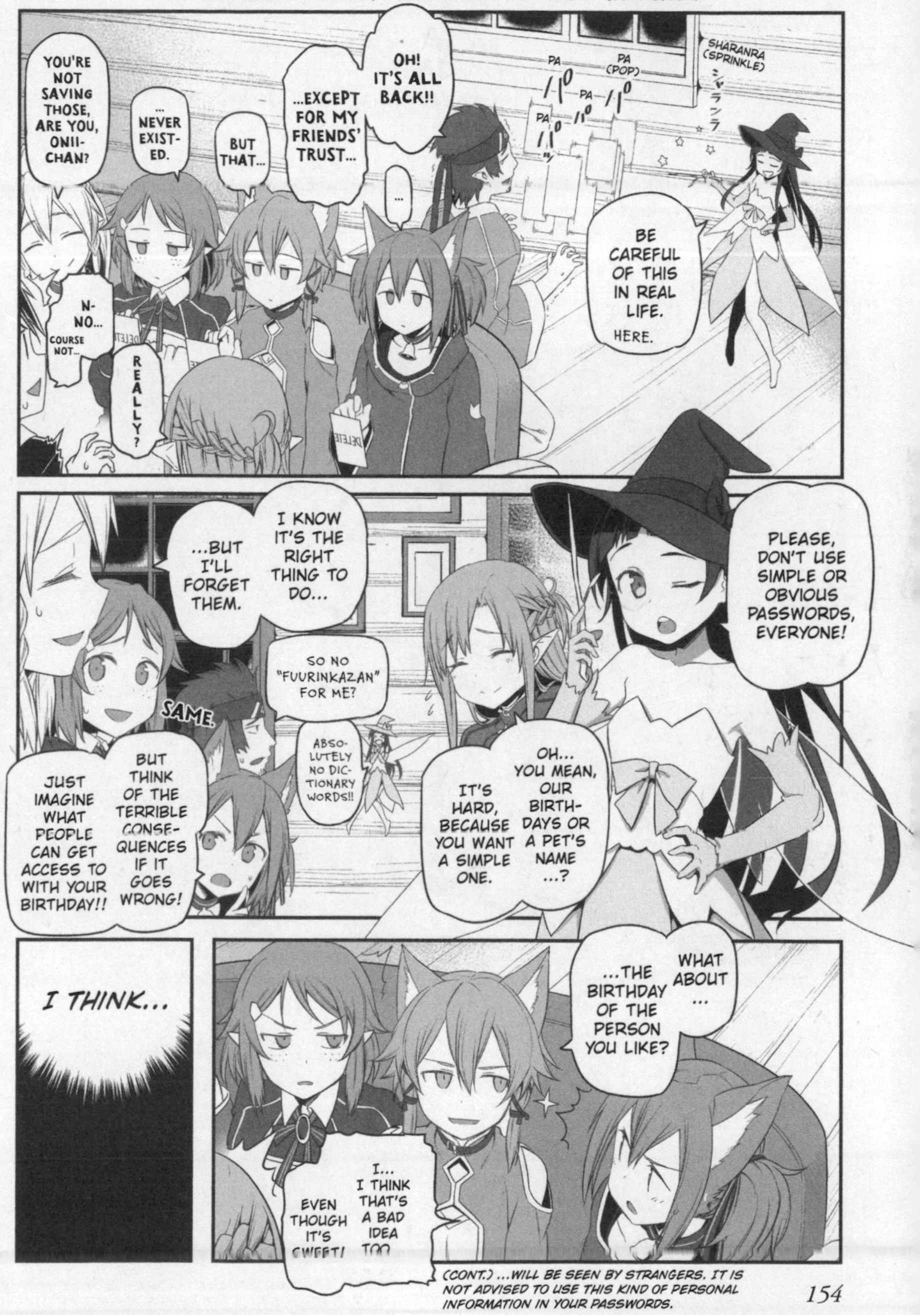
SHARANRA (SPRINKLE)
PA (POP)
PA
PA
PA
OH! IT'S ALL BACK!!
...EXCEPT FOR MY FRIENDS' TRUST...
BUT THAT...
...NEVER EXIST-ED.
YOU'RE NOT SAVING THOSE, ARE YOU, ONII-CHAN?
BE CAREFUL OF THIS IN REAL LIFE.
HERE.
...
N-NO... COURSE NOT...
REALLY?
DELETE
DELETE
PLEASE, DON'T USE SIMPLE OR OBVIOUS PASSWORDS, EVERYONE!
I KNOW IT'S THE RIGHT THING TO DO...
...BUT I'LL FORGET THEM.
SO NO "FUURINKAZAN" FOR ME?
ABSO-LUTELY NO DIC-TIONARY WORDS!!
SAME.
OH... YOU MEAN, OUR BIRTH-DAYS OR A PET'S NAME ...?
IT'S HARD, BECAUSE YOU WANT A SIMPLE ONE.
BUT THINK OF THE TERRIBLE CONSE-QUENCES IF IT GOES WRONG!
JUST IMAGINE WHAT PEOPLE CAN GET ACCESS TO WITH YOUR BIRTHDAY!!
WHAT ABOUT ...
...THE BIRTHDAY OF THE PERSON YOU LIKE?
I... I THINK THAT'S A BAD IDEA TOO
EVEN THOUGH IT'S SWEET!
I THINK...

(CONT.) ...WILL BE SEEN BY STRANGERS. IT IS NOT ADVISED TO USE THIS KIND OF PERSONAL INFORMATION IN YOUR PASSWORDS.

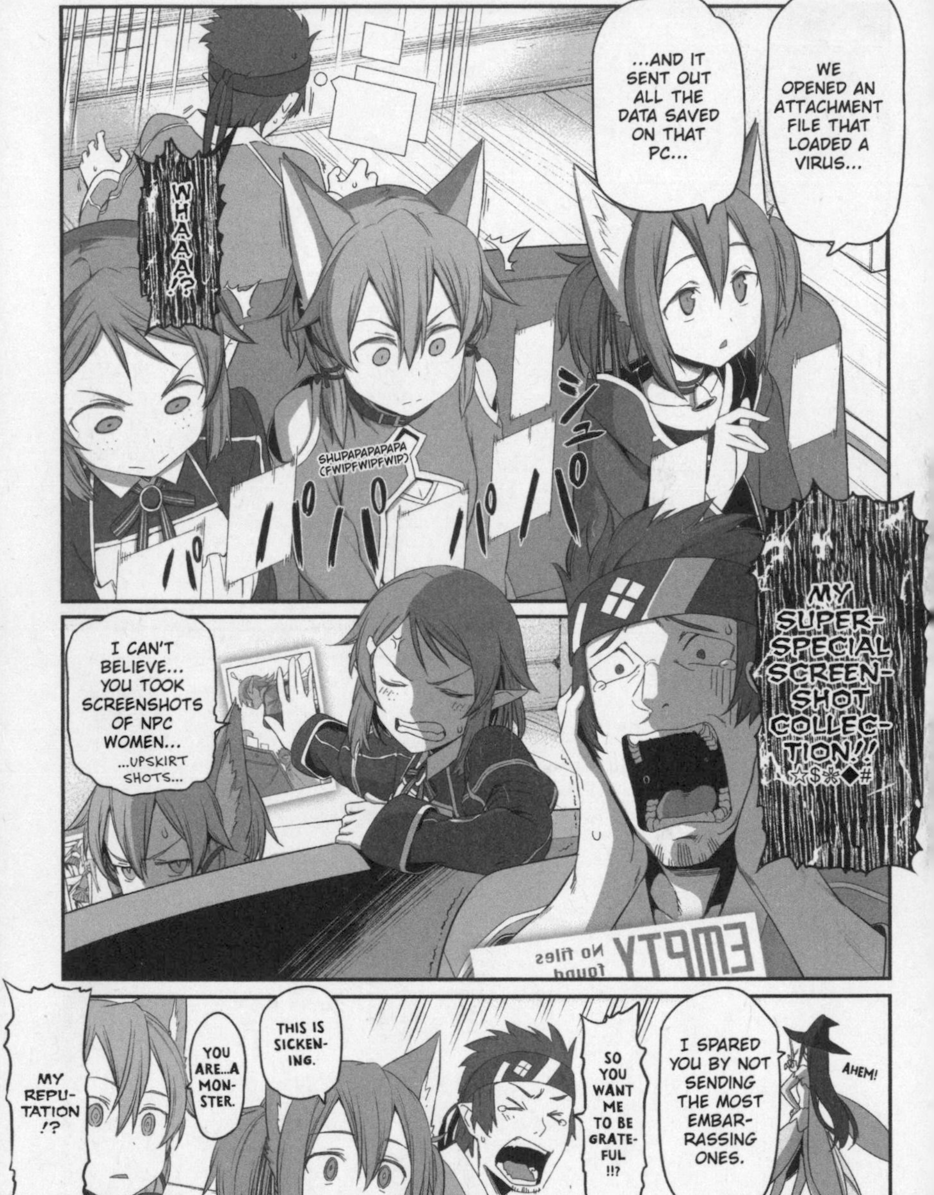
WE OPENED AN ATTACHMENT FILE THAT LOADED A VIRUS...
...AND IT SENT OUT ALL THE DATA SAVED ON THAT PC...
WHAAAA!?
SHUPAPAPAPAPA (FWIPFWIPFWIP)
MY SUPER-SPECIAL SCREEN-SHOT COLLEC-TION!! ☆$*◆#
I CAN'T BELIEVE... YOU TOOK SCREENSHOTS OF NPC WOMEN... ...UPSKIRT SHOTS...
EMPTY
No files found
AHEM!
I SPARED YOU BY NOT SENDING THE MOST EMBAR-RASSING ONES.
SO YOU WANT ME TO BE GRATE-FUL !!?
THIS IS SICKEN-ING.
YOU ARE...A MON-STER.
MY REPU-TATION !?

...THAT REMINDS ME, I CALLED OUT TO YOU THE OTHER DAY AND GOT NO RESPONSE.
I THOUGHT IT SEEMED WEIRD...
...
ASU-NA!
...?
OH NO...
I SUPPOSE THE AMUSPHERE ISN'T UNIQUE IN THAT REGARD.
IT'S THE SAME WITH SMART-PHONES, ISN'T IT...?
IT'S WHY YOU HAVE TO LOCK THE HOME SCREEN, SO NOBODY CAN GET IN THERE IF YOU LOSE IT...
I MUST PROTECT MY COLLECTION OF SLEEPING ONII-CHAN PHOTOS...
WHAT'S THE MATTER, KIRITO-KUN?
NO, NEVER MIND...
WAIT, WAS THAT LOG-IN THE OTHER DAY...?
WHAT!?
WHAT HAP-PENED!?
WHAT DID MY MOTHER DO WITH YOU, KIRITO-KUN!?
I... I CAN'T GET MARRIED NOW.
IT'S FINE! I'LL STILL MARRY YOU!!
SHE JUMPED HIM.
SHE SO DID.

ALWAYS TURN ON THE SCREEN LOCK FUNCTION OF YOUR SMARTPHONE, TO ENSURE THAT NOBODY CAN GET INSIDE OF IT IF YOU LOSE THE PHONE. ALSO, MAKE SURE THE LOCK-FEATURE INTERVAL IS SET TO NO MORE THAN A FEW MINUTES AT THE MOST, SO THAT THE LOCK WILL ACTIVATE SOON AFTER YOU LOSE IT.

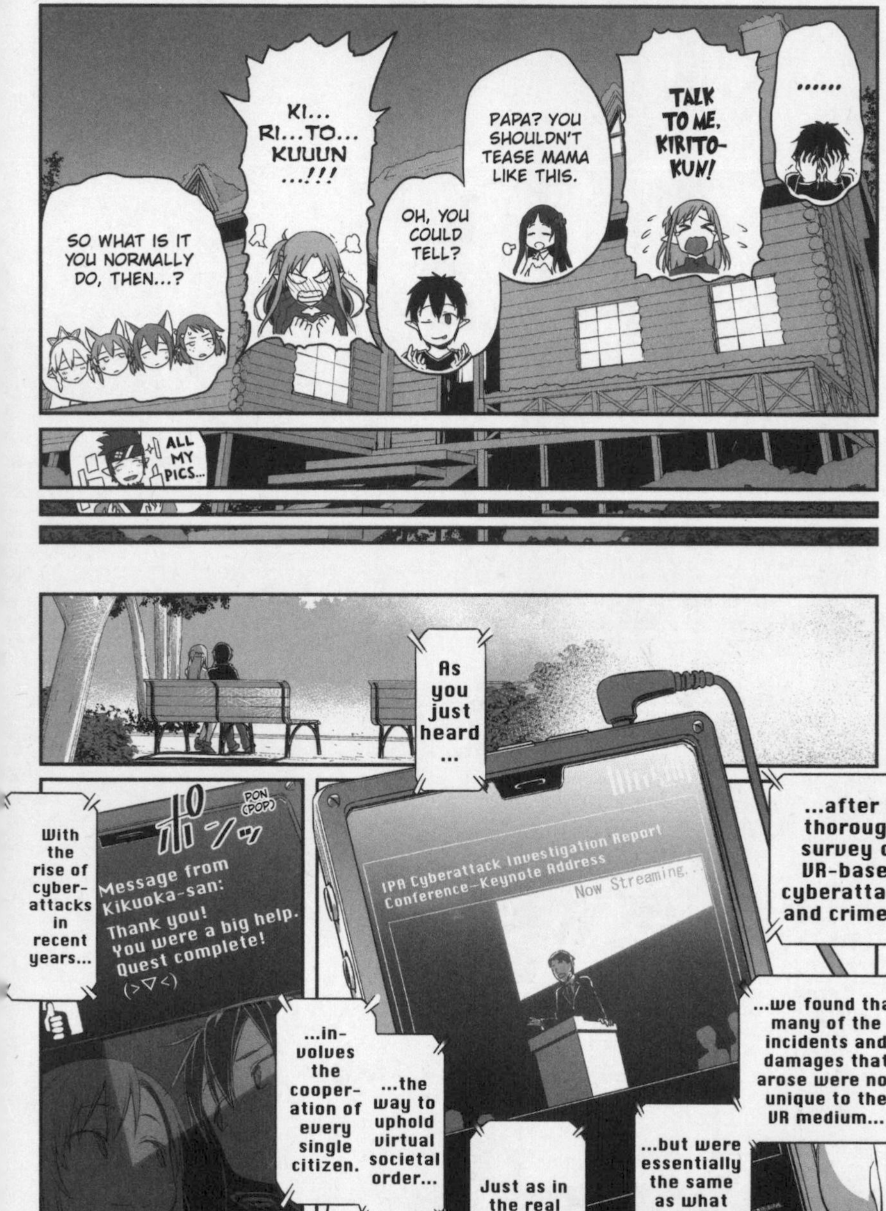

......
TALK TO ME, KIRITO-KUN!
PAPA? YOU SHOULDN'T TEASE MAMA LIKE THIS.
OH, YOU COULD TELL?
KI... RI...TO... KUUUN ...!!!
SO WHAT IS IT YOU NORMALLY DO, THEN...?
ALL MY PICS...
As you just heard...
IPA Cyberattack Investigation Report Conference—Keynote Address
Now Streaming...
...after a thorough survey of VR-based cyberattacks and crimes...
...we found that many of the incidents and damages that arose were not unique to the VR medium...
...but were essentially the same as what happens in the real world.
Just as in the real world...
...the way to uphold virtual societal order...
...in-volves the cooper-ation of every single citizen.
ポンッ
PON (POP)
Message from Kikuoka-san: Thank you! You were a big help. Quest complete! (>▽<)
With the rise of cyber-attacks in recent years...

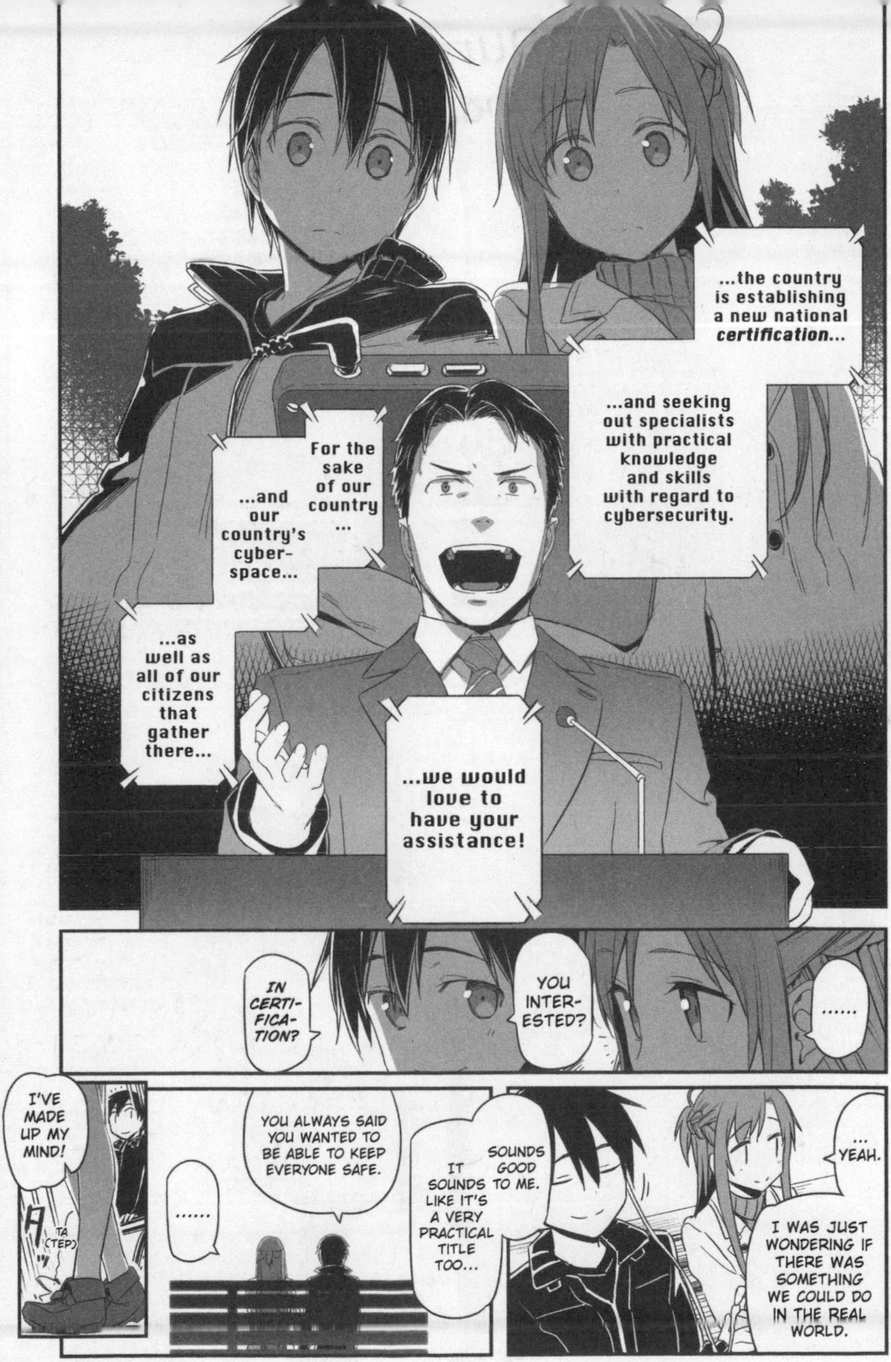
...the country is establishing a new national *certification*...
...and seeking out specialists with practical knowledge and skills with regard to cybersecurity.
For the sake of our country...
...and our country's cyber-space...
...as well as all of our citizens that gather there...
...we would love to have your assistance!
......
YOU INTER-ESTED?
IN CERTI-FICA-TION?
... YEAH.
I WAS JUST WONDERING IF THERE WAS SOMETHING WE COULD DO IN THE REAL WORLD.
SOUNDS GOOD TO ME.
IT SOUNDS LIKE IT'S A VERY PRACTICAL TITLE TOO...
YOU ALWAYS SAID YOU WANTED TO BE ABLE TO KEEP EVERYONE SAFE.
......
I'VE MADE UP MY MIND!
TA (TEP)

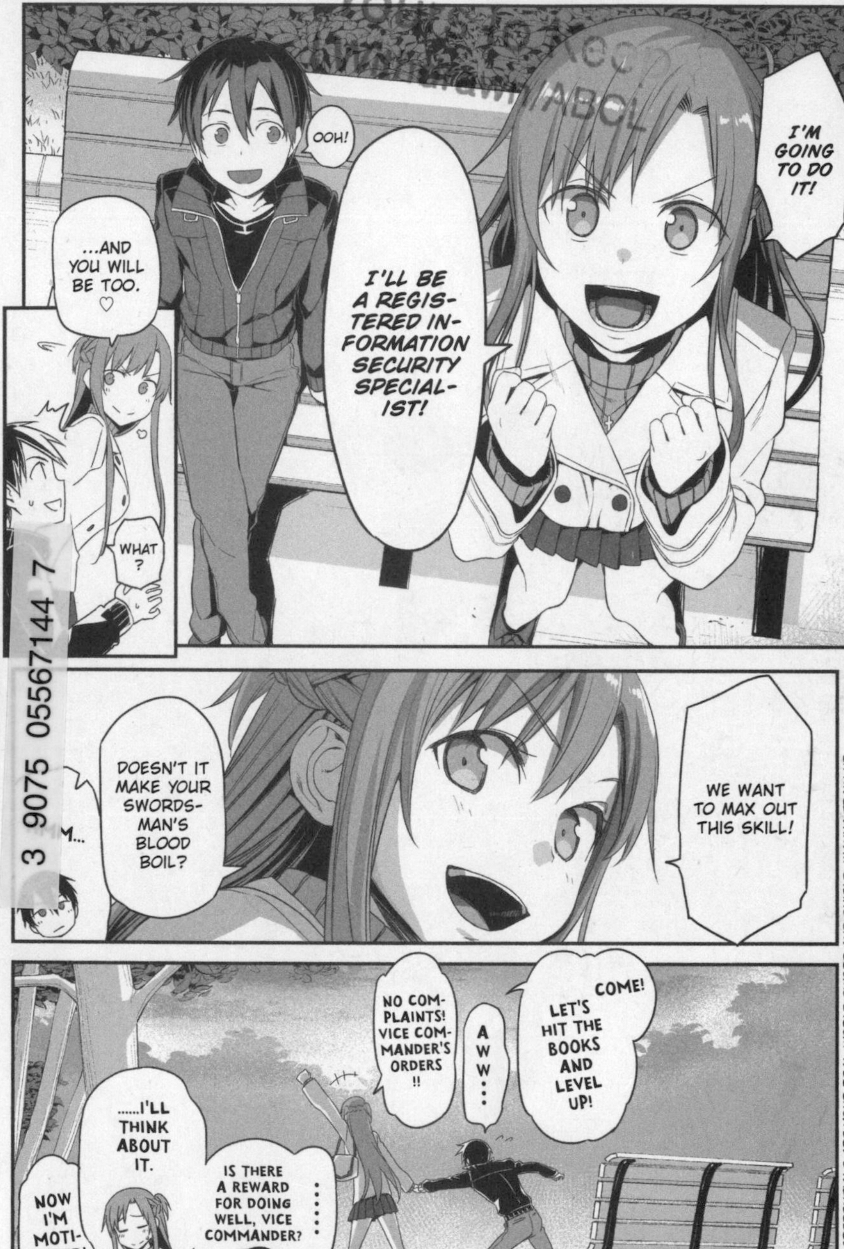
I'M GOING TO DO IT!
I'LL BE A REGISTERED INFORMATION SECURITY SPECIALIST!
OOH!
...AND YOU WILL BE TOO. ♡
WHAT?
WE WANT TO MAX OUT THIS SKILL!
DOESN'T IT MAKE YOUR SWORDSMAN'S BLOOD BOIL?
COME! LET'S HIT THE BOOKS AND LEVEL UP!
AWW...
NO COMPLAINTS! VICE COMMANDER'S ORDERS!!
IS THERE A REWARD FOR DOING WELL, VICE COMMANDER? ......
......I'LL THINK ABOUT IT.
NOW I'M MOTIVATED!

SECURITY CREDENTIALS ARE YOUR REAL-WORLD SWORD AND SHIELD. WANNA TRAIN UP, GATHER EQUIPMENT, DELVE INTO THE FUTURE WORLD OF SECURITY, AND WORK TOGETHER WITH EVERYONE ELSE TO PROTECT AGAINST CYBERATTACKS? WE'RE WAITING FOR YOU!

END